AT

Belleau Wood

AT

Belleau Wood

ROBERT B. ASPREY

University of North Texas Press
Denton, Texas

5 4 3 2 1

Permissions
University of North Texas Press
Post Office Box 13856
Denton, Texas 76203-6856

The paper in this book meets the minimum requirements of the
American National Standard for Permanence of Paper for Printed
Library Materials, Z39.48-1984.

Library of Congress Cataloging-in-Publication Data

Asprey, Robert B.
At Belleau Wood / by Robert B. Asprey.
p.   cm.
Includes bibliographical references and index.
ISBN 1-57441-016-4
[1. Belleau Wood, Battle of, 1918.] I. Title.
D545.B4A82   1996
940.4'34—dc20   96-25519
CIP

Design by Amy Layton
Maps drawn by G. Kelley Fitch
Cover art by Cyrus LeRoy Baldridge, Pvt. A.E.F., from
"I Was There" with the Yanks on the Western Front 1917–1919
published by G. P. Putnam's Sons, 1919. Originally published in The
Stars and Stripes. Used with permission of the National Tribune
Corporation, owner of the registered trademark, The Stars and Stripes.

This book is dedicated to my sister, Winifred.

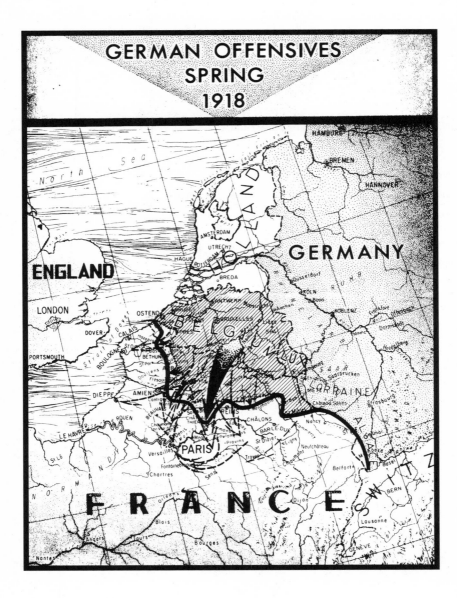

GERMAN OFFENSIVES
SPRING
1918

I have a rendezvous with Death
At some disputed barricade,
When spring comes back with rustling shade
And apple-blossoms fill the air . . .

—Alan Seeger
"I Have a Rendezvous With Death"

Table of Contents

Foreword and Acknowledgments / xi

The Wood / 1

1 The Americans / 7

2 "Cold, wet and hungry, on we marched . . ." / 17

3 "I would fight without a break . . ." / 30

4 "The situation bears much resemblance to the [1914] battle of the Marne." / 45

5 "We've been ordered up to the front at once." / 58

6 "The Seventh [German] Army will continue the attack until the enemy's resistance breaks between Soissons and Villers-Cotterêts . . ." / 69

7 "General, these are American regulars. In a hundred and fifty years they have never been beaten. They will hold." / 86

8 "The French line seems to be holding very well . . ." / 100

9 "Retreat, hell. We just got here." / 114

10 "All my officers are gone. . . ." / 137

11 "We now stood facing the dark sullen mystery of Belleau Wood. . . ." / 157

12 "Come on, you sons of bitches. Do you want to live forever?" / 172

13 ". . . make no further attempt to advance tonight." / 191

14 ". . . No numbers as to casualties are available. Losses known to be heavy." / 203

15 "OUR MARINES ATTACK . . ." / 215

16 ". . . Artillery has blown the wood all to hell." / 232

17 "In my judgement, the capture of the Bois de Belleau is the most important event that has taken place for the Allied holding in this vicinity . . ." / 250

18 "All objectives reached and we are consolidating. . . ." / 267

19 ". . . the spirit of the Brigade remains unshaken." / 287

20 "Belleau Woods now U. S. Marine Corps entirely." / 304

21 "The whole attack went off like a dress rehearsal . . ." / 325

22 ". . . The General commanding the Sixth [French] Army orders that henceforth in all official papers the Bois de Belleau shall be named 'Bois de la Brigade de Marine.'" / 339

Bibliography / 352

Index / 359

Illustrations to follow page 202

Maps

German Offensives, Spring 1918 / vi

The Situation, May 31st–June 1st, 1918 / 70

Allied Plan of Counter-Attack, June 6th, 1918 / 138

4th Marine Brigade Attack, Hill 142, Dawn, June 6th / 158

Marine Attack, June 6–7, 1918 / 158

23d Infantry Attack, Hill 192, June 6–7th / 158

Marine Attacks, June 10–11th, 1918 / 232

Marine Attacks, June 12–15th, 1918 / 268

Final Marine Attacks, June 25–26th / 304

Vaux, 3d U. S. Brigade Attack, July 1st, 1918 / 304

In another book, *The First Battle of the Marne* (Lippincott, 1962), I wrote:

> No great battle stands alone, a tactical mono-lith separate from the surging forces of either its strategic campaign or its parent war. The origin of each, the plan and purpose, the forces involved, the leadership, the outcome—all belong to a larger scheme of things, a politi-cal-military relationship that determines the final importance of a single battle.

Nothing in time's passage has caused me to alter these criteria, particularly when it comes to the series of actions culminating in the American capture of Belleau Wood and the village of Vaux in the spring of 1918.

But if criteria remain constant, treatment does not. In writing about the 1914 battle of the Marne, one perforce examined the issues in terms of French, German and British armies sprawled over hundreds of miles. The 1918 action compressed some very impor-tant issues into a few miles of battle front northwest of Château-Thierry where elements of one American division fought elements of several German divisions. Each battle was important, each perhaps decisive but for different reasons: the 1914 battle resulted in a strategic victory for the Allies and marked the turning point of the war from open, relatively fast action into trench stalemate. The 1918 battle resulted in a tremendous psychological victory for the Allies—by first helping to stop the Germans, then successfully counterattacking, the American action marked the turning point of the war from near Allied defeat to victory a few months later. As the British historian, John Buchan, later wrote, in the spring of 1918 "Ludendorff had stood as the apparent dictator of Europe; four months later he and his master were in exile."

Because of the massive issues at stake, both actions bred a good many legends remote from historical fact. In the 1918 instance some of the Americans who fought north of the Marne that spring died, either then or later, believing that by meeting and beating the flower of the German army they were responsible for saving the Allies.

This was not quite true. The men of the 2d U. S. Division, and to a lesser extent of the 3d U. S. Division, did meet some hardy German soldiers, did stop a part of an overall German advance, did ultimately gain the objectives of a limited counter attack. But while they fought, the French and Germans were also fighting elsewhere; in other words the war scarcely confined itself to Belleau Wood during the month of June.

The attention of the world, however, did confine itself to Belleau Wood. When the Americans went up to the Marne the world asked one question: Will the Americans fight? When the Americans did fight the world asked: Will they win? The dual answers gave not only new life to nearly dead Allies, but also time in which to continue and to exploit the vital transfusion of both moral and physical strength. That was the importance of the June fighting northwest of Château-Thierry.

Because this series of actions formed the first prolonged test of American arms in World War I and because of the subsequent and brilliant combat record of the 2d U. S. Division, a considerable postwar research effort was devoted to the history of this division. Under the auspices of the 2d Division Historical Section, military historians spent years putting together nine volumes of official sources. Each weighing several pounds, these contain a plethora of documents written at the time—of division, brigade, regimental and battalion orders; of pre-action, action and after-action reports; of field messages from squad level up; of daily brigade and division reports of operations. Another four massive tomes hold translations of German documents germane to the American fighting. To these must be added the several histories of the June action—some published, some not—and the numerous private accounts of the action, some in letters of the time, some in postwar accounts. Finally there are the living survivors.

I have frequently quoted from all these sources because I felt that the story could be better told by the men who wrote it. However, not all sources agree on all of the events of that crowded period. Where disagreements are serious, I have included them in the narrative; where they are possibly of interest to the student, I have placed them in footnotes; where they are minor I have resolved them on the plea of extensive research and study. I have also edited some of the documents, but only to make them more clear to the non-military reader. In case some readers find me unduly harsh to some commanders, I can only say that harsh battle rarely leaves professional reputations unchanged.

This work owes a great deal to a great many people. For services rendered I wish to thank Mr. Leo J. Bailey, Mr. Frank J. Cushner, Mr. John R. Hardin, Mr. Samuel W. Meek, Mr. and Mrs. William Wyly, Dr. Willard Morrey, Major General Melvin Krulewitch, USMCR (ret), Dr. Emil Kauder, Mr. A. E. Holden, and Mrs. Joan Saunders of Writers' and Speakers' Research, London. I am also indebted to General Graves B. Erskine, USMC (ret), who probably has forgotten that he originally interested me in this campaign; to General Alfred H. Noble, USMC (ret), Lt. General Keller E. Rockey, USMC (ret), and Mr. Fielding S. Robinson, who have supplied many germane details; to Colonel Frank J. O'Connor, USMCR, who placed a most valuable document at my disposal; to Mr. D. M. O'Quinlivan and his staff at Headquarters, Marine Corps, who as usual have been more than cooperative; to Mr. Victor Gondos and his staff at the National Archives; and to Mrs. Ray Spurling who typed a large portion of the final manuscript.

I want further to acknowledge the invaluable help of General Gerald C. Thomas, USMC (ret), General Lemuel C. Shepherd, USMC (ret), General Clifton B. Cates, USMC (ret), Mr. Louis F. Timmerman, Mr. William R. Mathews, Mr. Hanson W. Baldwin and Brigadier General Samuel B. Griffith, USMC (ret)—they have given freely of their time, their documents, their memories and their impressive critical acumen in trying to make this a better book. Throughout the long preparation of this work I have as always received the unstinted support of my parents and of my sister, to whom the book is dedicated.

Finally I am greatly indebted to the following writers and/or publishers for permission to quote from various sources as follows:

World War I: Hanson Baldwin; Harper and Row Inc.

1918 The Last Act: Barrie Pitt; W. W. Norton and Co.; Cassell and Co. Ltd.

Soldiers of the Sea: Robert D. Heinl, Jr.; Mr. A. Denis Clift and the United States Naval Institute.

With the Help of God and a Few Marines: Colonel A. W. Catlin; Mrs. Muriel W. Dyer; Doubleday and Co.

The Doughboys: Laurence Stallings; Harper and Row Inc.

Great Soldiers of the Two World Wars: H. A. De Weerd; W. W. Norton and Co.

The World Crisis: Winston Churchill; Odhams Press Ltd. and Charles Scribner's Sons.

French Headquarters 1915–1918: Jean de Pierrefeu; Geoffrey Bles Ltd.

Grandeur and Misery of Victory: Georges Clemenceau; Curtis Brown Ltd.

Dear Folks at Home—: K. F. Cowing and C. R. Cooper; Houghton Mifflin Co.

Haig: Duff Cooper; Faber and Faber Ltd.

My Experiences in the World War: General John J. Pershing; Mr. F. Warren Pershing.

Foch Speaks: Charles Bugnet; The Dial Press, Inc.; Editions Grasset.

The Memoirs of Marshal Foch: Ferdinand Foch; Mrs. T. Rowland Slingluff; Doubleday and Co.

"We Can Take It": E. D. Cooke; Mr. John B. Spore and the Association of the United States Army.

Suicide Battalions: Wendell Westover; G. P. Putnam's Sons.

Leaves From a War Diary: James C. Harbord; Mrs. Anne Whiting and Mr. Lewis Brown; Dodd Mead and Co.

The American Army in France: James G. Harbord; Mrs. Anne Whiting and Mr. Lewis Brown; Little Brown and Co.

"The Generals and the Downfall of the German Monarchy": E. Eyck; Royal Historical Society.

Memoirs of a Staff Officer 1917–1919: S. T. Hubbard; Mr. Samuel T. Hubbard III.

"I Have a Rendezvous With Death": Alan Seeger; Elsie Adams Seeger and Charles Scribner's Sons.

Fix Bayonets!: John W. Thomason, Jr.; Charles Scribner's Sons.

My War Experiences: Wilhelm, Crown Prince of Germany; The Hutchinson Publishing Group.

"Capture of Hill 142, Battle of Belleau Wood and Capture of Bouresches": E. N. McClellan; Lieutenant Colonel W. R. Traynor, USMC, and the Marine Corps Association.

"The Battles for the Possession of Belleau Woods, June, 1918": Ernst Otto; Mr. A. Denis Clift and the United States Naval Institute.

Generals and Politicians: J. C. King; University of California Press.

American Reporters on the Western Front 1914–1918: Emmett Crozier; Oxford University Press, Inc.

As I Saw It: Alden Brooks; Alfred A. Knopf, Inc.

The Supreme Command 1914–1918: Lord Hankey; Allen and Unwin Ltd.

Ludendorff's Own Story: Erich Ludendorff; Harper and Row Inc.

Out of My Life: Marshal von Hindenburg; Harper and Row Inc.

The Last of the Ebb: Sydney Rogerson; Arthur Barker, Ltd.

Belleau Wood today is an American shrine in the heart of France. Along its northern fringe the American Battle Monuments Commission maintains a large cemetery surmounted by an imposing, quite beautiful chapel towering over the graves—a silent sentinel of the dead.

North of the chapel neat rows of white crosses give way to a few hundred yards of open, undulating fields leading to the Bouresches-Torcy road and across it, in a small valley, to the ancient village of Belleau. Belleau has not greatly changed—a pleasant little cluster of stone houses, a church and a gushing spring whose crystal-clear, very cold water explains the name.

Behind the chapel a part of the wood has been made into a carefully groomed exhibition piece. Marked trails lead several thousand visitors a year through the dark quiet of shell-scarred trees and soft forest floor to lend some idea of the wood's personality, some slight notion of the light which gave a name to history.

A blue-smocked guide, an old man with wide mustache flowing above broken English words, will explain that by tradition the wood belonged to the château of Belleau. Until the village came in the way of war, a wealthy sportsman from Paris maintained the château as a country house and the wood as a shooting preserve generously stocked with birds, hare and deer.

The wood made splendid hunting. Large and irregularly shaped, it has been variously compared to a misshapen kidney, a distorted hourglass, even to a sea horse. More than anything else its old map profile resembled a jellylike glob of a green amoeba under a microscope. Just over a mile long from north to south, in 1918 its upper section stretched about a thousand yards from east to west. A thin neck connected this to an elongated lower section nearly a mile wide and some 600 yards deep—heavy woods and tangled nearly impenetrable undergrowth slowly thinning down into a large ravine flanked by wheat fields which led five or six hundred yards to the village of Lucy on the left, Bouresches on the right.

Its external shape in no way suggested its internal nature. The misbegotten son of a glacial writhing, it was a very old wood split severally by ravines and gullies and spotted with enormous boulders, some as large "as a small freight car." This together with a massive undergrowth provided an ideal breeding ground for birds and game, an ideal spot for shooting breakfasts where attractive ladies and cold champagne awaited the tired sportsmen at tables clustered around an octagonal lodge called the Pavillon that stood in the northwest corner.

Such parties, and they were many, constituted a major facet in a way of life which for decades sparkled for a privileged few. A hallmark of the Edwardian Age, they were scarcely confined to the Château Belleau or to the soft valley of the Marne. In those years Europe and its neighbor, England, furnished many counterparts to the Château Belleau, to the thick wood, the soft, green fields, the pipe-smoking, tolerant peasantry whose view of life was vastly circumscribed, provincial to the extreme.

As a way of life those years have been thoroughly scrutinized by historians and sociologists, some defending, some condemning. Certainly there was a great deal to defend and a great deal to condemn. In the end, however, the effort remains academic because in 1914 that portion of civilization went to war.

In 1914 the hunting parties stopped . . . and so did a way of life.

The Great War did not immediately involve Belleau Wood. Although each side had assiduously prepared for action, each side had first to undergo certain physical preliminaries. Men had to be called up, battalions formed and from them divisions and corps until finally vast armies moved in accordance with sophisticated plans long developed and rehearsed in the otherwise halcyon days of peace.

The French needed the better part of two weeks to mobilize and march to the attack. Less than a week later their armies along with the recently landed British Expeditionary Force had fought and lost a series of battles known as the Battle of the Frontiers—a disaster costing the French, according to some estimates, as many as 300,000 casualties. With the French and British in retreat along the line, the Germans continued pushing toward Paris and what they thought would be the end of the war.

The war now came closer to the Marne.

Hausen's Third German Army, carrying out its share of Moltke's drive on Paris, wheeled in from Belgium, crossed the Aisne, fought east of Soissons, pushed on to Bussiares, Torcy, Belleau, Bouresches, left rearguards there and continued on across the Marne. For a few days the farmers who remained fed the German troops, watered their horses, tried to come to terms with a new way of life. Then, suddenly, the first battle of the Marne—a German defeat. The Germans left as rapidly as they had come. Soldiers of the British Expeditionary Force tramped through the towns in slow pursuit, the war moved north, the other farmers returned.

The fighting had damaged the village of Belleau: the deserted château and the church scarred by shells, a small cemetery of German, French and British dead, the young men gone, neatly tended fields beginning to suffer, the trails in the now disused wood beginning to grow over. This was the backwash of war, it could be lived with, and it was.

At first the war remained quite close. Following the German retreat the Allies began a methodical attack against the Aisne position. When it failed, both Allies and enemy turned north in a desperate series of attempts to outflank the other. When these failed, both sides began to dig trenches along a line that for nearly three years would not vary more than a few hundred yards in either direction.

During those grim years of war in which futile, costly offensives succeeded each other with monotonous regularity, Belleau Wood remained unimportant: a place name utterly unknown to the world, probably not even familiar to the citizens of Château-Thierry to the east, scarcely remarked by the farmers of Bouresches, Lucy and Belleau or by those of the flanking Clignon villages to the west.

For nearly three years the whole area lived a war felt rather than seen. Diminishing returns characterized this type of war, not alone in the Marne valley but throughout the once prosperous country-side of France. Young men had early gone off, then older and still older men. Each spring a few had come back on furlough to help with the planting and sometimes a few had come back in autumn to help with the harvest. With each spring and with each autumn fewer returned—there had not been many to start with in the region of Belleau; by 1918 most of them had died. The women also had gone off to war, to work in the ammunition factories clustered around Paris: at first the younger ones, the maidens once destined to marry the swains who now were dead, then the younger widows without children, then even middle-aged women.

As a result it was a countryside of very old and very young try-ing to carry on a way of life just scarcely possible. The horses to pull the plows and to pull the produce carts to market had long since been taken by the army. A few old and sick ones remained, so did a few oxen, so did cattle and sheep and poultry; for despite neglect the land was rich and grew grass and grew what was planted to it. But in this dying community less and less was planted and more and more was taken by the army—a microcosm of the blight covering all the lands of all the war countries, not yet dead but dying in that winter's impasse.

The winter of 1917 was not pleasant. It was an unusually cold winter and as it spun itself across the fields and into the lives of tired and hungry peoples, it slowly became a winter of very little hope: the French and British armies momentarily beaten, the Italians barely holding on the Piave, in Russia the Communists negotiating an ar-mistice with the Germans already shifting vast forces to the western front.

As 1917 gave way to 1918, gloom covered France and England like a gigantic burial pall. Along with the rest of their countrymen and with their Allies, the people of the Marne held no reason to believe their lot would ever change. And yet as the toothless old grandfathers and the tired old women and the rapidly aging widows with the little children fed the precious stock against the winter's blast and rummaged in Belleau Wood for faggots to warm the farmhouses of weather-beaten stone, two factors were slowly forming toward change.

One was the German high command: Hindenburg and Ludendorff had decided that if Germany were to win the war she must do so in 1918 and on the western front. The plan as yet remained nebulous—even in its final stages there would be no mention of Belleau Wood.

The other was a portion of that slight trickle of men and supply which America had started sending overseas when she entered the war in the spring of 1917. It was called the 2d Division of U. S. Regulars. Although certain of its units were already in France, the division as yet existed mainly on paper. It would form, it would train and finally it would march to battle north of the Marne. None of its nearly 27,000 fighting men would hear of Belleau Wood until they saw it.

So in that dreadful, dreary winter two elements existed rather like stars which by accident were to explode one against the other. The explosion would prove as disastrous to the farmers of the Marne as it would prove important to a world at war.

It would occur at Belleau Wood.

Chapter 1

The Americans

In that late winter of 1917 the least imposing of the two collision factors was the 2d Division of U. S. Regulars, the bulk of whose soldiers and marines were regular in name only. Most of the Americans fated to fight on the Marne in the spring of 1918 were youths who less than a year before had been swept into local recruiting offices by the first flood of patriotism.

The division originally was to have been all army—regiments from Pennsylvania and Texas which, like those of the already organized 1st U. S. Division, had been hastily scraped together from garrisons at home and abroad, fleshed out with willing volunteers, rudely trained and equipped and sent overseas to fight the war to end all wars.

In the interim, however, several factors changed War Department plans. One was a lack of trained army units, another a shortage of shipping. But looming above these was the unwillingness of the United States Marine Corps to remain distant from battle.

Perhaps no world power has ever been so badly prepared for war as was America in 1917. That fateful spring the American army numbered less than 135,000. Scattered in garrisons at home and abroad this meager strength consisted of units no larger than regiments, none trained, organized or equipped to fight in France. The American economy had barely begun to convert to war production. The army lacked rifles, ammunition, automatic weapons, artillery, horses, trucks, airplanes, even hand grenades and gas masks. The navy was small, its ships few and mostly obsolete; the merchant marine was even less effective. Only by the most enormous effort were sufficient regiments formed to constitute the 1st Division, which followed the newly appointed commander of the American Expeditionary Force, Major General John J. Pershing, to France in the spring and summer of 1917.

Considering the War Department's military poverty, logic dictated the deployment of every available fighting unit. But such was the military intransigence of the day that the men who, ironically enough, were to suffer the lion's share of the Marne fighting—the marines—were at first shunted aside.

By tradition and law the marines represented only a fraction of America's military strength. Before the war they numbered but a few thousand; in 1916 Congress increased their ranks to just over 15,000; in late March, 1917, President Wilson used emergency powers to authorize a further increase to 18,000, of whom 693 were officers. In May Congress authorized a further increase to 31,000.[1]

As was the case with the army, regular marine units were scattered at home and abroad. But for several decades, and unlike the army, the marines had been practicing the precise art now required: the mounting out of regiments hastily organized from ship's detachments and from naval posts and stations. Although such expeditionary forces were integral to naval operations, as demonstrated in the Civil War, the Spanish-American War and the China and Mexican campaigns, no one could doubt the ability of the marines to fight alongside the army if the need arose.

In the mind of Major General George Barnett, Commandant of the Marine Corps, the need had clearly arisen. By a careful juggling of his units, he decided that he could not only meet naval requirements brought on by America's entry into the war but could also furnish at least two regiments of infantry for service with the AEF. The first of these, the 5th Marine Regiment, was hastily organized and, by order of President Wilson, transferred to control of the War Department, which included it in the first contingent of the AEF.

The second regiment, the 6th Marines, began assembling almost immediately at Quantico, Virginia, the new marine base.

Colonel Charles Doyen, a New Englander who had spent thirty-four of his fifty-eight years in the Corps, commanded the 5th Marines. He would eventually be succeeded by Colonel Wendell Neville, a younger man and a contemporary of the new commander of the 6th Marines, Colonel Albertus Catlin. These seniors would be assisted by other regulars in the forthcoming months: younger and vigorous officers such as Harry Lee, Hiram Bearrs, Logan Feland, Holland Smith, Julius Turrill, Littleton Waller, Jr., Ben Berry, John Hughes, Thomas Holcomb, Berton Sibley, Maurice Shearer, Frederic Wise, Edward Cole. Most of the company commanders were also veteran regulars, for example Captain Lester Wass, who had served nine years, or Captain John Blanchfield, a former enlisted man with more years of service than many of his seniors. Regular NCOs completed the list: Sergeant Major John Quick, First Sergeant John O'Brien, Gunnery Sergeant Dan Daly—names already legendary in the Corps, names mentioned almost reverently by the younger sergeants and corporals despite their own impressive hash.

These were rugged Americans. Among them there wasn't much they didn't know about the Marine Corps and what it expected from the younger officers and men. They and their contemporaries had served all over the world—had fought with Huntington in Cuba, with Tony Waller in China and on Samar, with Smedley Butler in Haiti and Nicaragua, with John Lejeune in Mexico.

Of different builds and varying temperaments, they were as individual in action as they were similar in devotion to their Corps. The elder, rather dignified Doyen contrasted strongly with the impetuous Butler, the flamboyant Waller, the vigorous Catlin, the quiet Neville, the younger, very intelligent Feland. Of the still younger battalion commanders, Turrill was short, stocky, rather dark in complexion, while Berry was tall, over six feet, sparsely built, of light complexion. "Johnny the Hard" Hughes was over six feet, slim and in perfect physical condition. One of his marines remembered him "drilling the battalion at Quantico where every few minutes he shouted an unorthodox but highly effective order: 'Heads up, goddamn it, heads up.'"[2] Tommy Holcomb was short, of compact build, quiet, rather aloof. Frederic Wise—some called him "Fritz," some "Dopey"—was a taskmaster, a heavy man who, to one of his platoon commanders, looked "seven months pregnant"; he was also tough—once in the tropics at the funeral of a troublemaking marine he had the band play "He Was Always in the Way." Catlin's adjutant was Major Francis Evans, an elderly officer who had come out of retirement to go to war—"a jolly fellow, always in good spirits, [who] possesses that sort of magnetic, dynamic personality that keeps things moving."[3]

Diverse though they were, they had long since subordinated themselves to an ideal represented by the globe and anchor surmounted by the scrawny-looking eagle. Heretofore they had protected this ideal with the regular Corps. But in 1917 this nucleus was no longer sufficient of itself. It was a big war now; they needed help.

The Commandant called for help with a massive recruiting campaign whose action posters challenged the youth of America to be the "First to Fight." Twelve hundred recruits were already in training at Parris Island when America entered the war. With that, volunteers flowed into recruiting offices throughout the nation. They came singly and in pairs and in groups. They came from every economic class, from colleges and universities, businesses, professions, factories, farms, lumber camps, the employed and unemployed, the rich and the poor. Colonel Catlin later wrote of the 6th Marine Regiment:

> The officers, from captain up, and fifty or so of the noncommissioned officers were old-time Marines, but the junior officers and all of the privates were new men . . . sixty percent of the entire regiment—mark this—sixty percent of them were college men. Two-thirds of one entire company came straight from the University of Minnesota. . . . Of our young lieutenants a large number were college athletes. . . .[4]

These early volunteers formed just as diverse a group, even more so, as the coterie of regulars. But youth and health and a desire for battle are powerful catalysts when mixed in the crucible of war. Various as were their backgrounds, as different their personalities, they were there to learn how to fight.

"There" was first of all Parris Island, off the coast from Port Royal, South Carolina, an isolated mass of acreage covered with stunted scrub pine—a wind-blown, sandy land utterly bereft of physical comfort. The drill instructors—hand-picked sergeants and corporals—owned it and they owned the youngsters who came to it.

To the youngsters the drill instructors were the "old" marines, the tall, straight, mustached professionals who dressed their pride in gaudy blue uniforms, decorated their bodies with salty tattoos, fed their thirst with chewing tobacco, frequently dipped snuff, assuaged fatigue with whiskey, cursed with the metric vigor of Kipling, drilled their troops night and day, held frequent and demanding inspections, and knew everything there was to know about the Springfield .03 rifle.

A week or two was needed to square away the new recruits, to organize them into platoons, shave their heads, shoot them with typhoid and smallpox vaccines, teach them the drill. It was a hard life at first, one neatly summed up by a recruit in a letter to his mother:

> The first day I was at camp I was afraid that I was going to die. The next two weeks my sole fear was that I wasn't going to die. And after that I knew I'd never die because I'd become so hard that nothing could kill me.[5]

This was the general experience. Despite the sand and flies they ate well and slept well and in surprisingly short order the civilian flab began giving way to solid bodies and minds increasingly imbued with a very old tradition. Part of the tradition, a large part, was marksmanship. The recruits spent fully half their time on the rifle range, a rigorous course which for most of them would pay off on the Marne the following spring.

Young officers were simultaneously trained, both at Parris Island and at Quantico where the recruits were sent from boot camp. These, too, came from around the country: Lem Shepherd and Dick Murphy from VMI; Cliff Cates from the University of Tennessee;

Graves Erskine from Louisiana; Lagore, and John Overton from Yale; the all-American end, Bastien, from Minnesota; Louis Timmerman and William Moore from Princeton; Arthur Worton from Harvard; Leroy Hunt from the University of California; Bill Mathews from Arizona.

Officers and recruits joined companies at Quantico, drilled, learned how to build trenches, worked with bayonet and rifle and Lewis guns. From here, contingents entrained for Philadelphia, boarded ship, waited as long as a week at anchor in New York for a convoy to form, then endured a ten- to twelve-day sea voyage. Sick or not, they drilled daily and practiced abandon ship routine twice a day. For the hearty ones there were shows and boxing matches, and for everyone there were rumors of enemy submarines.

In France only a few companies were into field training. The bulk of the marines found themselves performing stevedoring and guard duties at such places as Saint-Nazaire and Bordeaux where they survived rain and cold in rude barracks "with straw strewn over the damp floors of earth, knapsacks for pillows and sandwiched between army blankets."[6]

For men who had come overseas to kill Germans the new duty was altogether a dreary existence. But even as they worked on the ice-covered docks or patrolled the smelly bistros, even as they slept in rude, cold huts and drilled in the mud, even as they ate the corned willy and cursed the YMCA that sold Sweet Caporal cigarettes for twenty-five cents a pack—even as they endured their winter of cold discontent, their future was being determined in Pershing's new headquarters at Chaumont. Their future was the 2d Division of U. S. Regulars.

Neither Pershing's headquarters nor the War Department could ignore the presence in France of nearly two regiments of marines, particularly in view of increasing pressures brought by Congress and the President for their use. On September 20, 1917, the War Department authorized a brigade of marines to replace the army brigade originally planned for the 2d Division. Some five weeks later the senior marine in France, Brigadier General Charles Doyen, opened division headquarters in Bourmont, a village some 150 miles southeast of Paris. On November 8, 1917, he turned command over to an army officer, Major General Omar Bundy.[7]

Bundy found himself with an impressive paper command. Its heart consisted of two infantry brigades, each with two infantry regiments and one machine gun battalion, an artillery brigade with two regiments of 75mm guns and one of 155mm guns, an engineer regiment, an additional machine gun battalion and a signal battalion. Fleshed out by ordnance, motor transport, salvage, clothing, bath, laundry and bakery units, it was fed by a vast conglomeration of supply trains operating from rear area depots. Altogether it numbered more than 27,000 men, a size well over twice that of an Allied or German division.[8] (See charts pages 74 and 75.)

This was on paper.

When Bundy took command, none of his artillery had arrived, none of his trains, no signal units. Two machine gun battalions and one battalion of marines were still in America. The bulk of marines in France were performing rear area duties—only a battalion and a half were in field training in nearby Damblain.

Newly arrived army units, particularly the 9th and 23d Infantry regiments of the 3d U. S. Brigade, were as short of supply as their troops were short of training. Private Leo J. Bailey, M Company, 9th Infantry, is quoted by Laurence Stallings as saying that

> his company of "Regulars" contained not a single man who had ever fired a Springfield rifle, and few who had ever discharged a firearm of any kind. Not many of the 250 men in this outfit possessed scabbards; and Private Bailey, wearing thin barracks shoes and canvas leggings, arrived in the village of Soulacourt with his bayonet wrapped in a newspaper, ten round of live ammunition in his belt, ready to beat the German to his knees.[9]

With the exception of Major Thomas Holcomb's battalion of marines, the units still to come would not arrive in much better shape. Captain Wendell Westover of the 4th Machine Gun Battalion later wrote:

A sun tanned lieutenant paused before the bulletin board at Headquarters of the 48th Infantry at Syracuse early in September 1917. "Memo—Officers desiring early overseas service and having had experience with machine guns see the Adjutant." Three companies formed the provisional battalion. They had no machine guns—there were not enough available to equip them. Their training was to be carried out in France with French equipment.[10]

In fact, 87.2 percent of the soldiers and 74.3 percent of the marines consisted of youngsters in their first year of service. Only 4.8 percent of the soldiers and 9.3 percent of the marines were regulars with four or more years of service.[11] Speaking of his arrival at Soulacourt, Private Bailey wrote, "To have sent us to the front at that time would have been murder; but we were all willing to go. We were woefully ignorant of the basic principles of the soldier."[12]

Private Bailey and his fellows would learn these "basic principles." As each American unit, excepting certain of the marine battalions, arrived in France, it was attached to a French or British unit for instruction. Major Wise, whose battalion of marines was sent to the crack 115th French Chasseurs Alpins—the famous Blue Devils commanded by Major Touchon—later wrote:

> All our training that summer was along the lines of trench warfare. Early one morning, right after breakfast, we marched out to the training area, met the French officers, and the day's work started. We dug a series of trenches. We took up the new method of bayonet fighting. Long lines of straw-stuffed figures hanging from a cross beam between two upright posts were set up. The men fixed bayonets and charged them. British instructors, who had arrived shortly after us, stood over them and urged them on. . . . The British at that time were crazy about the bayonet. They knew it was going to win the war. The French were equally obsessed with the grenade. They knew it was going to win the war. So we also got a full dose of training in hand grenade throwing.

Then, Wise continued, after learning how to fire the rifle grenade and the one-pounder or 37mm gun:

> We were put through a series of shows to teach us how trench raids were conducted and repelled. We had gas mask drill and were put through a gas chamber. We were given a workout with those damnable French Chauchat automatic rifles. . . . The men worked their heads off at all this new stuff. They assembled and dismounted machine guns, learned the names of the parts and how to repair them. They made wire entanglements and dugouts. They looked upon the French instructors as gods, for they knew they were being trained by veteran troops.[13]

Not all battalions were as fortunate, but their time was coming. For as the old year gave way to the new, the 2d Division began receiving its delayed infantry units, its trains, artillery, two machine gun battalions, signal and medical troops. It was now ready to begin training as a division.

Notes

1. Robert D. Heinl, Jr., *Soldiers of the Sea*. Annapolis: U. S. Naval Institute, 1962. See also Clyde H. Metcalf, *A History of the United States Marine Corps*. New York: G. P. Putnam's Sons, 1939; E. N. McClellan, *The United States Marine Corps in the World War*. Washington: U. S. Government Printing Office, 1920.
2. William R. Mathews. Personal correspondence. After a distinguished World War I career, Mr. Mathews returned to newspaper reporting as publisher and editor of a large paper in Tucson, Arizona.
3. A. W. Catlin, *With the Help of God and a Few Marines*. New York: Doubleday, Page and Co., 1919.
4. Ibid.
5. Kemper F. Cowing and Courtney R. Cooper, *Dear Folks at Home—*. New York: Houghton Mifflin Co., 1919.
6. W. A. Carter, *The Tale of a Devil Dog*. Washington: The Canteen Press, 1920.

7. Oliver L. Spaulding and John W. Wright, *The Second Division American Expeditionary Force in France, 1917–1919*. New York: The Hillman Press, Inc., 1937.
8. Ibid.
9. Laurence Stallings, *The Doughboys*. New York: Harper and Row, 1963.
10. Wendell Westover, *Suicide Battalions*. New York: G. P. Putnam's Sons, 1929.
11. Spaulding and Wright, op. cit.
12. Stallings, op. cit.
13. Frederic M. Wise and Meigs O. Frost, *A Marine Tells It to You*. New York: J. H. Sears and Co., Inc., 1929.

Chapter 2

"Cold, wet and hungry, on we marched ..."
—Marine Private W.A. Carter

In January, 1918, the 2d Division began real training for war. At Le Valdahon the 2d Field Artillery Brigade moved into rude quarters where, as one of the young lieutenants later wrote, "Military preparations started with a whirl. Classes were formed, schedules put out, reveille and retreat, etc. . . ."[1]

The neophyte gunners had to master considerable theory before breaking their weapons out for firing. The war had produced a bewildering variety of artillery techniques. In 1917 density ruled, the result of the last German offensive in Flanders where a fantastic concentration of artillery pieces had produced *Prommelfeuer,* later called "hurricane" and "typhoon" fire by the Germans, "drum" fire by the Allies. In addition the peculiar requirements of trench warfare had produced "barrage" or "curtain" fire which called for a rain of shells on a designated zone; "raking" fire where shells literally raked a piece of ground; "encaging" or "box" fire used during raids across no-man's-land to box in either enemy or friendly troops; "bothering" or "harassing" fire; "sprinkling" fire; "combing" fire; and "destroying" fire. The young gunners had also to learn how to fire "special" shells containing either lachrymatory or asphyxiating gases—a delicate art since if the wind were wrong they could wipe out their own units.[2]

The rest of the division worked equally hard. New units arrived daily. Early in January, for example, a company of the 6th Marines in Saint-Nazaire

> moved out in very severe weather, but the French had covered the bottom of the box cars with straw. With our blankets and forty men to a car we managed to keep fairly warm. For four days we ate hardtack and corn bill. Why the relatively short trip required four days I'll never know, but it did.[3]

On January 12 Colonel Catlin opened 6th Regiment headquarters in Blévaincourt. A few weeks later Holcomb's 2d Battalion arrived from America. The 6th Regiment was intact.

The newcomers occupied an area northeast of the 5th Marine Regiment. Some of the units were split into groups of from ten men to a platoon and assigned to the stables and haylofts of Blévaincourt, Champigneulles, Chaumont-la-Ville, Robecourt and Germainvillers. These were drab little Vosges farming villages where the height of the manure pile in front of a house determined the owner's wealth. The troops disdainfully called it the "Manure Sector" and cursed when they had to drain the orange-colored water from the flooded streets. Still, their lot was better than units billeted in outlying Adrian barracks hastily thrown up by the 2d Engineers. These wooden structures, spartan in the extreme, each held 100 men. Cheesecloth covered the few windows; a small stove at either end provided a mockery of heat. Although some men attempted to heat water for a weekly bath, "most of us took a bucket of cold water and went out for a bath in the snow which we followed with a brisk rubdown."[4]

Training started immediately. As was the case with the marines and soldiers before them, the new arrivals had a great deal to learn. They had to get used to wearing two-pound helmets and to lugging two different types of gas masks, British and French—and neither worth a continental damn. Once the gas alarm sounded they had six seconds to put on the mask. Colonel Catlin later described it as a hot and stifling thing [that] seems to impede the faculties. The wearer takes in the air through his mouth, after it has been sucked through the purifying chemicals. His nose is not trusted and is clamped shut. Imagine yourself fighting with a clothespin on your nose and a bag over your mouth and you may be able to get some notion of what a gas mask is like.[5]

After a good deal of bayonet drill, the men had to learn how to throw the serrated cast-iron hand grenade. French instructors explained that it could not be thrown like a baseball, but had to be lobbed with a stiff-arm movement in order to gain the desired trajectory to reach a trench or shellhole and to remain in the air long enough so that the enemy could not throw it back.

They next learned how to fix a truncated cone which the French called a *tromblon* onto the muzzles of their Springfields and then arm it with a rifle grenade called the VB grenade, after its inventor, Vivien Bessières. The projectile weighed a pound, was fired with the rifle butt firmly held on the ground, and could reach from 200 to 500 yards. The launcher was also used to fire signal rockets.

Next came instruction in the light trench mortar, a crew-served weapon firing a heavier projectile about 300 to 500 yards. It was backed by the one-pounder or 37mm gun, also an infantry weapon, mounted on wheels and generally pulled by a mule to the action zone. There its crew manhandled it into a defilade position and, if employing it in battery formation, removed its wheels. A quick-firing weapon—twenty rounds per minute—it was extremely accurate at 900 yards and was generally used against enemy machine guns.[6]

The marines had brought their Lewis guns with them, and used them for the first weeks of training. In early January the Lewis guns were replaced with both the French Hotchkiss, a heavy machine gun demanding mule-drawn carts for transportation, and the French automatic rifle or Chauchat. One officer described the latter as "heavy, clumsy and inaccurate," while according to another, the only good thing about it was that you could lay it down for a day or two, then pick it up and fire it—rust and all.[7] Another officer described it as a pain in the neck. If you had put it in a vice and fired it at 100 yards range it would have dispersed twenty-five feet. Both the weapon and ammunition were very heavy. My platoon carried nineteen clip bags, each weighing fifty–sixty pounds. We had to rotate them on the march with the lieutenants taking their turn along with the rest.[8]

The day-in, day-out training was hampered by severe physical discomfort. According to one survivor:

The only place we were allowed to drill was in the swampy meadowlands where the ground could not be tilled. We drilled all day, usually in water half-way to our shoe tops. By night our feet were soaking wet and half-frozen. We dried our socks by pressing them under the blankets.

Later we made a great many forced marches. It was a real pleasure to get out of the swamps and march on a road where you could keep your feet dry.[9]

Another veteran later described one of the forced marches:

Cold, wet and hungry, on we marched, hour after hour, each man bearing a pack weighing about forty-five pounds, consisting of two blankets, a supply of underclothes, a pair of trousers, emergency rations of hardtack and "monkey meat" (canned corn beef), besides a heavy belt with 100 rounds of ammunition, a canteen, wire-cutters, gas mask, helmet and rifle . . . and two identification tags around his neck.[10]

Army infantry regiments and the 5th Marines were also sharing the experience. Lieutenant Lem Shepherd would never forget it:

. . . Colonel Wise really put it to us that winter. We were constantly on the alert. Sometimes at night we were called out without warning to make a hike in subzero weather. Around Christmas we marched to some mock trenches where we spent three days in assimilated trench warfare. It was rugged duty but we learned a great deal, and we became tough as nails. I personally learned something about Colonel Wise, whom we all regarded as something of an ogre. One night when I was OD I had to break up a fight between some French and American soldiers in a small café. I did this by sending the Americans to their billets. The woman who owned the café accused me of ruining her trade. She got so mad that she fell to the floor and started gnawing the rung of a chair. We had orders to report anything out of the ordinary to Colonel Wise so about 10 P.M. I went to his quarters. He heard the story, complimented me on my handling of it, then said, "Sit down, I want to talk to you."

He said it in a friendly way. I had never heard him talk like that and rather hesitantly took the chair he indicated. "Shepherd, you've been with me some time now and you know I'm considered a martinet. I know that you youngsters fuss because I insist on meticulous obedience of my orders. Some of them seem petty to you—the making up of the bunks to regulation, the correct uniform, my inspecting every rifle in the battalion. I insist on these little things because they make the big things. One of these days we'll be in combat and the only way we can win is by strict and unqualified obedience of orders. In combat you won't have time to think and deliberate over an order. You will have to execute it immediately without questioning your superior. When we go into battle this battalion will be so trained that there will never be any question about our disobeying an order or not carrying it out to the best of our ability."

It was a talk I remembered all my life. It was the only time he ever showed another side to me, the only time he explained that he had a purpose for being the way he was.[11]

Wise and other battalion Commanders could be forgiven for driving their junior officers and troops. They were living under a twofold responsibility: learning a new mode of warfare themselves and seeing that their green subordinates understood it. At times the abysmal ignorance of the juniors would have tested the patience of

Job. On one occasion Lieutenant Clifton Cates was attending a class
on field engineering held by his battalion commander, Major Thomas Holcomb:

> I hadn't read the book and hoped he would not call on
> me. Naturally he did.
> "Cates, how many entrances should a dugout have?"
> I had no idea, but thought quickly and answered, "Well,
> sir, at least one."
> "That's a hell of a bright reply," he grunted.[12]

During that first winter, only a few lucky ones gained temporary
surcease from the harsh environment by receiving liberty passes to
Paris. But Paris was drab and cold and, as they soon discovered,
General Pershing was doing everything possible to frustrate the natural desires of his men. When Monsieur Clemenceau graciously offered the AEF the freedom of French bordellos he was hastily and
abruptly turned down. Not only were the Americans to be the best
appearing and disciplined troops on the continent, but they were to
be the most moral, and it was up to the flocks of military policemen
who patrolled the streets of Paris and other major cities to carry out
the senior commander's desires.

Diversions in the training area were pathetically inadequate.
Again, a lucky few fell in with village maidens, but these were so rare
as to represent nothing more than an ephemeral dream to the bulk
of the Americans. During free hours and when weather permitted,
the troops turned to team sports; otherwise they endured the con-
fines of a small YMCA or Red Cross hut to smoke Sweet Caporals,
read the heavily censored Paris edition of the *Herald Tribune* (and
after February 8, 1918, the new *Stars and Stripes)*, write letters home
and sing songs that failed to survive another generation. One of the
current favorites was:

> My girl's a Lulu,
> Every inch a Lulu,
> Lulu, that old girl of mine . . .

Another was just coming into vogue:

Mademoiselle from gay Paree, parlez-vous,
Mademoiselle from gay Paree, parlez-vous.
Mademoiselle from gay Paree,
She had the clap and she gave it to me,
Hinky-dinky, parlez-vous . . .

That was their life until mid-March. The weeks of preliminary training had proven long, grim and miserable. But as one of the marines later pointed out:

> It was this period that made us tough. In my battalion we had one case of sickness in two months—a man evacuated for appendicitis. We had no colds—nothing. We got tough, we stayed tough. When we went to the trench we were so mean that we would have fought our own grandmothers.[13]

The 2d Division went to the trenches in mid-March. These lay in a so-called "quiet" sector—twenty miles of elaborate fortifications along a line between Verdun east to and around the enemy salient at Saint-Mihiel. Here, under French command, the army and marine battalions rotated between forward centers of resistance, intermediate backup trenches and rear area reserve positions, while machine gun and artillery units served under French command until sufficiently trained to occupy independent positions.

The major mission of such "quiet" sectors was observation. Enemy trenches, observation posts, gun positions, supply depots, roads, trails, railways—each was the subject of almost constant scrutiny by the soldiers in the trenches, by roving patrols and by aerial observation and photography. The Germans shared the mission, and war on both sides consisted largely of a game of elaborate and generally useless camouflage projects. At one point in a sector the French would hold the upper hand because of a commanding position, at another the German would look down on French positions. In the southern sector French soldiers used field glasses to watch their countrymen endure daily life in the German-held town of Saint-Mihiel; one unit even posted its guard by means of the Saint-Mihiel town clock.[14]

The Americans did not accept this way of life. They were there to fight a war and, being new to war, held slight brief for any mutual accommodation to ease its rigors. One can almost picture the French division commander, General Savatier, in a later interview, his mustache quivering and his hands thrown apart in that gesture of disapproval unique to the French:

They were irrepressible! If the night relief took place without a hitch and in the deepest silence, as soon as the sun was high enough some of the doughboys, who had no place in the front line, wanted absolutely to "see the Boche" and "to kill the Boche." They climbed like cats into the highest trees (the sector, as I have said, was in the woods), and began to fire on the enemy sentries or on the platoons which from the heights of their observation posts they could see running between the first and second line trenches.[15]

The Germans naturally retaliated, and the war grew warm. The Germans would send out a patrol to learn something of the newcomers; the Americans answered with counterpatrols. On April 6, a patrol of the 1st Battalion, 6th Marines, led by Lieutenant Carlton Burr and his intelligence sergeant, Gerald C. Thomas, ran into a large German force. A brisk fire fight ensued, with both sides calling down artillery, and a night of most awful confusion ended with Thomas saving Burr's life. A few days later German gas shells struck a marine rear area position, one of the deadly missiles falling into an Adrian barracks holding sixty troops. Quite naturally a few men panicked and most required some minutes to gain their senses. They were men already tired from war and yet men to whom war—at least this kind of war—was still new. Practically the entire company of 300 including all officers was evacuated. Forty of them eventually died.

The bombardments continued on both sides. Shortly after midnight on April 14 a large German raiding force struck Colonel Leroy Upton's 9th Infantry sector. For nearly two hours the soldiers of his surprised 3d Battalion fought with rifles, bayonets and even fists while in places the enemy penetrated up to half a mile. Finally a bugle call signaled the German retreat, but now the Americans laid a heavy barrage behind the enemy which disrupted their final maneuver and caused them to lose a number of prisoners and captured machine guns.

The fighting finished about 2:00 A.M. The 9th Infantry counted seven killed, three officers and thirty-six men wounded, and twenty-six captured including one surgeon and six hospital corpsmen. The Germans lost one officer and fifty-nine men killed, eleven men captured. One of the enemy officers later wrote:

> The Americans have offered embittered resistance with their machine guns, some even with their bayonets; a great many of them died fighting heroically.[16]

Considering that this was their first real action, the troops could only be praised for their behavior and spirit. At one point word filtered to the rear that the frontline companies were being wiped out. Upon hearing the news, Mess Sergeant Wiggins, a forty-year-old regular of Company I, grabbed a rifle and a carving knife and called to his mates: "Hell! I Company's never wiped out as long as I'm here."[17]

Colonel Upton was particularly impressed. On April 18 he reported to General Bundy:

> This action is an excellent example of what determined men can do to win success even when almost everything is to the advantage of the enemy. Attention is invited to the list of names of those who rendered conspicuous service. It will be noted that many of these are of foreign origin. In this brigade there are not less than twenty-five percent of this class. In the training area, organization commanders almost gave up hope of ever making soldiers of them, not through any lack of willingness on the part of the men themselves, but on account of their lack of knowledge of English. Since arriving in this area, this class of men have in every engagement with the enemy fully demonstrated that they have a fierce fighting ability and that they will stick to their work to the bitter end. . . . It is evident that with patience and painstaking

effort in the training of this class, we can develop fighters who will measure up to our best American traditions.[18]

It was a good lesson to learn, as were most of the lessons emerging from the bizarre environment of these weeks. For the first time the Americans faced real war. By the end of April most of them had experienced the indescribable sense of isolation from patrol duty in no-man's-land, the feeling of helplessness while lying in the mud to sweat out a barrage, the instinctive reflex actions upon hearing the dreaded honk of the klaxons and the whisper "Gas," the sound of a bullet's impact, the whine of shrapnel, the hatred of an enemy felt by a man saying good-bye to a dead friend.

They learned the utter, excruciating monotony of trench life and some of them caught it in letters home such as the one from Corporal Adel Storey of the 6th Marines:

> I do not know of much that is new or startling; it is just the same thing day in and day out. It manages to rain about every other day or so and keeps the trenches in continual mud. . . . We have to wear our gas respirator and helmet at all times. It seems to me at times that my neck will break, and I am sure that I am beginning to get round-shouldered. Our respirator and helmet weigh a little over six pounds, and with one on your head and the other hanging around your neck, you can imagine how it feels. . . .
>
> We nearly always have time to sleep in the daytime, but at night we either have to stay up all the time, or, if we lie down, we have to lie with cartridge belts and gas masks on, and rifle and bayonet by our sides.[19]

Adding to the boredom were the body lice, which caused men to scratch their bodies raw in an interminable entirely futile struggle to eliminate them. Nicknamed cooties, they were also called "arithmetic bugs" because, according to one marine, "they added to our troubles, subtracted from our pleasures, divided our attention, and multiplied like hell."[20] And if the cooties were bad, the trench rats were worse. For years they had been breeding on the corpses of both sides until they had evolved into sleek giants unafraid of man. Sergeant Thomas found

> the trenches alive with them. Jamey Johnson, my bunkmate, and I used to plug every hole we could find in our dugout. They still got in and crawled over our blankets at night. I was never bitten. Some men probably were but I don't believe anyone was seriously ill from it. I guess we were as tough as the rats.[21]

Corporal Storey noted in a letter home:

> Never in my life have I seen rats of such size as these are here. They don't run from us, either, like any ordinary rat does. They will fight like a good fellow when you fool with them. . . .[22]

Rain, mud, heavy helmets, respirators, enemy shells, an occasional patrol, boredom, cooties and rats—all part of the blooding process necessary to produce a better, stronger division of fighting men. The combined experience immeasurably aided the process of cohesion. Officers learned to know non-coms and the troops; all began to feel that immeasurable pride of individual units that produces first-class fighting machines. The process was helped when a new French commanding general reorganized the line, for the first time grouping the Americans into brigades.

The experience had not alone tested the junior officers, the non-coms or the men. Bundy replaced his chief of staff with Colonel Preston Brown, a Yale man who had enlisted in the army in the 1890s. Brigadier General Bill Chamberlaine came up to take over the artillery brigade; Brigadier General E. M. Lewis arrived to take command of the 3d Brigade. Doyen, commanding the 4th Marine Brigade, was relieved on account of illness[23] and replaced by Pershing's former chief of staff, James G. Harbord, who also had come up from the ranks and only recently had won his first star.

A few days after Harbord took command of the marine brigade, the 2d Division was relieved and sent south for additional field training. For the moment the soldiers and marines would again find themselves remote from the war, but not for long. A blooded division, they fitted nicely into the bigger scheme of things.

The bigger scheme of things had been and was being determined by the Allies and by an enemy whose last giant offensive of the war had begun a few days after the 2d Division entered the trenches.

Notes

1. Stanley W. Metcalf, *Personal Memoirs.* Auburn, N.Y.: Privately printed, 1927.
2. Jacques Rouvier, *Present-Day Warfare.* New York: Charles Scribner's Sons, 1918.
3. General Gerald C. Thomas, USMC (ret). Personal interview and correspondence. After very active roles in both world wars, General Thomas commanded the 1st Marine Division in Korea.
4. Ibid.
5. A. W. Catlin, *With the Help of God and a Few Marines.* New York: Doubleday, Page and Co., 1919.
6. Rouvier, op. cit.
7. Thomas, op. cit.
8. General Clifton B. Cates, USMC (ret). Personal interview. After a most distinguished service in both world wars, General Cates became the nineteenth Commandant of the Marine Corps (1948–1951).
9. Thomas, op. cit.
10. W. A. Carter, *The Tale of a Devil Dog.* Washington: The Canteen Press, 1920.
11. General Lemuel C. Shepherd, USMC (ret). Personal interview. After a most distinguished service in both world wars, General Shepherd became the twentieth Commandant of the Marine Corps (1952–1955).
12. Cates, op. cit.
13. Thomas, op. cit.
14. Oliver L. Spaulding and John W. Wright, *The Second Division American Expeditionary Force in France, 1917–1919.* New York: The Hillman Press, Inc., 1937.
15. G. S. Viereck, *As They Saw Us.* New York: Doubleday, Doran and Co., 1929.
16. Spaulding and Wright, op. cit.
17. Ibid.
18. Ibid.
19. Kemper F. Cowing and Courtney R. Cooper, *Dear Folks at Home—.* New York: Houghton Mifflin Co., 1919.

20. Carter, op. cit.
21. Thomas, op. cit.
22. Cowing, op. cit.
23. General Doyen returned to America where in October, 1918, he died from influenza.

Chapter 3

"I would fight without a break ... I would fight all the time."
—General Foch, Doullens Conference,
March 26, 1918

Germany had begun planning the final year of the war several months before the 2d Division went into the trenches. The plan was the work of two officers who held the military destiny of the Central Powers in their combined hands: Field Marshal Paul von Hindenburg and his *Oberst Quartiermeister,* or first deputy, General Erich Ludendorff.

Had they been a vaudeville team, the two could have made a fortune impersonating themselves. Hindenburg was the front man. At seventy years of age he was distinguished solely by his lack of professional distinction. Of massive build with hair cropped in the traditional Prussian fashion and with a sweeping bicycle mustache, he offered an appearance of comfortable solidity utterly lacking in his predecessor, the more realistic Falkenhayn. Speaking of the war on one occasion, he said that "it agrees with me like a visit to a health resort." Visiting dignitaries found him a quietly agreeable commander who offered a first-class table and a fund of good stories. Ludendorff, on the other hand,

> was never known to smile during the whole war. His conversation was unpleasantly dictatorial, harsh, obstinate and opinionated. He appeared irregularly at mess, his face drawn tight, his vacant, detached manner betraying his intense inward preoccupation.[1]

The relationship nonetheless approximated a military marriage of convenience mutually agreeable to each partner. Hindenburg later wrote of his deputy that he gave "as much latitude as possible to the brilliancy of my chief of staff, to his almost superhuman powers of work, and to his unweighed energies."[2] Ludendorff remarked in his memoirs that Hindenburg "agreed with my ideas and approved my proposed orders. . . . I honored him highly, served him faithfully, and esteemed his lofty sense of honor, his loyalty to the Emperor, and his joyful sense of responsibility."[3]

It was just as well that the two officers enjoyed such a *modus vivendi,* for in late autumn of 1917 they arrived at a decision which would yield them one massive problem after another until the war's end. In Ludendorff's words, the decisive question of that time was whether the Supreme Command should "utilize the favorable conditions of the spring [of 1918] to strike a great blow in the west or should it deliberately restrict itself to the defensive and make only subsidiary attacks say in Macedonia and Italy?"[4]

The answer emerged from a realistic appreciation of such factors as the perilous state of Germany's allies, the failure of the highly vaunted submarine campaign to loosen the tentacles of the Allied blockade's grip against Germany or to stop the flow of supplies and of American troops across the Atlantic, the material superiority of France and England, whose 1917 offensives had cost the Germans dearly, and finally the feeling engendered in the troops by German victories in Rumania, Galicia and Italy, victories which, taken with Russia's collapse, meant a host of blooded troops available for transfer west.

Ludendorff accordingly concluded:

The army all called for an attack that would bring about an early decision. This was possible only on the western front. All that had gone before was merely a means to the one end of creating a situation that would make it a feasible operation. . . . All that mattered was to get together enough troops for an attack in the west.[5]

In January, 1918, Ludendorff made a final decision: since for some time the British had played the preponderant offensive role on the western front, it would be necessary first to split the British and French armies, then destroy the British in detail. Simultaneously, other techniques, primarily aerial and cannon bombardment of Paris, would be used to smash enemy morale. The first blow, aimed at the British front between Arras and La Fère and code-named Plan St. Michael, would fall in late March.

To accomplish his overall plan Ludendorff rested his hopes on a series of storm offensives of highly trained troops attacking by infiltration. Surprise was the keynote of the tactic. After a short but very powerful shock artillery barrage including gas shells, groups of *Strumtruppen*—riflemen and light machine gunners—were to punch channels through enemy defenses to the immediate rear, thus disorganizing the defense before reserves came up. If necessary these storm troops would bypass isolated centers of resistance, leaving them to be neutralized by close support units of heavy machine guns, light and medium trench mortars, flame projectors and mobile artillery while the assault troops, aided by heavy artillery and tactical aircraft, continued forward. Meanwhile reserve troops would follow to enlarge the channels and consolidate gains against enemy counterattacks.

This brilliant concept of the coordinated assault needed only dive-bombers and armor spearheads to become the famous *Blitzkrieg* of World War II. By beefing up the firepower of the battalion with trench mortars, flamethrowers and a primitive version of close support artillery, Ludendorff and his Eighteenth Army commander, von Hutier, made it the tactical unit of the division with the assault groups the tactical units of each battalion—a brilliant innovation displaying a tactical genius hitherto unparalleled.

Brilliance, however, generally breeds problems. The bulk of younger German officers and troops had known only defensive warfare, while to the veterans who somehow had survived the last three years the old offensive concepts seemed a century away. The complete turnabout from defensive to offensive warfare meant that, from December of 1917 on, the German army was caught up in one vast training and reorganization program.

Special schools established behind each army stressed individual and small unit instruction in attack by infiltration. Throughout the winter special teams screened German divisions on other fronts to order the most suitable troops west. These, coupled with recruits scraped up from the civilian labor force, enabled Ludendorff to add thirty-four divisions to the western front by mid-March, 1918, with another fourteen divisions scheduled for later formation.[6] Altogether 194 divisions—about 3,600,000 men—would be serving on this front by the time of the attack.

To retain the essential advantage of surprise, Ludendorff ordered a score of harsh security measures. Construction of roads, railways and airfields was carried on along the entire front so as to allay Allied suspicions of a buildup in one area. Troop trains ran only at night; censors read all letters, monitored all telephone calls; camouflage experts constantly flew over positions to report violations. Under the overall direction of Colonel Bruchmüller, the artillery expert, gun emplacements were dug at night, carefully camouflaged. A young artillery genius, Captain Pulkowsky, worked out a mathematical method by which guns were registered without pre-firing.

These and other preparations for the great offensive seemed to breathe new life into tired German bodies. On December 14, 1917, the representative of the Foreign Office at the Supreme Command reported: "The generals are talking now very big and are full of the idea of smashing the enemy."[7]

For the generals, particularly Ludendorff, the campaign was nothing short of a do-or-die attempt. "That the attack in the west would be one of the most difficult operations in history I was perfectly sure," he later wrote.[8] But he rightly judged that it was the only way to victory, that the future of Germany depended on its success. What if it failed?

This question was put to Ludendorff by Prince Max of Baden in an interview at Kreuznach on February 19, 1918. "Then Germany must perish!" was Ludendorff's brutal answer.[9]

Although the Germans employed utmost secrecy in readying their divisions for the new offensive, the probability of a large-scale enemy attack was never far removed from the minds of Allied leaders. From the channel coast to the Swiss border—a battleline of nearly 450 miles—their tired and vastly depleted armies stood totally on the defensive. Aware that Germany even then was transferring large numbers of troops from the Russian front, their primary hope was to hold until American strength arrived in sufficient quantity to offset the German gains.

The earlier crisis in Italy had already led to their forming the Inter-Allied Supreme War Council which began meeting at Versailles in November, 1917. The civil side of the council held very real powers, enabling its members in the ensuing months to advantageously coordinate such vital matters as allotment of manpower, equipment, supply and shipping. The military side, however, lacked executive powers and functioned primarily in an advisory capacity, a function already performed by the respective chiefs of staff whose counsel was not always welcome to the Allied commanders in chief, Haig and Pétain.

Despite the best efforts of Colonel House, President Wilson's personal representative in France, and General Tasker Bliss, the President's military adviser, to effect a more central Allied leadership, the principals of all countries spent the winter in acrimonious argument. Nonetheless by February, 1918, a certain harmony of form had resulted:

Chief of Staff	*Versailles Committee*	*Commander in Chief*
America: Peyton March	Tasker Bliss	John Pershing
England: Henry Wilson	Henry Rawlinson	Douglas Haig
France: Ferdinand Foch	Maxime Weygand	Henri Pétain

Unfortunately the form did not extend to fact. Pershing detested March, who was his junior, and paid him scant attention. Haig loathed Wilson and ignored him when he could. Pétain held no more than lukewarm regard for Foch, resented Pershing's insistence on keeping his few U. S. divisions under his own control and regarded the strategical views of Haig with some suspicion. No arrangement would ever heal these relationships, but at least the first step toward establishing unity of command had been taken.

It was only a step. By mid-March, 1918, the front continued to resemble feudal fiefs ruled by separate barons. In the extreme north King Albert's twelve infantry divisions held eighteen miles of front. His right flank tied in with Haig's command—four armies that carried the line another 125 miles to the south. In turn the British right tied in with Pétain's domain: Franchet d'Esperey's Army Group of the North—three armies holding the next seventy miles—and, beginning at Verdun, Castelnau's Army Group of the East—four armies which carried the line south to its termination. Of the 312 miles of front held by the French, four American divisions—equal in size to about eight Allied divisions—held seventeen miles, and these in "quiet" sectors.[10] In all, 173 Allied divisions faced 194 German divisions, theoretically a satisfactory proportion of defender to attacker but one, in view of the elongated line, particularly prone to exploitation by concentration.

By March, 1918, Pétain believed that his front would be the target of enemy attack, specifically east of Reims in the Champagne country. To guard against this he kept sixty of his ninety-nine divisions in line, with another fifteen screening the Vosges sector. He held twenty divisions in reserve behind his center, another four in reserve to aid the British, the result of a private agreement with Haig.

Contrarily, Haig believed the attack would strike his line. To meet the threat he deployed sixty-three divisions, including two Portuguese divisions and the Canadian Corps. Because of his relatively compressed rear area which allowed scant room for withdrawal and maneuver, he retained only eight divisions in reserve. The remainder were parceled out to the armies of the line. The portion of front soon to be struck by von Hutier's Eighteenth Army was held by the right of Byng's Third Army and by Gough's Fifth Army. The latter consisted only of twelve infantry and three cavalry divisions whose defenses stood in a rude and partial slate of construction. On March 21, 1918, it was the weakest part of the British line.

At 4:00 A.M. on March 21 the German army unleashed the most powerful concentration of artillery fire in the war to date. On a forty-mile front between Croisilles and La Fère some 6,000 guns, firing high-explosive and gas shells under the overall direction of Colonel Bruchmüller, shattered the eerie quiet of the fog-filled night to announce the enemy's final bid for victory.

While British counter-batteries added to the furor, German shells tore into outposts and trenches, exploded ammunition and supply dumps, ripped up communications—a vast, seemingly omnipresent cannonade that hurled man and earth and defenses to the heavens while turning the gas-drenched land into a living hell. For five hours the cannon remorselessly combed from front to rear and back to front. At 9:35 mortars took the first trenches under direct fire while engineers blew charges planted beneath the protective barbed wire. At 9:40 the assault groups went over the top.[11]

The soldiers had trained well. With rifles slung over their shoulders they double-timed to an attack backed by hand grenades, machine guns, flamethrowers and, on occasion, bayonets to punch their way through outer defenses and across the trenches into the battle zone. In the south the same fog that held the gas to the ground blinded the defenders. From the Oise to Saint-Quentin the initial assault ended before the British knew what had happened. Squads and platoons, even companies and battalions, found themselves suddenly isolated, and if they were able to work to the rear they often found the enemy blocking the way. Farther north, the advance was not quite so easy, for here the fog lifted much earlier to reveal the crouching gray groups to British machine gunners and riflemen. Still, by evening assault groups along the whole line had at places penetrated deep into British defenses while following waves were consolidating the captured ground.

In the south and center of the battleline, the next few days seemed to the exhausted Tommies a horrible repetition of the first. Gough's right crumbled early on March 22, a rupture sending some of the troops in flight behind the Somme where Pétain's first reserve divisions were beginning to arrive. Others fell back to the rear of the battle zone, then to the ill-prepared defenses of the rear zone, fighting when and where they could—pathetic, isolated actions which saw entire battalions simply disappear from existence.[12] Gough's center and left lasted a little longer, but by March 23 chaos ruled his battle zone. No one knew who held what, runners reporting to regimental and division headquarters often found the Germans in possession, local commanders received either meaningless orders or no orders at all.

On March 23 Ludendorff added another perspective to the offensive: the bombardment of Paris. At 7:20 A.M. the first eight-inch shell, fired from a secret emplacement some seventy-five miles distant, harmlessly exploded on the pavement in front of House Number Six along the Quai de Seine. At 7:40 A.M. a second shell struck outside the Gare de l'Est, killing eight and wounding thirteen Parisians.[13]

While Paris lay under morale-shattering bombardment, the British continued to fall back. By March 24 Gough had yielded the battle zone of his entire army and Byng the battle zone of Third Army from below the Scarpe to the Flesquières salient. In a fourteen-mile advance, a gain unheard of since 1914, the Germans had reached Péronne. Ahead of them loomed the Albert-Bapaume line, on their left the vital rail junction of Amiens.

It was a major victory for the Germans, no doubting that. But so far it was a local success, a tactical victory requiring decisive exploitation. And in the north neither von der Marwitz's Second German Army nor von Below's Seventeenth German Army were finding such easy going as von Hutier's Eighteenth Army in the south. Here, behind the battle zone, were well-organized rear zone defenses augmented by reserve units from Horne's First Army to the north. Despite fighting of the most incredible ferocity, the German shock units could not rout the dug-in defenders, but could only push them back, and then very slowly and at tremendous cost to the attackers. So long as Byng retained his tactical integrity, there was still hope, faint though it may have seemed.

To Pétain it seemed very faint. The prisoner of his own deep pessimism, Pétain now became convinced that Haig was planning a withdrawal north to screen the channel ports. Despite Haig's frantic denials of any such action in meetings on March 23 and 24, Pétain, possibly acting under instructions from his government, announced a change in strategy. In Haig's words:

> . . . I gathered that he had recently attended a Cabinet meeting in Paris and that his orders from his Government are "to *cover Paris at all costs.*" On the other hand to keep in touch with the British Army is no longer the basic principle of French strategy. . . .[14]

The falling out of the two commanders was respected in a hastily summoned top-level conference at Doullens on March 26. While Haig was explaining the situation to Lord Milner, the Secretary of State for War, and to Henry Wilson, Chief of the Imperial General Staff, the President of France, Monsieur Poincaré, was walking outside in the garden with his premier, Monsieur Clemenceau. After a moment's silence the worried Clemenceau turned to the other man. "Pétain is annoying with his pessimism," he said. "You can't imagine what he said to me, and which I shall confide to no one but you. This is the phrase: 'The Germans will beat the English in the open country; after that, they will beat us also.' Should a general speak or even think in that fashion?"[15]

Before Poincaré could answer, a military car drove up to the town hall, aides saluted and from the interior sprang the short, stocky figure of the French chief of staff, the fiery Ferdinand Foch. In Clemenceau's later words:

> There was a bustle, and Foch arrived, surrounded by officers, and dominating everything with his cutting voice. "You aren't fighting? I would fight without a break. I would fight in front of Amiens. I would fight in Amiens. I would fight behind Amiens. I would fight all the time."[16]

Clemenceau turned again to the President of France. *"C'est un bougre,"** the Tiger grunted.

The joint meeting began soon after Foch's arrival. Clemenceau bluntly asked Haig if he intended to fight at Amiens or to continue falling back. After answering in a vein similar to that already offered

(*There's a good fellow.)

to Milner and Wilson—he was doing everything he could to prevent the enemy from reaching Amiens—the British commander in chief asked what the French intentions were. Pétain explained that he was bringing up a total of twenty-four divisions from the east at a rate of two per day. Foch then entered the discussion, stressing time and again that the war would be won by fighting, not withdrawing.

With Foch's blunt words ringing in their ears, Milner and Clemenceau conferred privately before announcing a decision which could have been made with profit nearly four years earlier: the Allies must coordinate present and future actions under one commander. The man chosen was Foch, and although his authority was very limited the move brought two immediate results. One concerned Pershing, who on March 25 had visited Pétain to offer him those American divisions which were ready for action at the time. On March 28 Pershing called on Foch at Bombon to place all of his forces at Foch's disposal:

> The acceptance of this offer meant the dispersion of our troops along the Allied front and a consequent delay in building up a distinctive American force in Lorraine, but the serious situation of the Allies demanded this divergence from our plans.[17]

The second result was another high-level conference held at Beauvais on April 3. In only a few days Allied representatives had seen the necessity of enlarging Foch's authority. On this occasion Foch was charged with "the strategic direction of military operations." Although each commander in chief, including Pershing, would have "full control of the tactical action of their respective Armies" and "the right of appeal to his Government, if in his opinion his Army is endangered by reason of any order received from General Foch," the appointment nonetheless gave a new and vital direction to the war.

Black though the picture, unified command or no, defeat could still be prevented. For even as the Allied representatives met at Doullens the German advance was slowing everywhere along the line. When von Hutier's and von der Marwitz's divisions had advanced over thirty miles in six days, two days were now required to push on another five or six miles. Farther north the German offensive claimed the Albert-Bapaume line, proceeded a mile or two beyond, then halted.

After a week's hard fighting the German troops were as tired as the Allies. In some cases divisions stood miles ahead of their supply trains, which lumbered with increasing difficulty over the pockmarked wasteland. Lacking ample reserves behind each front, Ludendorff had to move replacement units laterally, a slow task in view of the crowded conditions, then send them forward over the difficult terrain. The same terrain frequently prevented mobile artillery from keeping up with assault units. Disciplinary problems also existed: hungry and tired soldiers, existing mainly on nervous energy, thoroughly sick of war and its sacrifices, deprived of many basic necessities not to mention luxuries of any sort for at least two years, fell like scavenging hordes heedless of disciplinary measures on the villages and towns standing in the way of war.[18]

Faced with increasing resistance in the north and center, where he had hoped to obtain the crucial breakthrough, Ludendorff had transferred seven divisions to the south, partly to protect von Hutier's enlarged front, partly to try to keep von Hutier's advance moving. When it slowed anyway, he turned to an entirely new plan. For March 28 he ordered an attack against the extreme left of Byng's Third Army, a move previously worked out under the code name of Mars. But this offensive struck thoroughly alert British troops—six well-dug-in divisions—and within a day failed at tremendous cost to the attackers.

Thus frustrated, Ludendorff turned again to the south, ordering an all-out offensive to seize Amiens. With this decision, he failed to respect his loss of momentum. Although von Hutier's divisions fought to within seven miles of the vital rail junction, by April 4 they had halted and were not to advance farther in this sector. For the moment the German offensive had ended.

Long before deciding on Plan St. Michael, Ludendorff had been attracted to an attack against the northern fifty miles of British front, from La Bassée north. This plan, known as St. George I and II, called for attacks on either side of the Ypres salient to seize the commanding Mont Kemmel-Mont des Chats heights, converge on the rail junction of Hazebrouck and then wheel north to seal off the British and Belgian armies in that area. The probability of heavy spring rains and thus mud had caused Ludendorff to order first the St. Michael attacks, whose fundamental purpose was to set the scene for the grand finale of St. George.

A mild spring had made the ground very dry. In addition, even though Plan St. Michael had not succeeded in the original sense, Ludendorff correctly reasoned that Haig had greatly weakened his northern armies to meet the German attacks in the south. Ludendorff's own reduced strength now meant compressing the original Plan St. George to a major strike between La Bassée and Armentières with complementary attacks north; despite this disadvantage he ordered the new offensive to begin on April 9.

At first the German attack resembled the earlier effort to the south. Early on April 9, after a short but vicious artillery bombardment, von Quast's Sixth Army moved out. Whether by chance or design the bulk of his nine divisions struck a single Portuguese division, which instantly broke and fled. Early reports, received by Ludendorff while lunching with Emperor Wilhelm, seemed to justify his fullest expectations. Nor did subsequent reports dampen the optimistic air of the German headquarters. By evening the Saxons had advanced six miles to the River Lawe, which they crossed the next day. By the evening of April 10 they had also pushed across the lower Lys; in the north, units of von Arnim's Fourth Army had captured Messines and Ploegsteert. In but two days the assault groups were well on the way to obtaining their primary objectives.

But already the advance had begun to differ from the earlier offensive. Although the British line fell back, it did so in a methodical manner that exacted a very heavy toll of enemy infantry. On April 12, Ludendorff issued orders for an all-out attack against the primary objective of Bailleul which, if taken, would bring his Sixth Army forward for jointure with Fourth Army. But due to the superb British stand—it was here that Haig issued his famous "backs to the wall" order of the day—the plan required almost a week of very hard fighting to carry out. And now, contrary to Ludendorff's belief, Foch had bolstered the British line in the north with the first of several French divisions. Meanwhile such were von Arnim's losses that he persuaded Ludendorff to order an attack against the northern side of the Ypres salient in an effort to obtain a less costly breakthrough. Ludendorff agreed without knowing that General Plumer, in a desperate decision to gain additional reserves, had pulled this front back almost to its original dimensions, a voluntary evacuation of ground won the previous autumn at a cost of at least 250,000 casualties. The subsequent German attack, falling on a deserted front far too deep to exploit with available strength, was called off by nightfall.

By April 19 Ludendorff's entire offensive stood still. Although von Quast could claim a penetration of up to seventeen miles, he now held a line roughly double his original front and possessing none of its static defenses.

The impasse continued for a week. To break it Ludendorff ordered an attack in the original St. Michael sector to be followed by a final effort in his northern sector. On April 24 von der Marwitz's Second Army, spearheaded by thirteen of the first German tanks, the A.7.V.s, moved out on the Amiens front, an attack frustrated by a well-organized British counterattack. On the following day von Arnim's Fourth Army seized Mont Kemmel from its French defenders and in four days of fighting pushed a few miles beyond. By April 29 they too were stopped. The second great offensive had failed.

The dual offensives nevertheless accomplished a great deal. Psychologically Ludendorff had reversed the tables of the previous year. Now it was Germany who stood on the offensive—and not one which had gained a few hundred blood-soaked yards but one that in just over a month had seized far more territory than either side in three years of war in the west. Although the attacks cost the Germans heavily—estimated between 250,000 and 300,000 casualties—they inflicted over 240,000 casualties on the Allies, mainly the British, in addition to capturing another 85,000 troops.[19] Of fifty-nine British divisions, fifty-three had been engaged, twenty-five of them several times. Until replacements arrived from England and from outer theaters of war, the British army would remain on the defensive.

Nor could Foch, compelled to commit French reserves in the north, begin the offensive which he so heartily desired. And in attempting to repair their losses, the Allied commanders were widening an already serious rift with Pershing, who refused to commit his units in a piecemeal fashion by which they would be absorbed into the foreign armies.

More than anything else, fear characterized the Allied position. One of Pétain's staff officers, Jean de Pierrefeu, later described the prevailing mood at GQG:

> In truth we found ourselves confronted by a new condition. The rapidity of maneuver of the enemy was amazing; not only the speed with which the German command shifted the battle area and the assault against the spots they considered least protected, but also the efficiency of their method, the short and savage artillery preparation which paralyzed the defenders, and the skill of their units in making their way always to the point of junction of French and British corps. The Allied troops seemed ill adapted to these unexpected methods, and had no defensive parry corresponding to the offensive thrust. . . . For the future the brains of the Chiefs must find a method capable of counter-balancing that of our adversaries. Up till now the indomitable will of the joint command not to give way, transmitted to the troops, was merely a makeshift. Things could no longer remain in this state. The moment when the infantryman would weary of being one against six must be foreseen. . . . All General Pétain's cares were directed to the solution of the problem.[20]

Fortunately for Pétain's temper he did not know that even before the Lys offensive Ludendorff had been looking to the south. Here in a very short time he would exhibit, and strikingly so, that "rapidity of maneuver" which impressed Pierrefeu and his fellow staff officers at GQG. And here, also, he would find himself eventually fighting the Americans.

Notes

1. Harvey A. De Weerd, *Great Soldiers of the Two World Wars*. New York: W. W. Norton and Co., 1941.
2. Marshal Paul von Hindenburg, *Out of My Life*. New York: Harper & Brothers, 1921.
3. Erich Ludendorff, *Ludendorff's Own Story*. New York: Harper & Brothers, 1919.
4. Ibid.
5. Ibid.
6. Hanson W. Baldwin, *World War I*. New York: Harper and Row, 1962. See also Barrie Pitt, *1918 The Last Act*. New York: W. W. Norton and Co., 1963; Cyril Falls, *The Great War*. New York: G. P. Putnam's Sons, 1959; Basil H. Liddell Hart, *A History of the World War 1914–1918*. Boston: Little Brown and Co., 1930.
7. Erich Eyck, *The Generals and the Downfall of the German Monarchy 1917–1918*. Fifth Series, Vol. 2. London: Royal Historical Society, 1952.
8. Ludendorff, op. cit.
9. Eyck, op. cit.
10. American Battle Monuments Commission, *American Armies and Battlefields in Europe*. Washington: U. S. Government Printing Office, 1939.
11. Pitt, op. cit.; see also Liddell Hart, op. cit.; Falls, op. cit.
12. Ibid.
13. Henry W. Miller, *The Paris Gun*. London: Jonathan Cape, 1930.
14. Duff Cooper, *Haig*. London: Faber and Faber, Ltd., 1935. See also John Terraine, *Douglas Haig*. London: Hutchinson, 1963.
15. Jere Clemens King, *Generals and Politicians*. Berkeley: University of California Press, 1951.
16. Ibid.
17. General John J. Pershing, *Final Report of General John J. Pershing*. Washington: U. S. Government Printing Office, 1920.
18. Pitt, op. cit.
19. Ibid. See also Baldwin, op. cit.; Liddell Hart, op. cit.; Terraine, op. cit.
20. Jean de Pierrefeu, *French Headquarters 1915–1918*. Translated by Major C. J. C. Street. London: Geoffrey Bles, 1924.

Chapter 4

"The situation bears much resemblance to the [1914] battle of the Marne."
—Colonel Rozet to Major Clark,
May 30, 1918

Perhaps sensing the consternation pervading the Allied high command, Ludendorff chose a new and daring plan to break the impasse existing in the center and north: an attack by Crown Prince Wilhelm's army group across the formidable Chemin-des-Dames against Pinon and Reims.[1]

As developed in April and May, Plan Blücher[2] involved three armies, the Eighteenth, Seventh and First. On May 27 von Boehn's Seventh Army and the right of von Mudra's First Army were to attack along a twenty-two-mile line running southwest from Anizy to Berry-au-Bac, the objective being the line Soissons-Reims. A second phase would push the German right across the Ailette River toward its parent stream, the Oise, while the German left attacked as far south as Reims. Depending on developments, the Eighteenth Army was to plan an attack west of the Oise with the principal effort toward Compiègne. Simultaneously with the opening of the first phase, the Eighteenth and Second Armies were to feint with a large-scale attack in the Amiens sector. Meanwhile in Flanders, Crown Prince Rupprecht's army group would rest and refit—once Plan Blücher had sucked French reserves south, Rupprecht could recommence his offensive.

Ludendorff approved Plan Blücher toward the end of April. By mid-May Wilhelm's formidable army group was ready, and on May 20 the secretly assembled assault divisions began night marches to the line. All appeared ready for the massive blow. Up to this point Ludendorff still saw Blücher as a limited offensive designed solely to clear his Flanders front of French reserves. But now in a conference with his chiefs of staff of May 21 a new note appeared. As later described by von Unruh, chief of staff of von Conta's IV Reserve Corps which would play a major role in the action:

> . . . Ludendorff ended [his review of the situation] by asking whether any of us had questions to put.
>
> I asked whether, if the attack went according to plan, we could not push on to the Marne. Ludendorff asked when I thought we should have reached the objectives south of the Vesle, to which I replied: "We shall reach the Vesle on the morning of the second day." Ludendorff reminded me that it was twelve miles to the Vesle, and "how could I be so optimistic?" I answered that our preparations were so thorough that if the information of their [Allied] weakness was correct, we should overrun the English [the English divisions sent from the fighting to the north to recuperate in this "quiet" sector]. Ludendorff's opinion was that his information was absolutely reliable. We were actually up against a single English corps of four divisions, without reserves. He admitted it would be very welcome if my optimism were justified, but in spite of it he did not intend to go beyond the Vesle. . . .[3]

Had the Allies held more respect for Pershing and the American army he was desperately trying to form, von Unruh's optimism would have been misplaced. Unfortunately the command rift that had been developing throughout the summer, autumn and winter of 1917 was now, in the spring of 1918, reaching full-blown proportions.

The crux of the difficulty was Pershing's continued refusal to turn over raw American units to be trained by the Allies and then incorporated into their armies. As Ludendorff had also foreseen, Pershing realized that the war could only be won by first breaking the trench deadlock, then exploiting such a breakthrough with mass attacks in open terrain. In his mind the depleted, exhausted, morale-shaken French and British armies were no longer capable of either course of action. Success would depend on a new army—an American army which he stubbornly insisted on building.

Allied commanders including Foch, Pétain and Haig did not share this belief. Arguing that American military men lacked sufficient experience to field their own army and that the war would be lost before they acquired such experience, they wanted instead the raw material of American men. This desire, of course, collided head on with Pershing's ideas (not to mention his orders from Secretary of War Newton Baker), the more so because he disapproved of the doglike devotion to trench warfare which he believed Allied leaders to hold.

In view of Pershing's actual strength his insistence on a national army did seem somewhat vainglorious. When the American commander in chief called on Pétain and Foch during the March crisis, he owned four divisions in training and three more arriving—a total 300,000 men who ultimately would provide the equivalent of fourteen Allied divisions at a time when 175 Allied and 192 German divisions were serving on the western front.[4] Of these four divisions, the 1st and 2d occupied trench sectors on either side of the Saint-Mihiel salient; the 26th and 42d had just completed a month's trench training. At Foch's request, Pershing sent the 42d back in line to relieve French units while the 26th relieved the 1st, the latter moving early in April to Micheler's Fifth French Army in reserve near Beauvais.

Neither Pershing's offer nor Foch's acceptance of the temporary use of the American divisions implied the slightest change of mind on the part of the principals. At conference after conference the Allied representatives, often acrimoniously and always unsuccessfully, sought to coerce the American commander into a change of mind. During one stormy session, at Abbéville on May 1–2, an exasperated Foch asked Pershing if he were willing to stand by to see the French driven behind the Loire. Pershing thought a moment and replied, "Yes." Later, when collectively besieged, he banged a fist on the table: "Gentlemen, I have thought this program over very deliberately and I will not be coerced."[5]

Although Pershing was worshiping at the altar of the future, he scarcely remained blind to the Allied plight. During the March crisis he had given his few divisions to Foch, who placed them in the line to relieve French units for transfer to the threatened front. By May these divisions were holding thirty-five miles of front as compared to Belgium's twenty-three miles, a mild but still valuable assistance.

He was further cooperating with Foch during the lull after the second German offensive. Although the Allied commanders were primarily concerned over a new German offensive, Foch was even then studying the possibility of launching his own offensive between the Oise and the Somme.

At the suggestion of the French high command, Pershing had agreed to a preliminary operation by Bullard's 1st U. S. Division against the fortified town of Cantigny, an important German salient west of Montdidier. In late April the American division joined Debeney's First French Army to start preparations for the attack scheduled early on May 28. In the interim, the 2d U. S. Division, upon leaving the trenches and completing its field training, was turned over to Micheler's Fifth French Army. Ultimately it would relieve the 1st Division at Cantigny.

This slight accommodation scarcely repaired the already existent hard feelings. The typical French attitude at this time was reflected in a May report from Major Paul H. Clark, Pershing's representative at Pétain's headquarters, GQG:

> Colonel Rozet [of Pétain's staff] visited the 2nd U. S. [Division] last Thursday—23rd—returning here the 24th. He expressed many compliments for the division but manifested considerable impatience over what he described as the attitude, principally of the Chief of Staff, Colonel Brown, to hold aloof from French influence and to require too much exertion from the troops. . . . Rozet says there is disposition

on part of Chief of Staff, Colonel Brown, "to keep the French at arm's length and act with almost complete independence of them. However well instructed and capable Colonel Brown may be, he should not indulge the illusion that he can not profit by the counsel and example of excellent French officers who have made war for nearly four years; he has never made war."[6]

Since a similar attitude pervaded the French and British high commands, none of the Allied leaders was disposed to pay attention to an American estimate of German intentions.

And this was a very great pity.

In Pershing's headquarters a young captain of the military intelligence section, Samuel T. Hubbard, had been keeping a sharp eye on the flow of intelligence reports arriving daily from every line unit on the western front. A 1907 Harvard graduate and prominent cotton dealer, Hubbard enlisted as a private in the New York National Guard in 1911. Commissioned at the outbreak of war, he was assigned to Pershing's original G-2 section where eventually he took over the enemy order of battle section. With this unlikely background Hubbard now produced a masterpiece of intelligence analysis: by mid-May he concluded that the Germans were preparing an attack against the Chemin-des-Dames and would be able to strike at the end of the month.[7]

Hubbard's impressive (and very accurate) report, approved by Pershing and his staff, went to Colonel Farnum, liaison officer at Pétain's advance headquarters in Chantilly. Farnum relayed it to the appropriate French officer, Colonel de Conte. Hubbard later wrote:

> Farnum reported the next day over the telephone that Colonel de Conte was quite convinced that our arguments were sound and he had taken it up with the French high command, but they had expressed considerable doubt that the American intelligence service could be correct in their summary of what the Germans would do. . . .[8]

This major Allied error stemmed only in part from the French belief in their own infallibility and the consequent disregard of

Hubbard's analysis. Pétain's own intelligence section based its analyses on indications received from various frontline sectors. In the case of the Chemin-des-Dames sector, these were submitted by the French Sixth Army under the command of General Duchêne, a dreadful martinet whose position was attributed to his being the brother-in-law of General Anthoine, Pétain's right-hand man at Provins. One of Pétain's staff officers, Jean de Pierrefeu, later wrote:

> . . . the staff of the Sixth Army which was holding the Chemin des Dames had not the least idea of the preparations which the enemy had been making for a month on this front. It was declared at G.Q.G. that there was nothing surprising in this, that if General Duchêne had not unfortunately been in command in this sector, any sort of a staff, especially after the lesson of March 21st, should have been able to find out something of what was going on; that at least it should have made some effort in that direction; that in any case no other major general [Anthoine] not related to him could have had so blind a confidence in the commander of the Sixth Army, or could have neglected to inquire what was happening in this sector, which was obviously badly watched. . . .[9]

Even though German prisoners on May 19 and 22 "declared that an important German offensive was in course of preparation between the Oise and Reims," neither Foch, Pétain nor Anthoine felt it necessary to investigate Duchêne's sector. Had they done so they would have discovered that the intelligence failure represented only one of Duchêne's crimes.

To hold the sector, which the high command regarded as relatively safe due to the forbidding terrain, Duchêne commanded six French and four British divisions, each badly depleted and in the process of recuperation from the earlier fighting. Duchêne held four of the French and three of the British divisions in line with one British and two French divisions in reserve, a patent contradiction of Pétain's expressed policy of defense in depth.

Here was a major tactical failure which, along with the intelligence failure, must be credited not alone to Duchêne but also to

Anthoine and Pétain whose negligence in not inspecting this sector is downright incredible. The twin failures were going to cost thousands of French, British and American lives—a needless sacrifice that would result in the greatest Allied crisis since the German drive on Paris in 1914.

The horrible truth of the Allied intelligence failure exploded on May 26 when two German prisoners revealed the dimensions of the imminent attack to French intelligence officers. It was too late for satisfactory countermeasures. Shortly after midnight on May 27 the combined violence of nearly 4,000 German guns claimed the entire Sixth Army sector. Preceded by heavy gas, the three-and-a-half-hour barrage exploded seven to eight miles deep throughout the battle zone while trench mortars concentrated on barbed-wire defenses and on the densely packed trenches of the immediate front.[10] By dawn organized Allied resistance had turned to carnage and confusion as German assault teams plunged forward along the line. By 10:00 A.M. the German vanguard stood on the Aisne from Vailly to Oeuilly. By evening the center assault force pressed on to the Vesle River between Courlandon and Briane.

The brisk day's work, which killed and captured thousands of French and British soldiers, resulted in a twelve-mile advance. It surprised everyone but its prognosticator, von Unruh. In less than twenty-four hours Wilhelm had nearly gained his tactical objective and at the cost of very light casualties—an enormous achievement celebrated by everyone from the lowest German private to Emperor Wilhelm, who had moved his headquarters to the scene.

At first the crushing attack confused rather than alarmed the French high command, the result principally of poor communications. Clemenceau, upon confronting Foch, was told

> that such things are inevitable in war, that any one, soldier and civilian alike, may be found at fault, and that it was no good dwelling upon the fact. After this opening Foch changed the conversation. When he saw me insisting with my questions he wanted to know if I intended to court-martial him, to which I replied there could be no question of that. [11]

On May 28 Pétain's staff officers at GQG struck Major Clark as "very calm . . . angry, peevish, but not frightened or anxious."[12] One reason for this was that GQG was running far behind events— at the time the German vanguard approached the Vesle, a ranking officer told Clark that "we hope and expect to hold them on the Aisne." Another reason was Hanson Ely's attack at Cantigny where the 28th Infantry Regiment of the 1st U. S. Division began consolidating its objectives an hour after the initial attack.

Cantigny, however, soon became the only bright spot in the Allied sky. While the Americans were pushing in the German outposts there, the German center on the main front was thrusting across the Vesle to achieve its final objective: the high ground to the south. But Ludendorff now changed his mind. Surprised at the impressive gains, he began to wonder if this subsidiary operation could turn into a decisive victory in addition to its original purpose of sucking down French reserves from the north. For the moment he decided to push his right wing through and beyond Soissons while his center continued its advance to the Marne.

Meanwhile in the west the XI French Corps yielded the high ground commanding Soissons and even began to fall back from the city itself. Throughout the day a frantic Duchêne committed French reserves direct from railheads. Altogether his army received the battalions of four infantry and two cavalry divisions which, according to a French officer, "evaporated immediately like drops of rain on a whitehot iron."[13]

At last, faced with some notion of the German progress, Pétain began to commit fourteen more infantry divisions, four regiments of heavy artillery and three of horse-drawn 75s—"in fact, nearly every available French organization was set in motion towards the battle."[14] This meant the beginning of a serious readjustment of strength in the north, precisely what Ludendorff originally wanted.

But Ludendorff's ambition was growing radically. Dissatisfied with the progress on May 28, he began feeding in reserves while ordering "an accelerated rate of pursuit. . . . The infantry in the firing line were to be accompanied everywhere by trench mortars and field guns which were to blast away opposition by directly observed fire."[15]

Corps von Conta blasted off early on May 29. At first making excellent progress, the assault divisions met increasing resistance in the afternoon and asked corps headquarters if they should halt and consolidate. Having already learned from prisoners that the French were committing battalions and regiments independent of support troops, von Conta ordered the attack continued toward the Marne. Although the Germans drove on through Fère-en-Tardenois, where they captured an important American supply depot, and to Cierges, only six miles from the Marne, their push was visibly slowing by evening. When von Conta asked Seventh Army headquarters if he should facilitate the Marne crossing, the answer was no.

Ludendorff was already worried about his lengthening supply line, particularly in the center where von Conta's assault corps was rapidly forming a southern bulge. His supply facilities lacked either railroads or motor transport to support his forward corps, nor did the rugged heights of the Chemin-des-Dames help matters. His right wing had captured Soissons but was meeting heavy resistance from the French located on the southern heights. A lag was also developing on his left. Only the day before, von Conta had ordered his 5th Guards Division east to help von Schmettow's corps, which during May 29 was pushing the British remnants, still fighting valiantly, back to the road from Reims to Ville-en-Tardenois.

Ludendorff now faced a critical decision. He could slow the present action, which was increasingly consuming French reserves as planned, and revert to his northern offensive. On the other hand, the present offensive was achieving undreamed-of gains and it was beginning to look as if thrusts west toward Montdidier-Noyon and southwest toward Paris might very well bring him the desired decision, albeit over the French rather than the British. Still not sure of himself, he ordered up the first reserve divisions from Prince Rupprecht's northern forces; the Eighteenth and Seventh Armies would continue their push, the latter to the Marne.

The French high command could not yet see this picture in its true perspective, but by now at least the threat was very real. In Foch's later words:

> The divisions sent by the Sixth Army melted away as fast as they were flung into battle, and this army, consequently, re-

mained in such a disquieting state of inferiority that General Pétain began to wonder if he would succeed in the object at which he now aimed, namely, to hold the Marne, the Montague de Reims and the high ground south of Soissons.[16]

Pétain could hold only by throwing more troops into the battle. To gain these he asked Pershing for help and ordered Fayolle to strip his Reserve Group of Armies, which meant weakening the vital junction between the British and French armies. He next asked Foch for the Tenth Army and the Army Detachment of the North (the last French reserves in the British sector), a request refused because of still-present danger of German attacks on the Somme and farther north.

On May 30 the broad-front offensive began to approach its climax. On the German right, north of Soissons, hard-fighting French divisions fell back on the Nouvron plateau; on the left two German corps crossed the Soissons-Hartennes road to continue the attack toward the Ourcq River and the Forêt de Villers-Cotterêts. In the center von Conta, for his march to the Marne, put three divisions in line with a division screen on either flank. By evening the vanguard of his center divisions stood on the Marne with the 28th Division, its commander killed, battering its way through the Forêt de Ris between Jaulgonne and Treloup. But on von Conta's left the advance slowed—the result of General Micheler's Fifth French Army arriving to bolster the wavering British-French line south of Reims.

The arrival of Micheler's divisions and the partial stabilization of that portion of the front allowed the French high command to concentrate on the western portion of the battleline. Intelligence identification of new divisions from Prince Rupprecht's Group of Armies in the north plus aerial observation of German reserves marching west indicated this as the sector requiring urgent countermeasures. That afternoon Colonel Duffieux of the Third Bureau showed Major Clark the new plan for a two-pronged counterattack to check this drive: four divisions to attack north toward Soissons, three divisions to strike northeast toward Fismes. The attack, scheduled for May 31, seems to have been the principal subject of conversation at GQG. General de Barescut told Clark that "this is the greatest, most important battle of the war. We will do all in our power to arrest the German advance on Paris." Although Clark reported he found de Barescut in a "jovial mood," Colonel Rozet set a more sobering tone.

> He said: "We will launch our offensive tomorrow morning. We hope it will give good results." He gave details identical with Duffieux. "We must stop the drive for Paris. If Paris is taken, that probably means the end of war for France. The great trouble is that our reserves are so far away. It takes three or four days to get our troops here to the scene and now is when they are needed. . . .
>
> "If the counter-attack tomorrow A.M. does not halt the advance, then I think our next move must be to abandon the front Rheims to Switzerland, leaving perhaps a few [units] to make a pretense, and assemble all we can thus get together and fight an open battle for Paris."
>
> The situation bears much resemblance to the battle of the Marne [1914]. Then as now we were in a very difficult situation, in great strain to get our troops to the point of contact. We succeeded then and let us hope we can do it again. . . .[17]

Foch confirmed the planned counterattack to Pershing, who dined with him at his Sarcus headquarters that night. Pershing wrote in his diary:

> It would be difficult to imagine a more depressed group of officers. They sat through the meal scarcely speaking a word as they contemplated what was probably the most serious situation of the war. As we still had troops that were not actively engaged, I suggested personally to Foch, when we were alone after dinner, that an early counter-attack be made against the new salient, offering him the use of these disengaged troops. Most confidentially, he said, that was what he had in mind.[18]

Before launching any such counterattack, the French had first to stop the enemy in the south, that is on the line of the Marne. At Pétain's request Foch now ordered the Tenth French Army of four divisions to move at once from Haig's area to the Marne along with some recently arrived American divisions being trained by the British. To fill the interim gap Pétain turned to Pershing, who later wrote:

> The alarming situation had caused General Pétain to call on me on May 30th for American troops to be sent to the region of Château Thierry. The Third Division (Dickman), then in training near Chaumont, being the only division within reach besides the Second, was ordered to move north immediately. Dickman started his motorized machine gun battalion over the road on the afternoon of May 30th. The infantry and engineers entrained the same night, and the division's supply trains marched overland. . . .
>
> The Second Division (Bundy) on May 30th was near Chaumont-en-Vexin and was preparing to move northwards the next day for concentration near Beauvais to relieve the First Division at Cantigny. But its orders were changed late that night. . . .[19]

Notes

1. Erich Ludendorff, *Ludendorff's Own Story.* New York: Harper and Brothers, 1919.
2. A code name optimistically paying historical homage: in March, 1814, Field Marshal von Blücher had crossed the Chemin-des-Dames from the south, fought a fierce battle against Napoleon at Craonne, and then defeated him on the eastern slopes of Laon.
3. Sydney Rogerson, *The Last of the Ebb.* London: Arthur Barker, Ltd., 1957.
4. Barrie Pitt, *1918 The Last Act.* New York: W. W. Norton and Co., 1963.
5. James C. Harbord, *The American Army in France 1917–1919.* Boston: Little Brown and Co., 1936.
6. Paul H. Clark, "Letters and Messages to John J. Pershing, 1918–1919." Washington: Manuscripts Division, Library of Congress. Unpublished. See also Robert L. Bullard, *Personalities and Reminiscences of the War.* New York: Doubleday, Page and Co., 1925. Colonel Brown had fought in the

Philippine Insurrection where he survived a general courtmartial in which he was charged with illegally executing insurgents.

7. Harbord, op. cit.
8. S. T. Hubbard, *Memoirs of a Staff Officer 1917–1919*. Tuckahoe, N. Y.: Cardinal Associates, Inc., 1959.
9. Jean de Pierrefeu, *French Headquarters 1915–1918*. Translated by Major C. J. C. Street. London: Geoffrey Bles Ltd., 1929.
10. Ferdinand Foch, *The Memoirs of Marshal Foch*. Translated by Colonel T. Bentley Mott. New York: Doubleday, 1931.
11. Georges Clemenceau, *Grandeur and Misery of Victory*. Translated by F. M. Atkinson. New York: Harcourt, Brace and Co., 1930.
12. Clark, op. cit.
13. Pierrefeu, op. cit.
14. Foch, op. cit.
15. Rogerson, op. cit.
16. Foch, op. cit.
17. Clark, op. cit.
18. John J. Pershing, *My Experiences in the World War*, Vol 2. New York: F. A. Stokes Co., 1931.
19. Ibid.

Chapter 5

"We've been ordered up to the front at once. The camions will be here at five o'clock in the morning."
—Lieutenant Legendre by telephone to Lieutenant Colonel Wise, May 30, 1918

The order to move the 3d U. S. Division (less artillery) reached Major General Joseph T. Dickman in headquarters at Châteauvillain some 160 kilometers southeast of Château-Thierry. The division commander could scarcely have welcomed the new turn of events. The 3d Division had not even been organized until November 1917. Its major combat units were brought together for the first time in France. With less than a month's training in the Châteauvillain area, the division received orders to relieve the 26th U. S. Division on a "quiet" sector of front. Dickman was making a reconnaissance of the area on May 28 when his orders were changed: the division would now occupy a sector in the Vosges, a move scheduled for May 31. On the following day these orders were canceled in favor of the emergency move to Duchêne's Sixth French Army.[1]

Under the hastily drawn marching schedule Major James G. Taylor's 7th Machine Gun Battalion (motorized) moved out in the afternoon of May 30, destination Condé-en-Brie about twelve kilometers southeast of Château-Thierry, with orders to report to the XXXVIII French Corps. The infantry brigades would follow by rail to Montmirail, then by foot to the battle area.

Making excellent time, Taylor's vanguard units under the command of Captain Charles F. Houghton closed Montmirail about noon on May 31. While eating a hasty lunch the Americans were questioned by French officers as to their destination and were told to turn back, "that it was useless to try to stop the Germans whose artillery shells were exploding in the town of Condé-en-Brie" about fifteen kilometers farther north.[2] Disregarding this counsel, the Americans pushed on, a trip slowed by hundreds of refugees making their way south. In midafternoon they reached Condé where they found massive confusion, with no one expecting them or holding any notion of what to do with them—a contretemps finally solved by one General Renouard who ordered them to join the 10th French Colonial Division fighting at Château-Thierry.

Toward evening the columns reached Nesles, a village about a mile south of Château-Thierry, where Houghton conducted a quick reconnaissance before issuing his orders: Company A with eight guns to dig in before the main or wagon bridge spanning the Marne; Company B with nine guns to defend the railroad bridge some 500 yards east; Lieutenant John T. Bissell, a young West Pointer of Company A, to take a section of two machine guns across the main bridge to join the French colonials desperately fighting to hold there.

The fight continued into darkness. While the Americans south of the river dug in their guns, French engineers planted high explosives under the spans of the vital bridge. From the other side of the river the crackle of rifle and machine-gun fire punctuated by exploding grenades and occasional artillery shells grew ever more intense as the fighting approached the Marne. At 10:00 P.M. the French blew the main bridge. By now the rest of Taylor's battalion began arriving, a welcome force of machine guns which in the next two days helped prevent the Germans from crossing the river. Dickman's infantry units were meanwhile streaming into the area where the

French commander strung them along the ten-mile front from Château-Thierry east to Dormans. At Jaulgonne, where the enemy had pushed across the Marne, the Americans joined with the French in launching a counterattack that sent the Germans back over the narrow river. And on the night of June 2, at Château-Thierry, a young machine gun officer, Lieutenant Cobbey, heard his name being softly called from across the railroad bridge. Half wondering if he were proceeding into a trap, he sneaked over the bridge to find Lieutenant Bissell and thirteen men on the other side. They had lost one man and both guns but had put up a splendid fight that helped win the battalion the following citation from Pétain:

> Under command of Major Taylor, barred to the enemy the passage of the Marne. In the course of violent combat, particularly the 31st of May and the 1st of June, 1918, it disputed foot by foot with the Germans the northern outskirts of Château-Thierry, covered itself with incomparable glory, thanks to its valor and its skill, costing the enemy sanguinary losses.[3]

By June 2 the arrival of the 3d Division had helped stop the German advance from Château-Thierry east. This was only one danger spot, however. West of Château-Thierry the enemy also planned to reach the Marne—a plan interrupted by the arrival of other American troops.

Pershing's order to move up the 2d Division of U. S. Regulars did not reach Major General Omar Bundy's headquarters at Chaumont-en-Vexin until late on May 30.

The division had arrived in this new area only a week or two earlier, after having refitted and trained in the general area of Bar-le-Duc. Spread out in the pastoral countryside northwest of Paris, the battalions had been concentrating on unit exercises which terminated on May 29 with brigade maneuvers.[4] Now, on Memorial Day, it was again preparing to move—this time by shanks' mare to the Beauvais area, its mission to relieve the 1st Division still fending off German counterattacks at Cantigny.

For most of the troops the day meant respite from drill and other duties. To most it seemed a peaceful day, a day of well-earned leisure that not even rumors of still another German offensive could upset. In the morning units such as the 2d Engineers held contests in "running, jumping and swimming."[5] At noon the men gathered in regimental formations to hear bands play *Departed Days* while chaplains spoke sonorously of the dead. "For want of something better to do," Sergeant Gerald Thomas took some of his platoon to the 6th Marines service.[6] Martin Gulberg was there and remembered that

> we had services on a little hill just outside of town. Chaplain Darche, in his sermon, told us that pretty soon we were to see real action on a lively front and many of us would not come back.[7]

At Brigade headquarters, a private château called Le Bout de Bois (End of the Wood), General Harbord prepared for an afternoon's ride with one of his aides, Fielding Robinson.[8]

A few miles away at Courcelles, Lieutenant Shepherd spent the afternoon polishing the leather and brass of his best uniform. Two days earlier he had met "an attractive little French girl" who had presented him to her careful parents. Having passed this test he was now invited to dinner at their country home where undoubtedly a number of relatives were gathering to look him over.[9]

Shepherd's commanding officer, Colonel Wise, was spending the day at Neuilly, a Paris suburb, with his wife who had just come to France with a hospital unit.[10]

Lieutenant Metcalf of the 17th Field Artillery Regiment whiled away the afternoon watching "a pretty good show" put on by the troops.[11]

After a quiet day, Lieutenant Gordon of Berry's 3d Battalion, 5th Marines, joined his fellow officers who "were seated in small groups" in the garden at the Château de Vaudencourt where they were "waiting for dinner to be served."[12]

Elsewhere in the area men spent the day walking in the country-side bursting with wheat and mustard and alfalfa; some slept, others hung listlessly around YMCA huts to write letters home, a few for-

tunate ones called on attractive girls in nearby villages, a few spent
the day in Paris on leave.

Paris was not as safe that day as the area around Chaumont-en-
Vexin. In a letter of May 30, Lee Meriwether, special assistant to the
American ambassador, wrote:

> . . . The majestic Madeleine witnessed today what I am sure
> is a spectacle unique in its history—a service held by and for
> American soldiers. Monseigneur J. N. Connolly, Chaplain
> of the American Army in France, preached the sermon which
> was listened to by an audience consisting in great part of
> American soldiers. The boys in khaki occupied seats on the
> right half of the grand nave; on the other side were civilians
> and, although many of these were Americans, many also were
> French. The hundreds of young men in khaki had the joy
> and gladness and *thoughtlessness* of Youth in their eyes; to
> them War is the Great Adventure. As they stand at its thresh-
> old they see naught of its horrors, fear not of its dangers. . . .
> As Cardinal Amette was making his brief but eloquent trib-
> ute to the young American soldiers before him, the bursting
> of the seventy-five-mile gun shells was plainly audible. . . .
>
> After the services were over a shell from this seventy-
> five-mile gun did strike the Madeleine, passed between two
> of the huge fluted columns and buried itself in the massive
> masonry behind the altar in the process beheading the statue
> of St. Luke which occupied one of the niches on the exterior
> of the churches.[13]

While this service was going on, while chaplains spoke to the
men of 2d Division, a French staff car was racing from Provins to
Major General Bundy's headquarters. It arrived in Chaumont about
5:00 P.M.

Moments later an excited French staff officer was conferring
with Bundy and members of his staff. The situation, he explained,
had developed rapidly and catastrophically since the enemy launched
his latest drive across the Chemin-des-Dames on May 27. The attack was sweeping French and British divisions before it. It had al-

ready penetrated to the Marne. GQG was rushing all available French reserves to the front; even now the 3d U. S. Division was moving on Château-Thierry.

Pershing and Pétain, the officer continued, agreed that the 2d U. S. Division would march at once to the sound of cannon. Convoys of French trucks or *camions* were on the way to pick up the infantry and move them to Meaux, a town on the Marne about twenty-five miles west of Château-Thierry—as yet no arrangements existed for moving the artillery or supply trains.

His words changed the placid evening to orderly chaos. While division staff officers worked up march schedules and called them down to the brigades and regiments, runners circulated outlying areas to pass the word: return to units at once. Later another French officer reported the scheduling of trains to move the artillery and other units but added that the division's motor transport would proceed under its own power.[14]

Sergeant Thomas and his men had idled away the afternoon talking to friends over at regiment and were walking back to their camp. "On the road we passed a runner from our battalion who told me to tell everyone I saw to hurry back, that something was going on. When I reported to my platoon commander, David Redford, a hard-bitten little fellow from Rhode Island, he told me to make sure that the men drew cold rations at chow that night—that we were moving out though he didn't know where."[15]

Harbord and Robinson later said they "had been riding through the fertile fields and woods and had slowed down to walk through the gates into the long driveway of the château. A sergeant was hurrying toward us with the news of orders to move. Orders to the regiments were on the way and packing had started at a furious pace."[16]

Lieutenant Shepherd got the word just as he was climbing on the bicycle that would carry him to his rendezvous. "I was told to turn out my platoon and stand by for boarding *camions*. I knew this meant action, otherwise we would have moved by foot. All I could do was send my orderly with a note of apology to my *marianne*."[17]

Colonel Wise was at dinner in Paris when he received a call from his adjutant: "We've been ordered up to the front at once. The *camions* will be here at five o'clock in the morning."[18] To make the trip the resourceful colonel persuaded his wife's hospital unit to lend him an ambulance.

Lieutenant Gordon was still waiting for dinner in the garden of the Château de Vaudencourt, when suddenly the "battalion's second in command, Captain Henry Larsen, came running to us and called out, 'The battalion is leaving, pass the word to your platoons to make their packs, as the *camions* are on the way, and we leave at ten o'clock tonight.'"[19]

Over at the 17th Field Artillery, Lieutenant Metcalf ate supper and "walked around for a while . . . at about nine o'clock orders were received that the regiment would begin to move within two hours. We had heard on the 29th that the Boche had broken through the Chemin des Dames and were driving another wedge in. We all thought that this was where we were going."[20]

With the passing of the word, confused and contradictory as it often was, officers and non-coms turned out their units, issued rations and ammunition, made final inspections of packs, then marched the troops to the designated embarkation points. At first they held the men in loose formation. By midnight when the *camions* still had not arrived they set the men at liberty to break out blankets and sleep as they could. Only a few units managed to divert rolling kitchens from the supply trains to provide a final hot meal. Most of the troops munched cold rations and swore at the delayed *camions*.

The empty convoys began arriving at 4:00 A.M. on May 31. Each consisted of fifty to seventy-five *camions,* the standard French army truck that held twenty to twenty-five men in a tarpaulin-covered bed provided with seats fore and aft and a bench running down the center. They were driven by French colonial soldiers, Annamese and Tonkinese, "little, yellow, dumb-looking fellows" perched on the front seats oblivious to the questions hurled by their new American passengers. Upon loading, each convoy, accompanied by a French staff officer in a separate automobile, roared off toward the little towns of Marines, Pontoise and Saint-Denis to join the Paris-Metz highway leading to Meaux.

By the time the first trucks were on the road the sun was up, harbinger of a clear, beautiful and very hot day:

The men were packed rather tight and the sun kept getting hotter and hotter. The dust arose in great clouds and the men were soon covered with a thick grayish powder. The truck train headed towards Paris, which fact gave rise to all sorts of speculations. Civilians all along the route waved and shouted, and at every halt gave the men water.[21]

At first it was all very exciting, humor and good spirits abounding. Private French later remembered passing a large cemetery: "Here's a quiet sector," someone shouted with a laugh, "let's take over here."[22] But, as Lieutenant Cooke, an army officer assigned to Wise's battalion of the 5th Marines, later wrote:

in a couple of hours we had very different ideas. The board seats were hard and narrow. The wheels of the truck had solid rubber tires and our vertebrae were constantly jerked and jarred like a string of box cars behind a switch engine. But the dust was worst of all.

It billowed in long funnels from the tail of each section. Clouds of grit swirled in through both ends of our truck and with each jounce of the springs, small geysers of dirt squirted up at us from between the floor boards. Some of the men tried wearing their gas masks, but decided that air with dirt was better than no air at all, so took them off again. On parallel roads other battalions could be spotted by the blankets of dust rising above the distant trees and small hills. The Annamese drivers of two columns, converging on a main highway, would race to get there first and avoid the other's dust.

"Lucky if we don't get killed before reaching the front," yelled Lieutenant Frazier, as we won a race and at the same time missed a tree by six inches.

Twice the columns were halted while staff cars and motorcycles rushed about furiously, like Collie herding sheep. About noon the driving became even more difficult when we ran into a continuous stream of refugees moving south . . . by late afternoon [we] rolled into the town of Meaux.[23]

The accounts of the ride are as many as the details are various, but each unfailingly mentions the refugees. For out of the intense heat and the dust and the dry throats and hungry stomachs and the certain prospect of battle that made men laugh hard at very poor jokes arose a common compassion for the very old and very young, for the women and children of the disjointed families that might have belonged to them but for an accident of time and continent:

> There were old men and old women, and children of all ages. They rode in farm wagons and carts, in old barouches and pony-traps, in quaint high-shouldered vehicles of another generation, drawn by oxen and cows and old raw-boned horses rejected by the army, or they went on foot, treading heavily through the dust. Some of them trundled wheelbarrows: an old bent woman pushed one, in which, atop a pile of household odds and ends, rode an ancient of days, clad in a blue smock, sucking with toothless gums at a cold pipe. Every conveyance was loaded with gear, things strangely assorted and precious to householders, not to be left behind; and things as absurd as people snatch when they run from burning houses. There were featherbeds and quilts and tall clocks, and ducks and chickens tied by the legs, and rabbits in crates, and chairs and bird cages and strings of garlic. The Mayor of a village passed: he limped in tight shoes and wore the high hat, the frock-coat, and the tricolor sash of ceremony. In the throng there were sheep and goats, herded anxiously: men remember a flock of sheep, which at a crossroads, went inescapably under the wheels of a battery of French artillery turning into the highway there, and the lamentable cries of the shepherds.[24]

By midafternoon these sights and others were familiar to the infantry and the engineers. Most of the artillery was entrained by then, but now the division entraining officer learned that only thirty-two of the fifty promised trains would arrive. They were enough to handle the rest of the artillery. That left the regiment machine gun companies and the animal-drawn supply trains. In late afternoon they began the trip on foot.

Notes

1. Joseph T. Dickman, *The Great Crusade*. New York: Appleton and Co., 1927.
2. Ibid.
3. Ibid.
4. U. S. Army, *Records of the Second Division (Regular)*. Vol. 6. Washington: The Army War College, 1927. (Hereafter referred to as *Records*.) None of my individual sources recall these brigade maneuvers with any exactitude; in view of the time limitation they must have been very rudimentary.
5. U. S. Army, *The Official History of the Second Regiment of Engineers and Second Engineers Train United States Army in the World War*. No place, no date. (Hereafter referred to as *Engineers*.)
6. General Gerald C. Thomas, USMC, (ret). Personal interview with the author.
7. Martin Gus Gulberg, *A War Diary*. Chicago: The Drake Press, 1927.
8. Fielding S. Robinson. Personal correspondence with the author.
9. General Lemuel C. Shepherd, USMC (ret). Personal interview with the author.
10. Frederic M. Wise and Meigs O. Frost, *A Marine Tells It to You*. New York: J. H. Sears and Co., Inc., 1929.
11. Stanley W. Metcalf, *Personal Memoirs*. Auburn, N.Y.: privately printed, 1927.
12. George V. Gordon, *Leathernecks and Doughboys*. Chicago: privately printed, 1927.
13. Lee Meriwether, *The War Diary of a Diplomat*. New York: Dodd, Mead and Co., 1919.
14. Oliver L. Spaulding and John W. Wright, *The Second Division American Expeditionary Force in France, 1917–1919*. New York: The Hillman Press, Inc., 1937.
15. Thomas, op. cit.
16. Robinson, op. cit.
17. Shepherd, op. cit.
18. Wise, op. cit.
19. Gordon, op, cit.
20. Metcalf, op. cit.
21. *Engineers*.
22. Craig Hamilton and Louise Corbin, *Echoes From Over There*. New York: The Soldier's Publishing Co., 1919.
23. Major E. D. Cooke, "We Can Take It," *Infantry Journal*, May–December, 1937. Before joining the U. S. Army, Lieutenant Cooke was a soldier of fortune in Central America. After a distinguished World War I career he stayed in the army and during World War II was promoted to major general.

24. John W. Thomason, Jr., "Second Division Northwest of Château Thierry, 1 June–10 July 1918." Washington: National War College, 1928. Unpublished manuscript.

Chapter 6

"The Seventh [German] Army will continue the attack until the enemy's resistance breaks between Soissons and Villers-Cotterêts ..."
—Contra Corps Order Ia Nr. 507,
11:30 P.M., June 1, 1918

Shortly after the first convoys moved out, the division chief of staff, Preston Brown, left for the front by private automobile. In Paris he telephoned the I U. S. Corps chief of staff, Colonel Malin Craig, informed him of the new development and asked him to send rations, ammunition and hospital supplies to Meaux. Not far out of Paris his car was slowed and at times blocked by refugees, whom he viewed with a sympathy tempered by a professional realization of the danger they represented to his oncoming convoys.

In Meaux he met his adjutant, Colonel Bessell, briefed him on latest developments, then drove another few miles to Trilport, headquarters of the Sixth French Army. French staff officers, their excitement compounded by fatigue, quickly dashed his hopes for orderly deployment. Everything was confusion and contradiction. There was no exact situation. No one held any real idea for the deployment of the 15,000

THE SITUATION
May 31–June 1, 1918

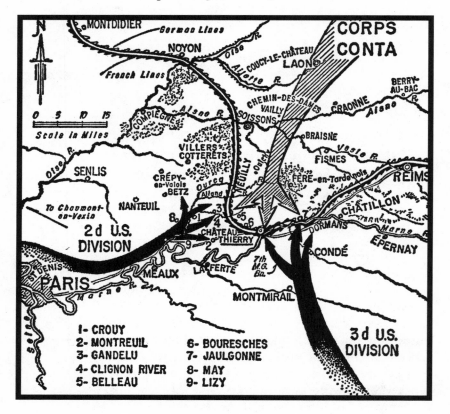

1- CROUY
2- MONTREUIL
3- GANDELU
4- CLIGNON RIVER
5- BELLEAU
6- BOURESCHES
7- JAULGONNE
8- MAY
9- LIZY

American infantrymen pressing hard behind Brown except that they should concentrate in the general vicinity of Meaux.[1]

Brown's temper was roiling by the time he located the harassed and very tired Sixth French Army commander, General Duchêne, whose own lack of specific plans frustrated him the more. To Brown's pointed questions, however, Duchêne did mention that the emphasis of the German attack seemed now to be coming increasingly from the direction of Soissons rather than from farther east. So far as was known, the present line ran almost directly south from outside Soissons across the Ourcq through Neuilly, then a few kilometers east of Gandelu, curved sharply toward Château-Thierry.

Brown's trained eyes studied the green-gray-brown hachures of the French map. The Ourcq River, a small stream rising above Château-Thierry in the vicinity of Fère-en-Tardenois, flowed west about twenty miles, then turned south for another fifteen miles where it paralleled the vital Meaux-Soissons highway before running into the Marne. Below the Ourcq, two creeks paralleled its east-west run, the Alland and farther south the Clignon.

The American officer at once suggested that the 2d Division should concentrate in the general vicinity of May-en-Multien. Why attempt a deployment at Meaux, a difficult if not impossible undertaking considering the hordes of refugees and the French troops jamming the Paris-Metz highway? Would it not be better to divert the convoys around Meaux to the west and then north along the Meaux-Soissons highway to May-en-Multien? From there the division could defend this highway with its left while its center and right spread out along the line of the Clignon Brook as far east as Gandelu.[2]

Duchêne seized on the plan with a Gallic alacrity that probably would have aroused Brown's suspicions in less hurried circumstances. Contrary to the original plan, Duchêne now told Brown to report to the VII French Corps on the left and deploy as suggested.

Returning to Meaux, the chief of staff sent out officers to divert the oncoming convoys to secondary routes. His brigade commanders, Harbord and Lewis, had already arrived and were given their new destination. Shortly after 2:00 P.M. Harbord learned:

> my brigade would go out to the northeast of Meaux and billet in four little villages to the west of the Ourcq River

and Canal, outposting toward Mareuil [sic]. The Germans were said to be not far away and we might expect to be attacked before morning. . . . We left, running out north through the green valley of the Ourcq. Every rod of the road was covered. All kinds of French units, artillery at a trot, straggling groups of infantry, lone engineers, Red Cross, trains, wagons, trucks, which sometimes would congest and bloat the road for half an hour so that there was no movement possible.

Hundreds of refugees crowded the roads, fleeing before the German advance. Men, women, children hurrying toward the rear; tired, worn, with terror in their faces. . . .

Meanwhile we passed a great many French officers and men, but all going from and none towards the front. All afternoon they passed, that motley array which . . . characterizes the rear of a routed army. Along towards nightfall there came one unit with its faces turned towards and not from the enemy: a brigade of French cavalry, neat, natty, horses well kept and equipment turned out, headed for the front. . . .[3]

Arriving at May-en-Multien in late afternoon, Harbord and his staff officers continued north to reconnoiter their assigned positions toward Mareuil, west of the Ourcq. Colonel Brown and the 3d Brigade commander, Brigadier General Lewis, next arrived, followed shortly by the first two battalions of Leroy Upton's 9th Infantry, which debussed in May-en-Multien, and Wise's battalion of the 5th Marines which passed through the town toward Mareuil.

While Upton's soldiers stretched cramped legs, shook the dust off their brown woolen uniforms and wondered what the hell was going on, Brown received a penciled order from General Duchêne. It directed the 2d Division to position between Montigny and Gandelu, east of the Ourcq, with an advance guard pushed out to Alland Creek. Its mission was to close a break in the French line along the Alland while preparing to counterattack north of the creek. It would establish liaison with a French division on the right and a French cavalry corps on the left—the latter undoubtedly the destination of the cavalry brigade earlier observed by Harbord.[4]

Brown's new order sent the two battalions of 3d Brigade infantry across the river to Crouy-sur-Ourcq where Lewis established brigade headquarters. While the infantry began digging in, Lewis and Upton left for a reconnaissance north toward Saint-Quentin to contact the French line. Instead they found the now familiar massive confusion of retreating units. Only late in the afternoon they learned that Saint-Quentin had fallen a few hours earlier. With that they turned back to Crouy-sur-Ourcq.

While Lewis and Upton were so engaged, Harbord and his party, returning from their reconnaissance, were intercepted by a French staff officer who informed them of the change of orders: upon arrival of his troops, Harbord would outpost on the right of the 3d Brigade, specifically toward Chézy-en-Allier, northeast of the Montigny-Gandelu road. Harbord immediately turned toward the new area where, because of heavy road congestion, he arrived about dusk. After selecting forward positions for his troops, he left two members of his staff to establish brigade headquarters and with an aide, Norris Williams, began threading his way back through retiring French infantry to the Meaux-Soissons road. At one of the crossroads a French division commander overtook their car. Williams, who spoke fluent French, asked the general the location of the Germans.

"I don't know," he replied.

Well, then, continued Williams, where was his own command? *"Je ne sais pas,"* was again the answer.

At Harbord's request Williams asked the old gentleman where he was going. The stern, troubled face broke into a smile: *"La soupe,"* he replied.[5]

By late twilight Harbord reached the main highway where he encountered the division chief of staff, Preston Brown, surrounded by a confused group of French and American officers.

In Harbord's absence, Brown had received a third order from Duchêne, a frustrating document contradicting the earlier one: the 2d Division was now to concentrate *west* of the Ourcq. For this reason, Malone's 23d Infantry, which arrived that evening, passed through May-en-Multien toward Mareuil.

Before Brown could issue further orders, he received still another order, the fourth, from Duchêne: the weight of the German

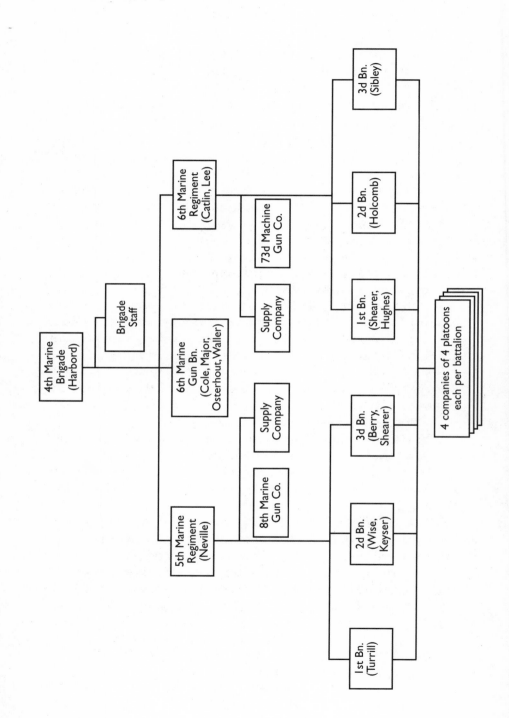

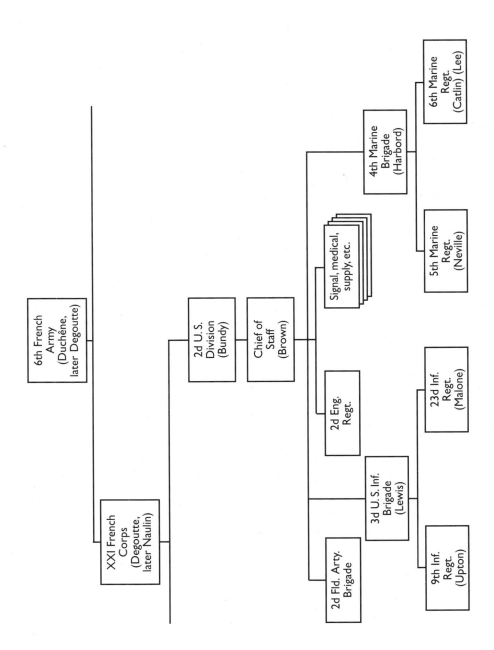

attack had shifted to Château-Thierry and the area immediately west, a strong attack having developed in the afternoon against the line Epieds-Etrépilly-Bouresches. Accordingly, the second Division would not concentrate on *either* side of the Ourcq but instead would march on Montreuil-aux-Lion—a day's march—to go into XXI Corps reserve between there and Château-Thierry.[6]

Harbord learned the details of the new plan from Brown's Field Order Number Five: the 3d Brigade with headquarters at Montreuil to deploy north of the Paris-Metz highway extending from in front of Belleau Wood to the line of the Clignon Brook; Harbord's brigade with headquarters at Bézu to deploy on the right or south of the Paris-Metz highway facing Vaux and Hill 204; artillery to emplace at Cocherel; ancillary units behind Montreuil.[7]

For the moment these ultimate dispositions would have to wait. The first problem was the general transfer to the Montreuil area, nearly a day's march distant. While Brown's staff officers carried the word to Upton and Malone commanding the army regiments, Harbord scouted the highway to find units of the 5th Marines and the 6th Machine Gun Battalion waiting impatiently for orders. Recognizing their disorganized, fatigued state and prompted by a German air raid—the result of Brown using his headlights to brief the division trains officer—Harbord told them to bivouac in the adjoining fields until 4:30 A.M. when they would march east.[8] Lieutenant Cooke of Wise's battalion later wrote:

> "I would like to see one German at least," barked Captain Wass.[9] He couldn't have gotten his wish any quicker if he had rubbed a magic lamp. A lone airplane came scooting low over the treetops, banked swiftly and *wham! wham! wham!* laid a string of eggs right down the road where we were sitting. Wass and I dove for the ditch, but before I landed, a fragment of hot steel smacked against the seat of my pants.
>
> "Pipe down," Captain Wass interrupted my heartfelt cursing while he helped to ascertain the extent of my injury. "You'll get a wound chevron for this."
>
> "And what do I say when people ask where I got hit?" I demanded with all the sarcasm permitted a junior officer.

The Captain offered several curt suggestions, all to the point, if a little crude. . . .

As we moved off down the road some kids in the first platoon broke out with a new version of the *"Parlez Vous"* song.

"The lieutenant, he saw an airplane pass," they caroled, and went on happily to describe in detail just what happened to the lieutenant.[10]

Harbord meanwhile motored to Bremoiselle, picked up his staff officers and returned to the highway, where he continued to sort out his units. In the interim General Lewis and Colonel Upton returned from their northern reconnaissance, received Brown's new orders and decided that Upton should march his 9th Infantry at once, a task made the easier since it was grouped in the vicinity of Crouy-sur-Ourcq.

The only infantry unit now lacking was Catlin's 6th Marines. When Catlin reached Meaux at 8:30 P.M. his first convoys were already proceeding toward May-en-Multien, a fact he learned at division headquarters in Meaux where he stopped for instructions and maps:

Then followed a series of misadventures that tried my soul. From Meaux my first orders were to proceed north, but those orders were changed twice during the night. About ten o'clock a French staff officer stopped my car and told me that the troops had been shunted off. I started in a new direction and was switched again to Montreuil-aux-Lions. I was a lost colonel, hunting around in the dark for his command, and hunting with an anxiety that, in this crisis, approached panic. There is no use trying to conceal the fact that it was a sorry mix-up. The French were on the run, and the staff came pretty close to being up in the air. Orders were given and countermanded in the effort to get the reinforcements to the spot where they were most needed, while a dozen spots looked equally dangerous.[11]

Other unit commanders of the division were sharing Catlin's sentiments. Colonel McIndoe's 2d Engineers reached Meaux about dark, slowed to a crawl in a gigantic traffic jam of French army convoys and refugees, then stopped altogether during a German air raid. Conditions did not improve on the Meaux-Soissons highway where, tired, thirsty and hungry, they spent a cramped night in trucks jolting ahead a few hundred yards at a time. Most of the 6th Marines shared this experience in trucks inching along between Meaux and Montreuil-aux-Lions. Private Carter's battalion managed to reach Montreuil where it bivouacked on the side of a hill along the road. The troops were just asleep, "when we were ordered to re-roll our packs and march further on, about five kilometers, to a place called White Farm.[12] Some of us slept here in barn lofts and others in the woods nearby."[13]

The artillery spent the day of May 31 and part of the night on uncomfortable trains which perforce approached by circuitous routes. The train carrying Lieutenant Metcalf's battery of the 17th Field Artillery arrived at Ormoy-le-Daviens, some twelve miles *northwest* of May-en-Multien, about 9:00 P.M. Metcalf described it this way:

We could hear the guns very plainly here so we knew we were pretty close to the show. It seemed to take an age to shunt our train around but we finally got detrained and ready to move at 11 o'clock. It was a beautiful, clear and starry night, and we could hear some planes in the air. Archie's [antiaircraft shells] were breaking in the sky in different places and we knew that Ormoy was an unhealthy spot due to the bombing parties of the last few nights. We had just left the station and were moving on the road when suddenly we heard a Boche avion very near us. We pulled over to the side of the road and stopped. The plane was almost over the station when a magnesium light was dropped and they commenced to bomb the station. It was a terrible feeling, as the rear of our column was hardly one hundred meters out of the station, and the terrific crashes sounded too close for comfort. . . . It was a great relief when they flew off as nobody had been able to move. . . . About four o'clock in the morning we came alongside of a village and were ordered to pull to the right and halt. We unharnessed, fed and watered the horses and then everybody turned in for a few hours sleep.[14]

During May 31 the French high command became especially concerned with the Montdidier-Noyon area northwest of Soissons. Intelligence reports of a building German attack along this line coupled with the heavy fighting of May 30 east of the Oise suggested that, as Foch later wrote, the Germans "intended to open up the road to Paris at all costs."[15]

The events of May 31 heightened this fear. Although the French beat off a German attack north of Reims, the planned counterattack toward Fismes failed to materialize. Instead the three divisions were "used for local purposes,"[16] a euphemism for fighting to hold what they had. South of Soissons the other counterattack kicked off with four divisions at 11:00 A.M., gained a little ground, captured several hundred prisoners, was checked and then thrown back. North of Soissons the enemy seized the important Nouvron plateau and in the Ourcq valley continued pushing the French back toward the Villers-Cotterêts Forest.[17]

Foch, Pétain, and Duchêne reviewed the situation that afternoon in a conference at Trilport. Foch found the pessimism of the two field commanders little to his taste. To Pétain's request for additional reserves including the American divisions training in the British zone, he answered with a sort of military pep talk while putting off any immediate action. But he later told Haig that if the present situation continued to deteriorate he, Foch, would have to transfer French, American and even British divisions from the north.

Pétain's own headquarters, or at least those officers sounded out by Major Clark, regarded the situation as very grave but not hopeless. But in response to Clark's question as to what the loss of Paris would mean to the prosecution of the war, the answers of three officers, although varying in degree, allowed him to conclude to Pershing "that they really feel that the loss of Paris . . . probably means the conclusion of the war for France."[18]

Pershing did not need this tidbit of intelligence to confirm his own assessment of the situation. Obviously he believed it grim— otherwise he would never have released the divisions essential to the formation of his own army. But his reactions to the pleas of Foch and Pétain for these troops stemmed more from a realistic understanding of the approaching crisis than it did from sympathy with the French defeats. As was the case with the earlier defeats on the Somme and Lys, Pershing thought the present disaster largely the result of the Allied marriage to trench warfare. He was not impressed when Foch on the previous day repeated a desire "that only infantry and machine gun units should be brought over from the States," nor was his temper improved by a visit on May 31 from Monsieur Tardieu, a politician who, according to Pershing,

> no doubt with good intent, undertook to comment adversely on our staff and our organizations. As these were subjects he could not possibly know about, I replied that he had an entirely erroneous impression and that our General Staff was composed of men selected for their ability and efficiency. I intimated that we had had quite enough of this sort of thing from the French, either military or civilian, and suggested that if his people would cease troubling themselves so much about our affairs and attend more strictly to their own we would all get along much better.
>
> I fully appreciated M. Tardieu's ability and his eagerness to be helpful, and I really had a high regard for him, but the constant inclination on the part of a certain element among the French to assume a superiority that did not exist, then or at any later period, added to the attempts of some of them to dictate, had reached the limit of patience.[19]

A further report from Clark read a little more optimistically. The Operations Section of GQG was already working on the counterattack briefly discussed by Foch and Pershing at Sarcus on the previous evening. In brief, this called for a stop line running from Noyon to the Marne, then east along the river. If this line held, GQG hoped to concentrate a force of fifteen to twenty divisions around Beauvais to attack the enemy salient from the east while another force of about fifteen divisions, concentrated around Chalons, would strike northwest toward Reims. Commandant Laure estimated to Clark that the forces could be assembled, ready to attack, inside of fifteen days.[20]

An enthusiastic plan, this, and, in view of enemy dispositions and intentions, a remarkably sound plan with the possible exception of the time factor. Considering that the enemy had advanced from the Chemin-des-Dames to the Marne in just four days, fifteen days seemed an optimistic period of grace. For to the west of the Marne the enemy was continuing an advance that at its present rate would put it well beyond Paris in another fifteen days.

Despite the distorted and delayed communiqués from GQG the calculation was obvious to the most unmilitary Parisian. Thousands of them were already leaving the capital, thousands more were soon to leave. Paris, indeed the western world, was scared.

For the Germans the battle seemed to be shaping well.

By June 1 the Crown Prince's offensive had brought his vanguard divisions within thirty-nine miles of Paris. The advancing troops had taken over 65,000 prisoners and quantities of matériel, an enormous victory.

But like Ludendorff's other recent victories, this one was scarcely complete. Although German troops stood before Reims they still had not taken the ancient town. They had reached the Marne between Dormans and Château-Thierry but they still had not crossed it in force. Elsewhere in the center and on the right they were continuing the advance, but now it was slowing, just as it had earlier slowed on the Somme and the Lys.

And for similar reasons.

One was overextended supply lines. The failure to take Reims restricted Seventh Army's major supply route to the single Soissons-Fismes railroad. This not only dictated a restricted quantity of supply and replacement troops, but a long and difficult march over congested roads from the railhead to the vanguard divisions.

The partial supply failure occurred at a bad time. Corps Conta's impressive gains, including the capture of 12,000 prisoners, came only at considerable cost. On May 31 the 28th Division reached the Marne where it was forced to rest in the thick forest north of Passy. On the same day, the 10th and 231st divisions fought their way along a line stretching from Château-Thierry to Etrépilly, but here their progress visibly slowed, as did that of the 5th Guards Division on the left. So essential was the supply line to these continuing actions that in an order of June 1 von Conta wrote:

> I forbid the resting of marching columns in villages, on bridges or similar narrow places. With the exception of villages, wherever possible troops will rest on the side of the road. Only in that manner is an uninterrupted frictionless traffic on roads possible.[21]

In the same order the corps commander concerned himself with malingering and drunkenness, a major problem shared with other corps commanders.[22]

Each of these factors contributed to the general slowing of momentum. Command reports of gains along the bulging battleline, though still comforting, markedly decreased on May 31. On the extreme left the attack against Reims was bogging down while von Schmettow's right reached the Marne only with the help of the 5th Guards Division of Corps Conta, whose chief of staff, von Unruh, later wrote:

> . . . a reconnaissance on our left flank showed me that von Schmettow's corps could not hope to advance much further [sic]. The resistance from the south bank of the Marne had become too strong, and every attempt to make ground toward the east broke down under the heavy flanking fire it encountered. The only way out would be to cross the river and gain possession of the heights south of it, for by so doing, the ring around Rheims would be drawn closer.[23]

Ludendorff did not believe that this was "the only way out." By June 1 this and other difficulties appeared as more shadow than substance. The failure to take Reims was annoying—Ludendorff termed it a "strategical disadvantage"—but scarcely decisive. To continue the action as von Unruh desired would have meant considerable delay. Not only had Corps Conta out-run most of its organic artillery, but the heavy Seventh Army guns essential to a crossing of the Marne were being shifted to the northern sector. Far better in Ludendorff's mind to keep the attack moving southwest, primarily to free the area around Soissons which would facilitate support of a major attack planned by von Hutier's Eighteenth Army against the Noyon-Montdidier line.

Ludendorff's plan meant that the right of the First Army and the left of the Seventh Army would assume the temporary defensive with the impetus of attack shifted west. To Corps Conta it meant a shift of strength from left to right primarily to support von Winkler's drive southwest.

Von Conta dictated the new dispositions in a corps order written at 1:30 A.M. on June 1. This placed five divisions in line and two in reserve: from right to left the 197th Division, which was being taken over from von Winkler's corps; the 19th and 36th divisions; the 231st fighting at Château-Thierry; and finally the 28th, soon to be relieved by an extension of von Schmettow's right; two divisions, the 237th and 5th Guards, to position slightly behind the right wing.

The same order directed the divisions to attack on June 1: the 197th to take the hill north of Courchamps-Licy Ferme-Licy-Clignon; the 237th to attack Monthiers-north edge of Etrépilly; the time to be decided by the divisions but not "later than twelve noon"; the 231st Division to take Hill 204 west of Château-Thierry and establish a bridgehead south of the Marne at about the railroad right of way; the 36th Division to establish a bridgehead south of the Marne on Hill 219 one and a half kilometers south of Courtmont.[24]

The actions began as scheduled. On the right the 197th Division took its objectives by afternoon and was ordered to extend its advance to the heights of Hautevesnes to complement the advance of one of von Winkler's divisions on its right toward Clignon Brook. A corps order issued in midafternoon read in part:

> to utilize the Clignon Sector, outposts must be established, and an outpost zone must be extended in front of the main line of resistance. At Château-Thierry and Jaulgonne, bridgeheads must be established on the south bank of the Marne, but these will only be held by a weak force. It is especially suggested that echelonment in depth and the establishment of a machine gun zone in depth be made.[25]

Corps Conta obviously was expecting counterattacks.

In the event, a bridgehead was not to be established at Château-Thierry, and the one that was established at Jaulgonne would not last long. All that day units of the 3d U. S. Division were coming into line. Conta did not know this when late that night he issued a new corps order. After noting that "the day's objective has been reached. The enemy has been forced back step by step, although tenaciously defending the ground . . ." this order clarified the corps' mission:

> The [Seventh] Army will continue the attack until the enemy's resistance breaks between Soissons and Villers Cotterêts. The left flank of Winkler's Corps is advancing in a westerly direction to the Clignon Brook.
> The [Conta] corps is covering the left flank of the [Seventh] Army by advancing as far as the line Gandelu-Château Thierry.

This meant no rest for the now weary German divisions. On June 2:

> The line Gandelu-Marigny-Bouresches-Vaux must be reached. The attack will start at 9 A.M. after a short artillery preparation.[26]

Once again German commanders read the order, studied maps and issued their own orders designed to take the objectives decreed by corps. They did not know that those objectives were already being defended by the 2d U. S. Division.

Notes

1. John W. Thomason, Jr., "Second Division Northwest of Château Thierry, 1 June–10 July, 1918," Washington: National War College, 1928. Unpublished manuscript.
2. Ibid.
3. James G. Harbord, *Leaves from a War Diary*. New York: Dodd, Mead and Co., 1925.
4. *Records*, Vol. 4. The complete order is given.

5. James G. Harbord, *The American Army in France, 1917–1919*. Boston: Little Brown and Co., 1936.
6. *Records*, Vols. 1 and 6; see also Thomason, op. cit. A great deal of confusion surrounds the chronology of these orders. Thomason states that the order to concentrate west of the Ourcq arrived around midnight. The 3d Brigade War Diary, whose statement I have accepted, has the particular order arriving shortly after the 3d Brigade reached May-en-Multien, thus the only logical reason for the 23d Infantry continuing north. The 2d Division's Journal of Operations, on the other hand, states that the order to move east to Montreuil arrived at midnight. This is refuted by Brown's extant order which carries the date-time group, 7:40 P.M., 31 May 1918.
7. *Records*, Vol. 1.
8. Harbord, *Leaves from a War Diary*.
9. Captain Lester Wass commanded the 18th Company. He was later killed at Soissons.
10. Major E. D. Cooke, "We Can Take It," *Infantry Journal*, May–December, 1937.
11. A. W. Catlin, *With the Help of God and a Few Marines*. New York: Doubleday, Page and Co., 1919.
12. This would be La Maison Blanche south of Lucy-le-Bocage.
13. W. A. Carter, *The Tale of a Devil Dog*. Washington: The Canteen Press, 1920.
14. Stanley W. Metcalf, *Personal Memoirs*. Auburn, N.Y.: privately printed, 1927.
15. Ferdinand Foch, *The Memoirs of Marshal Foch*. New York: Doubleday, 1931.
16. Paul H. Clark, "Letters and Messages to John J. Pershing, 1918–1919." Washington: Manuscripts Division, Library of Congress. Unpublished.
17. Ibid.
18. Ibid.
19. General John J. Pershing, *Final Report of General John J. Pershing*. Washington: U. S. Government Printing Office, 1920.
20. Clark, op. cit.
21. U. S. Army, *Translations of War Diaries of German Units Opposed to the Second Division (Regular), 1918. Château Thierry*. Vol. 1. Washington: Army War College, 1930–32. (Hereafter referred to as *Translations*.)
22. Barrie Pitt, *1918 The Last Act*. New York: W. W. Norton and Co., 1963.
23. Sydney Rogerson, *The Last of the Ebb*. London: Arthur Barker, Ltd., 1937.
24. *Translations*, Vol. 1.
25. Ibid.
26. Ibid.

Chapter 7

"General, these are American regulars. In a hundred and fifty years they have never been beaten. They will hold."
—Colonel Preston Brown to General Degoutte,
June 1, 1918

At 4:30 A.M. on June 1 the first columns of the 5th Marines stepped out, the 23d Infantry following, the 2d Engineers bringing up the rear—destination: Montreuil.

Harbord motored on ahead of the troops to report to General Degoutte, XXI French Corps commander, headquartered south of Coupru. A little past 6:00 A.M. he reported his brigade situation to Degoutte, who told him:

> Things have been going badly with us. They have been pressing us since the morning of the 27th and have advanced over fifty kilometers in seventy-two hours. I know that your men need rest. Let them get something to eat. If it can be avoided I shall not call on you today but it may become necessary. Your troops must be ready to go into line any time after eleven if called on.[1]

Shortly after Harbord's call, Bundy, Preston Brown and Upton arrived at Degoutte's headquarters where the old colonial general gave them the situation as he saw it. The enemy had just taken Château-Thierry and Hill 204 which gave him command of the Paris road and the Marne valley to the south and west. His first line continued west through Vaux, then northwest along the railroad to Bouresches, Torcy, Bussiares and Chezy-en-Orxois.

Degoutte's corps, flanked by VII Corps on the left and XXXVIII Corps on the right, consisted of two divisions, Michel's 43d on the left and Gaucher's 164th on the right. Each had been rushed up to meet the enemy, each had seen its battalions committed piecemeal to the battle, and in several days of hard fighting each had suffered very heavy losses which Degoutte, lacking reserves, could no longer repair. His artillery, however, "was keeping up the fight with fine spirit."[2]

The immediate danger, Degoutte continued, lay in the north and east, particularly the latter where the enemy on Hill 204 stood only a bit over four miles from his very headquarters. The Americans should join the French units here and attack at once.

The Americans, particularly Preston Brown, would have none of it. Any such action, Brown pointed out, could only lead to catastrophe. Due to the flux of Sixth Army orders the previous evening, only one regiment, the 9th Infantry, had joined the immediate area—the others were strung out west and south of Montreuil. The men were tired and hungry, they carried only 100 rounds of rifle ammunition, they lacked artillery and machine guns, their supply trains stood miles away. Surely the best plan was to form a defensive line behind the French divisions and attempt to hold until division support arrived.

For a considerable time Degoutte refused Brown's arguments, nor was that unnatural for one who worshiped at the tactical altar of Ferdinand Foch. Foch and his disciples believed primarily in offensive tactics, a belief compatible in a general sense to Pershing and his school. The difference was in method. In wanting to send in driblets of Americans, Degoutte was following the practice established by the earlier Somme and Lys defensives, a tradition of muddling through by piecemeal commitment, by plugging holes when and where possible, by finally stopping the advance (or letting it run out of steam), then by somehow striking back—a course perhaps dictated by the French inability to find sufficient reserves with which to strike back effectively.

And now on June 1 Degoutte wanted to follow such a course. For five long days he had been looking at defeat. He stared now at disaster. He and his staff were tired, nervous and frightened. When earlier they had learned of the approach of the 9th Infantry they were immensely relieved because at first having seen the foreign uniforms they thought the Germans were to their rear.[3] That possibility was still very real in their minds; it followed that any action which could prevent this disaster should be taken.

Neither was the American stand unnatural. Several factors existed in addition to the arguments voiced by Brown, and if they weren't expressed in so many words they nonetheless lost little of their potency. The French and British may have scorned the American claim to a tactical doctrine, but the Americans still believed in it. Nothing observed since their arrival in France had caused them to throw over their basic ways in preference to Allied methods. And for twenty-four hours their general observations had been reinforced by very specific contacts with French soldiers, many of whom regarded the present position as hopeless. *"La guerre est fini"* and *"Fini la guerre"*—the war is over—were called out time and again to the Americans, defeatist words spoken just as frequently by officers and non-coms as by the lower ranks, many of whom had abandoned their weapons and sought salvation from plundered bottles of wine. If they reflected the condition of Degoutte's divisions, it would be suicide to commit any division, French or American, in part or whole, to the fighting line. And even if the situation had been static, a final factor would have prevailed in the American attitude. For Degoutte's expressed desire represented a tactical attempt to absorb the American identity, which Pershing had been fighting so hard to retain. This was the real crux of the matter, and on that morning of June 1 Preston Brown was saying no more than Pershing had been saying for a good many months—we'll fight, but by God we'll fight on our own terms.

Whether Degoutte recognized his match in the jut-jawed Brown or whether his own confidence was shaken, he finally resolved the impasse in favor of the Americans. The 9th Infantry would take up a line to the east, facing Château-Thierry, while the other regiments assembled to the west and prepared to go into line north of the Paris-Metz highway. Degoutte was still not convinced that this was the right move, and in a final question the doubt in his mind found expression in his plaintive voice: Could the Americans really hold?

Preston Brown raised red-rimmed eyes to answer: "General, these are American regulars. In a hundred and fifty years they have never been beaten. They will hold."[4]

This dramatic but still unproven declaration ended the conference. Colonel Upton headed back to his regiment, met one of his battalion commanders on the road and at 8:10 A.M. on the morning of June 1 dictated a field order incorporating the decision reached in Degoutte's headquarters:

1. The Boche have advanced west of Château Thierry. The French hold the line between us and them.
2. The regiment takes up a position between here and Château Thierry.
3. The 2d Battalion advances to first crossroads northeast of here (Ferme Paris) then east through fields Ferme Paris to Le Thiolet and takes up a position as indicated on the map, three companies in line one in support. 1st Battalion advances southeast from the crossroads Domptin and takes up position as indicated on the map. Its right resting on Mount Debonneil. The 33d French on his right (liaison with flank forces and each other).

P.C. [command post] of regiment on road bend 100 metres north of Aulnois.

3d Bn hqs company now en route east on this road, will join regiment and constitute regimental reserve.

Men will be cautioned to make every cartridge count. Patrols to east of our line to connect with French forces reported between us and the Boche.

Special attention to ravine. Be prepared to repel hostile
aeroplanes and minimize losses by open formation of attack.
Liaison group to P.C. [command post] regiment as soon as
P.C. battalion is established.
Regimental aid station Domptin.
Ample protection provided on all sides, 100 metres between
companies advancing, each company to have wire cutters at
hand.[5]

Meanwhile Bundy and Brown returned to Montreuil, rounded
up Harbord and Lewis and proceeded to a council of war at the
Hôtel de Ville. They were discussing the situation when a motorcycle slid to a halt and a French officer handed Bundy the following
corps order:

The enemy is attacking on the front Etrépilly-Hill 190—la
Gonetrie and a little farther south. We have lost la Gonetrie
and the enemy is gaining ground in the direction of
Bouresches. Hence it is absolutely necessary that the line
agreed upon this morning be occupied without a moment's
delay by one of your regiments. If the 23d has not yet arrived, I beg that you direct your first available regiment to
that line. As agreed upon with you this morning, this regiment will be under the orders of General Michel, commanding the 43d Division, until you take over command of a part
of the front.[6]

Bundy acknowledged the new turn of events by ordering Brown
to put in Malone's 23d Infantry. But aside from general knowledge
that the 23d stood on the march, no one knew its exact location.
When French couriers continued to arrive, each urging haste, Bundy
ordered Harbord to put in Catlin's 6th Marines.[7] Bundy's order
thus reversed the intended deployment of Field Order Number Five—
henceforth, the marines would fight north of the Paris-Metz highway, the infantry south. This seemed at the moment a minor matter,
but minor matters often cause major consequences, and this was to
prove no exception.

Harbord's mission demanded drastic action since some of Catlin's battalions were still on the march. After briefing the regimental commander, Harbord drove to the lead battalion which he found a few hundred yards east of Montreuil unloading rations from seventeen trucks. Harbord ordered the motor transport to move forward, drop the rations along the road, then return to the rear to pick up the marching columns of Tommy Holcomb's 2d Battalion and bring them up to Ferme Paris about a half mile from the designated line. By the time Holcomb's battalion arrived the other battalions were closing the area on foot. Holcomb marched his companies forward, tied in his right with the 9th Infantry at Le Thiolet and extended the thin line north to Triangle, then west to Lucy-le-Bocage. Cole's 6th Machine Gun Battalion deployed behind the 2d Battalion with gun sections assigned variously along the line. Simultaneously, Shearer's 1st Battalion began extending Holcomb's left from Lucy-le-Bocage through Champillon to Hill 142.[8]

Harbord meanwhile hurried on to Lucy for his first meeting with General Michel, commanding the torn 43d French Division. He found the village under shellfire punctuated by the crackle of small-arms fire in the distance. Michel told him, "hold the line at all hazards." Harbord continues:

That was the order I transmitted to the brigade. The companies were hardly more than in place when a message from the same general suggested that I have a line of trench dug several hundred yards back of them, "just in case." My reply was that, with the orders our men had, they were prepared to die if necessary to hold the line, but if started to digging trenches they would know it could have but one purpose and that my orders were not to be taken as given. So, I said: "We will dig no trenches to fall back to. The Marines will hold where they stand."[9]

At 4:10 P.M. Harbord reported to Bundy by field message:

Have reported to C.G. [Commanding General] 43 Div. (French) and established liaison. Troops arriving by camion going in between Thiolet and Lucy. Important that available engineers with plenty of tools come as soon as infantry finish with camions. Should debuss at Ferme Paris and march in small columns about evenly distributed from Thiolet to Lucy. Hurry them.[10]

Less than an hour later, at 5:05 P.M., Harbord again reported to Bundy:

Second Bn. 6th Marines in line from le Thiolet through Clerembauts woods to Triangle, to Lucy. Instructed to hold the line. 1st Bn. 6th Marines going into line from Lucy through Hill 142. 3d Bn. in support at La Voie du Châtel which is also P.C. [command post] of the 6th Marines. 6th Machine Gun Bn. distributed at line. No instructions as to the evacuation of wounded.[11]

While these two regiments were deploying, most of the other units were closing the area. Of the tactical troops only the regimental machine gun companies and the 4th Machine Gun Battalion were encountering serious delay. Nothing could be done about the latter unit, whose train was blocked at Compans-la-Ville by a rear end collision between two refugee trains.[12] Far more serious was the delay in the regimental machine gun companies which, together with field kitchens and regimental supply trains, were marching overland— the result of only thirty-two of the promised fifty trains having appeared in the Chaumont area. When division headquarters learned of this in the afternoon, the supply officer hastily diverted division trucks to the rear to pick up what units they could while the others were ordered to forced marches.

On the favorable side, McIndoe's 2d Engineers, separated from their horse transport, were in bivouac outside Montreuil by early afternoon. A short time later Neville's 5th Marines and Malone's 23d Infantry, after a march succinctly described by one veteran as "heat-dust-rifle-pack,"[13] began arriving. By evening the 5th Machine Gun Battalion was completing a long march as were the gun batteries of Chamberlaine's artillery brigade slowly closing on Cocherel.

Signal, hospital and other supporting units were already establishing themselves throughout the area. Certain division trains, some carrying precious ammunition and rations, began setting up dumps behind Montreuil.

As quickly as the tactical units arrived Bundy pushed them forward to support his thin line: Neville's 5th Marines in reserve around Pyramide on the left rear of the 6th Marines and close to Harbord's new brigade headquarters at Yssonge Farm: Malone's 23d Infantry similarly positioned in support of Upton's line; a battalion of engineers to each of the two frontline regiments now digging in against the expected German onslaught.

For the troops in line and going in line, the worst blow was the absence of the field kitchens. Men who had marched anywhere from thirty to sixty miles in two days in stifling-hot weather needed food of a better-balanced and more palatable nature than the primitive field rations of the day. At first they successfully supplemented the official diet by constant, generally successful forage. For miles around, the French farms and houses now stood empty, livestock, chickens, rabbits alive and unfed. At Cocherel, a few kilometers west of Montreuil, General Chamberlaine established artillery brigade headquarters in a farmhouse whose door bore the scrawled message: *Papa, nous sommes parties à Rue, _____, Lizy-sur-Ourcq*—obviously written while Papa was in the fields, it told him where to find his fleeing family.[14]

Throughout the concentration area, foraging proved the order of the day. But as the troops moved forward to frontline positions, such opportunities significantly decreased and more than one soldier or marine was forced to an evening meal of the French ration, a foul-smelling tin of Madagascar beef which the troops called monkey meat, a few dry biscuits and a canteen of tepid, probably impure water.

Despite the supply breakdown, Bundy could count the day a positive gain, practically a miracle considering the situation twenty-four hours earlier. Although he still faced many problems, he was well on his way to gaining the inestimable advantage of division cohesion. From his new headquarters—"a schoolroom where staff officers used children's desks for writing orders"—he issued Field

Order Number Six at 6:00 P.M., June 1. Besides confirming the dispositions described above, this order established a specific division reserve, directed signal units to the task of communications between XXI Corps and division and between division units, established ambulance companies and field hospitals at suitable support points and, in one abrupt paragraph, provided for area integrity:

> The Commanding Officer, Military Police, will establish a barrier on the line Ste. Aulde–Montreuil-aux-Lions–Germigny–Gandelu; arrest all stragglers and send them to their organizations. You will cause a detail of one officer and twenty-five men to take post in Meaux.[15]

It was a complete order, a good piece of staff work, but an order that would read more comfortably in later years than on the night of issue. It did not encompass, for instance, any more than the 2d Division's immediate front. Yet while it was being written the battleline from Château-Thierry to the Ourcq was writhing like a poor soul damned to eternal perdition in Hades. To the north between Montigny and Gandelu, one of the earlier destinations of the 2d Division, the writhing became convulsive, the line broke. And to fill a two-mile gap between XXI Corps and VII Corps, Degoutte owned no more reserves, a fact hurled at Bundy's headquarters late that night.

Bundy had to respond—a breakthrough here could easily turn his still tenuous left flank. He responded with Malone's 23d Infantry, Turrill's 1st Battalion, 5th Marines, part of the 5th Machine Gun Battalion and a company of engineers—a powerful task force, thus a powerful loss to the main line. About midnight Malone began moving out on a forced march toward Coulombs where division trucks were already heading with 500,000 rounds of caliber .30 ammunition for his rifles.[16] Details arrived in an order from his new commander, General Michel, in headquarters at La Loge. The order, as complete as it was confused, contained a single recommendation: "Go quickly."[17]

This was the last flurry of activity for the night. Now the line stood even more thinly, the soldiers and marines tired, hungry and woefully ignorant. Most of them did not know where they were. What maps existed were obsolete, badly drawn, inaccurate, difficult to read. Most frontline units still lacked adequate amounts of rifle ammunition. The regimental machine gun companies still stood miles away, the artillery was still moving up.

The Americans felt awfully alone that night, isolated and insecure, comforted only by their intense belief in themselves and their buddies. They did not know, they had no way of knowing, that the eyes of the world were upon them.

The Allies were frightened now.

The fall of Château-Thierry on June 1 plus further reverses to the west placed the issue squarely in doubt. At a stormy session of the Supreme War Council, Monsieur Clemenceau attempted to blame the disaster in part, and in quite a large part, on the failure of the Americans to carry their share of the war. Ernst Otto reported that after vigorous, generally acrimonious discussion the representatives of France, Italy and England joined in a blunt appeal to President Wilson:

> There is danger that the war will be lost unless the speedy arrival of additional American troops serves to restore the weakened Allied reserves. Thus only can defeat be avoided because of the exhausting of the Allied reserves long before those of the Germans.[18]

Pétain left no doubt of the crisis in a letter to Foch stressing the need for American and British divisions in the threatened sector. According to Foch, Pétain's letter contained

> a report from General de Castelnau [commanding the Eastern Group of Armies] informing him that, if the Germans attacked in force on the front of the Eastern Group of Armies, at this moment denuded of all reserves, he would have no other course open to him but "to retire as rapidly as possible the divisions which were not attacked, regroup them, and maneuver to contain the enemy while waiting for better times."[19]

A similar air prevailed at Pétain's advance headquarters at Provins, only thirty miles by road from Château-Thierry. Pierrefeu later wrote:

> Although the bridges had been cut, it was thought that a raid by German armored cars, fording the river and taking disadvantage [sic] of our disorganization, might be able to reach G.Q.G. without meeting any obstacles on their way. There were no troops to stop them. The suggestion was made to General Anthoine, who gave orders, and I was told that barriers had been erected at various points on the road. Measures were concerted for removal [evacuation], a dismal project.[20]

Despite GQG's delayed and generally noncommittal press releases, the public was scarcely deceived. The loss of Château-Thierry, Pierrefeu later wrote,

> was sadly received by the country. Some names have a symbolic value, and Château-Thierry is one of them. Until this town was taken, the people of Provins [Pétain's forward headquarters] were calm, but after that there was much uneasiness. A lawyer from Provence, who had taken up his abode at Paris, replied with a sort of offended dignity to an officer who wished to prove to him that, since the enemy had not crossed the Marne, the danger could be met: "They have reached it, and you can tell the gentlemen of the Staff that that is bad enough."[21]

At GQG Colonel Rozet, talking with Major Clark "was at times optimistic and at times expressed discouragement." The trouble was, he explained:

> French morale is subject to change on short notice. It is capable of great heights and likewise of great depths. If we do not do something to inspire the troops with confidence their present good morale will tumble.[22]

The key to that something lay in the arrival of American troops at the line of the Marne. Pierrefeu later described a feeling shared by the downhearted officers of Pétain's forward headquarters:

> At this time swarms of Americans began to appear on the roads. At Coulommiers and Meaux they passed in interminable columns, closely packed in lorries, with their feet in the air in extraordinary attitudes, some perched on the tilt, almost all bare headed and bare chested, singing American airs at the top of their voices amid the enthusiasm of the inhabitants. The spectacle of these magnificent youths from overseas, these beardless children of twenty, radiating strength and health in their equipment, produced a great effect. They contrasted strikingly with our regiments in their faded uniforms, wasted by so many years of war, whose members, thin, their sunken eyes shining with a dull fire, were no more than bundles of nerves held together by a will to heroism and sacrifice. We all had the impression that we were about to see a wonderful operation of transfusion of blood. Life was coming in floods to reanimate the dying body of France.[23]

Would it come in time?

The beaten ones thought not. There were a great many beaten ones—soldiers who had left the battle convinced the war was over, France defeated. They wore tattered rags of uniforms, they carried no rifles; some clutched precious articles plundered from their countrymen's homes; most were drunk—drunk from battle, from plundered wine, from defeat. *"Fini la guerre,"* they called to the Americans; *"Pas fini,"* the Americans replied.

The beaten ones were not important; eventually they would be rounded up, herded into new units, fed back into battle. The important ones, and there were many, were fighting on and it was their morale which so concerned Rozet. One of them, a young American named Alden Brooks, watched the first troops of the 3d Division coming up on the march. An artilleryman in Duchêne's Sixth French Army, Brooks was a dirty, hungry and very tired survivor of the long retreat from the Chemin-des-Dames:

It was a pleasure to stand by the road side and watch the long, double files of them come in, watch them pass by, each man with that tightly rolled knapsack on his back, many a clean young head bare, all their khaki legs and arms and shoulders moving in a slow easy rhythm, and the dust ever drifting away from them over the hedges.[24]

The word passed quickly to the fighting lines. The soldiers there had already been told of the American victory at Cantigny. That was good enough, but where was Cantigny and how was that victory helping them? For six days they had fought alone, suffering defeat after defeat, yielding mile after mile to a relentless, seemingly superhuman enemy. But now they learned that Americans were fighting at Château-Thierry, that Americans were coming into line along the whole Marne front.

It was a healthy but very temporary development. No one watching the French divisions could doubt their waning strength. Very soon the battle would be willed to the Americans—the Americans of limited quantity and untried quality. Could they hold?

Notes

1. James G. Harbord, *The American Army in France, 1917–1919*. Boston: Little Brown and Co., 1936.
2. Major General Omar Bundy, "The Second Division at Château Thierry," *Everybody's Magazine*, March, 1919.
3. Jean de Pierrefeu, *French Headquarters 1915–1918*. Translated by Major C. J. C. Street. London: Geoffrey Bles Ltd., 1929; John W. Thomason, Jr., "Second Division Northwest of Château Thierry, 1 June–10 July, 1918." Washington: National War College, 1928. Unpublished manuscript.
4. Oliver L. Spaulding and John W. Wright, *The Second Division American Expeditionary Force in France, 1917–1918*. New York: The Hillman Press, Inc., 1937.
5. *Records*, Vol. 3.
6. Spaulding and Wright, op. cit. Although this order forced Bundy's hand, Brown's arguments had still penetrated. In sending a copy of the order to General Michel, Degoutte added: "The mission of this regiment will be to organize and if necessary to defend the support line indicated above. It will not be engaged for any other purpose."

7. Harbord, op. cit.
8. Major John Hughes was still in Gondrecourt. On June 5 he arrived to assume command of the 1st Battalion, 6th Marines.
9. Harbord, op. cit.
10. *Records*, Vol. 8.
11. Ibid.
12. *Records*, Vol. 8.
13. General Lemuel C. Shepherd, USMC (ret). Personal interview with the author.
14. *Records*, Vol. 9.
15. *Records*, Vol. 1. The complete order is given.
16. Ibid.
17. *Records*, Vol. 4. This order is dated 1 June, an obvious error in reproduction.
18. Ernst Otto, "The Battles for the Possession of Belleau Woods, June, 1919," *U. S. Naval Institute Proceedings*, November, 1928.
19. Ferdinand Foch, *The Memoirs of Marshal Foch*. New York: Doubleday, 1931.
20. Pierrefeu, op. cit.
21. Ibid.
22. Paul H. Clark, "Letters and Messages to John J. Pershing, 1918–1919." Washington: Manuscripts Division, Library of Congress. Unpublished.
23. Pierrefeu, op. cit.
24. Alden Brooks, *As I Saw It*. New York: Knopf, 1929. Failing to gain a commission in the American army, Brooks joined the Foreign Legion from which he was eventually transferred to the French army.

Chapter 8

"The French line seems to be holding very well ..."
—Colonel Malone to General Lewis,
June 2, 1918

On June 2 the soldiers and marines of the 2d Division awakened to interim war: the crack of French artillery, the random explosions of the German reply, the crackle of assorted small-arms fire not far to the front, a breakfast of cold rations and tepid water followed by the onerous, confusing task of consolidation.

All through the hot day men were to dig in, move, dig in again while their commanders frantically tried to keep in touch. Men were to find this a day of vast ignorance; in their frustration they were to swear at the French, at the enemy and at themselves, and while they were cursing the vital line into a semblance of cohesion some were going to be wounded and killed.

Bundy's main line that morning stretched nearly from the Marne at Azy northwest toward Hill 142, an elevation that, south of Bussiares, was to cause considerable confusion during the next two days. On the right of the Paris-Metz highway General Lewis's 3d Brigade, consisting momentarily of Upton's 9th Infantry, held the line with two battalions forward, one in reserve. Left of the highway General Harbord used Catlin's 6th Marines, also with two battalions up, one back, to carry the line toward Hill 142. Harbord backed his line with two battalions of Neville's 5th Marines. Cole's 6th Machine Gun Battalion stood in direct support of the line as did units of Degoutte's artillery—five groups of 75s (sixty guns) and one group of 155s (twelve guns).[1]

The most crucial mission of the morning, or so division headquarters believed, belonged to Colonel Malone, commanding the "Detachment, AEF" that around the previous midnight had been ordered to march northwest. Malone's orders were to fill a four-kilometer gap from the left flank of Michel's 43d French Division at the Bois de Veuilly west to the vicinity of Brumetz where he would tie in with the right of the French VII Corps.

Turrill's battalion of marines led the ten-kilometer night march across the dusty roads and through the small, deserted towns of Le Pletrière, Grand Cormont and Ecoute Plet.[2] Around 6:00 A.M. his leading columns reached Les Glandons, turned off the road and began closing a position from the front of Vaurichart Wood west to Prémont. At 6:30 A.M. Malone notified Bundy's headquarters by runner:

> Marines moving towards objective, rest of column proceeding towards next objective. No hostile detachments encountered. Constant reconnaissance to our right flank, rest of column proceeding towards Germigny. Line towards north seems to be held.[3]

Some ninety minutes later Elliott's 3d Battalion, 23d Infantry, began extending Turrill's line west to Moulin-du-Rhône. The remaining columns closed Coulombs a short time later. From here Waddill's 1st Battalion marched north to position between Elliott's left and the town of Brumetz. While Waddill and Turrill sent out patrols to contact the French on their respective flanks, machine gun and engineer units filed up to begin strengthening the new line. Meanwhile Malone set up headquarters in Coulombs where he retained Whiting's 2d Battalion and the remainder of the machine gun battalion as reserve.

While Malone's units were moving into position, enemy artillery opened fire against the French line stretching from Vaux to Gandelu. At 9:00 A.M. (8:00 A.M. French time), the first units moved to an attack designed to extend Corps Conta's right flank directly west from Château-Thierry to Marigny, then northwest to Gandelu. To accomplish this, General von Diepenbroick-Grüter's 10th Division would attack toward Vaux-Bouresches, General von Jacobi's 237th Division between Bouresches-Torcy and General Wilhelmi's 197th Division between Torcy and Gandelu along the line of the Clignon Brook.[4]

At first the advance went smoothly. On the extreme left Lieutenant Colonel Rotenbücher's 47th Regiment pushed through Rochets Wood to probe the Paris-Metz highway south of Vaux, an action too distant to be contested by Captain de Roode's two machine gun companies in support of the infantry and marines defending from Le Thiolet to Lucy-le-Bocage.

On Rotenbücher's right the 398th Infantry at first made good time in its attack toward Belleau Wood, Bouresches and Triangle. But French fire from Bouresches and from the highway north quickly slowed the center and right. And as the German left fanned out in the wheat fields south of Bouresches the massed columns fell within range of de Roode's guns. At 1,600 meters, just under a mile, the gunners raised sights, then opened a rapid, murderous fire.

The fire surprised the Germans, stopped them while they dispersed, hurt them when they advanced small groups which rushed forward a few yards to drop in the waist-high wheat while others came up beside them. They made another 400 yards before the heavy slugs cutting through the young wheat prompted them to break off the attack and fan out on either side to the cover of convenient woods and boulders.[5]

Simultaneous with this action the 237th Division moved against Belleau and Torcy where, again to their surprise, they found a determined defense only slowly yielding as the morning wore on. Similarly the 197th Division on the right advanced without difficulty toward the line of the Clignon only to be slowed and in some places stopped by an equally determined if scattered defense.

The delay proved valuable to the Americans. Malone perhaps benefited most of all since his recently arrived units faced the task of consolidation in strange and generally rugged terrain. Although the enemy took Coulombs and the soldiers of Waddill's 1st Battalion under intermittent artillery fire early in the day, the other units remained untouched. On the right Turrill quickly made contact with the French. At 9:50 A.M. he reported to Malone:

> We have gotten in touch with the colonel commanding the 133d Infantry, the left unit of the 43d Division. . . . Have placed one officer and platoon at Prémont with instructions to get in touch with your right company. . . . Have patrolled entire front. Reported by French Liaison Officer that no enemy south of Clignon River. French front covered by cavalry outpost line. Enemy having taken Hautevesnes yesterday, request Chauchat and Springfield ammunition. Rations for tomorrow. We are not yet connected by phone. Just received word that our left company is in liaison with the right company, Company I, 23d Infantry.[6]

Shortly after sending this message by runner, Turrill received an order from General Harbord. Earlier that morning Harbord had believed Malone's movement a division affair, a mistake quickly corrected by division headquarters. Nonetheless, Harbord kept a close eye on Turrill's battalion even though division had attached it to Malone's special force. Partly because of this concern, the brigade commander made his own early reconnaissance—wisely as it turned out. After checking in at General Michel's headquarters, he continued to the front. North of the 23d Infantry he found a French column of infantry which "did not impress me as being able to hold very long."[7] Between Vaurichart Wood and Hill 142, the latter being the left flank of Catlin's 6th Marines, "it appears that there is not much infantry but a few dragoons. . . ."[8]

Harbord now ordered Turrill to extend his new line to the northwest corner of Vaurichart Wood, if this were not "in conflict with some orders from higher authority." He also ordered Neville, commanding the 5th Marines, to take his headquarters company and Wise's 2d Battalion forward to fill the gap between Turrill on the left and Shearer's battalion of the 6th Marines on the right.

To strengthen the new line he asked Catlin to release a company of machine guns and send them to Veuilly Wood. In midmorning he reported this action to Malone and added:

> That gives us then American connection clear around from the 9th Infantry, inclusive, to the neighborhood of Prémont. I told Neville that when he got out there to that place, it was strictly an American proposition around to his left and included Turrill and to hold that line. Then I reported all to General Michel and told him what was done.[9]

Malone received this message at his new headquarters in Coulombs where he was busily trying to determine the location of his units and arrange for their supply. Up to noon all units had reported their fronts quiet, but shortly after noon enemy shells found Company A of Waddill's 1st Battalion, killed Private Charles Maggione, wounded Corporal Sam Meyers and Privates Sam Mathews and Prozet Zachio. Malone reported this information in an otherwise favorable message of 1:30 P.M. to General Lewis:

> The Chauchat ammunition—100,000 rounds, and the Hotchkiss—in clips—100,000 rounds, have arrived by French machines and have been distributed. . . . Also the 450 boxes rifle ammunition arrived and have been distributed thus making a possible 220 rounds for every man.
> The position was occupied without incident. . . .
> Liaison has been established with all units.
> Thus far no serious attack has been made. . . .
> The French line seems to be holding fairly well and I am not apprehensive.[10]

Malone was correct. The French line to his front was holding very well, the work mainly of determined French machine gunners dug in along the southern heights of the Clignon. According to the war diary of Corps Conta:

> The advance of the 197th and 237th Infantry Divisions . . . came to a halt in the afternoon as their inner flank was un-

able to advance because of the flanking effect of Hill 126. The Corps Headquarters ordered both divisions . . . [to] place their main effort on the inner flank and attach another field artillery detachment of the 5th Guard Infantry Division for this purpose.[11]

Malone's quiet situation was already contrasting with the rest of the 2d Division's front.

Shortly after Neville received Harbord's order to move up, he motored to Wise's position south of Marigny near Pyramid Farm. Handing his plump subordinate a map, he told him to march immediately "to establish a line from Hill 142 to the northeast corner of the Bois de Veuilly." The French, he explained, were defending along the railroad to the north and would probably fall back on the new line. Whatever happened, the marines were to hold.[12]

It was an order that appealed to the impatient Wise and his equally impatient troops. Before Neville's car was out of sight the bugles were erasing the hasty bivouac in favor of companies drawn up in columns of squads. A two-mile march brought them to Marigny, a village deserted except for a couple of batteries of French 75s whose fire was bringing a few enemy shells in reply.

While Wise set up his P.C. on the edge of town "against the cemetery wall," the columns continued forward over rising ground spotted with heavy woods and fields of growing wheat neatly separated by young hedgerows. A short distance out of Marigny company commanders looked to their objectives: Lloyd Williams to Hill 142 in front of Champillon on the right; John Blanchfield straight ahead toward Les Mares Farm, its spread of buildings now plainly visible; Lester Wass and Charley Dunbeck to Veuilly Wood. As Wass's company halted in the southern edge to execute right by file, the German artillery suddenly awakened. According to Cooke:

Shells struck in the treetops and fragments glittered in the air, like a shoal of small silver fish. The blow was quick, sudden, destructive, and eleven of our men went down. One or two cried out in surprised pain, but four lay inert and silent.

Faces turned white and the company showed a tendency to huddle and mill about.

"Get going!" Captain Wass sprang at them, a regular terrier for action. "What do you think this is, a kid's game? Move out!"

We scuttled through the woods, ducked and dodged as more shells pounded a shallow trench to our right, and then threw ourselves face down in the north edge of the Bois de Veuilly. To our front was a wheat field falling away gently to a narrow little valley and rising again to a forward slope some eight hundred yards ahead.[13]

On the, right Dunbeck's company was no more in position when a fresh barrage killed Sergeant Rogers and three privates. Cooke continued:

The larger sea-bags [nine-inch shells] came creaking along a rusty arc and unloaded in our woods like a ton of dynamite, while the smaller whiz-bangs [77mm shells] arrived with the speed of rifle bullets . . . we all took to digging fox-holes. Each excavation was made according to the owner's individual taste, or idea of safety. Some were long and narrow, others short and deep.[14]

On Dunbeck's right Captain Blanchfield halted his 55th Company in the woods bordering Champillon while he and Lieutenant Lem Shepherd, his second in command, performed a hasty reconnaissance of the front. A former enlisted man—what marines call a "mustang"—Blanchfield read the strange French map with only the greatest difficulty. His subsequent orders to Shepherd to take the company forward were hasty and vague. Acting on his own initiative Shepherd led the men to a "very commanding position overlooking the valley on the nose of Hill 183" where they found isolated groups of French chasseurs, the remnants of two battalions commanded by a colonel wearing a magnificent white beard.[15] Shepherd had scarcely positioned the platoons when he received a message from Blanchfield ordering him to fall back—he was too far forward to tie in either with Dunbeck on the left or Williams on the right. His subsequent movement brought the elderly French colonel rushing up to implore him not to desert the battle in this hour of great need. The young lieutenant reassured him that he was retiring only a few hundred yards.

Under Shepherd's direction the 55th Company dug in on a line fronting Les Mares Farm, a tenuous position of individual foxholes—"little scooped-up hollows similar to a grave but about a foot deep, with the earth piled in front for a parapet"—behind a barbed-wire fence.[16] On the right the line extended to the Champillon-Bussiares road where it tied in with Williams's 51st Company. To fill the gap on his left, Shepherd halted a group of retiring chasseurs and ordered their lieutenant to dig in. He also told his men to relieve individual Frenchmen of their Chauchats—the important automatic rifles of which he had only a few.

By evening Wise's battalion was spread wafer thin across a front of nearly two and a half miles. He possessed no machine guns, no rations, limited ammunition for both rifles and Chauchats. On his left Wass had found no sign of the 23d Infantry; on his right, Williams no sign of the 6th Marines. This was partly Wise's fault: Williams's company stood considerably to the rear of Hill 142. Understandably concerned over his bare flanks, he telephoned regimental headquarters, now a couple of miles behind Marigny at Carrières. "They'll show up," he was told.[17]

They had not shown up by evening, nor had any rations. The French filled the food gap with hardtack and cans of the slightly spoiled, stinking, stringy monkey meat. Cooking made it slightly more palatable, but fires would only attract German shells. Instead they ate it cold. And as they forced it down they watched an immense artillery barrage creeping south out of Bussiares. It would get to them soon enough, they knew—there was nothing to do now but wait.

Throughout the afternoon the situation on Bundy's flanks remained fairly quiet. On the left Malone continued organizing his defensive line. By late afternoon his four battalions seemed reasonably well situated with Turrill's battalion in contact with the French on his right. Waddill, on the other hand, still had not contacted the VII French Corps on the left (he would report first contact at 7:45 P.M.). All units suffered from poor communications and inadequate maps, a frustration evident in a message of late afternoon from Waddill to Malone:

> I transmit herewith sketch showing rough lead pencil outline of trenches but can give no order because the maps are so inaccurate. Herewith is sketch founded on reports by company commanders, etc., and an airplane photograph which I have followed in *outlining what I think* are the I Company trenches.[18]

At the other end of the line, Upton's 9th Infantry continued digging in, a task unaided by the attached engineers who were busy blowing the Marne bridge at Azy. Late in the afternoon Upton tersely requested seven ambulances to evacuate about twenty-six wounded, the result of enemy shellfire. He added that he had relieved a battalion commander for inability to read a map and inefficiency, and a company commander for reasons not stated.[19]

The situation was not so calm in the center where Bundy was trying to build a solid line prior to taking over sector command, a move scheduled for 9:00 A.M. the following day. The same shellfire that played havoc in Upton's lines caused considerably more trouble on Upton's left. Early in the afternoon Cole's P.C. was knocked out, causing him to move to Montgivrault-le-Grande Farm, re-establish communications to the battalions he was supporting and transfer his supply train farther to the rear. Another crisis developed in midafternoon when the French 155s, the big guns, began running out of ammunition. Although division headquarters hastily scraped up a convoy and sent it to the rear, a considerable time would elapse before fresh supply arrived, and until that happened the guns would fire much more slowly.

Harbord's attempts to repair Wise's exposed and weakly held position were frustrated both by the fluid situation and by faulty communications. Many of the P.C.s still lacked telephones while those installed frequently went dead. The alternative was runners, who could travel only so fast, particularly in strange terrain covered by intermittent shelling. This failure, besides lending disproportionate weight to the usual battlefield rumors, hindered correction of errors caused from small-scale and very poor maps.

At 2:15 P.M. Harbord notified Neville:

> . . . Please close the gap between your line and Turrill, incorporating the two small French battalions, if they remain as they probably will. Feeling a little uncertain about Turrill's position as belief that he extended to northwest corner of Bois de Vaurichart is based on an order I sent him to do so, and I have heard nothing from him since he left last night. Get in touch with him, include him in your command.[20]

This message had just gone out by runner when Harbord learned from Michel's 43d French Division that Holcomb's 2d Battalion was "giving way a little at Triangle." Had telephones been working Holcomb would have immediately contradicted the report. But telephones were not working, which meant messages by runners: one to Holcomb enjoining him to "hold your line there at all cost," another to Catlin to send up appropriate reinforcement from regimental reserve. Before the young marines reached the respective headquarters, signalmen had repaired the wires and Harbord was talking to Holcomb. Never one to waste words, the taciturn Delaware-reared officer told Harbord that when the 2d Battalion ran "it would be in the other direction." At 3:50 P.M. the brigade commander notified Catlin:

> The French now acknowledge that report as to 2d Battalion was a mistake and telephone with Holcomb says there is nothing doing in the fall back line. . . . I have asked the French General to investigate thoroughly the person who started the false report about Holcomb's Battalion, which is most annoying.[21]

While this "crisis" was being resolved, Harbord was attempting to locate Shearer's battalion, supposedly on Wise's right flank. In midafternoon he wrote Catlin:

Note the statement that Shearer's Battalion has its left 1,000 meters southeast of [Hill] 142. Is this true? Please note also that Feland [lieutenant colonel; second in command of 5th Marines] says that there is a battalion of French troops on the right of Wise and that Wise is at 142. I am speaking of 142 as shown on the map, not any hill in the vicinity; the actual figures where the left of Shearer's Battalion is supposed to be. Are the troops that you put in to fill the gap [82d Company, 3d Battalion] between Shearer's Battalion and 142, or between 142 and Wise's right?[22]

The mystery of the flanks would continue for some time, but before either Neville on the left or Catlin on the right could worry further about it a new development compounded the already confused situation. During the afternoon a German prisoner reported under interrogation that a fresh division expected to attack the American right with two regiments north of the Paris-Metz highway and one south.

Alarmed by this information, the French Corps commander, General Degoutte, ordered Berry's 3d Battalion, 5th Marines, to position behind the junction of the 3d and 4th Brigades as corps reserve. To replace Berry, Bundy ordered Turrill's battalion and two machine gun companies to leave Malone's line on the left: Turrill to march to Pyramid to form Harbord's brigade reserve; the machine gun companies to report to General Lewis at Ventelet Farm to form his brigade reserve. Meanwhile division trucks were hurrying to the rear in an attempt to pick up the regimental machine gun companies still on the march. Other truck convoys were bringing up artillery ammunition for the division's artillery brigade, also still on the march, and for the French 155mm guns, now seriously short of shells.

From Bundy's viewpoint the position by evening was neither good nor bad. In all, his division was defending a line nearly twelve miles long, a commitment preventing anything more satisfactory than local defense in depth. On the right Upton held one battalion in reserve with the two machine gun companies from Malone's sector expected to arrive by morning; Catlin, who had furnished one reserve company to back up Holcomb, another to back up Shearer, held only two companies in reserve; Neville would own no reserve until Turrill's battalion from Malone's sector arrived the following morning; and on the extreme left Malone now retained only a few machine gun units in his reserve.

It was a long, thin line but French resistance during the day had given its commanders what Napoleon called "the precious commodity of time" with which to make a good start toward consolidation. Despite massive confusion, despite the hunger and thirst, morale continued high. Wire communications were beginning to take form, ambulance and hospital companies were evacuating the wounded. General Harbord's report to Bundy at 6:25 P.M. reflected an almost comfortable feeling:

> Our communications are in much better shape than at this time yesterday. The liaison by runner is working regularly and efficiently. I have telephone communications now with both Regimental Headquarters and with the Headquarters of my Machine Gun Battalion and through the latter with the battalion nearest it [Holcomb's 2d Battalion], which is the battalion at the critical point on the line. The Regimental wireless stations are up and the signal officer sent to establish wireless stations at these Headquarters reports it will soon be in.
>
> It seems well established that the Germans have been repulsed today along our entire Division Front. Two attacks were made over in front of our lines and were stopped principally by the fire of my Machine Gun Battalion. There were also two attacks in the region south of Hautesvesnes. The French liaison officer here informs me the reports are that dead Germans pile the slopes. There is every indication that the French morale has been greatly stiffened by the presence of our men.[23]

Unfortunately the day's fighting was not over. Even as Harbord was writing these words the Germans in a final burst of evening effort were everywhere pushing back the French. By darkness, Corps

Conta claimed a line running from Vaux to Bouresches to Belleau, then west through Torcy and Bussiares to Eloup on the Clignon. By 11:00 P.M. German troops had penetrated Belleau Wood, the area south of Belleau-Torcy-Bussiares and had taken Hill 126.[24]

But now the French failed to submit gracefully. For the first time since May 27 they had held their own against the enemy, had given more than they had taken. Shortly after midnight Degoutte postponed Bundy's scheduled take-over of the sector and ordered a counterattack for the following day. Michel's 43d Division notified Harbord:

> The French troops received the order to retake the position they have just lost. The American troops will maintain at ALL COSTS the line of support they occupy: Bois de Clerembauts-Triangle-Lucy-le-Bocage, Hill 142, north corner of Bois de Veuilly.
> They will not participate in the counter-attack which will be made to retake the position of the French.[25]

At about the same time Degoutte and his staff were issuing orders for the counterattack, von Conta and his staff had decided to continue the attack: the 197th Division on his right to capture the high ground at Marigny and the heights of Veuilly; the 237th Division "with its main effort from Torcy on Lucy-le-Bocage" to "roll up the Bois de Belleau from the north and east with a simultaneous advance of the right flank on the hills of Marigny." The 10th Division, badly hurt during the day, would consolidate its present position from west of Vaux through Bouresches; the 231st and 36th divisions would prepare to cross the Marne; the 5th Guards Division to remain in reserve and "to automatically counter-attack in case the enemy should break through."[26]

These orders were important, even historic, for by them von Conta would bring his troops against the Americans.

Notes

1. Oliver L. Spaulding and John W. Wright, *The Second Division American Expeditionary Force in France, 1917–1919*. New York: The Hillman Press, Inc., 1937; John W. Thomason, "Second Division Northwest of Château Thierry, 1 June–10 July, 1918." Washington: National War College, 1928. Unpublished manuscript.
2. *Records*, Vol. 3.
3. *Records*, Vol. 5.
4. *Translations*, Vol. 1.
5. U. S. Marine Corps, *History of the Sixth Machine Gun Battalion*. Neuwied, Germany: 1919.
6. *Records*, Vol. 5.
7. Ibid.
8. Ibid.
9. Ibid.
10. Ibid.
11. *Translations*, Vol. 1.
12. Frederic M. Wise and Meigs O. Frost, *A Marine Tells It to You*. New York: J. H. Sears and Co., Inc., 1929.
13. Major E. D. Cooke, "We Can Take It," *Infantry Journal*, May–December, 1937.
14. Ibid.
15. General Lemuel C. Shepherd, USMC (ret). Personal interview with the author.
16. Wise, op. cit.
17. Ibid.
18. *Records*, Vol. 5.
19. Ibid.
20. Ibid.
21. Ibid. The report was made by a French officer who mistook a returning working party for Holcomb's troops.
22. Ibid.
23. *Records*, Vol. 6.
24. *Records*, Vol. 4.
25. *Records*, Vol. 5.
26. *Translations*, Vol. 1.

Chapter 9

"Retreat, hell. We just got here."
—Captain Lloyd Williams, USMC, to a French major,
June 3, 1918

June 3:

As on the previous day the troops roused from damp, chilly foxholes, stretched, relieved themselves, opened a tin of the hated rations, listened to the artillery duel, tried to judge the progress of battle from the sound of small-arms fire closer than the day before.

Strident voices of junior officers and NCOs quickly ended their speculations in favor of the now familiar tasks of digging holes or stringing wire or falling in to move God knows where and in all probability to move again shortly after reaching the new position.

Activities considerably varied on this hot, sunny day. Sergeant Major Matthew Ausborn of the 9th Infantry noted in his diary: "Foraging party goes out and returns with chickens, rabbits, potatoes, cider and a cow."[1] Sergeant Joseph Gleeson of Battery D, 12th Field Artillery noted:

Slept most of the A.M. At 1:30 P.M. regiment pulled out for line. Halted in woods. Thousands of troops went into position in an open field in the night. No chow, sleep or rest. Swiped a gallon of jam and six loaves of bread.[2]

Over at Battery C, 15th Field Artillery, Private John Hughes noted:

A German aviator was circling over our heads. We stopped, expecting every moment to hear something drop. He kept flying around and I suppose he had seen the column coming up the hill. Finally he flew away but in about twenty minutes was back again. By this time the battery was pulling into a courtyard where there was a big chateau. The aviator kept flying around. There were several French soldiers in the village, and I guess most everyone was firing his rifle at the plane and he was flying very low; in fact, we could see the Iron Cross painted on his plane. I kind of admired his nerve with all the bullets whizzing around him. Someone made a lucky shot as he flew over the chateau. We could see the observer looking over the side of the plane. I thought that he was going to take a "Brodie" but they managed to land in a field close by.[3]

In places the war was very real: the marines of Wise's battalion, for example, watched German artillery batteries approach at the gallop from the Clignon ridges, wheel off the road into firing positions, an activity hotly contested by French artillery units firing from immediately behind the marine line. But for most of the soldiers and marines the day meant facing an unseen enemy who confirmed his presence only by high explosive shells and by the increasing number of French soldiers who, alone or in twos and threes, stumbled toward the rear.

The Americans did not know that in front of them some very brave Frenchmen, far more tired and hungry than themselves, had forced their bodies from sleep to turn once more against the enemy of seven long days and nights. The counterattacks by units of Michel's 43d French Division centered south of Gandelu, Bussiares and Torcy. To no surprise of the French, the weak, disjointed efforts soon bogged down. By afternoon the survivors were falling back onto hastily organized defensive lines that in the center would crumble before the day was out.

In this sense the French effort failed, but in another it succeeded. The soldiers on the German right were already suspicious of the new resistance encountered on the previous day. Like the French, they were tired and hungry, their ranks greatly thinned. In the last forty-eight hours Corps Conta had suffered over 2,000 casualties, mostly on the right.[4] They had already seen enough activity behind the French lines to suspect that reinforcements were coming up. Despite the major gains of the night they faced the new day with a certain doubt now exploited by the French attacks. No matter how weak and disjointed the French effort, no matter how easily stopped, it confirmed German suspicions: obviously the French had gained new strength.

The knowledge upset the Germans. By causing frontline commanders to pause, then proceed slowly, it deprived them of their fresh momentum. On the left of the attacking line the 237th Division moved carefully through and down the flanks of Belleau Wood. On the right the 197th probed south from the heights of the Clignon. In the center both divisions pushed south from Bussiares and Torcy, but cautiously, slowly.

Once again the delay greatly benefited the Americans. By early morning the regimental machine gun companies, Chamberlaine's artillery brigade and the trains of the infantry brigades and the 2d Engineers began closing the division area. Truck convoys brought up urgently-needed 155mm shells for the French guns while adding to the new artillery dump at Lizy where an impressive million and a half artillery shells awaited the American units.[5]

By midafternoon the machine gun companies, although deficient in ammunition and lacking animals, were providing welcome reinforcement from left to right of the thin line. Simultaneously artillery commanders began reconnoitering assigned positions: Lieutenant Colonel Davis's 15th Field Artillery south of the Paris-Metz highway in support of the 3d Brigade, headquarters at Domptin; Colonel McCloskey's 12th Field Artillery north of the highway in support of the 4th Brigade, headquarters at La Loge Farm; Colonel

Bowley's 17th Field Artillery splitting to provide a battalion of 155s for each brigade with the third battalion assigned to counter battery fire.[6]

Just as welcome to the infantry were the supply trains, including the precious rolling kitchens, which moved up as far as practicable. The delivery of officer baggage and enlisted bedding rolls brought comfort to some units; to a few fortunate ones the kitchens offered the first hot meal since boarding the *camions* back at Chaumont-en-Vexin.

But time could not solve everything. Many of the problems of yesterday remained the problems of this day. Inadequate communications, poor maps and lack of patrol initiative on the part of concerned commanders continued to hinder proper liaison between units. Although Malone and Upton managed to tie in with the French on either flank of Bundy's line, the center of that line remained patchy.

The chief problem concerned Wise's marine battalion which stretched two and a half miles from Veuilly Wood across Les Mares Farm to the road a kilometer north of Champillon, a most vital line whose flanks connected neither to Malone's 23d Infantry on the left nor to Catlin's 6th Marines on the right.

The nub of the problem on the right was stated in an early morning message from Neville to Catlin:

> Wise [commanding 2d Battalion, 5th Marines] and Shearer [commanding 1st Battalion, 6th Marines] are in touch but Wise reports his right company (Captain Williams) has not been able to get in touch with Shearer's left company. Wise has gone this morning to his right to establish this liaison. He thinks there is a gap of some extent between Hill 142 and your left. Have directed him to find where your left is and to extend to the right if he finds that any gap exists.[7]

The strange terrain, coupled with considerable enemy artillery fire, prevented the battalions from tying-in during the morning. Shortly after noon Shearer notified Wise:

Have been trying to connect with your right flank. My left flank is on [Hill] 142. Liaison man states your right rests on Champillon-Bussiares [road] about 1 kilometer north of Champillon. My line runs from 142 southeast to Lucy, so if the above is true the vacancy is yours. I am trying to extend to reach your right. Please advise me exactly where your right is as I cannot spare men to run line past 142 as I understand your battalion line runs from 142 to Veuilly.[8]

In early afternoon Neville reported to Harbord:

Feland [second in command, 5th Marines] reports that his reconnaissance shows the right of Wise's battalion on road in edge of woods at [Hill] 142 and the two companies properly disposed to hold right of my line. A battalion of French troops is on the right of Wise.
While Feland was at 142, scout of Wise's battalion reported in, having located left of Shearer's Battalion just about 1,000 meters southeast of 142.
Twelve machine guns of 8th Machine Gun Company supporting Wise's left. Eight machine guns of Sumner's company and four of Kingman's company are supporting Wise's right.[9]

Similar confusion prevailed on the left where on the previous night Whiting's 2d Battalion of the 23d Infantry had relieved Turrill's battalion of marines.[10] Just after midnight Malone notified Whiting:

Send me report at once as to situation. Has any attack developed on your front or flank? Is your communication with Marines on your right [Wise's battalion] well established? Answer at once and investigate at once as to situation on front and flank and report later.[11]

Around 4:00 A.M. Whiting replied:

. . . No attack or demonstration on our front or flanks. . . .
French cavalry patrols well out in our front—liaison by runner to right and left flank units.
Telephone out of order all night . . . artillery fire in every
direction.[12]

Whiting accompanied this report with a sketch showing his battalion positioned to the right of the Prémont-Les Glandons road, its
right covering the northwest corner of Veuilly Wood where it tied in
with the 133d French Infantry Regiment.

Malone did not again refer to Whiting's contact with the marines until the afternoon. Upon learning that the enemy was attacking the 43d French Division in force and that General Michel,
contrary to his earlier orders, now wanted a solid American line behind him, Malone ordered Whiting "to gain contact with the Marines on your right and hold the lines at all costs. . . . Institute an
immediate reconnaissance to locate left of the Marines, and insure
continuous American line."[13]

About the time Malone was dictating this message Harbord
notified Neville:

The French Division Commander [Michel] desires that you
send out someone to establish the whereabouts of the right
of the 23d Infantry Battalion [Whiting's battalion] . . . also
to report if you are "elbow-to-elbow" with people on the
right and left of you.[14]

Michel's concern was well founded. The French center, hammered by German artillery and coordinated infantry attacks, was
rapidly crumbling. In early afternoon Captain Williams reported to
Wise that "all French troops on our right have fallen back, leaving a
gap." On Williams's right, Shearer's troops reported similar information. To plug the gap Shearer sent in two platoons from his reserve which shortly made contact with Williams's right. Catlin further
responded by starting two companies of his regimental reserve to
the threatened area.

By the evening of June 3 the American positions were full of retreating French soldiers. One of them, a French major of Chasseurs, stumbled up to Williams's second in command, Captain Corbin. In broken English the major informed Corbin of the German attack and told him to withdraw his line. When Corbin paid no attention he took a pad from his tunic and in English wrote a direct order to retreat. Corbin gave this to Williams, who exploded: "Retreat, hell. We just got here."[15]

It was a good sentence, one which tired, confused and somewhat frightened fighting men could grasp and take comfort from. One of Williams's platoon commanders, Lieutenant Hagan, later remarked that it "spread like wildfire through the units."

Because it was a good sentence and because Williams was killed not long after, his words were later questioned. After the war Colonel Wise claimed to have spoken it; a recent writer attributed it to Colonel Neville.[16] The evidence backs Williams, for in addition to Feland's and Hagan's testimony the record contains Williams's message of 3:10 A.M. to Wise:

> The French Major gave Captain Corbin written orders to fall back—I have countermanded the order. Kindly see that French do not shorten their artillery range.[17]

On that same afternoon a company commander on Williams's right also ignored an order to retire. Most of the marines and soldiers carried a disdain of retreat or defeat that would have won Foch's heart. For over a year they had been training for a single purpose of combat. They were now approaching their purpose. They may have been tired and hungry, their units confused and isolated, but they were not going to turn from what they had sought for so long.

And on that hot, sunny, explosive afternoon what they sought was rapidly approaching.

For the ones in the front line it was a matter of waiting, of huddling in the crude holes against exploding shells, of now and again taking a long shot when some German showed himself in the woods 800 yards away. The retreating French plainly announced the enemy's intention; and in late afternoon the enemy underscored it by suddenly increasing his artillery fire to dimensions heretofore unknown to the Americans.

In Wise's center the barrage found Captain Blanchfield talking with his second in command, Lieutenant Lem Shepherd. Blanchfield did not like the look of things. An old man, relatively speaking, he thought he was soon going to be killed, and he was right. His assistant, too young to be unsure of life, sensed his mood, tried to help him. That morning with Blanchfield's permission he had established an observation post of about a dozen men on a small hill from where, a few hundred yards ahead of the line, he found a commanding view and a good field of fire. And now, Shepherd stated, during the freshening barrage:

> Blanchfield gave me permission to go out and check this outpost. I don't know why I suggested it. It was one of those foolish ideas without reason because my men had orders to withdraw when they no longer could hold the position. For some reason, however, I wanted a personal look at the situation. My orderly and I started across the field and I said to myself, we'll never make it. Shells were exploding all over the place. One fell six feet to our front, a dud. We got to the observation point about 4 P.M. The barrage was now passing to the rear. Behind it the Germans were beginning to appear. We watched them come. . . . [18]

The marine outpost watched them come. They numbered only fourteen, they had no machine guns, no telephone to call up artillery. They could have run, and perhaps they should have. With a word, with just a sign of the hand, Shepherd could have taken them back. The little group did not know that the gray figures to their front were standing the closest to Paris since the German drive in 1914.[19] They probably wouldn't have cared. To them the issue was much simpler: like Lloyd Williams on their right, they had just gotten here and they did not wish to retreat.

> We watched them come on. A thousand yards, seven hundred, five hundred. I held our fire. Our sights were set for three hundred yards. . . .[20]

Considerably to the right of Shepherd an unnamed machine gunner of Catlin's 6th Marines was sharing the experience:

> Up to this time we had been under some pretty severe bar-rages, but this time we must have gotten under Fritz's skin because it started to rain shells of every caliber from one-pounders to the big "seabags," or nine-inch howitzers. It lasted just an even hour and then Fritz came at us with blood in his eye. I estimated them at about 500 and they were in fairly compact masses. We waited until they got close, oh, very close. In fact, we let them think they were going to have a leadpipe cinch.
>
> Oh, it was too easy; just like a bunch of cattle coming to slaughter.
>
> I always thought it was rather a fearful thing to take a human life, but I felt a savage thrill of joy and I could hardly wait for the Germans to get close enough. And they came arrogant, confident in their power, to within 300 yards. . . .[21]

Colonel Catlin and his adjutant, Major Frank Evans, sweated out the barrage in their new P.C., a house in the little village of La Voie du Châtel. Then, in Evans's words:

> From one side we had observation of the north, and when the Germans attacked at 5 P.M. we had a box seat. They were driving at Hill 165 from the north and northeast, and they came out, on a wonderfully clear day, in two columns across a wheat-field. From our distance it looked flat and green as a baseball field, set between a row of woods on the farther side, and woods and a ravine on the near side. We could see the two thin brown columns advancing in perfect order un-til two thirds of the columns, we judged, were in view. . . .[22]

To Evans's front the marines watched the enemy work through the wheat. Suddenly the young machine gunner received the order to fire:

. . . Rat-tat-tat-tat full into them, and low down, oh! But it was good to jam down on the trigger, to feel her kick, to look out ahead, hand on the controlling wheel, and see the Heinies fall like wheat under the mower. They were brave enough, but they didn't stand a chance.[23]

Shepherd and his marines did not have quite such an easy time of it:

Just over the crest of our hill there was a lone tree. I stood just in front of the tree where I could see and not be seen. About dusk the enemy began working around our hill. I gave the order to fire.

We opened up with what we had. They countered with a machine gun. A bullet from its first blast caught me in the neck. I spun around and dropped to the ground. My first reaction was to see if I could spit. I wanted to know if the bullet had punctured my throat. I figured if I could spit I was all right. I could spit. I crawled up beside my men. Several had been hit but the rest kept firing. They fired until dark. Just after dark we fell back to our main line, bringing our wounded with us.[24]

While Shepherd and his marines defended the little hill, Catlin and Evans kept on watching:

The rifle and machine gun fire were incessant and overhead the shrapnel was bursting. Then the shrapnel came on the target at each shot. It broke just over and just ahead of those columns and then the next bursts sprayed over the very green in which we could see the columns moving. It seemed for all the world that the green field had burst out in patches of white daisies where those columns were doggedly moving. And it did again and again; no barrage, but with the skill and accuracy of a cat playing with two brown mice that she could reach and mutilate at will and without any hurry. The white patches would roll away, and we could see that some of the columns were still there, slowed up, and it seemed perfect suicide from them to try.

You couldn't begrudge a tribute to their pluck at that! Then, under that deadly fire and the barrage of rifle and machine gun fire, the Boches stopped. It was too much for any men. They burrowed in or broke to the cover of the woods.[25]

For a time the fire fight continued from the woods, then slowly died. While snipers on both sides continued to fire on the careless ones, while stretcher-bearers snaked through the fields to collect the wounded, the artillery took over the battle.

The failure of the German attack left von Conta's right wing considerably short of its assigned objectives. In view of the day's casualties, something over 800, the now disorganized attacking divisions and the increasingly vigorous defense, these objectives seemed considerably less attainable than they had twenty-four hours earlier.

Von Conta admitted the unpleasant fact in his new corps order. At midnight on June 3 he directed his division commanders to "fight for a position that is especially suited for defense," namely the line Veuilly-Marigny-La Voie du Châtel-Le Thiolet-Hill 204, about one kilometer west of Château-Thierry. The attempt could only succeed by committing a reserve division, the 5th Guards, to the right wing. Consequently, he stated: "The time for the attack will be ordered later. The attack will not occur before June 7th. Reconnaissances and preparations will be started at once."[26] "Preparations" included priority marches for the artillery of the two reserve divisions which would add to the already heavy fire being hurled on the Americans. "Reconnaissances" meant continuing isolated attacks along the line.

By the time this order reached the German units a major change was taking place on the opposing side. The breakdown of the French counterattacks and the subsequent hard fighting had nearly eliminated the bulk of Degoutte's two French divisions as effective fighting forces. Although French units continued to screen his flanks, from Neville's left at Veuilly Wood across Catlin's front to Upton's right the exhausted *poilus* used the night to pass through the American line, which at 8:00 A.M. on June 4 would fall under Bundy's command.

That line, thanks to the time gained by the French stand, was growing stronger. On the extreme left, Schmidt's 167th French Division was moving up to relieve the remainder of Michel's 43d Division as well as Malone's 23d Infantry, which would mean a further strengthening of Bundy's main position. On Bundy's right, units of the XXXVIII French Corps relieved a battalion of Upton's infantry between Bonneil and La Nouette, which slightly shortened the American line. By early morning Wise at last tied in his left with the 23d Infantry while fresh units from Catlin's reserve strengthened his right. Both Neville and Catlin now held a reasonable reserve as did Upton to the east. Behind the line the newly arrived artillery was fast moving into support positions; communications and supply were steadily improving.

It was just as well, because early on June 4 the Germans continued their attack against the marine line. For two days they would strike from left to right, sharp, vicious attacks preceded by artillery barrage and supported by machine guns and in turn halted by artillery and machine guns and the superb rifle fire of the marines.

Accounts of the divergent actions are numerous enough. Each tells the same story and in the telling reveals the fantastic spirit prevailing on the battleline. On Catlin's right a young private in Holcomb's battalion described one attack:

The German barrage lifted; the French guns almost ceased firing. The men about me were cursing and swearing in that choice collection of profanity that belongs to the Marines. It took me back swiftly, on the wings of a memory to a lonely walk in the woods I had taken, as a boy, when I had whistled to keep up my courage.

The German troops were clear of the woods. On they came with closed ranks in four lines. One looked at them with almost a friendly interest. No particular hate or fear. And yet there was a queer sensation along the spine, and the scalp seemed to itch from the tug of the hair at the roots. The fingers bit into the rifle.

"Hold your fire!"

As the command rang in my ears with the sharpness that enforced obedience, I seemed to be standing on Bunker Hill and hearing the command: "Wait till you see the whites of their eyes!" I think I know how those old Yanks felt that day, as the enemy drew nearer and nearer.

The next I recall is firing. Firing. Firing. My fingers were tearing greedily at more ammunition, then the instinct of the hunter restrained me. I began to fire slower, looking for my mark, making sure they hit. The Huns now appeared to be almost on top of us and then, all of a sudden, there was nothing more to aim at. A few scattered groups with hands held up, racing for our lines and shouting "Kamerad! Kamerad!"[27]

A member of Shearer's battalion on Catlin's left remembered another attempt:

They came out of the wood opposite our position in close formation. They came on as steadily as if they were on parade. We opened up on them with a slashing barrage of rifles, automatics and machine guns. They were brave men—we had to grant them that. They had a good artillery barrage in front of them, but it didn't keep us down. Three times they tried to break through, but our fire was too accurate and too heavy for them. It was terrible in its effectiveness. They fell by the scores, there among the poppies and the wheat. Then they broke and ran for cover.[28]

The marines were determined that the enemy was not going to pass, and they were not alone in their determination. Shortly after moving up in support of the 3d Brigade, Lieutenant Elmer Hess of the 15th Field Artillery noted in his diary:

I went over to Major Bailey's headquarters and was there when he was visited by a French colonel and his adjutant. Through the interpreter, Major Bailey was begged to remove his battalion across the River Marne to the hills overlooking the river on the south bank. This Major Bailey refused to do, stating that his orders were to take these positions, and until his colonel countermanded his orders, he would stay here. The French colonel then informed us that outside of the detachments of French cavalry, there was no infantry in front of the 1st Battalion; the Germans at any moment might sweep through this sector. He begged us to cross the river immediately as he expected to blow up the bridge which he said was our only avenue of escape. Again Major Bailey refused to withdraw. An hour later we heard a terrific detonation which we knew meant the destruction of the bridge over the Marne and our supposed last avenue of escape. Lieutenant Peabody who was in the kitchen of the farm house, raised a bottle of wine and drank a health to the bridge in which we all joined before the reverberations of the explosion had passed away.[29]

The defiant and aggressive mood owned by the Americans reflected itself in acts of individual heroism which, sometimes recorded, sometimes lost, stood far beyond the call of duty.

At Les Mares Farm, Gunnery Sergeant Buford warned his men to keep a sharp eye against the favorite enemy trick of infiltration. Shortly before noon on June 5, Corporal Dockx, in charge of an outpost some thirty yards forward, crawled back to report a suspicious movement of the wheat to his front. Taking a squad, Buford wormed his way through the field until he sighted a group of Germans fanned out around two machine guns. When the marines opened fire Buford rushed forward with two men. His strength, reinforced by snipers firing from rear haystacks, put the bulk of the enemy into retreat across an open patch. Buford, an old bushwhacking marine and a crack pistol shot, ran to a flanking position. In the school stance, crouched with .45 automatic in hand, he killed several of the retreating Germans before rejoining his marines to take the machine gun crews under attack. A fierce rush surprised the first crew, who either surrendered or died. In the attack on the second crew, Dockx and one other marine were killed.[30]

The action had just finished when Lieutenant Mathews, now the battalion intelligence officer, came up and noticed Dockx's body:

> "Let me have a couple of your men," I [Mathews] asked, "so I can go out and see what's left out there."
>
> "Oh, no, Mr. Mathews," Buford replied. "We are all too unnerved now, we can't do it."
>
> I saw he was telling the truth, so I asked him to post Corporal Knapp and Sergeant Britton, both expert shots, on top of the hay under the shed so they could cover my advance. With my sergeant following me I crawled out to the hay stack where Dockx had had his listening post. A beautiful Jersey cow was grazing peacefully only a few feet away. We crawled on past the stack and had not gone fifteen yards when we came upon at least a half dozen enemy corpses lying in the wheat. . . . [W]e crawled over them and a few yards further came upon a body lying across one of the paths in the wheat. I stopped because I could see the torso of the body rise and fall as it breathed. The upper part of the body was covered, head and all, with a German shelter half, while the lower part wore French sky blue britches and puttees. I called to him in a low voice to surrender several times before he pulled the shelter half off and turning his head murmured in French, "Merci." We did not dare stand up straight as we would be exposed to enemy fire, and after several attempts to move the wounded man, we had to give it up, as he let out loud yells. He was badly wounded in the leg and thigh. One ankle was very badly broken. He kept murmuring, *"Feldwachen,"* and kept pointing with one arm. We heard a groan a little farther off and got what he meant. We left him and crawled only a few feet when we came upon a young blond German lying on his back rolling back and forth groaning. He too was badly wounded in the thigh. He was barely conscious. I saw then that the only way to get them in would be by stretchers. I sent my sergeant in to get them. There were none at the farm so Buford sent a couple of his men after some. My sergeant waited quite a while, and realizing

the pickle I was in, saw a woven wire gate to a chicken coop, tore it off and crawled out to me dragging the gate after him. We brought in the two wounded Germans.[31]

During still another attack against the farm, Lieutenant Lem Shepherd (who despite his neck wound refused evacuation) found himself in Blanchfield's P.C. After calling for artillery fire on his front, he took his orderly, Cable, and headed for the line.

On the left of the farm he found that a platoon of French colonials, earlier assigned to cover this line, had withdrawn to leave a gap of a couple of hundred yards. Hastening after the French, the two marines were almost at once taken under German rifle and machine-gun fire. They flung themselves into a protective copse. But now the French, slightly to the rear, returned the German fire. Trapped in the middle, Shepherd and Cable hugged the ground. Suddenly the orderly jerked convulsively from a bullet in the foot. Shepherd dressed the wound, helped the man crawl through the fire to a dressing station behind the buildings, then returned to the line. There he found Gunnery Sergeant Babe Tharau fully exposed, completely calm, pointing out a target to one man, directing a range adjustment to another. With considerable difficulty Shepherd diverted part of the fire to cover the exposed portion of line until the Germans broke off the attack. Back at battalion headquarters he arranged for reinforcements, had his wound freshly dressed, then returned to the firing line.[32]

In terms of comparative casualties the two-day action appeared relatively insignificant—it cost the Germans of Corps Conta just over 200 casualties,[33] the Americans of the 2d Division slightly more than 250.[34] Such small actions, however, can sometimes lend a war a new direction: a German breakthrough would have greatly altered the subsequent fighting, undoubtedly to the enemy's benefit. Contrarily, his failure marked the turning point of the southern offensive.

This was an incredibly heartening development to the Allies. On June 2, after a conference with Pétain, Foch had summarized his urgent instructions: "The line of conduct to be followed by the French Command is to stop the enemy's advance on Paris at all costs, especially in the region north of the Marne."[35]

On the same day Major Clark wrote Pershing from Pétain's head-quarters:

> I talked last evening with General de Barescut just before dinner; he described the situation as very serious, seemed very uncommunicative with regard to details, but insisted that the French were fighting hard and would mount the difficulties.[36]

Although the German advance began to show signs of slowing, it was still far from halted. On June 3 Pershing noted in another "personal and confidential" cable to General March: "Consider military situation very grave." By now, however, news of the American actions was filtering into Pétain's headquarters. On June 3 Clark wrote Pershing:

> . . . Colonel Duffour said he had talked this date with the French commander [Duchêne] and he is immensely pleased with 3d Division especially with the conduct of the machine gun battalion at Château Thierry. . . .
>
> Commandant Millet made many compliments regarding the 2d [Division]; said that division is held in very high esteem.[37]

During the next two days French enthusiasm grew until on June 6 Clark reported:

> Colonel Rozet praised the behavior of the American troops. . . . Colonel Paillé returned tonight from liaison with the Sixth Army and was full of praise for the 2d U. S. [Division]. . . . My impression of the 3d Bureau today is that they are in very good *moral* [sic]. . . . They are very enthusiastic over the American troops. It is in some instances touching to hear their expressions of praise and gratitude over the rapid arrival of the Americans.[38]

A rather different mood was claiming the German headquarters. To von Conta the dismal reports from his frontline commanders added an exclamation point to a rapidly deteriorating situation. On the left his bridgehead across the Marne in the vicinity of Jaulgonne had been beaten back by the French and by units of Dickman's 3d U. S. Division. In the center he was stopped by a line which he knew to be formed by more Americans. On the right the French were not only holding but were beginning to counterattack. He lacked essential supply, his divisions were woefully understrength, his request for replacements ignored. The 10th Division, fanned out around Bouresches, was in particularly bad shape. Five rifle companies in the 47th Regiment were fighting without officers; on June 4 the 398th Regiment reported an average company strength of forty men and these "not fit for front line service." The 6th Grenadier Regiment reported itself "exhausted and incapable of further effort." The division artillery was "worn out." General Sydow, commanding the division, estimated a total deficit of 2,700 to 3,000 men.[39]

Von Conta's unfavorable situation accurately reflected the overall position of von Boehn's Seventh Army. On his left the First Army had been completely contained in its attack against Reims. On his right, von Winkler's and Wischura's effort had slowed to what Crown Prince Wilhelm described as "a step by step advance."

Aside from the noteworthy French-American defense, Ludendorff was largely to blame for this loss of momentum. Blinded by his initial victories, he was trying to do too much with too little. His error had plunged him into a vicious circle where hesitation and delay served more to dissipate than to concentrate his strength at a decisive time and place. Crown Prince Wilhelm later wrote that Ludendorff, after abandoning the attack against Reims on May 31,

> played with the idea of letting the left wing of the Seventh Army cross the Marne and advance on Epernay with a view to setting the First Army's attack against the Rheims hill region in motion again. In view of the failing strength of the troops and the ever increasing enemy resistance Schulenburg and I opposed this idea, which was then soon dropped.[40]

Ludendorff replaced it with orders to launch a major attack by von Hutier's Eighteenth Army against the Noyon-Montdidier line while von Boehn's right pushed through southwest of Soissons. Since the northern attack depended on the transfer of heavy artillery from Seventh Army, it was scheduled for June 7. But von Boehn, attempting to gain his objectives against ever-increasing resistance, was forced to retain the artillery, thus altering Ludendorff's timetable. Ludendorff later wrote:

> At a conference early in June at the Eighteenth Army Head-quarters I became convinced that its preliminary artillery work would not be done in time. The arrival of the reinforcing artillery from the Seventh Army had been delayed. The attack was, therefore, postponed to June 9. This was a draw-back, since it thus lost much of its tactical connection with the great action between the Aisne and the Marne, for which a local operation southwest of Soissons could form no complete substitute.[41]

By building up von Hutier at Seventh Army's expense, Ludendorff in effect forced Wilhelm to temporarily abandon his southern and southwestern offensives. The German Crown Prince later wrote:

> From June 2 onwards the resistance stiffened in both directions of our attack, after our outer wings had already had to be content with a step by step advance. Moreover, both the extensive forest of Villers-Cotterêts and the wooded heights on the west and southwest of Rheims were favorable for defense, and the difficulties of supply, which could only be brought up to the divisions engaged in the attack by motor and horse transport, made themselves felt to an increasing degree.
>
> In view of this situation my Army Group staff as early as June 3 opposed the continuation of the offensive in the form of open warfare. The attack must not be resumed except after systematic preparation and then only at a particularly

favorable point, or in parts of the line where local straightening out was necessary. The resumption of the offensive in a southwesterly direction was to await the result of the attack on the southern front of the Eighteenth Army.[42]

The decision came as no surprise to von Hutier's commanders. Von Conta's chief of staff, von Unruh, later wrote:

Though we told ourselves and our men, "On to Paris," we knew this was not to be. . . . [O]ur casualties were increasingly alarming; ammunition was running short and the problem of supply, in view of the large demands, became more and more difficult. It became all too clear that actions so stubbornly contested and involving us in such formidable losses would never enable us to capture Paris. In truth the brilliant offensive had petered out.[43]

It was an unpleasant fact and it placed von Hutier's commanders in a difficult situation. Having promised the troops a victory that many believed would end the war, they were now forced to indulge in some fancy linguistic gymnastics in an attempt to preserve what morale still remained in their tired and disorganized divisions. Von Conta's corps order of June 4 began:

Corps Conta . . . is compelled to temporarily assume the defensive, after positions most suitable for this purpose are captured. I insist that all commanders inform their troops, leaving no doubt in their minds, that our attack up to this time had passed far beyond the objectives that were first assigned, and had achieved far greater successes than had been anticipated. The offensive spirit must be maintained even though a temporary lull in the attack seems to exist. In the general picture of the operations, no halt or lull exists. We are the victors and will remain on the offensive. The enemy is defeated and the High Command will utilize this great success to the fullest extent.[44]

Considering the situation, these words must have seemed in-congruous to his generals, particularly when they read further that "the infantry must organize itself in depth and dig in," and that besides organizing for defense,

> the main task of the commanders for the present is to reor-ganize their units, and commanders to regain strict control of their troops again, and replace the shortage of officers, men and equipment. The temporary halt is further to be utilized to reorganize the service of supply and rearrange the rearward communications.[45]

All but two of von Conta's divisions were engaged in just such activities at this time. His order primarily applied to the 237th and 197th divisions which on June 3, along with the 5th Guards Divi-sion, he had directed to prepare for an attack designed to gain a suitable line of defence.

The new order did not quite shut the door on this operation. But on June 5, when his right failed to make even limited advances, when its extreme portion was hit by French counterattacks, he was forced to end the masquerade. He now indefinitely postponed the planned attack and ordered his commanders to dig in along the line.

Notes

1. Oliver L. Spaulding and John W. Wright, *The Second Division American Expeditionary Force in France, 1917–1919*. New York: The Hillman Press, Inc., 1937.
2. Ibid.
3. Ibid.
4. *Translations*, Vol. 1.
5. James G. Harbord, *Leaves from a War Diary*. New York: Dodd, Mead and Co., 1925.
6. *Records*, Vol. 9.
7. *Records*, Vol. 5.
8. Ibid.
9. Ibid.
10. Ibid. German artillery fire during the relief cost Turrill one killed and ten wounded.

11. Ibid.
12. Ibid.
13. Ibid.
14. Ibid.
15. Logan Feland, "Retreat Hell!" *Marine Corps Gazette*, June, 1921. See also Lieutenant Colonel J. A. Hagan, USMC (ret). Personal correspondence with the author.
16. Laurence Stallings, *The Doughboys*. New York: Harper and Row, 1963.
17. *Records*, Vol. 5.
18. General Lemuel C. Shepherd, USMC (ret). Personal interview with the author.
19. E. N. McClellan, "The Nearest Point to Paris in 1918," *Sea Power*, June, 1921. See also William E. Moore, "The 'Bloody Angle' of the A.E.F.," *The American Legion Weekly*, February 24, 1922.
20. Shepherd, op. cit.
21. A. W. Catlin, *With the Help of God and a Few Marines*. New York: Doubleday, Page and Co., 1919.
22. Kemper F. Cowing and Courtney Riley Cooper, *Dear Folks at Home—*. New York: Houghton Mifflin Co., 1919.
23. Catlin, op, cit. He places this on June 2 but from the rest of his account it was obviously a day later.
24. Shepherd, op. cit.
25. Cowing, op. cit.
26. *Translations*, Vol. 1.
27. Craig Hamilton and Louise Corbin, *Echoes From Over There*. New York: The Soldier's Publishing Co., 1919.
28. Martin Gus Gulberg, *A War Diary*. Chicago: The Drake Press, 1927.
29. Spaulding and Wright, op. cit.
30. Shepherd, op. cit.; Moore, op. cit.; McClellan, op. cit. Dockx was posthumously awarded the Distinguished Service Cross, Buford the Distinguished Service Cross, Navy Cross and Croix de Guerre. Buford was later killed at Belleau Wood.
31. William R. Mathews, "Official Report to Headquarters, U. S. Marine Corps, September 28, 1921." Knapp was later killed at Belleau Wood, Britton at Blanc Mont.
32. Shepherd, op. cit.
33. *Translations*, Vol. 1.
34. *Records*, Vol. 6.
35. Ferdinand Foch, *The Memoirs of Marshal Foch*. New York: Doubleday, 1931.
36. Paul H. Clark, "Letters and Messages to John J. Pershing, 1918–1919." Washington: Manuscripts Division, Library of Congress. Unpublished.
37. Ibid.
38. Ibid.
39. *Translations*, Vol. 1.

40. Crown Prince Wilhelm, *My War Experience*. London: Hurst and Blackett, 1922.
41. Erich Ludendorff, *Ludendorff's Own Story*. New York: Harper & Brothers, 1919.
42. Wilhelm, op. cit.
43. Sydney Rogerson, *The Last of the Ebb*. London: Arthur Barker, Ltd., 1937.
44. *Translations*, Vol. 1.
45. Ibid.

Chapter 10

"All my officers are gone...."
—Captain George W. Hamilton to Major Julius Turrill,
June 6, 1918

Equally important changes were meanwhile taking place on the other side of the German line where the arrival of Schmidt's 167th French Division had greatly strengthened General Degoutte's hand.

On June 5 his XXI French Corps consisted of two divisions: the 167th French on the left and the 2d U. S. on the right. During the preceding night, Schmidt had relieved Colonel Malone's task force and was in the process of taking over Wise's front to just west of Champillon. The 2d U. S. Division extended this line southeast to La Nouette Farm.

Malone's return caused Bundy to reorganize his sector. By replacing Holcomb's 2d Battalion, 6th Marines, with Malone's 23d Infantry, Bundy split the line between the two brigades: Lewis's 3d Brigade between La Nouette Farm and Triangle, Harbord's 4th Brigade from Triangle to the road north of Champillon.[1]

Once the brigade commanders effected these and other changes, Bundy would own a fairly strong if somewhat exposed defensive position. Backed by ma-

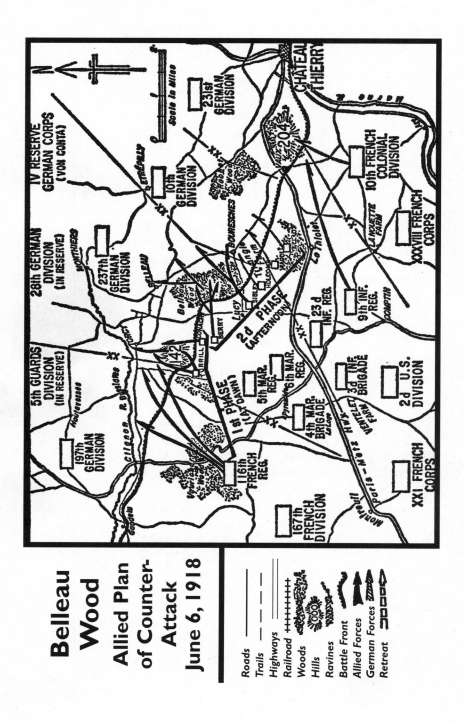

Belleau Wood

Allied Plan of Counter-Attack June 6, 1918

Roads
Trails
Highways
Railroad
Woods
Hills
Ravines
Battle Front
Allied Forces
German Forces
Retreat

chine guns and artillery, each of the four infantry regiments would finally hold about 2,000 yards of front with two battalions in line, one in reserve.

Degoutte, however, had no intention of remaining on the defensive. On the afternoon of June 5, with the American reorganization far from complete, he ordered a general advance for the following day. Designed to straighten his line and seize certain strongpoints, it would occur in two phases.

Before daylight on June 6, the 167th French Division was to attack the high ground south of the Clignon Brook while Harbord's marines advanced on Hill 142 to eliminate its flanking fire against the French. A second phase, to be carried out as soon as possible after the first, directed the 2d Division to seize the ridge dominating the towns of Torcy and Belleau, to "occupy" Belleau Wood and to capture the town of Bouresches on the right of the wood.[2]

Nothing was wrong with these objectives. The heavy, wooded terrain fronting the Clignon and terminating at Belleau Wood offered natural concealment to the enemy infantry who up to this time had shown every inclination to pursue the attack. By depriving the enemy of these natural concentration areas, Degoutte would partially prevent a surprise attack and at the same time gain a much less exposed line. His desire to seize the menacing heights was therefore logical enough. The illogic lay in his timing.

A commander cannot switch from the defense to the offense with the ease of turning a water tap on or off. The necessary change in combat posture is difficult enough for seasoned troops even in today's slimmed-down formations. The bulky organization of the 2d Division taken with the relative inexperience of its commanders and troops meant a most difficult task.

Degoutte's order primarily concerned Harbord's brigade. At the time it had not yet reorganized. West of Champillon, Wise's 2d Battalion, 5th Marines, scheduled for relief by the 167th French Division, still occupied the Veuilly-Champillon line, as did two companies of Turrill's 1st Battalion, 5th Marines, supported by the 8th Machine Gun Company. Earlier in the day Harbord, who had moved brigade headquarters to La Loge Farm, had ordered Berry's 3d Battalion, 5th Marines, to relieve Shearer's 1st Battalion, 6th Marines, which would go into corps reserve while Malone's 23d Infantry relieved Holcomb's 2d Battalion, 6th Marines—all reliefs to take place after dark on June 5.[3]

The bulk of the marines were tired, many of the units were still foraging for meals, communications between units remained far from perfect. Maps were still in short supply and those that existed fit the *Punch* definition of the Boer war map: "a chart upon which names are sprinkled without any special significance as to exact locality"[4]— they were in fact the 1:50,000 hachured maps made by the Dépôt de la Guerre in 1832 and corrected in 1912; in some cases roads had since been built and forests had grown.[5]

Harbord and his commanders also lacked any precise knowledge of enemy positions. Harbord later wrote that despite his orders to send out patrols:

> Little or no reconnaissance or scouting appears to have been done by the companies in front of their positions between June 4th and 6th, the responsibility having been ours since the withdrawal of the French on the 4th. This was probably due to inexperience. Maps were scarce, almost unobtainable, and the hachures gave no real information as to the physical features of the ground.[6]

Contrarily, by maintaining air superiority the enemy held a fair idea of American dispositions. Preston Brown's "Report of Operations" for June 5 noted "eighty-nine flights of enemy aeroplanes made over our lines during the day . . . ten hostile balloons were in observation at different points."[7]

These very real deficiencies could only have been cured with time—which Degoutte refused. His official reason for the extreme haste—to strike before the enemy reinforced his artillery—was probably not the major working factor in his mind. The enemy's artillery fire was already heavy; it had caused and was causing numerous casualties and for some days it had prevented troop movement during daylight hours.[8]

A more plausible explanation emerges from two considerations: Degoutte and the Americans. A disciple of Foch, the French corps commander believed first and foremost in the virtues of the offense. For ten galling days he had been defending against heavy odds, with the issue generally in doubt. Now, suddenly, he owned two fresh divisions—tactical riches beyond the dreams of avarice. Now at last he could strike back. He would waste no time.

The Americans were obviously of the same mind, possibly more so, as indicated by Bundy's later words:

> . . . The Germans had been prompt to see its value [Belleau Wood] as a place of concealment for the assembly of infantry and machine guns to continue their attack. They had occupied it immediately with a regiment of infantry and numerous machine guns and trench mortars. It had the protection of their artillery, placed in concealed positions to the north. As long as they held it, it would be an ever-present menace to our line. A successful attack launched from it would force us off the Paris road, our main source of supply, and compel us to fight with our backs to the Marne, with probably disastrous results.
>
> *General Degoutte . . . saw the importance of Belleau Wood, and was in full accord with our desire to take it as soon as possible. . . .*[9] [author's italics]

Apparently none of the American commanders questioned the order. On Bundy's case this was not surprising. He was an old man, relatively ineffectual, who remained generally remote from the action. The same could not be said for either Preston Brown, who had earlier defied Degoutte, or for James Harbord. But Brown was a rugged, hard-charging officer who held both the French and Germans in contempt and who seems to have believed that the 2d Division was going to win the war single-handedly. Harbord was an equally determined commander whose pride in his marines was flowing over from their recent magnificent stand. Together the two officers shared an aggressive confidence that, normally a virtue, now became a grave defect.

Brown and Harbord met at 3:00 P.M. on June 5 to discuss the order. The conference did not last long. After reviewing the first-phase objectives, Brown stressed two points: attack by infiltration rather than by waves, and close liaison between the infantry and artillery.[10] The artillery was to begin interdiction and raking fire that evening, continue it through the night and at thirty minutes prior to H-hour change over to preparation and destruction fires on the intermediate objectives. They evidently did not discuss the second phase of the attack.[11]

During the afternoon General Chamberlaine's headquarters fixed the artillery support at three groups or six batteries of 75s and two of 155s, an American-French effort commanded by Colonel McCloskey, who shared General Harbord's headquarters at La Loge Farm. This order informed McCloskey that "there will not be any [artillery] preparation properly speaking, so as not to attract the attention of the enemy."[12] Instead, his 75s would first rake Hill 142, the north slope of Lucy and the hill south and west of Torcy; they would then interdict the ravines on either side of Hill 142 across to and including the western edge of Belleau Wood. The 155s were to interdict primarily road crossings and communication routes from the towns of Lucy-Clignon, Bussiares, Torcy and Belleau. Following this:

> At H-5 a violent annihilation fire on the first objective of the attack will be made. This fire will be lifted 400 meters ahead of the hour H, and will be placed as much as possible on the second objective, and so on. During the operation a boxing fire enclosing the whole area of attack will be made.[13]

McCloskey's guns were already firing and the German guns were answering when Harbord learned that Degoutte had set H-Hour at 3:45 A.M. on June 6. Despite the early hour, Harbord was unable to issue Field Order Number One until 10:25 P.M. The order directed Turrill's 1st Battalion, 5th Marines, supported by the 8th and 23d Machine Gun Companies and a company of engineers to attack "between the brook of Champillon, inclusive, Hill 142, and the brook which flows from one kilometer northeast of Champillon, inclusive." Berry's 3d Battalion, 5th Marines, would tie in to Turrill's right "to conform to the progress made by the 1st Battalion in its attack." Upon reaching the objective, a line on the far side of the hill, the two battalions would consolidate against counterattack.[14]

Colonel Neville, commanding 5th Marines, received this order, reduced it to regimental proportions and at thirty-five minutes past midnight issued his own order. It read quite similarly to Harbord's except that it told Turrill to tie in with the French 116th Regiment and it accurately identified the flanking brooks as ravines. It told the battalion commanders to evacuate wounded and prisoners to Champillon, and to carry "panel and signal equipment available for communication with aeroplanes."[15]

The two orders supposed that things had been moving on schedule, that for example Turrill's battalion would already have relieved Sibley's battalion dug in along the edge of the woods south of Hill 142.

This was not the case.

Neville's order found Turrill and his second in command, Captain Keller Rockey, in the battalion P.C., a concrete powerhouse belonging to an adjacent château.[16] Only two of Turrill's companies, Crowther's 67th and Hamilton's 49th, were on hand. The remaining two rifle companies and the 8th Machine Gun Company were still in line at Les Mares Farm where, since 9:00 P.M., they had been awaiting relief by the French. There was no sign of either the 23d Machine Gun Company or D Company of the 2d Engineers.

The officers were now joined by Lieutenant Colonel Logan Feland, Neville's second in command. Supposing that the delayed units would soon arrive, Feland told Turrill to call in his two company commanders. When Hamilton and Crowther reached the basement P.C., Feland ordered them to march their companies north to Sibley's line, where in attack formation Crowther would deploy on the left, Hamilton on the right. To the five officers gathered in the musty-smelling room, the 1:50,000 map showed a reasonable enough picture. Hill 142 was actually an elongated crest running north-south—difficult terrain of open, rolling wheat fields alternating with patches of woods, the whole enclosed by two ravines. To gain the stated objective, the forward line of woods where Hill 142 broke to an unimproved road jutting west from the Champillon-Bussiares road, Crowther would attack north with his left along the western ravine, Hamilton along the crest and right flank on a nearly due north bearing.[17]

Because of Hill 142's commanding position (see map p. 158), the enemy held it in considerable strength. The boundary between the 237th and 197th German divisions, it was defended on the east by a battalion of the 460th Regiment, 237th Division, reinforced by an additional company; on the west by a battalion of the 273d Regiment, 197th Division. A small command dispute over the exact boundary had prevented the battalions from tying in for maximum defense, a serious error which they would soon regret. Still, the separate units were defending in depth, their infantry fanned out around a series of machine-gun nests sprinkled throughout the wooded areas. The artillery fire of the previous evening and night, while causing considerable casualties, had also alerted the commanders to possible attack. And now, as night gave way to early light and as the enemy barrage began to concentrate solely on the hill, those commanders passed the word to their foremost gunners to keep on guard.[18]

While McCloskey fired his pre-assault barrage and while guns of the 15th Machine Gun Company hurled position fire on the immediate front, Crowther's and Hamilton's marines deployed in front of the wood, the platoons of each company ready to move out in four attacking waves. Still chilly from the damp night air, the men stood ankle deep in ground mist, rifles loaded, bayonets fixed, their eyes on the exploding terrain through which they soon must pass.

Turrill was still not ready to attack. None of the delayed companies had arrived, Crowther and Hamilton had tied in neither with the French on the left nor with Berry's 3d Battalion on the right. Time, however, had run out. At 3:45 A.M. the whistles of the company commanders cut the din of exploding shells to start the first waves forward. Nervous young platoon commanders, their sticks pointing to the unknown, shouted, "Follow me." Turrill reached the first-line trenches at this point. He later reported that he: "Went down the front line and found some of the men over the top and about twenty-five yards out—so I gave the word to advance to the whole line. . . ."[19]

The whole line advanced, as described by John Thomason:

The platoons came out of the woods as dawn was getting gray. The light was strong when they advanced into the open wheat, now all starred with dewy poppies, red as blood. To the east the sun appeared, immensely red and round, a hand-breadth above the horizon; a German shell burst black across the face of it, just to the left of the line. Men turned their heads to see, and many there looked no more upon the sun forever. . . . It was a beautiful deployment, lines all dressed and guiding true. Such matters were of deep concern to this outfit. The day was without a cloud, promising heat later, but now it was pleasant in the wheat, and the woods around looked blue and cool.[20]

They advanced through the mist for fifty yards. Then the Maxims in the wood cut loose, a staccato fire killing some, wounding others, sending the rest prone in the protective wheat. But for one man the attack would have stopped.

The man's name was Captain George Hamilton. He was a young man, exceptionally well built, an outstanding athlete.[21] His battalion adjutant, Keller Rockey, remembered him as "well qualified professionally, sound, brave, a fine leader respected by his men, his contemporaries and his seniors."[22]

It was Hamilton's day to prove himself in combat and for the rest of his short life he held the knowledge that he had done so. In a letter to a friend he later and very modestly described the attack:

I realized that we were up against something unusual and had to run along the whole line and get each man (almost individually) on his feet to rush that wood. Once inside, things went better, but from here on I don't remember clearly what happened. . . .[23]

What happened was that the marines, or those who made it to the wood, ran forward, unseeing and uncaring but to thrust the cold steel of the standard issue U. S. Army bayonet through whatever enemy body came in their way. A few Germans threw up their hands and screamed *"Kamerad"* in time to miss death. Most of them found it, a savage death greeted with the undignified squeals that marine after marine later recalled. But while this terribly fast, brutal action was running, Crowther's 67th Company, passing by the left of the wood, was hit by Maxims concealed in a small thicket off the flanking ravine. Crowther went down, as did 1st Sergeant "Beau" Hunter—both dead.[24] Again the marines charged, again a few made it. By the time they cleared the position, Hamilton had reorganized his shattered platoons to lead them from the wood to another field:

> I have vague recollections of urging the whole line on, faster, perhaps, than they should have gone—of grouping prisoners and sending them to the rear under *one* man instead of several—of snatching an iron cross ribbon off the first officer I got—and of shooting wildly at several rapidly retreating Boches. (I carried a rifle on the whole trip and used it to good advantage.) Farther on, we came to an open field—a wheat-field full of red poppies—and here we caught hell. Again it was a case of rushing across the open and getting into the woods. Afterwards we found why it was they made it so hot for us—three *machine-gun companies* were holding down these woods and the infantry were farther back. Besides several of the heavy Maxims we later found several empty belts and a dead gunner sitting on the seat or lying near by. It was only because we rushed the positions that we were able to take them, as there were too many guns to take in any other way.
>
> After going through this second wood we were really at our objective, but I was looking for an unimproved road which showed up on the map. We now had the Germans pretty well on the run except a few machine-gun nests. I was anxious to get to that road, so pushed forward with the men I had with me—one platoon (I knew the rest were coming, but thought they were closer). We went right down over the nose of a hill and on across an open field between two hills. What saved me from getting hit I don't know—the Maxims on both sides cut at us unmercifully—but although I lost heavily here I came out unscratched. I was pushing ahead

with an automatic rifle team and didn't notice that most of the platoon had swerved off to the left to rout out the machine guns. All I knew was that there was a road ahead and that the bank gave good protection *to the front*. . . .[25]

Hamilton did not yet realize it, but he had overrun his objective and was approaching the main road leading into Torcy. An unidentified corporal and two men continued on into the town where a German company was organizing a counterattack. When a bullet wounded one of the marines, the corporal sent him back to report the town taken and to ask Hamilton for reinforcements. The two marines continued the attack. As they approached the first house of the village, heavy enemy fire drove them to a large hole from where they continued their fire. Two of the enemy rushed the hole. They never returned—nor did the marines.[26]

Hamilton, meanwhile, was catching fire from the company in Torcy, from a battalion on his right and from another battalion coming up on the left. He wrote later to his friend:

I realized that I had gone too far—that the nose of the hill I had come over was our objective, and that it was up to me to get back, reorganize, and dig in. It was a case of every man for himself. I crawled back through a drainage ditch filled with cold water and shiny reeds. Machine-gun bullets were just grazing my back and our own artillery was dropping close (I was six hundred yards too far to the front). Finally I got back, and started getting the two companies together.[27]

This was no easy task. In just over two hours Hamilton had lost all five of his junior officers. On his left only one lieutenant remained of the 67th Company's original five. The platoons, shredded down in some cases to a few men led by a corporal, were dispersed and disorganized. Neither the French on the left nor Berry's marines on the right had shown up. Enemy artillery was pounding the scrub-covered hill. At utter disregard of his own safety, Hamilton ran from group to group, ordering a strong point established here, an outpost there. After setting up a rudimentary defensive line, he sent out runners to look for the units supposedly on his flanks.

And then came the first counterattack.

Using their favorite trick of infiltration, the Germans approached the marine position without being observed. They announced themselves with exploding hand grenades. Momentarily stunned by a rock thrown up by one of the grenades, Hamilton heard a bloodcurdling yell from the right where Gunnery Sergeant Charles Hoffman was trying to organize a strong point. Hoffman, a quiet, forty-year-old career marine, had seen a line of twelve German helmets moving through the heavy brush some twenty feet away. His yell preluded a personal bayonet assault. Before the enemy knew it he was on them. A short thrust killed the lead German. Pulling back the dripping blade, the lithe sergeant whirled and caught the next man. Hurtling into the melee, other marines effectively dispersed the remaining Germans about to set up five light machine guns on the flank. But for Hoffman's quick action the 49th Company would undoubtedly have been wiped out.[28]

Meanwhile considerable activity had been taking place to Hamilton's rear. Shortly after 4:00 A.M. Turrill was still watching the fourth wave of the attacking companies enter the woods when Lieutenant Gilfillan reported the arrival of his platoon, the vanguard of the units delayed at Les Mares Farm. Turrill placed the reinforcement on the north edge of the first woods in a field heavy with Hamilton's wounded. While Navy corpsmen began dressing wounds, Gilfillan's platoon was reinforced with the rest of the 66th Company which Turrill now ordered forward. By 5:30 A.M. the 8th Machine Gun Company was backing this line and Captain Winans' 17th Rifle Company was approaching it via the ravine on the right. At 5:37 A.M. Captain Keller Rockey, Turrill's adjutant, notified Neville's headquarters by field message:

> 17th Company going into deployment from old first line—
> 8th Machine Gun Company already forward. Things seem
> to be going well—No engineers are in evidence. Can some-
> thing be done to hurry them along. The advance is about
> one kilometer. Major Turrill is up forward with the line.[29]

Turrill was soon joined by Logan Feland, second in command of the 5th Marines. Upon learning of the exposed left flank, Feland notified Neville at 6:00 A.M.: "Send one company of reserve to Champillon to connect Turrill's left with the French. He is ahead of them. Am with Turrill but will go back to Champillon to put reserve company in."[30]

Neville's only reserve, Wise's 2d Battalion which had just been relieved at Les Mares Farm, now stood as brigade reserve under Harbord's control. At 6:30 A.M. Neville telephoned the brigade commander, repeated Feland's message and persuaded Harbord to release Lloyd Williams's 51st Company which would come up the ravine on Turrill's left.

Turrill and his company commanders would have been surprised at the situation as pictured in Harbord's headquarters. Just after 7:00 A.M. the brigade commander learned from Neville that

> both Turrill and Berry have reached their objectives; that there was heavy shell fire, rifle and mitrailleuses [machine guns] and some rifle firing; that a few men were killed and quite a number wounded but only lightly. Turrill advanced faster than the French and had to halt to gain touch. Our front line has thrown strong points in front of the line and are consolidating their position as rapidly as possible. Champillon is being shelled heavily.[31]

At 7:10 the American liaison officer with the French, Lieutenant Hunt, reported by telephone that the "French division on our left has practically obtained all its objectives, though fighting still continues. About 100 to 150 prisoners."[32]

At the same time the brigade intelligence officer, Major Holland Smith, reported from Turrill's P.C.: "[We have] reached our objectives. We are throwing out strong points and are consolidating our positions."[33]

These inaccurate reports were giving Harbord a dangerously optimistic picture. Turrill had gained his objectives, but not at the slight loss reported. In front of his line Hamilton's group was fighting for its very life. On the left the French had not yet reached most of their objectives, which meant a continuing gap. A similar situation existed on Turrill's right, supposedly guarded by Berry's 3d Battalion.

Berry's advance, which was supposed to conform to Turrill's, was primarily the concern of Captain Conachy's 45th Company on Berry's left. Instead of pushing his left to the ravine, where it was to have tied in with Turrill's line, Conachy moved forward considerably to the right of the ravine, which placed his leading platoons under the fire of two companies of the 460th Regiment defending the fronting woods. The left platoon, far from conforming to Turrill's advance, was pinned down almost immediately after starting its own advance; on its right, Lieutenant Hope's platoon pushed forward about 200 meters before the German Maxims pinned it down. Twenty minutes after Neville reported Berry as reaching his objective, Berry wrote a message reporting himself short of the objective and obviously confused as to the exact situation: "Ravine of creek will be occupied as soon as Major Turrill has gained his objective."[34]

At 8:10 Turrill notified Neville:

French 115th Infantry [*sic*] was at 6:40 A.M. outskirts north of Bois de Mares hill 165. This information from Verry (interpreter). . . . Have a thin line on what I think is our last objective. Am building it up. Have four machine guns there now. Cleaning out ravine on our left. Would like a company (at least). . . .[35]

Not knowing these details, Harbord assumed the major action was over. At 8:40 he reported to Bundy's headquarters:

The French did not relieve elements on left of my line until 3 A.M. this morning instead of 9 o'clock last night as expected. Our attack between brooks [*sic*] on either side of Hill 142 started with two companies and half a machine gun company [*sic*] in the first line. At 6:30 our line was considerable distance ahead of the French and had to be halted to wait for them. At 7:01 A.M. report was received that both 1st and 3d Battalions of the 5th Regiment had reached their objectives. There had been some heavy shell fire, rifle and machine gun fire. Several men killed and quite a number wounded. Figures as to casualties will be hurried as soon as received. Sixteen prisoners, including one officer, were reported as captured by 5:50 A.M. All young, ragged and badly fed. Three deserters from the Germans surrendered. Of the foregoing, nine prisoners, including the officer, reached Brigade Headquarters and have been forwarded to Division Headquarters. At 7:10 reported that our position was being consolidated as rapidly as possible and that our front line had thrown out strong posts in front of the position. Incident to the attack, the villages of Lucy, Champillon, Montgivrault, have been under heavy shell fire.[36]

Without further appraising himself of the exact situation Harbord next sent Neville an incredibly inept letter that, excepting the final paragraph, has been excised from the official record. Written at 9:00 A.M., June 6, it read:

DEAR COLONEL NEVILLE:
It is no time to deliver a lecture on liaison during a fight, and I couldn't take a chance on cramping Major Turrill's style by not giving him that extra company [Captain Williams's 51st from brigade reserve] to fill the gap between him and the French at that time. The facts appear to me to be however:
1. The French attacked through a battalion in line which remained in position and effectually guarded Turrill's left flank no matter what the gap appeared to be.
2. All that was needed was proper runner liaison between his left and the French either ahead or behind him.
3. A company of Wise's battalion, tired, sleepy, entitled to rest, and which may be sometime today really needed in

support had to be sent to do the duty that might have been done by two or three runners if Turrill had observed the orders which so many times have been given him and the other battalion commanders.

Please take the first opportunity to make the necessity of liaison to both flanks and from front to rear, absolutely clear to Major Turrill, as well as the other battalion commanders.

I congratulate you and the 1st Battalion and 3d Battalion on doing so well, what we all knew they would do.[37]

The patent unfairness of Harbord's criticism was emphasized by a message from Turrill to Neville written at precisely the same time as Harbord's letter:

Hear French got under own artillery fire and retired. Can't they be persuaded to come up to our left. Williams' company coming up. Suggest shelling *beyond* our objective. Need Chauchat ammunition and Springfield ammunition, also stretchers—also machine gun ammunition. Berry is fighting in woods on my right. Woods not shown on map.[38]

To this message, which got through very quickly, Neville replied:

Have arranged for 30,000 Springfield, 20,000 Hotchkiss and 20,000 Chauchat to be sent to Champillon immediately.[39]

At this point Champillon could have been a thousand miles from the front for all its proximity meant to Turrill. He replied: "I have no men to carry this up. . . ." At 9:45 he prefaced another message with: *"NEED AMMUNITION."*[40]

Turrill had just dispatched this when he received a frantic message from Hamilton to his front:

Elements of this Company and the 67th Company reached their objective, but because very much disorganized were

forced to retire to our present position which is on the nose of Hill 142 and about 400 yards northeast of square woods. . . .
Our position is not very good because of salient. We are intrenching and have 4 machine guns in place.
We have been counter-attacked several times but so far have held this hill. Our casualties are *very* heavy. We need medical aid badly, cannot locate any hospital apprentices and need many. We will need artillery assistance to hold this line to-night.
Ammunition of all kinds is needed.
The line is being held by detachments from the 49th, 66th and 67th Company and are very much mixed together.
No Very pistols. All my officers are gone.[41]

The tense situation continued throughout the morning. Although Turrill's front slowly gained cohesion, the position, its flanks still open, lay under constant enemy bombardment and frequent counterattack. At 12:10 Hamilton wrote Turrill:

Think it important that artillery have our position and get busy to the front in order to stop constant enemy activity and save our ammunition. Ammunition now is the big point and we need as much as can be gotten up. Several hospital apprentices should come forward to *dress* wounds. We could evacuate later.
Need water badly. . . .
Need Very pistols and illuminating rockets.[42]

At 12:40 Turrill bluntly notified Neville:

Unless Berry comes up to my right I will have to fall back, there is nothing on my right between the front and way back to where we started from, as far as I can find out.[43]

A half hour later, in a message enclosing situation reports from Hamilton and Winans, he wrote:

. . . Our first line is on our objective—left weak—right un-
covered. Think French are slowly advancing on our left. As I
said before a strong attack on our right would finish us.[44]

Turrill's concern is understandable. He had already lost the better part of a total nine officers and 325 men, his units were very
disorganized, his wounded were lying all over the scrub-covered
hill, he lacked ammunition, water and food.

Nor could he know that he had already won the battle for Hill
142. Although the action was not quite finished—Lloyd Williams's
51st Company would take nearly fifty more casualties on the left—
the enemy was by now in no position to launch an attack in force
against any part of his thin line.

Winan's company, facing east, stood in excellent if unknown
juxtaposition to Conachy's line, facing north. If Conachy could not
advance on the wood holding German machine guns, he could fire
on anything emerging from those woods to attack Winan's line.
Apparently aware of this, the two enemy companies remained in the
protective cover of the woods.

They could not be reinforced. The dawn attacks by the Americans and French had caused the flanking regiments of both German
divisions to commit their local reserves early in the action. When the
counterattacks by these units were beaten off, the 197th Division
was forced to ask corps for additional support troops, a request finally met by two battalions of the 5th Guards Division coming up
behind the left of the 273d Regiment.

The severe fighting, not only in the vicinity of Hill 142 but as far
west as Eloup, had already extracted a heavy toll. The 197th German Division later reported some 2,000 casualties from June 4 to 6,
the bulk of them sustained on the last day; on June 6 the 273d
Regiment of this division reported over 400 casualties, including
prisoners, most of them suffered before noon.[45]

This would not be the last of the casualties taken by either side
on June 6. To "Jule" Turrill and his company commanders the issue
may still have been in doubt. But to Generals Bundy and Degoutte
the advance along the line seemed eminently satisfactory. The fighting had not yet finished on Hill 142 when Degoutte ordered Bundy
to move into the next phase of the attack.

Notes

1. John W. Thomason, Jr., "Second Division Northwest of Château Thierry, 1 June–10 July, 1918," Washington: National War College, 1928. Unpublished manuscript.
2. *Records*, Vol. 4.
3. *Records*, Vol. 2.
4. Rayne Kruger, *Good-Bye Dolly Gray*. New York: J. B. Lippincott Co., 1960.
5. Thomason, op. cit.
6. James G. Harbord, *The American Army in France, 1917–1919*. Boston: Little Brown and Co., 1936.
7. *Records*, Vol. 6.
8. Ibid.
9. E. N. McClellan, "Capture of Hill 142, Battle of Belleau Wood, and Capture of Bouresches," *Marine Corps Gazette*, September–December, 1920.
10. *Records*, Vol. 4. This seems to have been the last mention of "infiltration"; in any event the troops were not trained in this German battle tactic.
11. Ibid.
12. *Records*, Vol. 9.
13. Ibid.
14. *Records*, Vol. 2.
15. *Records*, Vol. 3.
16. Lt. General Keller E. Rockey, USMC (ret). Personal correspondence with the author.
17. Ibid. See also *Records*, Vol. 5; Thomason, op. cit.
18. *Translations*, Vol. 1.
19. *Records*, Vol. 5.
20. John W. Thomason, Jr., *Fix Bayonets!* New York: Charles Scribner's Sons, 1925.
21. Rockey, op. cit. After the war Hamilton left the Corps, returned in the early twenties and was killed in an air accident a year or two later.
22. Ibid.
23. Kemper F. Cowing and Courtney Riley Cooper, *Dear Folks at Home—*. New York: Houghton Mifflin Co., 1919.
24. Rockey, op. cit.
25. Cowing, op. cit.
26. Thomason, "Second Division Northwest of Château Thierry." Nine years later a French farmer found the four corpses, arms and equipment undisturbed, at the bottom of the hole.
27. Cowing, op. cit.
28. U. S. Navy, *Medal of Honor, The Navy*. No place, no date. See also Jane Blakeney, *Heroes, U. S. Marine Corps, 1861–1955*. Washington: 1957. Hoffman, whose real name was Ernest Janson, was awarded both the Navy and Army Medals of Honor for this deed.

29. *Records*, Vol. 5.
30. Ibid.
31. *Records*, Vol. 6.
32. *Records*, Vol. 4.
33. Ibid.
34. *Records*, Vol. 5.
35. Ibid.
36. *Records*, Vol. 6.
37. James G. Harbord, "Personal War Letters." Washington: Manuscript Division, Library of Congress. Unpublished.
38. *Records*, Vol. 5.
39. Ibid.
40. Ibid.
41. Ibid.
42. Ibid.
43. Ibid.
44. Ibid.
45. *Translations*, Vol. 1.

Chapter 11

"With the information we had had that the woods were unoccupied by the Germans, we gave it [sic] no artillery preparation, thinking thereby to take it by surprise or to find it unoccupied...."
—General James B. Harbord

"We now stood facing the dark sullen mystery of Belleau Wood....That the wood was strongly held we knew...."
—Colonel Albertus Catlin

Taken with the prevailing ambition of the French and American commanders, the reports of the morning attack exercised an effect not unlike that of a first drink on an alcoholic. By the time these reports reached higher headquarters, they had been largely cleansed of the confusion still surrounding the frontline positions. Together they offered a crystal-clear elixir of victory which, once quaffed, dissipated whatever remaining doubts may have been found in command minds.

Had time allowed and had anyone been so inclined, an analysis of the morning's action would have

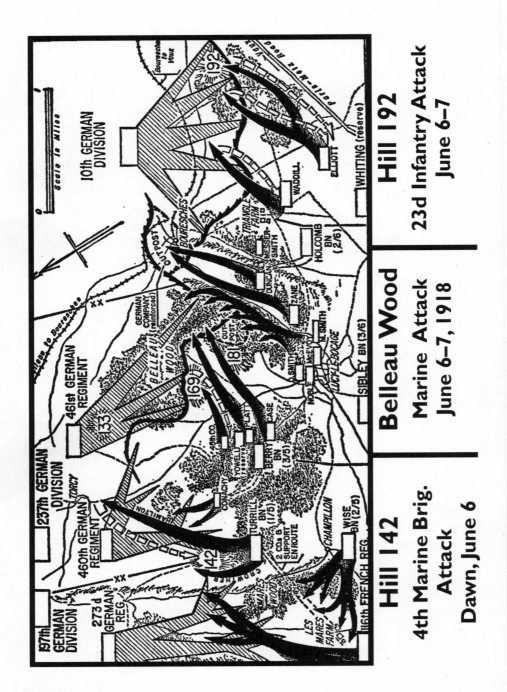

Hill 192

23d Infantry Attack
June 6–7

Belleau Wood

Marine Attack
June 6–7, 1918

Hill 142

4th Marine Brig.
Attack
Dawn, June 6

produced some grave conclusions. A competent analyst would have first discovered that the marine success in seizing and holding Hill 142 stemmed from a combination of fantastic courage and sacrifice plus the good fortune of striking parts of the two enemy divisions at their weakest point, their boundary. A competent analyst would have pointed out that success should have been aided by other more pro-saic means, for example, by reconnaissance prior to attack, by ample artillery preparation, by proper coordination of attacking units, by proper offensive weapons such as hand grenades and trench mor-tars. A blunt analyst would have concluded that it was quite proper for men to die—that was one reason they were there—but for God's sake why slaughter them?

Unfortunately no such analyst emerged in the higher headquar-ters on June 6.

Around noon, with the action still very hot along the entire line, General Degoutte issued order XXI C. A. 87/PC: the 167th French Division to continue its push to the line of the Clignon; the 2d U. S. Division to proceed with the second phase of its attack: the seizure of the ridge west of Belleau Wood, the wood itself and the town of Bouresches on its right.

Bundy had already assigned the second phase to the 4th Bri-gade. At 2:05 P.M., after having alerted regimental commanders to the general idea, General Harbord issued Field Order Number Two directing a two-phase attack, the first to take Belleau Wood, the second Bouresches and the heights west of the wood.

To accomplish the first phase, Berry's battalion (less Conachy's company attached to Turrill's battalion), would attack the west side of the wood while on his right Sibley's battalion struck at the south-western hook. Holcomb's battalion was to advance its left to con-form to Sibley's progress. Supported by the 77th Machine Gun Company and by an artillery preparation "made in accordance with orders" from the commanding general, 2d Field Artillery Brigade, the attack would kick off at 5 P.M. under the overall command of Colonel Catlin.[1]

Once Catlin attained his objectives, he would begin the second phase: Sibley to continue east to the railroad line north of Bouresches while his right took the town itself; simultaneously Berry to push through the northern portion of the wood to put his right at the railroad bridge on Sibley's left, a line extended northwest to Hill 133 on the Bouresches-Torcy road. At the same time Logan Feland would kick off a separate attack from Hill 142. Here Turrill's battalion, reinforced by two companies and supported by additional machine gun units, was to advance about 650 yards to the north to claim a line running from east of Bussiares to tie in with Berry's left at Hill 133.[2]

In effect this very ambitious plan called for the entire 4th Brigade, less one battalion in corps reserve and three-fourths of another battalion in brigade reserve, to pivot on the anchor of Holcomb's battalion and Lewis's brigade: a wide sweep designed to extend Degoutte's defensive line from east of Bussiares in a curve around the north of Belleau Wood and thence south past Bouresches.

As was the case with the earlier attack, the objectives were entirely logical. The fault again lay in the timing.

Harbord was not ready to attack. At noon on June 6 Sibley's battalion lay in reserve in the wood north of La Maison Blanche Farm, which placed it over a mile from its designated attack position north of Lucy. Berry's battalion, in line from Lucy northwest toward Hill 142, was irregularly disposed with three companies facing east, north and northwest, and its fourth, Conachy's, committed to Turrill's battalion. Turrill was still actively engaged on Hill 142, his flanks open, two of his companies decimated—casualties greatly at odds with Preston Brown's entry in the "Report of Operations" for June 6: ". . . Our casualties light."[3] Holcomb, in line from Triangle to Lucy, was still in the process of shifting two companies freed by Malone's 23d Infantry. Holcomb had moved Zane's 79th Company into the left of his line at Lucy, but had ordered Captain Duncan's 96th Company, relieved only that morning, to spend the day in the wood behind the 23d Infantry.

Of the remaining units, Wise's battalion, in brigade reserve behind Turrill, had been shot up in the earlier defensive actions. Wise lacked Williams's 51st Company, in line on Turrill's left; his other companies were tired and depleted. The most static unit, Hughes's battalion, was committed to corps reserve.

To have placed these battalions in proper cohesion, to have repaired Turrill's and Wise's ranks, to have issued essential attack items such as hand grenades and trench mortars, to have worked out an adequate artillery plan—all would have required at least a day, probably longer.

For reasons already given, neither Harbord nor the other top commanders were inclined to wait. Harbord later wrote:

> It was supposed to be a surprise attack and was, therefore, not preceded by any unusual artillery activity. The French had informed us that Belleau Wood was not occupied except by a very short line across the northeast corner which was intrenched. Little or no reconnaissance or scouting appears to have been done by the companies in front of their positions between June 4th and 6th, the responsibility having been ours since the withdrawal of the French on the 4th. This was probably due to inexperience.[4]

When after the war a German officer remarked on Degoutte's tactical failures, Harbord replied:

> I am obliged to acquit General Degoutte of any responsibility as to the tactical methods employed on that date. . . . With the information we had had that the woods were unoccupied by the Germans, we gave it no artillery preparation, thinking thereby to take it by surprise or to find it unoccupied. . . .[5]

This testimony is contradicted by an entry in the 4th Brigade's War Diary at 5:00 P.M. on June 6:

> . . . Artillery starting with raking fire on Bois de Belleau and on the northern and eastern slopes. 2nd, interdiction fire on the ravine, railroad, and road between Bouresches and Belleau-Torcy-Lucy-Clignon and Bussiares, with the 75's. . . .[6]

Harbord's words also stand at variance with the later testimony
of Colonel Catlin:

> We now stood facing the dark, sullen mystery of Belleau
> Wood. . . . That the wood was strongly held we knew, and so
> we waited. . . . That something was going on within those
> threatening woods we knew, for our intelligence men were
> not idle. Every day my regimental intelligence officer ren-
> dered a report of the enemy's movements to the divisional
> intelligence department and also to me, and I reported in
> turn to Brigade Headquarters. The report on this morning
> [June 6] was to the effect that the Germans were organizing
> in the woods and were consolidating their machine gun po-
> sitions, so that a sortie in force seemed not unlikely.
>
> As a matter of fact, we had been prepared for something
> of the sort for nearly two days. On the night of the 4th
> Lieutenant Eddy, the intelligence officer of the Sixth [Ma-
> rine Regiment], with two men stole through the German
> lines and penetrated the enemy country almost as far as Torcy.
> They lay in a clover field near the road and watched the
> Germans filing past them. They listened to the talk and ob-
> served what was going into the woods. . . .[7]

Eddy's patrol report was not all this informative, but it did suggest
that the woods were occupied.[8]

Division had already received several indications that this was
the case. As early as June 2 a division intelligence report stated: "At
present the Boche are believed to be concentrating in the woods
just north of Bouresches. The French are concentrating on this point
with 75s."[9]

On June 3 a French pilot of Escadrille Sol 252, flying for the 2d
Division, reported:

> . . . Fire is heavy enough southeast of the Bois de Belleau.
> Due to the density of the woods little could be seen in them.
> I am under the impression that they are occupied by the

Boche. I was fired on by machine gun from the rear of the woods.[10]

Preston Brown's "Report of Operations" for June 4–5 noted: "A patrol of one officer and two men [Eddy's patrol] of the 6th Marines sent from Lucy-le-Bocage at 9 P.M. [June 4] found the Bois de Belleau and the high ground south of Torcy occupied by Germans. Strength unknown. . . ."[11]

Another French pilot reported to division headquarters on June 5: "Several Boche elements in the Bois de Belleau—enemy gun shots fire."[12]

Taken collectively, these reports were conclusive enough to have warranted further investigation, even at the expense of delaying the attack. By failing to respect the objective the commanders very nearly forfeited the objective, for as Bundy, Brown, Harbord and the marines were soon to discover, the Bois de Belleau was not just another wood.

On June 2 the village of Belleau had fallen to Major Bischoff's 461st Regiment, 237th German Division. Except for corpses of both sides, he found the place deserted, the château a shambles, the church gutted. But under the bluff of the gushing spring he found what soldiers call dead space—unobserved ground that can only be shelled by random, high-trajectory shells. Placing his kitchens in the vicinity of the spring, he set up headquarters to the west in the château's deserted stables, partially dug into the protective bluff.

Meanwhile his battalions fanned out from the town, climbed an old cart trail leading up the bluff, crossed the Bouresches-Torcy road, fought their way across the grass fields, pushed into and down the flanks of the wood. With the advance toward Lucy halted by the Americans, they turned back to the wood. On June 4 they began digging in.

Bischoff knew his terrain. Recognizing the defensive potential of the wood, he wasted little time in organizing it under the local command of Major von Hartlieb. With his right tied into the 460th Regiment, he placed two battalions in line and one in reserve in the wood proper. His main line of resistance ran from the extreme northwest corner south along the western front of the upper section and on down to the bottom of the connecting neck. Judging the western portion of the lower section too overgrown for good defense, he placed outposts here, then curved the main line of resistance to the extreme southeast corner. The natural features of the wood, particularly the giant boulders and ravines, made ideal machine-gun and trench-mortar positions to protect the entrenched infantry.

At the far corner of the wood Bischoff's line tied in with the 398th Regiment, 10th Division, which extended it east to the small railroad line, then south behind Bouresches and Vaux. Having been on the defensive since June 2, the 10th Division, despite its weakened condition, was well dug in on naturally commanding ground. Because of the ground the initial line had been pulled back from the towns which were left to outposts to defend. In the case of Bouresches, a reinforced company had dug in around the railroad station and the shattered houses, its machine guns claiming the fields to the north, west and south.[13]

This was the local German position on the afternoon of June 6.

Upon receiving Harbord's verbal orders in early afternoon, the regimental commanders alerted their respective battalions to the pending attack. To the north Berry spent the few hours desperately trying to reorganize his position, an attempt hindered by difficult terrain, local fire fights and a great deal of enemy artillery fire.[14] About 4:00 P.M. Floyd Gibbons, the *Chicago Daily Tribune's* flamboyant war correspondent, accompanied by Lieutenant Oscar Hartzell, one of Pershing's press officers formerly of the *New York Times,* reached Neville's headquarters at La Voie du Châtel where, according to Gibbons:

> Lieutenant Hartzell and I announced our intentions of preceding at once to the front line. . . .
> "Go wherever you like," said the regimental commander, looking up from the outspread maps on the kitchen table in the low-ceilinged stone farm-house that he had adopted as headquarters. "Go as far as you like, but I want to tell you it's damn hot up there."

The two men walked to Berry's front, and Gibbons later described what they saw:

> To the west and north another nameless cluster of farm dwellings was in flames. Huge clouds of smoke rolled up like a smudge against the background of blue sky. . . .
>
> Occasional shells were dropping in the woods, which were also within range from a long distance, indirect machine gun fire from the enemy. Bits of lead, wobbling in their flight at the end of their long trajectory sung through the air above our heads and clipped leaves and twigs from the branches. . . .[15]

A quieter air prevailed in Sibley's position, the woods north of La Maison Blanche Farm. Here men were stripping down their packs to combat rolls, cleaning weapons, writing what some felt would be final letters. Lieutenant Louis Timmerman was there. Having been in school at Gondrecourt when the division first moved out, the young officer accompanied by Lieutenant John Hardin had only just caught up to his battalion in which he commanded the 3d platoon of Noble's 83d Company. From Gunnery Sergeant Thompson he learned something of the past few days. The company had not seen too much action although on June 2 a heavy barrage had caused some casualties. Privates Snow and Collins had been killed then, and one of Timmerman's runners, Private Flanigan, later died of wounds. Timmerman had become quite fond of Flanigan, a tough little seventeen-year-old from Chicago. Timmerman learned from his men of Flanigan's ghastly wounds. They told him that when the aid men lifted the stretcher the young marine painfully raised his head to smile while counting marching cadence.[16]

At about 3:00 P.M. Major Sibley ordered his battalion forward. Moving in companies which by circuitous routes "skirted the edges of various small woods to keep under cover,"[17] it began deploying shortly before 4:00 south of Lucy on either side of the ravine leading toward Belleau Wood.

Sibley's battalion was deploying south of Lucy when a motorcycle bounced up to Catlin's P.C. It carried Lieutenant Williams, one of Harbord's aides, who brought the written brigade order for the attack. For the first time Catlin learned of his total command responsibility and didn't care for it:

I was supposed to direct Berry's movements, though he had also received the orders from his own regimental headquarters. I telephoned at once to Berry's P.C. at Lucy, but his battalion was beyond reach and he was himself in the woods in their rear, a mile away. It had been impossible, on account of the heavy shelling, to run a telephone out to him. I sent runners, but I was sure they couldn't reach him before the attack would have to be made.

I must confess that this situation caused me considerable anxiety. I don't know whose fault it was, but the communications were far from perfect. It looked as though we would have to attack without proper coordination.[18]

Catlin would have been more concerned had he known Berry's precise situation. In his official report, Wise's intelligence officer, Lieutenant Mathews, wrote:

About 4 P.M. we received orders to move over behind the 3rd Battalion and take up a reserve position in the woods northwest of Lucy. Enemy balloon observers spotted our movement and we were hardly in the woods before their artillery was inflicting casualties. Just after we got there Wise met Berry, commanding the 3rd [Battalion], at the southeast corner of this woods, and I saw them talking earnestly with Wise shaking his head and Berry looking quite worried. At 4:45 he [Berry] had received orders for his battalion to attack at 5:00. It was of course impossible for him to get word to all of his units in time.[19]

Obviously Berry never saw the brigade order. Perhaps it was telephoned down to him and he failed to understand that Captain Conachy's 45th Company was committed to Turrill's battalion for the second phase of the attack; or perhaps he thought that he was first to use the 45th Company, then lend it to Turrill. Whatever the case, when shortly before zero hour Conachy returned from a conference with Feland, commanding the second phase, he discovered only Lieutenant Conroy's platoon in his old position; in his absence Captain Larsen, Berry's adjutant, had shifted the other three platoons to form the left of Berry's new battleline. In the center Platt's 20th Company was to push through the fields leading to the waist of the wood while on the right the 47th Company would advance with Sibley's left. Captain Yowell's 16th Company was in reserve with Lieutenant Gordon's platoon in line supporting Platt. In spite of Berry's efforts during the afternoon the hasty reorganization left much to be desired and at least one platoon commander did not receive the order to attack until after the attack had started.[20]

Colonel Catlin meanwhile had his hands full with his immediate situation. After receiving Harbord's written order he called in Sibley and Holcomb, a hurried conference ending just shortly before McCloskey's guns started the pre-attack barrage. Catlin later wrote:

> With map in hand, I explained the situation to them without trying to gloss over any of its difficulties and gave them their orders. I found them ready. As we stood there, Sibley's battalion was filing by into a ravine, getting into position. . . .[21]

Catlin's orders to Sibley conformed to Harbord's basic order. The regimental commander, however, instructed Holcomb to put in a company on Sibley's right to take that part of the objective south of Bouresches.

Holcomb sent a runner with this word to Captain Don Duncan whose 96th Company was resting in the wood behind Malone's 23d Infantry. The thirty-five-year-old captain received the message less than half an hour before the scheduled attack. Completely unoriented, he quickly assembled his platoons and started them on the double to the departure line, over a thousand yards distant. Again the orders were hurried and ambiguous—a few days after the action Lieutenant Cates, one of Duncan's platoon commanders, wrote in a letter:

. . . at 4:35 P.M. we received word that we were to move in to position and to attack a certain town at 5 P.M. The entire line was to move forward—the town was my company's objective. . . .[22]

On Catlin's right a similar confusion prevailed in the 3d Brigade which theoretically was to play only a subordinate role in the attack. Upon learning of Harbord's plan, General Lewis issued his own field order at 3:15 P.M. Lewis directed Malone's 23d Infantry to "maintain close tactical liaison during the attack, advancing the left battalion where necessary to prevent a re-entrant angle in the line near Triangle Farm." His brigade reserve was to "be kept well in hand during the attack for use at any time if called upon."[23]

Colonel Malone received this order about 4:00. His line consisted of Waddill's 1st Battalion on the left, Elliott's 3d Battalion on the right and Whiting's 2d Battalion in reserve. In Malone's mind a marine advance into and south of Bouresches could very easily create a re-entrant angle between Holcomb's and Waddill's battalions. To prevent this he decided to advance his line several hundred yards to the northeast, toward Hill 192, the movement pivoting on Elliott's right.

At 4:15 Malone gave this order to Major Elliott. The young army officer protested that he did not have time to prepare for the attack, that the objective was useless and untenable. Brushing aside the objections, Malone hurried on to Waddill's P.C. nearly a mile away at Triangle. Repeating the order to Waddill, he told him to advance in conformance with the marines on his left. The meeting ended just five minutes before zero hour.

To further complicate matters, Lewis meanwhile had received another order. At 9:30 P.M. the 10th French Colonial Division on his right would attack Hill 204: "The right of the 2d Division [Upton's 9th Infantry] would maintain liaison with this advance, establishing a new flank halfway between Monneaux and Vaux."[24] Lewis at once informed Colonel Upton of the order.

While Upton began preparations for his limited advance and while Malone was racing around his sector, Major Sibley had returned to his battalion, called in his company commanders, showed them the map and given final orders: on the left of the ravine Dwight Smith's 82d Company followed by Noble's 83d to attack toward the southwest corner of the wood, push across its southern portion, then turn on Bouresches; on the ravine's right Mark Smith's 84th Company followed by Tom McEvoy's 97th to move out toward Bouresches; all companies to advance in line of sections.

Line of sections was a standard French formation well rehearsed by the Americans. It meant that each company formed a two-platoon front with two platoons in support. Each platoon, divided into four sections of twelve men, put two sections forward and two to the rear. These were carefully spaced vertical columns which, when ordered to deploy as skirmishers, would form a horizontal wave or line with a five-yard interval between each man. Some forty yards to the rear the remaining two sections would form a second line and so forth to the rear. In Sibley's case, and because the ravine separated the assault companies, this meant a total battalion frontage of about 900 yards with perhaps a 700-yard depth, a neat boxlike formation that on the approach march eliminated ninety-nine percent of the units' firepower.[25]

About the time the company commanders were passing on the word to their platoon leaders, Colonel Catlin arrived on his way to Lucy. He found Sibley's battalion

> waiting in the sheltered trenches, ready to go over the top. They were equipped for action. When Marines go into line they travel in heavy marching order, but when they go into fight it is in light marching order, with no extra clothing or any blankets. They carry twenty-odd pounds then. They all had their rifles and ammunition and some of the men were equipped with hand or rifle grenades. The machine guns were in position . . . just back of the front line. Each company had eight automatic rifles and eight in reserve. . . . The men seemed cool, in good spirits, and ready for the word to start. They were talking quietly among themselves. I spoke to several as I passed. . . .
>
> On my left I passed some of Berry's men, the right end of his battalion. They too seemed to be ready and waiting for the leash to be slipped. . . .[26]

Accompanied by Captain Laspierre, his French interpreter, Catlin continued on through Lucy, through a small wood to "a little rise of ground protected by a low line of bushes about 300 yards from the woods." McCloskey's perfunctory barrage was nearing its end. For some time the Germans had been replying with their own artillery and now Catlin heard the sound of heavy German machine guns.

And as he stood watching the wood to the front and the fields to either side the sweep hand of his watch ticked off the last few seconds.

At 5:00 P.M. the leash slipped, the marines attacked.

Notes

1. *Records*, Vol. 6.
2. Ibid.
3. Ibid.
4. James G. Harbord, *The American Army in France 1917–1919*. Boston: Little Brown and Co., 1936.
5. Ernst Otto, "The Battles for the Possession of Belleau Woods, June, 1918." *U. S. Naval Institute Proceedings*, November, 1928.
6. *Records*, Vol. 6.
7. A. W. Catlin, *With the Help of God and a Few Marines*. New York: Doubleday, Page and Co., 1919.
8. *Records*, Vol. 7.
9. *Records*, Vol. 4.
10. Ibid.
11. *Records*, Vol. 6.
12. *Records*, Vol. 4.
13. *Translations*, Vols. 1, 2, 3. See also John W. Thomason, Jr., "Second Division Northwest of Château Thierry, 1 June–10 July, 1918." Washington: National War College, 1928. Unpublished manuscript.
14. George V. Gordon, *Leathernecks and Doughboys*. Chicago: privately printed, 1927.
15. Floyd Gibbons, *They Thought We Wouldn't Fight*. New York: George H. Doran and Co., 1918.
16. Louis F. Timmerman. Personal interview with the author. Mr. Timmerman distinguished himself in World War I, returned to private business, served in the OSS in World War II and later headed a large company in New York.
17. Ibid.
18. Catlin, op. cit.

19. William R. Mathews, "Official report to Headquarters, U. S. Marine Corps, September 28, 1921."
20. Gordon, op. cit. See also C. T. Lanham and E. F. Harding, "Infantry in Battle," *The Infantry Journal*, 1939.
21. Catlin, op. cit.
22. General Clifton B. Cates, USMC (ret). "Personal letters, 1918." Unpublished.
23. *Records*, Vol. 2.
24. *Records*, Vol. 6.
25. Timmerman, op. cit.
26. Catlin, op. cit.

Chapter 12

"Come on, you sons of bitches.
Do you want to live forever?"
—Gunnery Sergeant Dan Daly to members of his
platoon attacking Belleau Wood, June 6, 1918

To the hot, tired and hungry soldiers and marines, the attack meant many things. Pride, honor, duty, confusion, surprise, horror, bravery, fear, pain, death— each was present, each experienced in intermingling degree.

For those to the north, the platoons of the 45th Company (see map p. 158), the attack meant trying to cross a field full of exploding shells crisscrossed by the fire of heavy Maxims tearing indiscriminately through budding spring wheat to smash bodies into the soft ground, pin them there, the ones who lived, until they crawled back to where they started. Captain Larsen clarified their fate in a later message to brigade—"three platoons 45th Company went over. Only a few [men] returned. . . ."[1]

For Lieutenant Gordon's platoon zero hour meant a great surprise and a sudden reprieve. At 5:00 P.M., as he later wrote, he was standing with a friend in a fringe of wood, "watching the shells as they dropped along the edge of the woods across the wheatfield."

"I wonder what this is about," [his friend] said, as several more landed. "They must have something spotted over there."

A few minutes afterward, Captain Larsen [Berry's adjutant] came running over and said, "Get your platoons ready immediately, you should have started across with the barrage."

This was the first information we had received regarding an attack and did not know one had been planned. No objective was given as to where it was to stop and no maps had been distributed; the only thing we were sure of was the direction and we knew that.

Just as the platoon was being formed, orders came for us to remain in position to protect the flank, as we had the extreme left of the sector.[2]

To those on Gordon's right the attack meant watching a heavy fire that "nipped the tops of the young wheat and ripped the bark from the trunks of the trees three feet from the ground on which the Marines lay."[3] Then young platoon leaders stood up, blew whistles, pointed heavy canes to the wood, shouted "Follow me," and left the wood to charge into hell. In seconds German bullets were tearing into bodies, their force spinning men to the ground, smashing legs, arms, guts, faces, wounding and killing most of the first waves. The following waves found that hell had not changed. The Maxims were hot now, very accurate, the gunners as cool and determined as the American gunners a few days before. In the center the fire pinned down the Americans; farther south small groups braved fast rushes forward. Gunnery Sergeant Dan Daly was leading a platoon here. When his people wavered he suddenly rose, moved his bayonet-tipped rifle over his head and in a voice with twenty-five years of parade ground authority behind it roared, "Come on, you sons of bitches. Do you want to live forever?"[4] They did not at that moment want to live forever, they wanted only to live to gain the cover of the wood to kill those who were killing them.

A lot of them died in the attempt. Many more fell wounded and many of the wounded were killed when trying to crawl back from whence they came. Shortly after the initial attack Pharmacist's Mate 2d Class Frank Welte was treating one group in a field about 130 yards short of the wood. According to Navy records:

> He had dressed four wounded marines, calmly writing their tags, and had started on the fifth man when he was struck in the back and right heel, while kneeling over his patient. Fragments of a bursting high-explosive shell painfully wounded him. He continued dressing his patient and filled in the diagnosis tag when his head was pierced by a machine-gun bullet. He gave his book of diagnosis tags to his patient, asking him to "turn them over to the chief" when he arrived at the battalion station. With the delivery of the tags to the patient, Welte died.[5]

Only a few made it to the wood. Early in the action Major Berry notified brigade: "What is left of battalion is in woods close by. Do not know whether [we] will be able to stand or not. Increase artillery range."[6]

Wanting more exact information, Berry went forward to try to find his nonexistent line. Floyd Gibbons and Lieutenant Hartzell followed him down the wooded hillside across a V-shaped oat field lying under enemy machine-gun fire. Gibbons later told the story:

> Major Berry had advanced well beyond the center of the field when I saw him turn toward me and heard him shout: "Get down everybody."
> We all fell on our faces. And then it began to come hot and fast. Perfectly withering volleys of lead swept the tops of the oats just over us. For some reason it did not seem to be coming from the trees hardly a hundred yards in front of us. It was coming from a new direction—from the left. I was busily engaged flattening myself on the ground. Then I heard a shout in front of me. It came from Major Berry. I lifted my head cautiously and looked forwards. The Major was making an effort to get to his feet. With his right hand he was savagely grasping his left wrist.

"My hand's gone," he shouted. One of the streams of lead from the left had found him. A ball had entered his left arm at the elbow, had traveled down the side of the bone, tearing away muscles and nerves of the forearm and lodging itself in the palm of his hand. His pain was excruciating.

"Get down. Flatten out, Major," I shouted, and he dropped to the ground. I did not know the extent of his injuries at that time but I did know that he was courting death every minute he stood up.

"We've got to get out of here," said the Major. "We've got to get forward. They'll start shelling this open field in a few minutes."

I lifted my head for another cautious look.

I judged that I was lying about thirty yards from the edge of the trees in front of us. The Major was about ten yards in front of me.

"You are twenty yards from the trees," I shouted to the Major. "I am crawling over to you now. Wait until I get there and I'll help you. Then we'll get up and make a dash for it."

"All right," replied the Major, "hurry along."[7]

Prone on the fire-swept field, Gibbons dug toes and elbows into the soft ground—a slow, prehensile movement. He had advanced only a yard or two when a bullet caught the upper part of his left arm. Aside from burning it did not hurt. He kept on. A second bullet hit the top of his left shoulder, another burning sensation over a larger area. To his surprise he found he could still use his arm. He shouted once or twice to the major, who he feared was mortally wounded. He kept going. This time he rested the left side of his face on the grounds, his helmet tipped accordingly. Then he got the big one. He remembered his world going white, not black. He didn't think he lost consciousness but he wondered if he were dead. He moved the fingers of his left hand, then his left foot. He wasn't dead. He was not far from it, but he didn't know that. Sending his right hand to the left side of his face, he discovered blood. He next discovered that he could not see out of his left eye. He assumed it was momentarily closed. He did not know that a bullet had gone through the eye and crashed through his forehead.

For the moment he could not move, he could not even shout to tell Berry what had happened. From his peculiar position in the world he watched Berry stumble to his feet, wade through the fire and disappear into the woods. Later he learned that the officer had directed an attack against the machine guns before being evacuated.

Gibbons continued to lie as motionless as possible in the field. In a little while he gained voice communication with Hartzell to his rear. They decided to stay where they were until dusk. Gibbons was in pain now, his face hurt, his left arm was useless. He began to resent a wounded marine not far away; the occasional writhing of the unconscious man kept drawing German fire. Sometimes the fire died down:

> During those periods of comparative quiet, I could hear the occasional moan of other wounded on that field. Very few of them cried out and it seemed to me that those who did were unconscious when they did it. One man in particular had a long, low groan. I could not see him, yet I felt he was lying somewhere close to me. In the quiet intervals, his unconscious expression of pain reminded me of the sound I had once heard made by a calf which had been tied by a short rope to a tree. The animal had strayed round and round the tree until its entanglements in the rope had left it a helpless prisoner. The groan of that unseen, unconscious wounded American who laid near me on the field that evening sounded exactly like the pitiful bawl of that calf.[8]

The hours passed very slowly and with them Gibbons felt a waning optimism. He exchanged his wife's address with Hartzell, then he lay there until Hartzell called over that they could start back. He could scarcely see now; it took a little time for Hartzell to orient and then find him. As Gibbons later remembered:

> "Hold your head up a little," [Hartzell] said, "I want to see where it hit you."

"I don't think it looks very nice," I replied, lifting my head. I wanted to know how it looked myself, so I painfully opened the right eye and looked through the oats eighteen inches into Hartzell's face. I saw the look of horror on it as he looked into mine.

Twenty minutes later, after crawling painfully through the interminable yards of young oats, we reached the edge of the woods and safety.[9]

To those on Berry's right the attack meant a more orderly departure. Somewhat shielded by an elevation on the southwest corner of the wood, Sibley's companies moved out to the same whistles, the same pointed canes, the same command from young voices, "Follow me." Once clear of the orchards the lead companies formed line of skirmishers. Not far away the tall figure of Colonel Catlin watched them:

It was one of the most beautiful sights I have ever witnessed. The battalion pivoted on its right, the left sweeping across the open ground in four waves, as steadily and correctly as though on parade. There were two companies of them, deployed in four skirmish lines, the men placed five yards apart and the waves fifteen–twenty yards behind each other.

I say they went in as if on parade, and that is literally true. There was no yell and wild rush, but a deliberate forward march, with lines at right dress. They walked at the regulation pace, because a man is of little use in a hand-to-hand bayonet struggle after a hundred yards dash. My hands were clenched and all my muscles taut as I watched that cool, intrepid, masterful defiance of the German spite. And still there was no sign of wavering or breaking.[10]

Behind Catlin and on either side the American machine guns were chattering, the German guns answering. In a nearby gully Lieutenant Fielding Robinson, sent up by Harbord to observe the attack, noted that "lead was flying all over." Catlin's interpreter, Captain Laspierre, begged the colonel to leave his observation point and take cover. His eyes glued to field glasses, the colonel refused. His men were still short of the wood, a few were dropping.

The guns were chattering very fast now, the fields filling with the destructive puffs of German artillery. It was 5:37 P.M. and Catlin was watching the last of Sibley's left merging with the shady fringes of Belleau Wood. Very proud and very interested, he remained oblivious to the fire, to Laspierre's pleas to take cover. So far he had been lucky.

His luck ran out. A German bullet caught him in the chest, swung him around, toppled him to the ground. He tried to get up, he could not move; the bullet had paralyzed his right side.

Laspierre saw him fall, left his own foxhole, ran to the colonel's side and with considerable effort dragged the bigger man back to a small shelter trench. He opened Catlin's tunic and shirt. Catlin was still conscious. He told Laspierre to send a runner to Lucy to telephone his P.C. and inform his second in command, Lieutenant Colonel Harry Lee, to come forward.[11]

Most of Sibley's left made it to the wood. Dwight Smith's company pushed through the long southwestern tongue, shot down or bayoneted a few outposts, battered their way east several hundred yards in a tangle of undergrowth that made contact between sections at first very difficult, then impossible. Moving slightly uphill they penetrated a couple hundred yards of the main section of the wood before the German machine guns opened fire. The heavy fire hit the leading wave, slowed them, turned them from east to north.

Coming from the rear, Noble's company almost at once lost contact with Smith's 82d Company and with its own units. His left continued forward through the wood, ran into the German fire, halted and turned north. His right, guiding on the ravine, continued due east as ordered. This consisted of two platoons, Lieutenant Hurley's followed by Lieutenant Timmerman's.

Having seen the lead company enter the woods safely, Timmerman did not deploy his platoon in line of skirmishers. With files connecting him to Hurley's platoon he led his people across the field in line of sections. Inside the wood he lost contact with Hurley and very shortly with his own two sections on the left.

Timmerman had not gone far when he passed some American machine gun units going into action. A few minutes later he heard heavy machine-gun fire to his left rear. He thought it was the American guns he had just passed. He was wrong. It was German fire; it was pinning down Smith's 82d Company, his own two sections and Sibley's other two companies advancing on the right of the ravine.

Content in his ignorance, Timmerman continued to move rapidly east. His momentum plus the protection offered by the sharp slope of the wood on his left saved him for the moment.

Midway through the wood Timmerman almost stepped on a German outpost, two surprised enlisted men who at once surrendered. Scarcely pausing he sent them back under one man, continued his push and suddenly emerged on the far side of the wood just north of Bouresches. Here Private Henry reported himself wounded. Timmerman instructed him to return to the rear.

Noble's hurried orders had directed the right platoons to advance through the wood, turn and take Bouresches. Seeing no sign of either Mark Smith's 84th Company or Hurley's platoon, Timmerman assumed he was behind time for the assault. He ordered his two sections, just over twenty men, into line of skirmishers and with Corporal Larsen and Private Swenson ahead as scouts led them from the wood, through the ravine into an open wheat field stretching no more than 200 yards to the town. Timmerman's diary records:

> The wheat field was thrashing to and fro with the machine gun bullets. About fifty yards out was sort of a mound of earth parallel to our line of advance. I could see some of Hurley's men ahead of the connecting files. Cpl. Larsen and Pvt. Swenson signalled halt here. I put my platoon behind the rocks and I noticed that we were coming under fire from all directions although we were sheltered from the enemy in front.
>
> We were there about a minute when Pvt. Henry came running back yelling something. I told him to come over and he said the woods in back of us were full of Germans. At first I didn't believe him as we had just come through there.

But just then I saw the bullets kicking up dust and landing all around on our side of the barricade. I gave the order to form skirmish line to the rear. I heard a man to my left groan and drop his head forward to the ground. We had been behind the mound three or four minutes now and I saw that we could not stay there. I jumped up and yelled to the platoon—there were only two groups—about fifteen men—with me, . . . and we charged into the woods. Luckily I hit the edge of the woods just where the Germans were.[12]

The Germans, seventeen conscripts under two older NCOs, were digging in two machine guns in a depression leading off the ravine. Lieutenant Timmerman was slightly ahead of his men when he came on them. Giving a shout he waded into the group with the best weapon he could summon: steel-tipped boots that sent two of them sprawling unconscious by the time his men arrived with fixed bayonets. Stunned and terrified, the remaining enemy threw themselves to the ground, some ripping open their shirts to show themselves unarmed. Timmerman stood them to, ordered all equipment dropped, their shirts torn off. As he was assembling them, Sergeant Groff of Hurley's platoon came up with a couple of men. Groff had become separated from the platoon, did not know where it was. He and his men had obviously been through hard action. Timmerman ordered them to take the prisoners back.

Timmerman still thought that Mark Smith's company and the rest of Hurley's platoon was attacking toward Bouresches. Thinking he had cleared the wood of the annoying Germans, he again formed a line of skirmishers and returned to the field. His diary continues:

I again advanced out to the mound. The machine gun fire from the town opened up all around. I halted the platoon behind the mound.

Immediately a terrible fire from the left flank was opened up from a little rise of ground about fifty yards away, also from our left rear by machine guns. I faced around and saw Swenson lying dead with a bullet hole through his forehead. At the same time I shouted to "Open fire to the right" pointing toward the hillock where a terrific fire was coming from. At this moment we had only been at the mound a minute or so while all this happened. I was hit in the left side of the face and fell forward thinking, "I've got mine," as I thought a bullet had ripped through under my eye. It knocked me out for a minute and then I felt better and although I was covered with blood I realized I had not been dangerously hit. My men were dropping around there so I told them to follow me and we ran back for the shelter of the woods.[13]

Timmerman's force now consisted of about six men defending the depression earlier taken from the group of Germans. He held no idea of the general situation. He knew only that one hell of a battle was going on ahead, behind and on either side of him and that he might be attacked at any moment. Fortunately Sergeant Fadden, who had become separated from him, came up with enough men to work the captured German machine guns. Fadden was just going into position when Timmerman saw a file of troops coming up on his left front. At forty yards he decided they were Germans, ordered his men to open fire. The newcomers dispersed, subsequently disappeared.

After organizing his position, Timmerman sent a situation report to Major Sibley whose P.C., he knew, was in the ravine leading back to Lucy. Meanwhile lost remnants of other platoons started stumbling on his position. They came from left, right and center. One man, Private Arbuckle, crawled in from the field to the rear, his wounds having been neatly bound by a German medic who was too busy to capture him. Others came from Hurley's old platoon, others from as far away as Captain Case's 47th Company of Berry's battalion.

Eventually they numbered about forty. Timmerman had just finished organizing them into a center of resistance when Sibley's intelligence officer, Lieutenant Marshall, arrived from the battalion P.C. Upon learning the details of Timmerman's position, Marshall told him to hold what he had until Marshall could get him some reinforcement from the rear.

To Sibley it was obvious that Timmerman's unit alone stood on any of the objectives. Dwight Smith's 82d Company and the rest of Noble's 83d Company were still held up by the German line in the southern part of the wood. On the right his other two companies, badly hurt in the initial advance, had been forced to slowly turn from east to north against the heavy fire from the wood. Sibley now ordered Noble to move his company over to Timmerman's position.[14]

Sibley's initial advance pivoted on Holcomb's left. In theory this was to have been Captain Duncan's 96th Company; in fact it was Captain Randolph Zane's 79th Company which almost immediately was struck by heavy German fire including gas. One of the early casualties was Lieutenant Arthur Worton. Another of Zane's platoon commanders, Lieutenant Graves B. Erskine, later wrote:

> We jumped off after about ten minutes of very light artillery concentration in and around the area of Bouresches and were met with murderous fire, mainly automatic weapons, some artillery and some mortar. My platoon consisted of fifty-eight men in addition to myself when we jumped off. About forty minutes later, five of us were left. A wounded Marine passed my platoon P.C. with a wound in his nose. I asked him to tell my captain, some distance in the rear, that we were pinned down and could advance no further. About an hour later this poor kid crawled back to report the captain's words: "Goddamnit, continue the advance." This was at early night-fall. We continued the advance.[15]

Meanwhile on Erskine's right, zero hour found Duncan's men moving at a hot, tiring trot through La Cense ravine that led his platoons into Triangle Wood on the ravine's left, a small wood already being whipped by German machine guns from Bouresches. Directing three of his platoons to the eastern edge, Duncan told his fourth platoon commander, Lieutenant Clifton Cates, to push out left and contact Sibley's people.

Cates moved out, found Zane's right flank. Thinking Sibley must be forward, Cates turned east and made his way to the far edge of the wood. To his front he found a field gently sloping some six or seven hundred yards to Bouresches. There was still no sign of Sibley but on his right he saw the rest of his company leaving the wood in line of skirmishers, an advance he at once joined.

Captain Duncan had already decided that Sibley must be ahead of him, hence he should advance. Leaving the wood he told the men around him, "All right, men, the guide is left, remember, hit their line together, boys."[16]

In the first hundred yards Lieutenant Bowling was hit, other men fell, the advance slowed. On the right Lieutenant Lockhart's platoon found slightly easier going and began moving ahead of the others. Captain Duncan and First Sergeant Sissler strolled through the murderous fire to Lockhart's position. A friend who had grown up with Duncan in Kansas, Sergeant Al Sheridan, watched him come down the slope and later wrote his family:

> . . . Don had on his best suit carrying a swagger stick and smoking a straight stem pipe, and the coolest man on the field always giving orders and smiling all the time. . . . Don came over and made us halt till the rest of the Co. [company] got on the line with us. At that time we were within 600 yards of our objective. While he was talking to Mr. Lockhart our platoon leader the bullets were singing all around us and I ask him as a joke if he thought we would see much action, he said "oh! yes we will give and take but be sure you take more than you give." I guess he meant lives anyway he started away up the hill and it was not a minute till down he went. . . .[17]

The captain fell from a Maxim bullet through his stomach. While Sissler called for a corpsman, Sheridan ran back to his friend. Dental Surgeon Weedon Osborne and an unnamed navy corpsman ran through the heavy fire. Then, Sheridan went on:

> [We] carried him to a small clump of trees, all the time he was gasping, hit through the stomach, we no more than laid

him on the ground when a big 8 in. shell came in and killed all but myself, I was knocked down but my helmet saved me, so I left them and rejoined my platoon.[18]

The word quickly passed: the captain was down. Duncan's second in command, Lieutenant Robertson, took over. Lieutenant Cates saw him suddenly jump up in the field. "He waved his pistol and said, 'Come on, let's go.' We really didn't know where we were going but this town was right in front of us."[19] Cates got to his feet, his men behind him. The thin line moved down the slope and across the field, the casualties increasing with each yard. Halfway through the wheat a bullet caromed off Cates's flat helmet. When he went down, his nose in the dirt, Robertson took command of his platoon and continued on toward Bouresches.

Cates was not out long. Coming to, he felt the contusion on his head, found his helmet, noted the life-saving dent, put it back on and looked around:

The German machine gun fire reminded me of hail hitting the ground. My first thought was to run like hell to the rear. I couldn't see anyone around me except the wounded and dead. Then I looked to the right front, saw four men in the ravine and beat over to them.[20]

The four marines were Sergeant Belfry, Corporals Finn and Dorrell and Pfc. Tom Argaut. They watched the tall, thin lieutenant make his way like a drunken man, staggering, falling and finally landing in their midst. Argaut took off Cates's helmet, opened his canteen and began to pour wine over the lump of bloodied hair. "Goddamn it, Tom," Cates told him, "don't pour that wine over my head, give me a drink of it."[21]

Slightly revived, Cates picked up an abandoned French rifle, found ammunition in it and led his new command down the ravine. Just short of Bouresches they spotted a group of enemy in the southern fringe of buildings. They opened fire, saw the Germans run and pushed on into the village. From this vantage point Cates looked across the wheat field to see what was left of his own platoon leaving the western portion of the town. Recognizing Lieutenant Robertson, Cates yelled, then blew his whistle. When they came over he told Robertson, "Come on, let's take the rest of the town. There's no one in there now." Robertson told him to take the men on in while he went back for reinforcement.

Cates divided his command of some thirty men into three groups: Gunnery Sergeant Moorey to take one group in from the west to occupy the northwest corner of the town; Sergeant Belfry to take another down a road leading east and secure that portion. Cates led the rest of the men up a road leading north to the railroad station. Halfway through town he struck a machine-gun nest, lost several men, caught a bullet through the rim of his helmet, another through his tunic which struck his lieutenant's bar and grazed his shoulder. Pulling back, he split his force into two fire teams which, working around from left and right, neutralized the German position, captured one German and the gun.

Lieutenant Cates was now occupying Bouresches with twenty-one effectives. He established four Cossack or independent posts: one to his left in the apple orchard, one behind the stone wall facing the railroad station, one on the right and one on the extreme right. It was still very early; he was not far from the better part of a German regiment; he had taken an objective designed for capture by three companies.

But Robertson meanwhile had passed the word to isolated groups on his way to the rear. In about half an hour the survivors of the 2d and 3d platoons began filtering in, the 1st platoon followed; sometime later Captain Zane brought in what was left of the 79th Company including Erskine's shattered platoon. Cates posted the reinforcements as received until turning over command to Zane.[22]

At zero hour the marines of Captain Messersmith's 78th Company stood fast according to plan. On their right Waddill's battalion was preparing to move out. Colonel Malone, still in the vicinity, later reported to division: "At 5:00 P.M. the Marines were seen advancing in splendid order. The spectacle was inspiring. . . ."[23]

By runner Malone asked Waddill why he was not moving forward. Waddill answered that the marines on his immediate left, Messersmith's 78th Company, were in a support position and were not supposed to advance. After directing Waddill to stand fast until the marines moved, Malone left for a conference at brigade headquarters.

During the conference Malone told Lewis of his orders to Waddill and Elliott. A surprised Lewis replied that it was anything but his intention for Malone's regiment to advance unless the marines on the left made it necessary. Malone at once telephoned his headquarters to stop the movement where it was. He was too late. By the time runners reached Waddill and Elliott, they were forward, their battalions already in action.[24]

On Waddill's right Major Elliott had been making frantic efforts to attack in conformance with Malone's orders. In the brief time available he alerted his two frontline companies, Captain Valentine's K Company on the left and Captain Green's M Company on the right, moved his support company to the front and called up his reserve company. Assuming that Waddill, with whom he still lacked liaison, was planning to attack, at zero hour he ordered his two frontline companies forward.

Once in front of the protective wood, the two infantry companies entered the hell now familiar to most of the long battleline. Dug in behind the small railroad east of Bouresches, the Germans held splendid observation of Elliott's movement. Almost at once they opened heavy machine-gun fire followed by artillery shelling which slowed but did not stop his advance.[25]

By 6:00 P.M. Elliott had established his advance P.C. in the northern edge of Bourbetin Wood. Seeing the German machine-gun nests dug in behind the small railroad line, he ordered his special weapons officer, Lieutenant Kaemmerling, to bring up trench mortars and 37mm guns. Shortly after Kaemmerling arrived a German barrage killed him and Captain Hearington, the medical officer, wounded the French liaison officer and numerous others of Elliott's headquarters. Elliott now moved his P.C. back to an open field and at 6:40 reported to Malone: ". . . I have received no message from companies on the line but have sent runners forward to get information as both companies look as if they are holding their objectives."[26]

On Elliott's left, Waddill still had not advanced. But around 7:00, when Waddill saw Elliott's men on the ridge to his far right, he ordered his line forward to tie in with Elliott's left. By 9:30 Waddill's people were digging in along the line earlier indicated by Malone, his right was in contact with Elliott's support company and he had taken almost no casualties.

By now Elliott's companies were on their objectives, Captain Green's company had taken particularly severe casualties, his right was hanging in the air and Elliott was sending Malone a stream of messages asking for support, including artillery fire. At 8:55 Elliott notified Malone:

Lieutenant Filley reports heavy casualties on our right and support will be needed to hold same. Runner just brought message from 1st Battalion [Waddill] stating support is needed there. Artillery is still causing us losses and Sergeant Medical Department reports need of men to assist him and many bandages. Rush us assistance.[27]

Malone did not receive this message until 10:10. In the interim he had ordered Elliott to "maintain your liaison with the 9th Infantry" and "to hold your present position and consolidate strongly." He had also informed Waddill to "maintain close contact with the Marines on your left." Malone obviously did not know that Elliott had long since lost liaison with the 9th Infantry and that Waddill had been forced to refuse his left flank toward the marines.

Shortly after Malone received Elliott's new message, word came to him that Elliott's line had broken. He at once notified General Lewis who at 10:25 telephoned 2d Division Headquarters:

The right of the 23d [Infantry] has been heavily attacked and suffered heavy losses. The Germans have gotten through his line. Regimental Commander has reinforced him with his regimental reserves. I am sending two companies of the Brigade reserve to reinforce him.[28]

Although the report proved false, it was sufficient either to give Malone severe doubts about the entire operation or to have these prompted by General Lewis. At 10:55 Malone notified Elliott: "Use your utmost endeavor to restore the situation and get your battalion back in its original position by dawn."[29]

Because of the time lag between messages written and messages received and because of the darkness, the strange terrain and the heavy action, Elliott did not begin to disengage. At 1:00 A.M. his companies or what was left of them were struck by a German counterattack which pushed his right out of the wood east of Hill 192. Soon thereafter he began moving his force back, as did Waddill on his left.

On Malone's right, Upton was having his own troubles. Although his advance started smoothly, he soon ran into heavy artillery fire. The counterbarrage from Davis's 15th Field Artillery now began to fall along the *American* line. After four runners failed to get through to the rear, a young machine gun officer, Lieutenant Lambert Wood, voluntarily braved the exploding terrain to stop the American fire— an act which later won him a Distinguished Service Cross.[30] Shortly after midnight Upton's battalions stood on the new line. By 3:00 A.M. his right was in touch with the French and his men were digging in.[31]

Waddill and Elliott meanwhile were back in their old P.C.s where at 3:15 Malone informed them:

It is desired that you merely reoccupy the position which you occupied before the advance this afternoon.
Major Waddill with left at Triangle and connection by detachments north toward Bouresches. Major Elliott in the trenches now occupied by him until broad daylight and full reconnaissance develop the situation. No advance is desired.[32]

At 3:45 one of Bundy's staff officers called 3d Brigade:

I asked General Lewis how far Malone's left had advanced in order to keep contact with the right of the 4th Brigade. He said that the maximum was about 250 yards, and that merely to take a little "tit" out of the line.

I asked him why Major Elliott's battalion left its trenches. He said he did not know, as it was not intended, but he supposed that Elliott thought it was a general advance.

General Lewis then told me he understood perfectly that there was to be no advance.[33]

But there was an advance, a very costly one that accomplished absolutely nothing. Waddill's battalion was not badly hurt—he lost one man killed, eleven wounded. Elliott lost twenty-seven killed and 225 wounded or missing. Upton's battalions suffered another seventy-six casualties, mostly from artillery fire.

Notes

1. *Records*, Vol. 5.
2. George V. Gordon, *Leathernecks and Doughboys*. Chicago: privately printed, 1927.
3. Floyd Gibbons, *And They Thought We Wouldn't Fight*. New York: George H. Doran and Co., 1918.
4. Ibid.
5. U. S. Navy, Bureau of Medicine and Surgery, *The Medical Department of the United States Navy with the Army and Marine Corps in France in World War I*. Washington: U. S. Navy Department, 1947. Hereafter referred to as *Medical Department*.
6. *Records*, Vol. 5.
7. Gibbons, op. cit.
8. Ibid.
9. Ibid.
10. A. W. Catlin, *With the Help of God and a Few Marines*. New York: Doubleday, Page and Co., 1919.
11. Ibid.
12. Louis F. Timmerman, *War Diary, 1917–1919*. Unpublished manuscript.
13. Ibid.
14. Lieutenant Timmerman was later awarded the Distinguished Service Cross for the afternoon's work.

15. General Graves B. Erskine, USMC (ret). Personal correspondence with the author. Lieutenant Erskine was wounded later in the action, again at Soissons and finally at Saint-Mihiel. In World War II he became an outstanding division commander.
16. André Maurois, *Semper Fidelis*. New York: Marine Corps League of New York booklet, no date. See also *St. Joseph Gazette*, June 8, 1919.
17. Mr. and Mrs. William Wyly. Personal correspondence: copy of Sergeant Al Sheridan's letter.
18. Ibid.
19. General Clifton B. Cates, USMC (ret). Personal interview with the author.
20. Ibid. See also General Clifton B. Cates, USMC (ret). "Personal letters, 1918." Unpublished.
21. Ibid.
22. Ibid. See also Oliver L. Spaulding and John W. Wright, *The Second Division American Expeditionary Force in France, 1917–1919*. New York: The Hillman Press Inc., 1937.
23. *Records*, Vol. 7. Just what marines Malone saw is not clear. He could not have seen Sibley's companies, but perhaps he glimpsed Duncan's men advancing up the ravine.
24. John W. Thomason, Jr., "Second Division Northwest of Château Thierry, 1 June–10 July, 1918. Washington: National War College, 1928. Unpublished manuscript.
25. *Translations*, Vol. 1. The 47th and 398th German regiments used up their entire supply of small-arms ammunition by nightfall. The 40th German Fusiliers in reserve hastily formed working parties to carry up the vital resupply.
26. *Records*, Vol. 5.
27. Ibid.
28. *Records*, Vol. 4.
29. *Records*, Vol. 5.
30. Lambert Wood, *His Job—Letters written by a 22-year-old lieutenant in the World War to his parents and others in Oregon*. Portland, Oregon: Metropolitan Press, 1936. Lieutenant Wood was later killed at Soissons.
31. *Records*, Vol. 4.
32. *Records*, Vol. 5.
33. *Records*, Vol. 4.

" . . . make no further attempt
to advance tonight."
—Brigadier General Harbord to
Lieutenant Colonel Lee, June 6, 1918

General Harbord's P.C. at La Loge Farm received only bits and pieces of the fast-moving action. Twenty minutes after zero hour Lieutenant Moore of the 6th Marines "telephoned that the 6th P.C. was moved forward and telephonic communications would soon be established. Communications working well." A minute later Captain Gill of the 5th Marines "reported nothing to report. Everything in line set and the communications working well up and down." Preston Brown called to wish the brigade commander good luck, so did Colonel Malone's headquarters. At 5:39:

> Major Cole [commanding the 6th Machine Gun Battalion] reports troops started out in beautiful deployment in beautiful line and entered into woods to the attack as far as he could see with absolutely no loss. One casualty at the dressing station. Things are going fine.[1]

The first bad news arrived at 5:50. The runner sent by Laspierre to report Catlin's wound failed to find the 6th Marines' P.C., instead reported in to Colonel Neville. Neville telephoned Harbord, told him Catlin was "wounded in right shoulder." Harbord ordered an ambulance forward. Ten minutes later he directed Lieutenant Colonel Harry Lee, Catlin's second in command, to take charge "if Colonel Catlin too badly wounded to continue."[2]

Lee left the permanent P.C. at 6:10, drove to Lucy and then on foot spent considerable time before finding Catlin stretched out in a small shelter trench awaiting evacuation. In the midst of very heavy fire Catlin gasped out what he knew about the situation and turned over his command. About then the enemy started using gas, which forced the small group to put on respirators and take cover against the increasing artillery fire. When Catlin was finally evacuated, Lee returned to Lucy where he set about trying to learn something of the situation.

Meanwhile a barrage of generally inaccurate messages was falling on Harbord's P.C. Although the brigade commander learned that Berry's battalion had been badly hurt, other messages received from 6:30 to 7:00 made him believe the attack was going quite well:

a French liaison officer reported "Americans on road from Bouresches to Belleau";

Lieutenant Moore reported "German prisoners are just being brought in . . . and the men who brought them in state German equipment is lying all over front. Our people have knocked hell out of them and they are running";

Major Evans, Catlin's adjutant, telephoned that "German prisoners are from 461st Regiment, 237th Division. They are attached to no Corps; are a reserve outfit. It is the first time they have been in the fight; they have been here one day. They [the captors] said that when they brought these Germans back they were about 500 yards from Bouresches. They could see the town. There was a great deal of machine gun fire but very few casualties as far as they knew";

a French liaison officer reported marines in the town of Torcy.[3]

Most of this information was false: the Americans were not on the road from Bouresches to Belleau; the Germans were not running anywhere; American casualities were already numerous. And far from marines being in the town of Torcy, Logan Feland had not yet attacked.

At 6:45 Feland notified Harbord: "Send Chauchat ammunition to us as soon as possible. Needed badly. Everything is set for successful attack. . . ." But Feland now learned from Captain Williams on his left that the French, instead of attacking as scheduled, "have withdrawn from the hill on our left and there is no indication of their activity in that direction." Forwarding this information to Neville, Feland added, ". . . it is hardly possible for his [Williams] left which is refused to a point in the ravine opposite 165 Hill to progress without being in the air. Am awaiting instructions as to progress of first phase since Catlin wounded. . . ."[4]

Harbord received all this information at 7:57. Not knowing the progress of the first phase, he could not order Feland to the attack. He did approve Feland's request for an artillery barrage to be fired at 8:30, which would indicate that he still planned to launch the second phase. Meanwhile even more confusing messages were raising his temper to the boiling point. As he had excoriated Turrill that morning, so now at 8:55 P.M. he leveled off—in a message to Colonel Lee:

I am not satisfied with the way you have conducted your engagement this afternoon. Your own regimental headquarters and this office have not had a word of report from you as to your orders or your positions. Major Sibley under your command is asking your regimental adjutant for orders. Major Berry, over whom you should have asserted your authority, is reporting to his own Regimental Commander. I want you to take charge and to push this attack with rigor. Carry the attack through the woods from Hill 133 south along the Bouresches-Torcy road and send Sibley to take Bouresches. Holcomb is instructed to advance his line to conform to the movement. If necessary you can use the left half of Holcomb's battalion to assist. If as reported Sibley had a small nest of machine guns surrounded in the wood, leave somebody to contain them, go around it and go on with the attack in the second phase. I want reports from you every fifteen minutes. Send them by runner if necessary. Major Sibley has had telephone connection with your regimental headquarters all afternoon.[5]

At that particular moment Lee was in Belleau Wood desperately trying to take charge of an already mutilated action. Had he received Harbord's most unfair message, he could have reported little. No one knew the present situation: at 9:45 Cole notified Harbord that "the whole outfit was held up in the north edge of the wood by machine gun nest." Sibley needed a trench mortar and hand grenades—had these been available the marines "would have been over it two hours ago." According to Cole, "Lee is now on the north side of the Bois de Belleau."[6]

Cole was wrong. The marines were nowhere near the north edge of Belleau Wood but rather in the southern edge of the southern portion.

Harbord next learned from Holcomb that Lieutenant Robertson was in Bouresches with two and a half platoons. This was substantially correct except that Lieutenant Cates was in Bouresches, a fact overlooked weeks later when Cates stood in formation to watch Robertson decorated for being where he wasn't.

At 9:50 Neville forwarded a message from Berry's adjutant: Berry was missing, his attack had failed, no word from the 47th Company. Twenty minutes later Lee informed the brigade commander:

Sibley reports unable to advance infantry because of strong machine gun positions and artillery. He had heavy losses. Ordered him hold position at far edge Bois de Belleau, 47th Company, 3d Battalion, 5th Marines reorganizing at this point. Seems impossible to attack hostile gun positions without artillery. Request instructions.

Harbord replied to Lee's adjutant, Major Evans:

Tell Colonel Lee two companies engineers coming up with tools. Use them to consolidate positions now attained. Make no further attempt to advance tonight. Give me report of conditions at daylight or before if you can form reliable information. Direct Sibley to try to get in touch along the east edge of Bois de Belleau with Berry's battalion [*sic*]. Stokes mortars are expected to arrive soon and effort will be made to get grenades. With reference to Holcomb's report of occupation of Bouresches, tell him straighten his line from Bouresches straight south to Triangle Farm and consolidate on that line, extending from the left from Bouresches to connect up with Sibley whose companies on the Lucy-Bouresches road a little way west of Bouresches [*sic*]. Tell Holcomb Colonel Lee has engineers and tools in Lucy. Call on him for help in consolidating position.[7]

These orders in part reflected Harbord's ignorance of the general situation. The bulk of Berry's battalion was not in the eastern edge of Belleau Wood nor were Sibley's companies as far east as he believed them to be. Not knowing this, however, Evans passed on the orders to Lee and the battalion commanders who were already attempting to carry out part of them.

Lee pushed one company of engineers into Bouresches, another up to Sibley who put them in a close support position. Sibley had already ordered Noble to consolidate Timmerman's position in the southeast corner of the wood. Upon learning that Holcomb needed help in holding Bouresches, Sibley ordered his two right companies forward to the town. Holcomb in turn moved up one company on the left of Bouresches, another on the right.

With Zane's authority, Cates meanwhile was organizing a satisfactory defense in the shell-torn town. In the confusion, however, someone reported a critical shortage of ammunition to regimental headquarters, a crisis met by Major Evans who loaded a truck with bullets and tools and sent it off in the capable hands of Lieutenant William Moore and Sergeant Major John Quick. After a horrendous ride, the volunteers dumped their cargo on the outskirts of town and returned to the rear—a courageous act for which they were duly decorated. Legend has it that this saved the town of Bouresches. It did nothing of the sort: the town's defenders had "plenty of ammunition"—for four days the fresh supply remained where it had been dumped.[8]

Crisis and confusion continued throughout the night. Most of the company commanders were already mixed up and could only become more so in attempting to move their units in darkness through unfamiliar terrain smothered by small-arms fire and bursting from enemy shells. In trying to move forward from Lucy, Companies A and B of the engineers under Major Fox soon encountered very heavy shelling during which part of Company B became separated from the main column and halted just outside of Lucy. Eventually oriented, the platoon commander led this detachment not up to Sibley's position but into Bouresches, an error that cost him two men killed and seven wounded.[9]

Lieutenant Noble, while bringing up the rest of his company to Lieutenant Timmerman's position, ran into a heavy barrage that nearly wiped out his company headquarters. Although Noble and his second in command, Lieutenant Holladay, escaped injury, Lieutenant Murphy was mortally wounded, several other men badly wounded.

The confusion did not end here.

While Sibley and Holcomb attempted to consolidate their positions, one of Harbord's aides, Lieutenant Fielding Robinson, returned from Feland's position on the left. Feland still had not attacked and wanted another artillery barrage. At 10:25 Robinson left the brigade P.C. with Harbord's reply:

> Barrage was put down at your request about 8:50. Your later request, through Lieutenant Robinson, for barrage cannot be honored because of ignorance of your whereabouts. If you have not advanced your position on receipt of this, consolidate it tonight and be prepared to hold it tomorrow morning, using Wise (2d Battalion, 5th Marines) to connect up from your right to the left of the Berry Battalion [*sic*], presumed to be near [Hill] 133, and north end of Bois de Belleau.[10]

Wise's battalion minus Lloyd Williams's 51st Company was in reserve in the wood south of Champillon. The marines had been under heavy shelling the previous night and intermittent shelling throughout the day. At 10:00 P.M. the Germans started in again. Lieutenant Cooke later wrote:

> ... One shell landed right in the headquarters group and three more exploded in the trees overhead.
>
> Steve, a company runner, was blown against me by the concussion, knocking us both to the ground. I grabbed him and rolled into a hole, but Steve was dead. Two other fellows were killed and a half dozen more torn and bleeding.
>
> Captain Wass raged about, making men scatter, take cover, and dig in. Frazier and Jackson pulled the wounded behind trees while Ashurst and Zischke worked with the litter bearer. It was a messy ten minutes.
>
> From then on we kept digging and ducking shells. Every few minutes there was a wail from someone in the battalion for first aid. Fritz was pouring it to us. A grim business, crouching in a shallow hole, wondering if it were to prove a selfdug grave. It was with no regrets that we pulled out shortly after midnight to accomplish the relief of the 3d Battalion.[11]

Harbord had already sent the order to Wise by runner:

> Take three companies of reserve north on road to Torcy and go into the line on right of Feland between him and the 3d Battalion, 5th Marines [Berry]. Feland's right is supposed to be about one kilometer south of Hill 126. Berry's left near Hill 133.
>
> When you arrive approximately in position report by runner to Feland who is on road Champillon-[Hill] 142-Torcy. Orders will be sent to Feland.[12]

In Wise's words:

> That was the damndest order I ever got in my life—or anyone else ever got. It went on the calm assumption that all

the objectives of the First and Third Battalion had been se-
cured. Starting at two A.M. I was to go along the Lucy-Torcy
road, find Colonel Feland, second in command of the Fifth
Marines, whose P.C. was supposed to be somewhere near
Champillon, and get orders from him what to do. . . .

I was between the devil and the deep sea. If I didn't
move, I knew I'd catch hell. If I did move, I knew I was
going right down into Germany.

It was dark as pitch. Finding Feland would be a miracle.
Getting the men together after that blasting we'd just had
was no easy job. I started to do it, after sending runners out
to try and find Feland, inform him of my orders, and tell
him I would get under way as near two A.M. as possible.

That might have been a fine order to have sent out on a
maneuver field. I didn't see exactly how it was going to work
in war. But, being disciplined, we started. I had received no
word from Feland. Evidently my runners hadn't been able
to find him.[13]

The night was "black as pitch—impossible to see even one foot
ahead."[14] Accompanied by Lieutenant Bill Mathews and his scout
section, Wise led his battalion out of the wood in single file, each
man holding on to the man in front of him. The long column headed
northeast toward the Lucy-Torcy road. For about a half mile north
of Lucy high ground sheltered this road which then gave way to
"sloping grain fields, like a bottle-neck opening into a bottle."[15] On
the right lay Belleau Wood where units of Berry's battalion were
presumably holding a line from Hill 133 at the north end of the
wood west to the ridge on the other side of the road.

Just beyond the bottleneck Wise stopped the column. He was
acting on a hunch. Something about the deadly quiet of the night
disturbed him—and he was right.

He took his adjutant, Lieutenant Legendre, and a couple of
squads forward down the road. They had made about 200 yards
when rifle fire opened from their left. Instantly recognizing the sharp
bark of Springfield rifles, Wise shouted to the unseen riflemen to
hold their fire. Realizing their error they ceased fire. One of them

called, "Look out. The Germans are on your right in the Bois de Belleau."[16]

Wise turned his small group around. The Germans, perhaps thinking they were being attacked, opened a heavy machine-gun fire followed by an artillery barrage that claimed about half of Wise's group on its way back to the column. To the waiting officers Wise shouted: "About face to the rear—on the double."[17]

The word traveled down the line to further confuse the waiting marines. Lieutenant Lem Shepherd

> wondered what all the firing was about, then we got the word to "about face to the rear." We had been taught never to do that without saying, "By whose command?" This word now went all the way back up the line and was answered with, "By Colonel Wise—we're in the wrong spot."[18]

At the tail of the column Lieutenants Jackson and Cooke, who had been watching the exploding enemy shells, received the order. According to Cooke:

> Jackson and I looked at each other inquiringly. We knew there wasn't any such thing as going to the rear because of shells.
>
> "To the rear!" word came back insistently as the shelling increased, but Jackson and I made the tail of the column stand fast.
>
> Then we saw a man coming towards us at a dead run and we recognized the voice of Captain Wass.
>
> "To the rear! By order of Lieutenant Colonel Wise. To the rear!"
>
> That was different. We couldn't run from the Boche, but if Fritz Wise and Captain Wass said to run it was time to get going. We picked up our feet and galloped back in the direction from which we had come.[19]

Cooke's people may have galloped but the tail of the column did not. "We would move a few steps and then halt, then a few steps and halt. This kept up until day was just breaking."[20]

Wise now halted the column, about-faced it and prepared to deploy, Blanchfield's 55th Company going ahead to take up a position adjoining the woods. With first light showing in the east, Blanchfield moved up fast, came to a bend in the road and moved his platoons into a small wood on the left. Lieutenant Lem Shepherd suggested he make a reconnaissance to the front. He had just identified the fire as coming from an outgrowth of wood some 200 yards away when other guns opened from the western face of Belleau Wood proper. One of the bullets caught Blanchfield, spun him around and down. Private Paul Bonner saw him fall,

> right on the road. Everybody scattered. I started to run, then I thought of Blanchfield and started back. I rushed across the road, machine gun bullets whipping the air everywhere, and I made the captain's side. He was still alive. He was twice my size, but I picked him up and carried him back. I got him into the woods to a doctor and left him to look for the company. . . . Many weeks later I heard that an officer saw me carry Blanchfield away and had recommended me for the Distinguished Service Cross. Isn't it funny to get that for doing a thing at a time when I was more scared than at any time during the war.[21]

Shepherd meanwhile had skirted the sector deciding where to position the platoons:

> About then I got word from a runner that Captain Blanchfield had been killed along the side of the road up there. I carried on getting the platoons in position along the edge of the woods. Fire was coming from the little woods to my front and also from Belleau Wood on the right. My orderly, Private Martin, suddenly went down. In trying to help him I got one in my left hip. Martin wasn't hit too badly. One of my men came along, pulled us back to the edge of the road, then got us to a dressing station.[22]

Meanwhile Wise was trying to get the other companies into position in the woods on the left of the road. At the rear of the column Lieutenant Cooke's platoon, according to Cooke,

wound down a steep hill and out into a wheatfield where the column halted. The men lay down and many went to sleep. Daylight came suddenly as we lay alongside of the road.

Up ahead I heard some talking, then shouts and the chug-chug of a heavy machine gun. Several other guns joined in and the air was full of bullets.

"Down!" I yelled at the men. "Keep down!"

They were down already, their noses buried in the dirt, for just above our heads death was weaving a fancy pattern in the air. Then, from the woods to our left rear, more guns opened up. Our own guns—firing into our column. . . .

Panic sent the blood pounding into my head and emptied my stomach of courage. It was bad enough to be shot at by the Boche but there was no sense in being killed by friendly troops. My men looked wild and fingered their triggers, ready to return the fire of our other battalion. Something had to be done and done quick. And Captain Wass did it. Unintentionally, but still he did it.

"Jackson!" he yelled.

"Yes, Captain."

"Where are you?"

"Right here. Across the road."

"Stand up, so I can see you."

"Captain," Jackson shouted above the crackling roar of machine gun bullets, "if you want to see me, you stand up."

American humor can lick anything. Smothered chuckles ran down the line. Orders were given and listened to. Men wriggled backwards out of the zone of fire. The first to reach the trees dashed down the line of the 3d Battalion, shutting off the guns.[23]

There were still the German guns to worry about. The intensity of the fire caused Wise to expect an attack at any moment. But it did not materialize, and shortly before daybreak his companies were in position, the men digging in, runners on the way to report his situation to Feland. Although his right remained open, by 6:00 A.M. he had tied in his left with the remnants of Berry's battalion. In turn this force was joined to Captain Conachy's group of marines and engineers which in the early morning had attacked the woods on Turrill's right only to find the enemy gone.

Notes

1. *Records*, Vol. 6.
2. Ibid.
3. Ibid.
4. Ibid.
5. Ibid.
6. Ibid.
7. Ibid. See also *Records*, Vol. 5.
8. General Clifton B. Cates, USMC (ret). "Personal letters, 1918." Unpublished.
9. *Engineers.*
10. *Records*, Vol. 6.
11. Major E. D. Cooke, "We Can Take It." *Infantry Journal*, May–December, 1937.
12. *Records*, Vol. 5.
13. Frederic M. Wise and Meigs O. Frost, *A Marine Tells It to You*. New York: J. H. Sears and Co., Inc, 1929.
14. William R. Mathews, "Official Report to Headquarters, U. S. Marine Corps, September 28, 1921."
15. Wise, op. cit.
16. Ibid.
17. Mathews, op. cit. See also General Lemuel C. Shepherd, USMC (ret). Personal interview with the author.
18. Shepherd, op. cit.
19. Cooke, op. cit.
20. Mathews, op. cit.
21. Craig Hamilton and Louise Corbin. *Echoes From Over There*. New York: The Soldier's Publishing Co., 1919.
22. Shepherd, op. cit. Private Martin lived.
23. Cooke, op. cit.

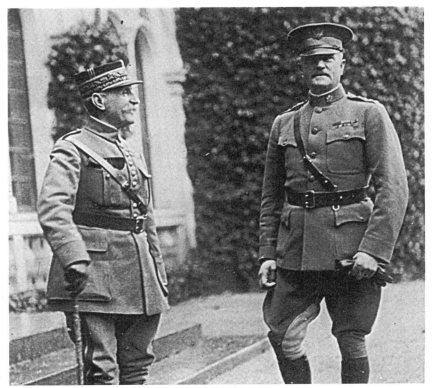

Generals Foch and Pershing.

Major General Bundy, commanding 2d U. S. Division, and Colonel Catlin, commanding 6th Marines.

Colonel Neville, on left front, commanding 5th Marines, Lieutenant Colonel Feland, right front, and staff officers.

U. S. Signal Corps

Colonel Lee, left, who replaced Colonel Catlin as Commander of 6th Marines.

Defense Dept. Photo (Marine Corps)

Left to right: Major Holland M. Smith, Brigadier General Doyen, original commander of 4th Marine Brigade, and Lieutenant Colonel Wise, commanding 2d Battalion, 5th Marines.

U. S. Signal Corps

U. S. Signal Corps

June, 1917. Marines of the 5th Regiment arrive in France and depart for training camps. An army private later spoke to them: "To have sent us to the front at that time would have been murder; but we were all willing to go. We were woefully ignorant of the basic principles of the soldier."

U. S. Signal Corps

France, winter of 1917–18: "It was day-in, day-out training, the monotony relieved only by further physical discomfort."

France, winter of 1917–18, gas mask instruction: "They had to get used to wearing two-pound helmets and to lugging two different types of gas masks, British and French, and neither worth a continental damn."

France, winter of 1917–18: "Long lines of straw—stuffed figures hanging from a cross-beam between two upright posts were set up. The men fixed bayonets and charged them."

France, spring of 1918. Marines of the 5th Regiment stand inspection after leaving the Verdun trenches: "Rain, mud, heavy helmets, respirators, enemy shells, and occasional patrol, boredom, cooties and rats—all part of the blooding process necessary to produce a better, stronger division of fighting men."

National Archives

Belleau Wood, June 6, 1918: "Through the mist the forest loomed up as a grim shadow."

National Archives

"No Man's Land" as viewed from the lines established by the First Battalion, Fifth Marines, after Hill 142 was captured on June 6th.

Marines on the way to Belleau Wood.

Belleau Wood, June 1918. 75mm gun crew prepared for gas attack. A marine later described the mask as "a hot and stifling thing that seems to impede the faculties."

Defense Dept. Photo (Marine Corps)

A part of Bouresches, one of the original marine objectives on June 6, 1918.

Defense Dept. Photo (Marine Corps)

Church of Lucy-le-Bocage. The crucified Christ remains untouched amid the ruins of the village.

Defense Dept. Photo (Marine Corps)

Belleau Wood, June 8, 1918: "The waves moved forward through a partial clearing gradually thickening to a wooded slope spotted with huge, irregularly shaped boulders frowning out from a mass of heavy undergrowth."

Defense Dept. Photo (Marine Corps)

Belleau Wood, June 12, 1918: "On the left Milner and most of the 43d Company somehow crossed Cooke's front to end at the hunting lodge in the northwestern corner of the wood."

Belleau Wood, June 6, 1918. "Most of Sibley's left made it to the wood. Dwight Smith's company pushed through the long southwestern tongue, shot down or bayoneted a few outposts, battered their way east several hundred yards in a tangle of undergrowth that made contact between sections impossible."

Belleau Wood, June 12, 1918. Bundy to Pershing: ". . . Approximately 250 prisoners, including 3 officers, have been taken, and a number of machine guns and two 7-inch minenwerfers trench mortars."

U. S. Signal Corps

"The wounded presented an enormous task. On June 6 the 4th Marine Brigade suffered casualties of 31 officers and 1,056 men."

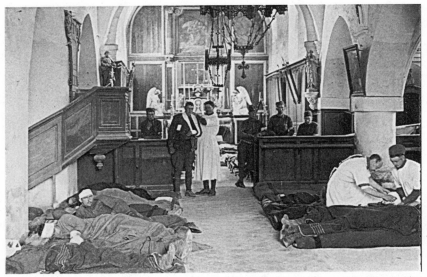

Defense Dept. Photo (Marine Corps)

Defense Dept. Photo (Marine Corps)

Belleau Wood, June 12, 1918. Wise to Harbord: "We have lost quite a few officers."

U. S. Signal Corps

Belleau Wood, June, 1918. The survivors of Jule Turrill's 1st Battalion, 5th Marine Regiment, en route to rest camp after 16 days in Belleau Wood: "The marines went back with pride justified by official reports of the enemy."

Vaux, the final objective of the 3d Infantry Brigade, 2d U. S. Division: "By 5:00 P.M. all American and French guns were firing, a murderous barrage finally consuming 21,000 75mm and 1,600 155mm shells of which 6,000 held mustard gas."

Paris, July 4, 1918. Lieutenant Clifton Cates: "Most of all Paris witnessed the parade, and it was one grand sight and adventure for us—one that I will never forget."

Chapter 14

"... No numbers as to casualties are available.
Losses known to be heavy."
—Brigadier General Harbord to Major General Bundy,
8:30 A.M., June 7, 1918

Early on June 7 Harbord reported his tactical position to General Bundy:

> The line is as follows at this time of writing:
> From the right: Triangle Farm in liaison with
> the 23d Infantry, north to Bouresches, inclu-
> sive (railroad station still in possession of en-
> emy) through the wood, then practically a line
> east and west through the Bois de Belleau from
> the northern edge of the town Bouresches to
> about Hill 181. This part of the line to Hill
> 181 is held by the 2d Battalion [Holcomb]
> and 3d Battalion [Sibley] 6th Marines. The
> remnant of the companies of the 3d Battalion
> 5th Marines [Berry] is to the left and com-
> munication with the 3d Battalion 6th Marines
> [Sibley] in a line running southeast—north-
> west to near north edge of woods about two
> kilometers north of Lucy. Late last night, to
> establish connection from the left to this shat-

.tered battalion, I sent the remaining three companies of the
2d Battalion 5th Marines [Wise] which is now in there. The
line is practically continuous from the brook near the little
square wood southeast of Bussiares to Triangle Farm. I am
withdrawing the remnant of the 3d Battalion 5th Marines
[Berry]. No numbers as to casualties are available. Losses
known to be heavy. . . . It is presumed that the edge of the
woods Bois de Belleau has in it still some wounded un-
evacuated. Effort will be made to get them out at the earliest
practicable moment. . . . The Brigade can hold its present
position but is not able to advance at present.[1]

Harbord's major tasks, consolidation of his meager gains and
evacuation of wounded, were already those of his commanders who
had been fighting chaos and confusion in trying to carry them out.
None was easy, for each demanded movement—and movement, any
movement, more than likely attracted a sniper's bullet, a burst of
machine-gun fire or the deadly smack of a 77mm gun, a flat trajectory weapon which gave no warning and which the men were already calling a whiz-bang.

The wounded presented an enormous task. On June 6 the 4th
Marine Brigade suffered casualties of thirty-one officers and 1,056
men; of these, six officers and 222 men were killed or later died of
wounds. In the forward areas nothing could be done for the dead;
in the fields to the left of the wood and far to the right where Major
Elliott had attacked, the bodies would lie for weeks in the hot June
sun, they would bloat and stink until the living could give them the
dignity of burial. Some of the wounded managed to get away from
those fields. On Wise's left, volunteers from Lieutenant Gordon's
platoon had spent the night crawling out in the fields to bring them
back:

Sergeant Patterson had carried back several of the wounded
lying out in the field whose cries for help attracted him. As
daylight was breaking an arm was seen through the waving
stems as the man would raise himself up and signal for help.
He was very tired from his previous tasks but wanted to go

out again. Another man volunteered to go out and started crawling the distance but probably had been seen because of the heavy fire he attracted.

Patterson insisted he was able to make it and crawled the entire way to the wounded man and carried him back and placed him on a stretcher to be taken to the hospital. Just as the stretcher bearers started away with him, Patterson chanced to sit on the edge of a fox hole, to talk to his group and was hit in the throat as he was taking a chew of tobacco, receiving a ghastly wound from a shell fragment, and died instantly.[2]

On Wise's front, Lieutenant Legendre and three enlisted volunteers snaked from the wood across the road and through the fields to where the earlier reconnaissance party had been hit. They found all but two of the men dead. They left the dead but safely brought back the two wounded.[3]

On Wise's left at Hill 142 Private Steck was a member of another rescue mission. While looking for American wounded, Steck and others, according to Catlin,

came across a German officer seated comfortably with his knees crossed. Before him was spread a little field table on which was cake, jam, cookies and a fine array of food. A knife and fork was in either hand.

Beside the officer was seated a large, bulky sergeant who had been knitting socks. The darning needles were still between his fingers. Both their heads had been blown off by a large shell.[4]

In Belleau Wood proper men were dropping all over the place. One of them, Private Smith, later told Catlin:

Every blamed tree must have had a machine gunner. As soon as we spied them we dropped down and picked them off with our rifles. Potting the Germans became great sport. Even the officers would seize rifles from wounded Marines and go to it. On the second day of our advance my captain and two others besides myself were lying prone and cracking away at 'em. I was second in line. Before I knew what had happened a machine gun got me in the right arm just at the elbow. Five shots hit right in succession. The elbow was torn into shreds but the hits didn't hurt. It seemed just like getting five little stings of electricity.

The captain ordered two men to help me back. I said I could make it alone. I picked up the part of the arm that was hanging loose and walked.

It was a two mile hike to the dressing station. I got nearly to it when everything began to go black and wobbly. I guess it was loss of blood. But I played in luck, the stretcher bearers were right near when I went down.[5]

The flood of crushed bodies was already taxing the best efforts of stretcher-bearers, medical corpsmen, surgeons and ambulance drivers. One stretcher-bearer, Private Robert R. Stanley of the 16th Ambulance Company, though severely gassed and working with difficulty, "begged his comrades not to mention the matter to anyone in authority, and continued to carry on for the whole of one day, always under intense fire, until he became so weak as to utterly collapse."[6] On June 6 a battalion surgeon noted in his log:

. . . Advance dressing stations established just behind first line where wounded were collected and ambulatory sent to the battalion station. Litter cases transported a distance of about 500 yards. At the battalion station examinations and sorting done. Evacuated from battalion go through regimental aid station where a check on each case is made. Returning ambulances bring fresh supplies, litters and blankets, so at no time have we been short of these necessities. Some cases of diarrhea developing. Only a few evacuations because of sickness made. The Second Battalion station located in Lucy le Bocage. Their position enabled them to care for all casualties of their battalion in line. Lucy likewise was under heavy shellfire and gas. A direct hit made on this station set the building on fire, necessitating evacuation. A new station soon established in a cellar, and evacuations continued from this point. . . .

The character of the wounds encountered here fall chiefly into the tearing, lacerating, crushing, and amputating types, accompanied by all degrees of fractures, hemorrhage, and destruction of soft tissue. Injuries of the extremities were most common, followed by those of the abdomen and chest. Despite massive injury, shock has not been common. This is probably due to early treatment, given by company hospital corpsmen, and undelayed evacuation through the regiment to field hospitals. Great attempts have been made to control hemorrhage, immobilize fractures, secure adequate dressings on all wounds, give morphine, antitetanic serum, hot coffee, cover patients with blankets, and promptly evacuate them from the area.[7]

Throughout June 7 dressing stations and field hospitals remained jammed, the wounded sometimes dying before they could be treated, the surgeons working around the clock, their aprons drenched with blood, trying to cope. There were simply not enough of them, not enough orderlies, not enough ambulances. A working party sent back to fill the canteens of one platoon found itself impressed as stretcher-bearers. The men worked throughout the day finally to return without the canteens they had been sent to fill.[8]

Despite such interruptions, consolidation of the front lines continued. During the morning of June 7 Harbord asked the French 167th Division to "take the little square wood about one kilometer south of Bussiares and hold it so that I may depend upon connection there with my left. . . ." He called for artillery fire north of Wise's new position and at 3:00 P.M. notified Bundy:

> . . . It is the intention to endeavor to straighten out the line north of Lucy. . . . This is a rectangular wood about 200 yards in depth and about 400 yards long as described. Artillery playing on it now and when it is considered advisable attempt will be made to straighten the line a little here.[9]

He gave the task to Wise who sent his 55th Company, commanded now by Lieutenant Cooke, an army officer, to relieve Captain Conachy's hodgepodge force of marines and engineers on his far left. Around 5:00 P.M. Cooke and his new command followed a guide through the fringes of Champillon Wood:

> The odor of arsenic tingled in my nose—an indication of recent shelling. Men were sprawled about among the trees. We had seen enough of war to know that they were dead. Arriving at the edge of the woods the guide halted and looked about. There were plenty of fox holes scattered around, but they were empty. Not a sign of American soldiers, except dead ones.[10]

Cooke had just sent the guide back to report his situation to Wise when one of Conachy's runners arrived to lead him several hundred yards through open field to another wood—the one Harbord wanted held. Suspecting a trick, Cooke debated for a moment whether he should follow. He decided to go ahead but also decided to kill the runner if he were led into a trap. He pulled out his automatic, ordered his men to follow him:

> Breasting the ripened wheat north of the Bois de Champillon we passed dead men—plenty of them. A German here and there, and whole squads of Americans. . . . Behind a handful of saplings lay an officer and three men. The officer had been hit high up on the thigh, had pulled down his pants to dress the wound but had died before being able to stop the blood.[11]

Minutes later Cooke's force reached the wood and relieved Conachy:

> A handful of engineers, who had dug a small P.C. and covered it with saplings, also said goodbye. The only ones to stay with us were two men with a machine gun, and they didn't look very happy about it. I felt sort of lonely and

inadequate. If any friendly troops were across the ravine on my left I didn't know where they were [the right flank of Turrill's battalion was located there]. . . . There was no one on my right and the Lord only knew how many Germans in front of me. Dead men littered the ground—four Germans spread around a shell hole out in front, and in the woods were three more and a dozen Yanks laid in a row, waiting to be buried.

Night was coming on and there I was with a company of men I didn't know anything about and who didn't know anything about me. We were out of touch with all friendly troops and the United States of America was three thousand miles away. I all but burst out crying. I had to do something so I assembled my platoon commanders.[12]

In desperation Cooke ordered them into an old-fashioned British square, each side consisting of a platoon, with the machine gun set up in the northeast corner. It probably served as well as any other kind of defense—when his position was attacked much later that night he held without difficulty.[13]

On the other end of the line Sibley's and Holcomb's battalions spent the day dodging bullets and shells in attempting to build up their defensive positions along the southern edge of the wood and in Bouresches proper. Harbord described his intention in this sector in the same message to Bundy quoted above:

We hold the town of Bouresches with a few more men than I consider necessary. I will endeavor to withdraw a company or two when night comes to enable me to get a little echelon in depth; something which is now lacking with the length of line held. The artillery is playing on the Bois de Belleau. There are understood to be eighteen machine guns and some infantry in the wood. It is now under a very heavy fire. If conditions permit the line will be straightened here.[14]

Still misled by his estimate of enemy strength, Harbord decided upon another attack. Later in the afternoon he ordered Sibley to prepare to advance early on June 8. Although Harbord provided no particular artillery support, he did promise a Stokes Mortar platoon from Lee's headquarters.

Sibley waited until darkness to organize the action. The elements of Noble's 83d Company on the right were ordered back to the ravine to form on the left of the 82d Company, the two companies to attack in waves of skirmishers. A detachment of Captain Dederer's engineers would cover the extreme right, advancing up the eastern edge of the wood in conformance with the marine progress. Two platoons of the 80th Company, on temporary loan to Sibley, would cover the left; the remaining two platoons and the rest of the engineers would constitute Sibley's reserve with two additional companies held in support.

Part of Dederer's engineers were still in Bouresches, the result of the previous night's confusion. Dederer meanwhile had sent a guide to the town with orders for this detachment of nearly two platoons to rejoin its company after dark.

The small group started out in a single-file column. The night was very dark, the ravine a difficult route of boulders and tangled underbrush prohibiting man-to-man connection. About 300 yards out of Bouresches the ravine forked, one branch turning sharply left to lead back toward Lucy, the other continuing north to parallel the small-gauge railroad line which was the ultimate marine objective. The guide, of course, led the column to the left. But in the darkness Sergeant Wood and seven men failed to see the fork and continued straight ahead. Some 200 yards later they marched through a culvert on the Bouresches-Belleau road, discovered an outpost of three Germans engaged in tired conversation, decided that something was wrong and left the ravine for the nearest wood. During the night two soldiers of the group became separated; on the following day four more were killed. For three days Sergeant Wood and Private Destler roamed the enemy lines, killed at least one German and wounded several others and, half starved, finally stumbled back to their own lines.[15]

Sibley was still reorganizing his position when a heavy artillery barrage struck the wood, the marines in Bouresches and the soldiers of Malone's and Upton's lines. So intense was the following machine-gun fire that Noble, believing an attack imminent, ordered his marines to open up with everything they had. The crashing fire fight was soon joined by the marines in Bouresches and Malone's soldiers, who met the first attacks shortly after midnight. From left to right the enemy advanced in mass formation but was quickly smashed by American machine-gun and rifle fire. Failing to find a weak spot here, the probing action shifted east to Upton's line where, meeting the same solid resistance, it slowly petered out.

Now it was Sibley's turn.

Noble's 83d Company stumbled back through the darkness to the ravine, its line taken over by Dwight Smith's right. Back in the ravine the hungry, exhausted marines found a pleasant surprise: food. It wasn't much: corned beef, bread and coffee brought up in clay vessels called marmites which kept the meat and coffee lukewarm. But for men who had not eaten for over twelve hours it was a temporary godsend of Lucullan proportions.

The men ate fast, for time was running out. They ate while listening to the hasty orders for attack, the sentences punctuated by the crump of trench mortars to the front. Then it was 4:00 A.M. Lieutenant Timmerman, commanding a platoon in Noble's company, reported:

> I was eating a piece of the warm, stringy beef and drinking coffee from a canteen cup. I hooked my cane over one arm and led the men forward, and I must admit I was more interested in finishing the meat and coffee than in the attack.[16]

The waves moved forward through a partial clearing gradually thickening to a wooded slope spotted with huge, irregularly shaped boulders frowning out from a mass of heavy undergrowth. For a moment it seemed as if the mortars had done their work. But when the first waves started up the slope the Germans opened fire from skillfully placed, hidden machine guns supported by riflemen armed with grenades.

Stopped by the heavy fire, commanders frantically tried to identify its source, then to send small groups forward to encircle and charge the machine-gun nests. By 6:00 A.M. each company had captured two machine guns but at terrible cost and with little gain, for as quickly as one gun fell another opened up. On the right Captain Smith and several of his officers were wounded; on the left Lieutenant Timmerman's platoon, among others, was hopelessly pinned down. As Timmerman later described it:

> We were trying to dig some little shelter against this awful fire. Not having any mess gear I was digging in with my fingers. Then Noble sent a runner over to tell me to take some men and flank the guns. I had already seen that we were up against intersecting fire, in other words there weren't any flanks to take. I found myself unable to even attempt to carry out the order.[17]

As with the earlier attacks, the reports filtering back to brigade were at first optimistic, then confusing and contradictory. At 5:45 A.M. Major Evans informed Harbord: "Some machine guns out of action. Mowing our men down pretty fast. 83d Company [Noble] reports many machine guns delaying advance. Good progress in some points. This information from wounded."[18]

At 6:10 brigade learned: "Sibley's advance has been checked at points and they are finding many more machine guns than expected and may be necessary to employ part or all of one of the support companies."[19] At 6:55 A.M.: "From conversation of prisoners, [Major] Cole reports progress is being made by Sibley. Losses severe. Morale good. Men in fine fighting mood. He has taken several guns and is going after the rest."[20]

Sibley tried to go after the rest. He brought up two 37mm guns, sent in the 84th Company, exhorted his commanders to push on. They did their best. Dwight Smith's line was held up primarily by one gun which his men attacked again and again. Captain Zane in Bouresches heard the marines in the wood calling, "Get that son of a bitch." They couldn't get him or others, neither could Noble's people. By 8:00 the line from left to right was pinned down. Shortly after 10:00 Sibley telephoned regiment:

> They are too strong for us. Soon as we take one machine gun, another opens. The losses are so heavy that I am re-

forming on the ground held by the 82d Company last night. All of the officers of the 82d Company wounded or missing and it is necessary to reform before we can advance. Unable to do much with trench mortars because of being in the woods. These machine guns are too strong for our infantry. We can attack again if it is desired.[21]

It was not desired. Sibley's message merely emphasized other evidence that the attack had failed; furthermore, German reinforcements were reported entering the wood from the north. At 12:30 P.M. Harbord notified Sibley:

Get cover for your men in the ravine (gully) at south edge of woods. Let your men rest. I will have artillery play on the wood. Any further orders will be given you later for other movement by you. Send reply by the runner who brings this as to the hour at which you will be in your gully.

Harbord received Sibley's reply at 2:30 that afternoon:

Will have men under cover for artillery fire south edge of woods (within 125 yards of edge) by 3:00 P.M. Regret to report officers and men too much exhausted for further attack on strong resistance until after several hours rest. Enemy shelling our position now. Damage not serious at present.[22]

For the moment Harbord and his marines were finished. Two costly attacks had netted a few hundred yards of ground, a thin line along the extreme southern edge of Belleau Wood and a precarious position in the town of Bouresches: gains that in contrast with command objectives spelled a tactical failure.

Tactical failures, however, can sometimes play a part in producing strategic victories, and this was the case with Belleau Wood. By opening a Pandora's box of attack on June 6, 1918, Degoutte, Bundy, Harbord and the marines had released qualitative forces that already were affecting friend and enemy alike.

Notes

1. *Records*, Vol. 6.
2. George V. Gordon, *Leathernecks and Doughboys.* Chicago: privately printed, 1927.
3. Frederic M. Wise and Meigs O. Frost, *A Marine Tells It to You.* New York: J. H. Sears and Co., Inc., 1929. Lieutenant Legendre later received the Distinguished Service Cross for this act.
4. A. W. Catlin, *With the Help of God and a Few Marines.* New York: Doubleday, Page and Co., 1919.
5. Ibid.
6. *Records*, Vol. 8. Private Stanley was evacuated and as of August, 1918, was slowly recovering.
7. *Medical Department.*
8. Gordon, op. cit.
9. *Records*, Vol. 6.
10. Major E. D. Cooke, "We Can Take It," *Infantry Journal*, May–December, 1937.
11. Ibid.
12. Ibid.
13. Ibid. In this account Cooke refers to Captain Carnegie. He could only have meant Conachy.
14. *Records*, Vol. 6.
15. *Records*, Vol. 7.
16. Captain Louis F. Timmerman. Personal interview with the author.
17. Ibid.
18. *Records*, Vol. 6.
19. Ibid.
20. Ibid.
21. *Records*, Vol. 5.
22. *Records*, Vol. 6.

Chapter 15

"OUR MARINES ATTACK. . ."
—New York Times headline, June 7, 1918

To the American war correspondents in France the attack at Belleau Wood meant news. If they greeted it in the manner of suddenly rescued men gorging themselves into illness, it was because they were men suddenly rescued from a barren existence.

Pershing's press policy heretofore had offered little real news. Following Allied precedent, it was restrictive and unfair. A press section or G-2-D consisting of a group of army censors under Colonel McCabe at 10 Rue Saint-Anne, Paris, told the American correspondents where they could go, whom they could see and what they could write.

They could not write very much. According to Emmet Crozier:

> Censorship had forbidden them to identify any of the divisions; they could not write that American troops in any given action were from New England or Texas; they could not distinguish between branches of the service such as infantry, artillery, signal corps, cavalry; they could not refer to regiments or battal-

ions, only "units" or "elements" of U. S. forces. Nor could they distinguish between the Regular Army (First and Second Divisions and part of the Third), the National Guard (Twenty-Sixth "Yankee" and Forty-Second "Rainbow" Divisions) and the Selective Service (draft) divisions.[1]

In addition to these restrictions, neither Pershing nor his staff brooked any criticism. They had already withdrawn the credentials of several troublemakers, among them Westbrook Pegler and Reginald Kauffman. On one occasion they refused to accredit a well-known British journalist, Ellis Ashmead-Bartlett. In 1914 he had been recalled from Gallipoli where, as the Americans discovered, General Sir Ian Hamilton described him as a

> well-known war correspondent who possesses considerable gifts and is able to write dispatches on military events with great clearness and descriptive powers. Unfortunately he is not to be trusted. He has the habit of criticism and sees everything from a most pessimistic standpoint.[2]

If Hamilton found those qualities undesirable in 1914, to Pershing and the other commanders in the crisis-ridden France of late 1917 and early 1918 they were positively anathematic.

Even with a more generous command policy the correspondents would have been hard put to write interesting copy. One can only write so much about men in training, so much about trench warfare. What they wanted, and what the American public wanted, was action.

But when action arrived in the form of the 1st Division's attack at Cantigny, Pershing's policy made effective reporting impossible. McCabe's censors blue-penciled the Cantigny copy almost beyond recognition, then shrugged away the pleas of the furious correspondents. A few days later a group of reporters covering the defense of Château-Thierry received the same treatment. One of them, Don Martin who had just come over for the *New York Herald,* cabled his paper:

Have Ohl [*Herald* correspondent in Washington] take censorship matter up Washington. Impossible to send real news. Correspondents hobbled every way imaginable. Situation inexcusable. Must be remedied. Press treated absolutely no consideration. Details letter.[3]

A slight ray of hope appeared when the 2d Division went into action. Several correspondents pointed out to McCabe that since the marines represented a separate service as opposed to a branch of a service they should be identified in dispatches. McCabe agreed and referred the matter to Pershing's headquarters, which also agreed. This was an important decision, for beginning on June 6 the marines gained and held the headlines of nearly every paper in America, often to the general exclusion of the army.

Shortly after McCabe's section announced its new policy on June 5, Associated Press filed its story. On Thursday, June 6, the *Chicago Daily Tribune* ran banner headlines:

U.S. MARINES SMASH HUNS GAIN GLORY IN BRISK FIGHT ON THE MARNE CAPTURE MACHINE GUNS, KILL BOCHES, TAKE PRISONERS
With the American Army in France, June 5, by the Associated Press—American Marines wrote another glorious page in their history Tuesday night and Wednesday, beating off two determined German attacks on the Marne battlefield. . . .[4]

On June 7 newspapers throughout the western world broke the story of the marine attack in huge, boastful headlines. Americans in Paris read in the European edition of the *New York Herald:* MARINES IN GREAT CHARGE OVERTHROW CRACK FOE FORCES.[5] The citizens of Sioux City, Iowa, read in the *Sioux City Journal:* U.S. MARINES SINK WEDGE IN ENEMY FRONT.[6] The *Chicago Daily Tribune:* MARINES WIN HOT BATTLE SWEEP ENEMY FROM HEIGHTS NEAR THIERRY.[7] The *New York Times:* OUR MARINES ATTACK, GAIN MILE AT VEUILLY, RESUME DRIVE AT NIGHT, FOE LOSING HEAVILY.[8]

This was news in its very essence, it held a promise long anticipated by the Allies and the American public, and the correspondents held no intention of letting anyone down for the sake of accurate reporting. According to the staid *New York Times,* the marines attacked while singing "Yankee Doodle Dandy"; in the dawn attack of June 6 the marines advanced over two miles on a two-and-a-half-mile front; the enemy was so hard pressed that he threw in three new divisions.[9] Not to be outdone, the *Chicago Daily Tribune* reported bayonet wielding marines had routed Germans from three villages.[10]

Subsequent editions continued the banner headlines, the colorful, generally inaccurate accounts of the fighting. American readers learned the background of General Harbord (shown wearing his special trademark—the French coal-scuttle helmet), of the great Indian athlete, Peter Garlow, of Sergeant Dan Daly. They learned that the Germans had named the marines *die Teufelhünden*—the Devil Dogs—and that one German writer termed the United States Marine the greatest fighting man in the world. (The same authority placed the Canadian Mounted Police second, the Potsdam Guards third.)

Most Americans agreed. According to the *New York Times:*

> The United States Marines were the toast of New York. . . .
> Everywhere one went in the cars, on the streets, in hotels or
> skyscrapers, the one topic was the Marines, who are fighting
> with such glorious success in France. Reports received at the
> recruiting headquarters in New York show that everywhere
> in the district application for service . . . has increased more
> than 100 percent in the last two days.[11]

The rest of America eagerly drank to New York's toast. Throughout the country young men jammed recruiting stations which had just received greatly increased quotas by the special vote of an appreciative Congress. Marines in London and Paris found that like Byron they "awoke famous," the olive-green uniform and the globe and anchor ornaments suddenly acquiring a new and special significance to the civil populace.

The reaction was natural enough. Harbingers of hope are always popular. The marine attacks held the first suggestion of a turning tide, a realization that America after all was in the war and would fight, 'tide what may. This was terribly important to war-weary peoples, but to those in Paris the attacks carried a special significance. On June 8 Lee Meriwether of the American embassy summed up the feeling of the French capital in a private letter:

> . . . During the last week Paris has lived through seven fright-
> fully anxious days—the seventy-five-mile guns dropping shells
> on the city daily and Gothas [large aircraft] dropping bombs
> almost nightly. . . . A giant Gotha was captured a few nights
> ago; thinking they were inside their lines the Germans came
> to earth just in the rear of Betz where fortunately French
> soldiers were close enough at hand to capture the eight avia-
> tors and their machine, the wings of which have an expanse
> of 136 feet! The monster carried several tons of bombs, one
> of which weighed 2200 pounds! . . . Terrific fighting is still
> going on barely forty miles from here where I am writing
> these notes; thus far the enemy is being "held," but whether
> he will continue to be held, or whether he will succeed in
> advancing again, and near enough to put Paris within reach
> of his marine guns [long-range naval cannon], remains to be
> seen. Yesterday the French government appointed a "Com-
> mittee for the Defense of Paris." It is announced that this is
> only a precaution and that the public must not become
> alarmed or imagine that the government believes the Ger-
> mans will really enter the capital, or that they will even come
> close enough to bomb it with ordinary big cannon.[12]

In short, Paris remained a nervous city wanting some reassurance of its safety. The news from the front offered precisely that. No one stopped to analyze the extent of the American gains, the hazy content of such headlines as those of the June 9th *New York Times:* AMERICANS RESUME ATTACKS NEAR TORCY; HOLD BOURESCHES AGAINST FRESH ASSAULTS.[13] For the moment it was enough that the Americans were attacking.

The American attacks held a dual significance for the French high command, which on June 6 was standing in waters troubled both by the enemy and by the British ally.

Although both Foch and Pétain were greatly relieved when the French and Americans finally halted the German drive to the Marne, neither remained under any illusion that Ludendorff was finished. Pétain increasingly (and correctly) believed the enemy would soon strike between Montdidier and Noyon. In Foch's later words:

> The necessity of making haste forced [the Germans] to neglect the minute precautions that had enabled them to perfectly conceal their preparations for the attack of May 27th. Consequently their new intentions were quickly discovered by the French aviation and intelligence service. By May 30th, General Pétain knew the lines of the enemy's plan; one point alone remained obscure, the size of the forces that he would employ. In theory these might be very considerable, for, according to the calculations of the French staff, the German Supreme Command had some sixty divisions in reserve and could launch an offensive between the Oise and the Somme composed of forty-five divisions, a stronger force consequently than he had used on May 27th against the Chemin-des-Dames, and in any case one greatly exceeding the total of all we had available.[14]

Even before the Germans were held on the Marne, Pétain had begun to meet the new threat by building up Humbert's Third French Army, an effort accomplished only by drastic reorganization of the battleline. To meet Pétain's troop levies, Foch recalled several French divisions earlier provided to the British commander, Sir Douglas Haig, and he further persuaded Haig to release the five American divisions being trained behind the British front. By June 4 these and other radical measures gave Humbert seven divisions in the first line of defense, five in the second line with further support "by seven other infantry divisions and three cavalry divisions assembled farther in rear."[15]

By borrowing from Peter to pay Paul, Foch rendered other parts of the front vulnerable to enemy attack, most notably the junction point of the British and French armies. On June 4 Foch asked Haig to transfer three more of his divisions to the Somme to back up this weak spot. This probably would have been all right except that Foch did not stop here. Instead he told Haig that if

> the enemy pursued his maneuver without pause in the direction of Paris between the Marne and the Oise, or if he developed it on a wider front—between Château-Thierry and Montdidier, for example—all the allied forces in France would have to give their aid to a battle which, in all probability, would decide the fate of the war.[16]

Accordingly, he asked Haig "to make detailed preparations for moving toward the front all his available troops, general and local reserves, and also to consider an eventual reduction of his forces in the front line."[17]

In view of the known tactical situation, this was an extraordinary suggestion prompted more by fear than logic. The German drive across the Chemin-des-Dames had unnerved virtually everybody. On the same day Foch wrote to Haig, the French premier Monsieur Clemenceau stood in the Chamber of Deputies to answer the demands of certain "parliamentarians not to mention groups of people in Paris" for the "removal of certain high officers namely Foch, Pétain and so forth from the army." Clemenceau told the politicians:

> If, to win the approbation of certain persons who judge in rash haste, I must abandon chiefs who have deserved well of their country, that is a piece of contemptible baseness of which I am incapable, and it must not be expected of me. If we are to raise doubts in the minds of the troops as to the competence of certain of their leaders, perhaps among the best, that would be a crime for which I would never accept responsibility.[18]

The Tiger's blunt words saved Foch and Pétain but only temporarily, only if they averted another disaster.

Sir Douglas Haig's position was no more secure than Foch's. His old ally, General Robertson, was gone; his enemy, General Henry Wilson, was now Chief of the Imperial General Staff; another enemy, Lloyd George, was Prime Minister. One more disaster such as those of early spring would seal Haig's fate and no one knew that better than Haig. And no matter what Foch and Pétain thought about enemy intentions, no matter that they were right—on June 4 Haig was still facing Crown Prince Rupprecht's Army Group estimated at forty-nine divisions of which twenty-six were fresh and could attack.

Haig therefore was just as frightened as Foch, and with equally good reasons. In addition, Foch had already annoyed him by transferring the French divisions from the British sector without even notifying Haig's headquarters. In his reply to Foch's letter, Haig agreed to transfer the three divisions to the Somme but he did it under "formal protest," sending a copy of the letter to London. This was tantamount to appealing to his own government as provided under the Beauvais agreement.

His action caused the utmost concern in London where, as in Paris, fear ruled the government. Lloyd George and his principal military advisers had just returned from a three-day session at the Supreme War Council, a stormy experience satisfying no one and discouraging everyone. On June 4 his cabinet secretary, Lord Hankey, recorded in his diary:

> . . . As regards the [present] battle . . . I do not like the outlook. The Germans are fighting better than the Allies and I cannot exclude the possibility of a disaster. I see difficult times ahead.

On June 5:

> After lunch Milner and Wilson came to 10 Downing Street and we discussed the question of the reserves and the proposed evacuation of Ypres and Dunkirk. Decided that Milner

and C.I.G.S. [Wilson] should discuss the question with Foch. The latter refuses to budge an inch; Wilson says that, if he does not, there will be a disaster. We also discussed the possibility of withdrawing the whole Army from France if the French crack. It was a very gloomy meeting.[19]

At this point Haig's letter reached London. Lloyd George immediately asked for a top-level conference to which he sent Milner and Wilson to meet with Haig and his deputy, General Lawrence, Clemenceau, Foch and his deputy, Weygand. The meeting was scheduled for June 7.

This could have brought a first-degree crisis in which the newly born principle of unity of command might easily have perished. But by the time of the conference the German threat on the Marne had not only been neutralized, albeit temporarily, but the French and Americans were counterattacking. As in the case of the Paris civilians this fact provided a perhaps ineffable but nonetheless ineluctable hope—the first good news from either the British or French fronts in many a month.

The Paris conference thus convened in a relatively favorable psychological air which tended to ease tempers and modify strong wills. In reviewing the situation, the participants agreed that both Haig and Foch had strong cases, that henceforth Foch must first notify Haig before transferring units away from him, but that unity of command must be preserved. Haig summed up this vital conclusion in his diary:

> . . . The effect of the Beauvais Agreement is now becoming clear in practice. This effect I had realized from the beginning, namely, that the responsibility for the safety of the British Army in France could no longer rest with me because the "Generalissimo" [Foch] can do what *he* thinks right with my troops. On the other hand, the British Government is only now beginning to understand what Foch's powers as Generalissimo amount to. This delegation of power to Foch is inevitable, but I intend to ask that the British Government

should in a document modify my responsibility for the safety of the British Army under these altered conditions.[20]

As for the future conduct of the war:

> The C.I.G.S. [Wilson] asked Foch if he still adhered to the same strategical policy as he had enunciated at Abbéville on May 2nd. F. [Foch] replied that he did, namely, first to secure the connection of the British and French Armies, second, to cover both Paris and the Channel Ports. And in reply to F. I said I agreed with these principles.[21]

While the Allied high command conferred in Paris, Pétain's headquarters continued to report indications of a massive German buildup between Montdidier and Noyon. But here again a freshening air prevailed. On June 6 Major Clark reported to Pershing:

> My impression of the 3d Bureau [Operations] today is that they are in very good *moral* [sic]. They expect an attack on the Third and perhaps First French Armies. They were very enthusiastic over the American troops. It is in some instances touching to hear their expressions of praise and gratitude over the rapid arrival of the Americans. . . .
>   I enclose copy of Colonel Paillé's report of June 5. It will be noted statement of operation to be undertaken by 2d U. S. [Division] tomorrow as well as words of praise for 2d U. S. Colonel Paillé is personally very enthusiastic over the quality and conduct of the 2d U. S. I think I am justified in reporting him as wildly enthusiastic.[22]

The French attitude materially reflected itself in a suggestion by Pétain to Pershing to form an American corps on the battle front, specifically near Château-Thierry. As Pershing reported, in a subsequent meeting with Pétain the American commander

> suggested to General Pétain that we should bring other divisions to join with the 2d and 3d [divisions] for that pur-

pose, and accordingly the release of the 26th and 42d [divisions] from the inactive front was immediately ordered. The assembly of four American divisions on the Marne front would more than offset the recent French losses. General Pétain, in his letter accepting my offer, said in part: "I must express my deep gratitude for the prompt and very important aid which you are bringing in the present crisis. The American troops already engaged in the battle have the unanimous admiration of the whole French Army. The power of the effort which your country is at present showing, as well as the resolute and generous spirit with which you enter the struggle are, for the Allies—and above all for France—a comfort in the grave times through which we are passing and a crutch of hope for the future."[23]

The reports from the front, though often distorted and inaccurate, continued to impress Pétain's senior staff officers. Pierrefeu later wrote that the American action at Belleau Wood "delighted the 3d Bureau. Colonel Dufieux frequently said to me: 'Do not forget the Americans in the communiques; they are admirable.'"[24] On June 8 Major Clark reported to Pershing:

> . . . The *moral* [sic] of the 3d Bureau impresses me as good. Dinner last night and lunch today gave no indications of subconscious anxiety.
> Last evening, walking back to his office from dinner, Colonel Dufieux said to me that the French feel a deep sense of gratitude for the formidable effort being made by America, for the rapid arrival of American troops, for their splendid demeanor and fighting qualities and also for the broad philanthropic view which is guiding General Pershing. He said he hoped soon to see an American sector on the battle front commanded by an American general. He said the beneficial *moral* [sic] effect produced on the French troops at seeing Americans fighting at their side, and fighting with such success and valor, could not be overestimated and conversely the presence of so many Americans, fighting vigorously, must

be a very unwelcome and disheartening realization to the Germans.[25]

The appearance of the Americans in the battleline, first at Seicheprey and Cantigny, then on the Marne, did not unduly alarm the German high command. Perhaps because German intelligence quickly identified the American divisions as those in France for some time, or because Ludendorff and his staff officers were gradually losing touch with reality, they seemed to have missed the psychological import of the new development. In Ludendorff's later words:

> In spite of a few unavoidable temporary crises, our troops remained masters of the situation, both in attack and in defense. They proved themselves superior to both the English and the French, even when their opponents were assisted by tanks. At Château Thierry [sic], Americans who had been a long time in France bravely attacked our thinly held fronts, but they were unskillfully led, attacked in dense masses, and failed. Here, too, our men felt themselves superior. Our tactics had proved sound in every way, our losses, compared with those of the enemy and the large number of prisoners, though in themselves distressing, had been very slight.[26]

Ludendorff was whistling in the dark. The spring offensives, though successful locally, had nowhere proven decisive and had everywhere caused large casualties in the German ranks. And in the spring of 1918 the Germans, like the French and English, were hard put to repair human losses. Only by considerable effort had Ludendorff scraped together his latest replacements: 23,000 recruits from the 1899 class along with 60,000 troops transferred from various auxiliary services.[27] From east to west of his long battleline his divisions stood badly depleted in officers and men, and in supply and equipment, factors already altering tactics and adversely affecting morale. His casual, almost flippant dismissal of the American effort ignored the stand of the 2d and 3d U. S. Divisions which, along with the French, had helped to throw off his strategic timetable.

Admittedly the subsequent American attacks were as yet accomplishing but slight tactical gains and these at tremendous cost to the attackers. To Ludendorff this was still the important point because, not being a student of human nature, he was far more worried about the tactical influence of the Americans than about their effect on the morale of either side. He still believed he could win the war before this tactical influence asserted itself. For the moment it was sufficient to contain the Americans, as evidenced by his June 8 orders to all army groups: "American units appearing on the front should be hit particularly hard in order to render difficult the formation of an American army."[28] This course of action would in addition bolster the confidence of his own troops while neutralizing Allied propaganda based on the American presence in the firing line.

Meanwhile he would get on with the war. On June 9 he would strike the French between Montdidier and Noyon. If he punched through here, Paris would lie under his guns; if necessary, and it would probably not be, he could then strike at Reims and along the Marne to the east or, more preferably, against the British in Flanders. If his strategy worked, the war would be over before the Americans could grow into a major worry.

Thanks to Ludendorff's delay in resuming the offensive, General Fayolle had been able to organize Debeney's and Humbert's armies into a reasonably good defensive position in depth behind the Montdidier-Noyon line. On June 8 Lloyd George's newly appointed Minister of Munitions, Winston Churchill, visited this front and reported:

> . . . I followed with the closest attention the improved methods of defense which the French were adopting. Nothing of consequence was now offered to the German opening bombardment. A strong picquet line of detached machine-gun nests, carefully concealed, was alone in contact with the enemy. Behind these devoted troops, for whom an assault could only mean destruction, was a zone three or four thousand yards deep, in which only strong points were held by comparatively small forces. It was not until at least 7,000 yards separated them from the hostile batteries that the real resis-

tance of the French Infantry and Artillery was prepared. When one saw all the fortifications and devices, the masses of batteries and machine guns, with which the main line of defense bristled, and knew that this could not be subjected to heavy bombardment until the stubborn picquets far in front had been exterminated, it seemed difficult to believe that any troops in the world could carry the whole position from front to rear in a single day.

On the evening of June 8 I walked over the center of the French line in front of Compiègne. The presage of battle was in the air. All the warnings had been given, and everyone was at his post. The day had been quiet, and the sweetness of the summer evening was undisturbed even by a cannon shot. Very calm and gallant, and even gay, were the French soldiers who awaited the new stroke of fate.[29]

To carry the position was the task of von Hutier's Eighteenth German Army consisting of thirteen rested divisions. Shortly after midnight on June 9, nine of these divisions began moving to forward concentration areas under the cover of a thunderous barrage again carefully planned and commanded by Colonel Bruchmüller. For nearly four hours Bruchmüller's big guns shattered the night while consuming French outposts and strong points with the unrelenting appetite of some furious prehistoric monster.

At 3:45 P.M. the first waves of gray-clad *Sturmtruppen* struck along fifteen miles of French line between Ayencourt and Thiescourt; by 6:00 A.M. the German left extended to the Oise River. Although the French did not know it, von Hutier had kept his flanks purposely light to concentrate his strength in the center. And here, on a ten-mile front between Rollot and Thiescourt, he pushed through in just under three hours. Before noon his vanguard units had seized Fayolle's second line of defense in the center. Other divisions, working down the valley of the Matz River, had taken the Sainte-Claude plateau and Thiescourt Wood.

But now any hope held by von Hutier for a rout ceased. If here and there a French division broke and ran, the bulk of them yielded ground only grudgingly, only in terms of feet and yards while reserve divisions were rushed up to plug the gaps. By evening von Hutier's forward units held a seven-mile front between Méry and Vandélicourt, a forward gain of six and a half miles—impressive but not decisive.

Nor did June 10 bring the Germans any closer to ending the war in their favor. Their most important gain occurred on the left. Here a retreating French division opened the way to Ribécourt and, by allowing von Hutier's left to gain the west bank of the Oise, forced Fayolle's right back to the old 1914 lines east of the Oise. Until he could advance in the center, von Hutier could not exploit this development. He did not advance measurably in the center, and now he had run out of time.

Now it was Fayolle's turn. The French general had already decided to counterattack with five carefully hoarded divisions commanded by General Mangin. The only question was when. Fayolle remained cautious, wanted everything ready first. "Butcher" Mangin, an old colonial soldier whose star had temporarily eclipsed with the fall of General Nivelle, was anything but cautious. On the afternoon of June 10, Foch found Mangin in conference with Fayolle. Foch later told an aide:

> . . . He [Mangin] had to counter-attack on the Oise with five divisions. One had arrived, the second was just detraining, the third was expensed during the evening, the fourth at midnight, and the fifth later still. He said to me: "I shall attack tomorrow."
>
> Fayolle, who had made the preparations for this offensive, preferred to defer the attack. "You can never do it! Wait a couple of days!" I replied to Fayolle: "Let him go ahead!" Indeed, Mangin was fully prepared; he had summoned his divisional commanders, and his artillery officers had been instructed to reconnoitre the ground. He had arranged everything and was ready to act.[30]

Fayolle finally agreed, the importance of his decision plain in the final paragraph of his orders:

Tomorrow's operations should be the end of the defensive battle which we have been fighting for more than two months. It should mark the definite check of the Germans and the renewal of the offensive on our part. It must succeed. Let everyone understand this.[31]

It succeeded. At 11:00 A.M. on June 11 the tired Germans in von Hutier's center found themselves under attack from three directions. In but hours the French recaptured the villages of Méry and Belloy, cleared the valley of the Aronde, captured several guns and over a thousand prisoners. On June 12 Mangin "wished to push on." Foch later told an aide, "We had to stop him, and to keep on stopping him." Foch was still worried about Rupprecht's divisions facing the British and was further concerned about a fresh attack southwest of Soissons by von Boehn's Seventh Army. Justifiably pleased by the turn of events, he wisely decided to hold what he had until either Ludendorff played fresh cards or until he himself was ready to claim the deal.

Foch's pleasure was Ludendorff's disappointment. On June 11, "in consequence of the great accumulation of enemy troops," he ordered von Hutier to take up defensive positions. Ludendorff wrote:

It was quite evident that the attack commenced in the meantime by the Seventh Army southwest of Soissons would not get through.

The action of the Eighteenth Army had not altered the strategical situation brought about by the attack of the Seventh Army, nor had it provided any fresh tactical data.[32]

Ludendorff found himself temporarily stymied. To break the impasse he now decided on a fresh attack against Reims followed by another against the British in Flanders. But even as he set his staff to work, even as the vast machinery of reorganization churned into action, the hands of the clock continued to move. Time for Ludendorff was running out—the Americans were growing into a major worry.

Notes

1. Emmet Crozier, *American Reporters on the Western Front 1914–1918*. New York: Oxford University Press, 1959.
2. Ibid.
3. Ibid.
4. *Chicago Daily Tribune*, June 6, 1918.
5. *New York Herald* (Paris Edition), June 7, 1918.
6. *Sioux City Journal*, June 7, 1918.
7. *Chicago Daily Tribune*, June 7, 1918.
8. *New York Times*, June 7, 1918.
9. Ibid.
10. *Chicago Daily Tribune*, op. cit.
11. *New York Times*, June 9, 1918.
12. Lee Meriwether, *The War Diary of a Diplomat*. New York: Dodd, Mead and Co., 1919.
13. *New York Times*, op. cit.
14. Ferdinand Foch, *The Memoirs of Marshal Foch*. Translated by Colonel T. Bentley Mott. New York: Doubleday, 1931.
15. Ibid.
16. Ibid.
17. Ibid.
18. Georges Clemenceau, *Grandeur and Misery of Victory*. Translated by F. M. Atkinson. New York: Harcourt Brace and Co., 1930.
19. Lord Hankey, *The Supreme Command 1914–1918*. Vol 2. London: Allen and Unwin, 1962.
20. Duff Cooper, *Haig*. London: Faber and Faber Ltd., 1935.
21. Ibid.
22. Paul H. Clark, "Letters and Messages to John J. Pershing, 1918–1919." Washington: Manuscripts Division, Library of Congress. Unpublished.
23. John J. Pershing, *My Experiences in the World War*. Vol. 2. New York: F. A. Stokes Co., 1931.
24. Jean de Pierrefeu, *Headquarters 1915–1918*. Translated by Major C. J. C. Street. London: Geoffrey Bles Ltd., 1929.
25. Clark, op. cit.
26. Erich Ludendorff, *Ludendorff's Own Story*. New York: Harper & Brothers, 1919.
27. Barrie Pitt, *1918 The Last Act*. New York: W. W. Norton and Co., 1963.
28. Ernst Otto, "The Battles for the Possession of Belleau Woods, June, 1918." *U. S. Naval Institute Proceedings*, November, 1928.
29. Winston S. Churchill, *The World Crisis 1916–1918*. Vol. 4. London: Butterworth, 1927.
30. Charles Bugnet, *Foch Speaks*. New York: The Dial Press, 1930. See also Foch, op. cit.
31. Foch, op. cit.
32. Ludendorff, op. cit.

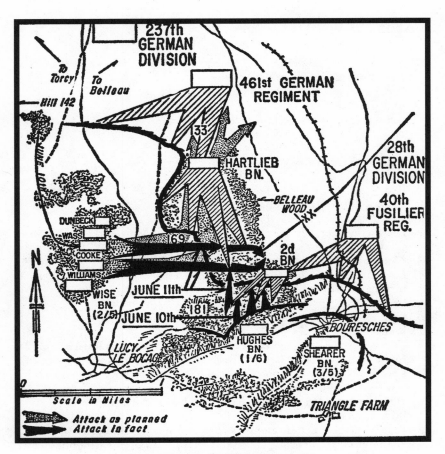

Belleau Wood
Marine Attacks
June 10–11, 1918

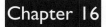

Chapter 16

" ... Artillery has blown the wood all to hell."
—Brigadier General Harbord to Major General Bundy,
June 10, 1918

In one sense Ludendorff was correct. By June 8 the American attack against Belleau Wood had tactically "failed." His conclusion, however, ignored two important facts: he did not understand that Pershing could now afford the human cost of continued effort, nor did he appreciate the tenacious quality of Americans to see a situation through, no matter how unpleasant, once they accepted it.

Having created this particular situation by throwing the American glove into the German ring, and having thrilled and inspired the western world by so doing, the Americans were in no mind to turn back. This was battle—the struggle of two wills, as Foch once defined it. And by June 8 the Americans were wholeheartedly in accord with another of the Frenchman's dictums: "A battle won is a battle in which one will not own oneself defeated."

Although the failure of Sibley's attack on June 8 nullified Harbord's hopes for an immediate and impressive victory, it in no way formed a seed of doubt as to that victory. Instead it brought him to a command reappraisal concerning past, present and future. He covered the past in a memorandum released to the battalions on June 8:

> The following suggestions occur from consideration of the week's fighting and are published for the information and action of company, battalion and regimental commanders:
> 1. Reports that do not show the time of sending are worthless.
> 2. "Losses are heavy" may mean anything. Percentages or numbers are desired.
> 3. Figures or conditions that are only estimated should be so stated.
> 4. Flanks of positions and any important peculiarities such as re-entrants, salients and refusals, should be described by [map] coordinates as far as practicable. Artillery cannot be called for with safety unless position of our Infantry is accurately known. . . .
> 5. The number of machine guns and prisoners captured to hour of writing reports is information that ought to be included in them.
> 6. Dispersion of troops is the fault of beginners as pointed out by all military authorities, and has in our Brigade, with the length of our line, deprived us of the necessary echelons in depth.
> 7. Officers given a task must plan to execute it with forces at their own command, and not count on reinforcements which may not be available. Only a grave emergency not apparent when the task is begun will justify requests for help. Supports have been thrown in during this first week at a rate not to be expected hereafter.
> 8. The enemy have been told that Americans do not take prisoners, which makes their men fight to the death rather than surrender when they think they will be given no quarters. This idea that we do not take prisoners undoubtedly costs us many lives.
> 9. The heavy losses of officers compared to those among the men are most eloquent as to the gallantry of our

officers, and correspond nearly to the proportions suffered by both the Allies and the enemy in 1914–15.
Officers of experience are a most valuable asset and must
not be wasted.
10. Recommendations for decorations should be made with
discretion but as promptly as possible. The "extraordinary heroism" which calls for the D.S.C. [Distinguished
Service Cross] must be liberally interpreted in cases of
officers and men who have met death or suffered the
loss of a leg, an arm, or an eye in action.
11. The French Corps Commander has asked for recommendations for awards of the Croix de Guerre. This
should be submitted promptly and in good faith.[1]

Harbord's memorandum could have held but slight appeal either to the units in line or to such as Berry's shattered battalion
attempting to re-form in the rear. Of far more importance to the
survivors was Harbord's wise if belated decision to try a fresh tactical approach—massive artillery preparation of the wood before attempting further infantry attacks.

Late on June 8 Harbord ordered Hughes's 1st Battalion, 6th
Marines, which Degoutte released from corps reserve, to relieve
Sibley's line in the ravine south of Belleau Wood. Later he changed
his mind to order the wood cleared altogether while fifty batteries of
guns blasted its defenses to shreds. At 9:45 P.M. he notified Lieutenant Colonel Lee:

The plan for relieving Major Sibley by Major Hughes' battalion has been changed. Major Sibley is to be withdrawn
tonight after dark with any engineers that may be with him.
The 80th Company [Captain Coffenberg] which it is understood has been moved to the woods southeast of Lucy
remains in those woods. Major Hughes will put there tonight one company of his battalion and as many more as the
wood will safely hold. The remainder of his battalion to be
in the wood southwest of Lucy. His P.C. to be in the wood
southeast of Lucy. At dawn tomorrow an artillery prepara-

tion will begin on the Bois de Belleau which by the late afternoon is expected to obliterate any enemy organization in that wood.[2]

This word also went to Neville with instructions for Wise to withdraw any part of his battalion lying east of the Lucy-Torcy road. Harbord further notified Holcomb on the right:

Much to my regret I am unable to relieve your battalion in its turn from its present place. The holding of that town [Bouresches] is too important for me to risk a change at this time. It will be done just as soon as conditions permit. You and your battalion have done fine work and it is much appreciated by the Division Commander and myself.[3]

Later that night Holcomb did receive some replacements whose behavior later caused Colonel Lee to write General Barnett in Washington:

The remarkable conduct of raw replacement troops which joined this organization on the night of June 8 when thrown into the line is transmitted for the information of the Major General Commandant. The replacement detail of 213 included among it a large majority who were enlisted two months before their reporting to this organization. It was necessary to replace immediately losses sustained in the 2d Battalion which was holding the right flank of our operations and the stronghold of the town of Bouresches, a line vitally important to the success of the present operations. The detail arrived at the Regimental Headquarters at 6:30 P.M. and were placed in the woods and organized for relief. . . . These troops were marched past the lines at 10:30 P.M. under detail from Regimental Headquarters to the point where they were met by platoon guides and conducted to their station. The Regimental Sergeant Major [John Quick] reports that the men obeyed orders without a word, moved in splendid order and across a terrain which was shelled by the enemy by high explosives and lighted up by flares. Their arrival in the lines of the 2d Battalion relieved a pressing need for men at a vital point. The remarkable steadiness of these men . . . under conditions that would have been trying to veteran troops, is eloquent evidence of the fine material from which the Marine Corps is drawing its men in a critical hour of the Nation's history.[4]

Harbord also alerted Major Shearer, who had replaced Berry in command of the 3d Battalion, 5th Marines, "to go over early tomorrow morning and familiarize yourself with the line he [Holcomb] is holding, including the town of Bouresches. It is the present intention that your battalion will relieve him tomorrow night."[5]

The first move in the reorganization belonged to Major Hughes whom Harbord had verbally alerted in the afternoon. Hughes directed Sergeant Gerald Thomas of his intelligence section to reconnoiter the route as far as the sunken trail north of Paris Farm; at that point his intelligence officer, Lieutenant "Waggy" Etheridge, would take over and lead the battalion to the concentration area.

Shortly after dark Thomas and Captain George Stohl, commanding the battalion in Hughes's temporary absence, started down the highway toward Paris Farm. All went well until the rear half of the column, becoming separated from its connecting files, turned left at a road junction, a mistake requiring some three hours to rectify. Once on the sunken trail Lieutenant Etheridge joined Stohl and Thomas. They had gone about a mile farther when, Thomas later reported,

we realized we did not know where we were going. At my question Etheridge said, "For God sake, don't you know where we're supposed to go?"

I told him, "I have no idea. Major Hughes said you would know the way."

"Hell," he said, "I don't know anything about it."

Daylight was just breaking when we left the trail, crossed a small wheatfield and a road and saw a wood beyond. We could hear plenty of artillery fire and realized we were under observation. We knew we were out of position but we also knew we had to take cover in those woods if we were to avoid losing most of the battalion to enemy fire.[6]

While Hughes's battalion marched toward the guns, Sibley's men began their exodus from the ravine bordering Belleau Wood. They were not sorry to go. They were exhausted, famished men, many with untreated wounds, their bodies filthy. Forty-two percent of their officers and forty percent of the men—some 400 total—were killed, wounded or missing. They needed replacements, food, a wash, a change of clothes, but mostly they needed sleep. In Lieutenant Timmerman's later words:

> We were all very much confused, but somehow we sorted out our units and started back toward Lucy. We were very glad to be ordered back because we had had almost nothing to eat or drink and very little sleep for almost a week. I had only nineteen people left out of my platoon and we were all just about out on our feet. I led them back through the ravine, heard the shells coming and going. From Lucy we struck out west to our new reserve position perhaps two miles away in Platerie Wood. Somewhere along this road a ration cart crossed my column and when I reached the wood I found only two men behind me. The others had all straggled in by first light. We found a large farm building with a concrete floor for a billet. We had just dozed off when a battery of 75s immediately to the rear commenced fire. I remember hearing the sharp thunder before sleeping.[7]

The marines and soldiers of the 2d U. S. Division would remember that sharp thunder for a long time. It came from every available American and French battery in the vicinity. It was pattern fire carefully distributed in and around Belleau Wood; a heavy, unrelenting, destructive fire which would send 28,000 75mm shells and 6,000 155mm shells at the enemy.[8] The enemy replied in kind though not in such fury. Throughout June 9 his shells fell in Bouresches and Lucy and in the other towns and along roads, a steady, even monotonous interdiction fire which made exploding terrain a way of life to American runners gamely carrying messages of war from one P.C. to another or to the beleaguered marines and soldiers holding the thin front line. In Bouresches a shell exploded "about every minute," a brutal fire mistakenly supplemented on June 9 by heavy shells from a long-range friendly cannon, probably a railway gun, somewhere to the rear.[9]

Shortly after the noon hour Harbord learned the new location of Hughes's battalion. In midafternoon he directed Hughes to move up to Sibley's old line after dark. At 6:30 P.M. the brigade commander issued attack orders: at 4:30 A.M. on June 10 Hughes, supported by heavy machine guns, to attack the southern portion of Belleau Wood, his objective an east-west line crossing the wood nearly at the top of its slim connecting portion. Once Hughes reached "X-line 261.70," he was to consolidate his position, his right tied in with the marines in Bouresches, his left with Wise's 2d Battalion.

Shortly after dark, Hughes led his battalion from the cover of the interim woods down the road toward Lucy, then up the semisheltered ravine to Sibley's old line across the southern edge of Belleau Wood. Simultaneously, Shearer brought his battalion forward, deployed one company southeast of Lucy as support for Hughes, and with the other three companies relieved Holcomb's line from Bouresches to Triangle.

At 2:45 A.M. Hughes reported himself in position. The American guns were firing faster now, the German guns answering. In Bouresches the crews of twelve Hotchkiss machine guns were standing by to open a curtain barrage between Belleau Wood and the town of Belleau; the crews of six other guns were waiting with the assault companies. For the moment there was nothing more to do.

Equally significant developments were meanwhile taking place on the German side of the battleline. Faced with a lack of replacements and with severe shortages of supplies and equipment, von Conta had been forced to reorganize his entire defensive line, first by relieving the 197th Division on his right with the 5th Guards Division, next by relieving the 10th Division with the 28th Division, finally by moving division sectors to the right, a shift drastically altering the defense of Belleau Wood.

Until the 28th Division began moving into line on June 8, Major Bischoff's 461st Regiment, 237th Division, had ably defended the entire wood.[10] Von Conta's new order, however, by shifting the 237th Division's sector to the right, split the wood's defense between Bischoff's left and the 28th Division's right. Bischoff's new line, which now ran north along the western face of the wood and then turned toward Torcy, forced him to leave only one reinforced battalion in the wood. This unit, commanded by Major von Hartlieb, was to tie in with a battalion of the 28th Division on its left.

At one time a first-rate fighting organization, the 28th Baden Division was tired and understrength when it began moving into the line running from west of Vaux to across Belleau Wood. Its soldiers had already fought against the Americans, had been amazed at the quality of their uniforms and equipment and depressed at the knowledge that more Americans, more supplies, more equipment, were on the way. After noting this, a member of the 40th Fusilier Regiment wrote:

> With us, however, each company consisted of barely five or even four detachments. For the first eight days, since the beginning of the offensive, our men were able to eat well; however, they appeared underfed. Uniforms and blankets began to look threadbare. Cartridge cases were made of tin; only those for machine gun ammunition were of brass with paper cartridge belts. Even shell cases were made of cardboard. The gun tubes were already so worn as to cause inaccuracy in firing. The straps of our kit bags were made of paper, sandbags and casings were of paper, our telephone wires were insulated with paper. . . .[11]

This did not mean that the German soldiers lacked will to fight, nor that they regarded their position as hopeless. On June 7 *Leutnant* Tillmann of the 2d Battalion, 40th Fusiliers, wrote in his diary:

> At the front. American troops have made counter-attacks. Have to move to the front again. . . . In the night of the 8th

and 9th we will relieve the front line. It must be a sad outfit which allows itself to be thrown out by the Americans.[12]

On June 8 his division commander, General von Boehn, issued a special order to the troops:

An American success along our front, even if only temporary, may have the most unfavorable influence on the attitude of the Entente and the duration of the war. In the coming battles, therefore, it is not a question of the possession of this or that village or woods, insignificant in itself [sic]; it is a question whether the Anglo-American claim that the American Army is the equal or even the superior of the German Army is to be made good.[13]

To answer the question in his favor, Boehn deployed two regiments in line, one in reserve. In turn the commander of his right regiment, the 40th Fusiliers, held one battalion in reserve with two battalions in line—one behind Bouresches and one in Belleau Wood.

The commander of the 2d Battalion assigned to Belleau Wood found himself responsible for about a 500-yard line running from east to west across the southern portion of the wood. In defending this line, Bischoff had deployed six infantry companies cored around six heavy machine guns with infantry reserves immediately to the rear. The new commander, although borrowing Bischoff's six machine guns for twenty-four hours, chose to deploy only two companies in line with two heavy machine guns and three trench mortars. He placed a third company in reserve well to the rear in the eastern edge of the wood, and his fourth and final company along the railroad line to the east where he also positioned two more heavy machine guns.

Bischoff at once protested this deployment to his own division commander. He had so far successfully defended this line only because of a strong, mutually supporting line with reserves close at hand. It was ridiculous, he argued, to suppose that two companies could do the work of six, particularly when reserves remained so far to the rear. When his division commander told him that neither the commanding general of the 28th Division nor von Conta agreed, he instructed von Hartlieb to begin building a switch line from west to east to protect his left flank.[14]

At 4:15 A.M. Chamberlaine's guns began to roll slowly back through the wood, a careful fire calculated to bring the shells on the objective line at 4:45. A few minutes later the machine guns in Bouresches opened curtain fire to seal Hughes's right from interference outside the wood. At 4:30 company and platoon commanders blew whistles, raised canes to the horizontal and started up the wooded slope ahead.

The attack went well. At 4:51 Hughes notified Harbord:

Artillery barrage working beautifully. Three or four casualties in 74th Company coming in. Otherwise all O.K. Kindly have artillery fire kept on machine guns firing down the line we have to cross.[15]

At 5:20 A.M. Lee's intelligence officer notified Harbord:

Action in woods deemed finished. Our barrage on woods is continuing. Guns are firing on enemy's batteries and towns. Only few short bursts of machine gun fire noted during advance.[16]

Twenty minutes later Lee notified Harbord:

All quiet in the Bois de Belleau. Our shells are falling further to the north and east. Occasional rifle fire in the Bois de Belleau. No machine gun fire there now.[17]

At 6:10 A.M. Lee reported "several sharp bursts of machine gun fire from center of the Bois de Belleau east of Hill 181. . . ." At 6:20 he forwarded a message from Lieutenant Perrin, a liaison officer attached to Hughes: "The line advanced obtaining objective without opposition. One trench mortar [captured] quite intact."[18]

Harbord next learned that Captain Fuller, commanding the 75th Company, had run into a nest of three machine guns in the northeastern portion of the wood; Major Cole, who as usual had come up with the forward machine guns, was helping in the attack against them. At 7:12 Lee reported a message from Hughes:

> Everything going nicely. No losses coming across. Have received no word from companies, but there is practically no firing. Artillery has blown the Bois de Belleau to mince meat.[19]

The situation remained unchanged at 7:54—the machine guns were still holding up Fuller, but Hughes had sent him two trench mortars to help in the attack. Two minutes later Harbord learned that Major Cole had been seriously wounded and was being evacuated.[20]

By 8:00 A.M. Harbord had reason to believe the attack had succeeded. Although no prisoners were coming in, the marines had captured two seven-inch mortars with ammunition besides suffering very few casualties. Except for isolated rifle and machine-gun fire, the wood remained quiet.

Harbord now heard from division headquarters: the French wanted a regiment of the artillery returned as soon as possible. At 10:02 the brigade commander notified Hughes:

> Very important that you give me your judgement on what is north of you in the Bois de Belleau. Push your reconnaissance and let me know at the earliest possible moment whether you think it possible to take part of the wood north of your present position. Let me know:
>
> 1st: Whether you think it will be practicable to take the part of the Bois de Belleau north of your present position with your force as it stands.
>
> 2nd: How much further artillery preparation should there be on that part of the wood.
>
> 3rd: If you think your forces are not equal to it with artillery preparation, give me your opinion on the forces necessary.
>
> All this on the assumption the machine gun fire along the railroad will be kept down by our artillery and that Wise can advance on the left of the Bois de Belleau.[21]

A few minutes later he wrote Preston Brown, Bundy's chief of staff:

> . . . I am hurrying all I can the reconnaissance in the north
> end of the Bois de Belleau. I have not been able to get any-
> thing definite as yet. My judgement is that the action of the
> artillery has very effectually silenced serious opposition in
> that part of the wood. I am of the opinion that I will want to
> attack the north end of the Bois de Belleau either today,
> tonight or tomorrow morning and request that the Corps
> not move this Regiment of field artillery within twenty-four
> hours.[22]

Neither official nor substantiative documents contain Hughes's
reply to Harbord's inquiry. It is doubtful if Hughes made a reply, for
had he sent a reconnaissance party to the north the Germans would
have quickly shot it out of existence.

The unfortunate truth was that the density of the wood coupled
with poor maps had caused Hughes to render a false report. Far
from gaining the specified objective line, he had simply reoccupied
Sibley's old position of June 8, a line roughly 800 yards south from
where Harbord supposed him to be. The machine guns holding up
Fuller's advance were located in the southeastern corner of the wood,
not the northeastern.

Colonel Lee's intelligence officer, the highly regarded Lieutenant Bill Eddy, learned something of the truth around noon on June
10 when, guided by Sergeant Gerald Thomas of Hughes's intelligence section, he made a personal reconnaissance. Thomas reported:

> [Eddy] asked me to lead him to these machine gun nests. I
> hadn't seen one up to this time, but knew about where they
> were located. We worked forward slowly through the dense
> wood. Finally we got to a place where I told Eddy I thought
> we'd gone far enough. He said, "All right, you keep watch
> while I climb this tree and take a look." He had no more
> gotten up there when he turned loose and came down with
> a thump. "My God," he whispered, "I was looking square

at a German in a machine gun nest right down in front of us." We got out of there fast. They evidently didn't see us—anyway they didn't open fire.[23]

Although Hughes didn't know it, his attack had not even involved Major von Hartlieb's defense on the left, except for isolated fire, nor had it seriously threatened the 2d Battalion's new defensive line across the wood. American artillery and machine-gun fire had made life a hell for members of the 2d Battalion. *Leutnant* Tillmann, who was on the line, noted in his diary:

> June 9th to 10th: The worst night of my life. I am lying in a thick woods on an open height in little holes behind rocks, for this is certainly heavy artillery fire, until six o'clock in the morning. It is a wonder that the fellows were all at their posts when the Americans attacked. The attack, thank God, was repulsed. God has mercifully preserved me. They fight like devils.[24]

Unfortunately the attack was not so much repulsed by the Germans as it was constrained by the Americans. Not only did the German line remain unbroken, but in many places it was not even contested. Although Harbord could not know this, he did hold two reasons for proceeding more cautiously than was the case.

The first reason was tactical. On the afternoon of June 8 he knew the wood was strongly defended. Aerial observers subsequently had reported no troop exodus; contrarily, prisoners had stated that the enemy was carrying out a relief within the wood proper. Further indications reached him during and after Hughes's attack: machine-gun and rifle fire were reported from the wood's center, while early in the afternoon Wise's intelligence officer, Lieutenant Bill Mathews, reported: "Enemy one pounder probably located at Point 173.2–262.2. Has been firing into 43rd Company sector all morning."[25] The particular map coordinates placed the gun in the lower portion of the northwest part of the wood, rather an isolated emplacement for an artillery piece unless infantry was guarding it to the south.

The second reason concerned the physical and mental condition of his command, described in his evening report to division:

> I desire to call attention of the Division Commander to the fact that this Brigade has been in the line since June 1st to date and has been almost continually fighting. Its line has receded nowhere and has everywhere advanced. Officers and men are now at a state scarcely less than complete physical exhaustion. Men fall asleep under bombardment and the physical exhaustion and the heavy losses are a combination calculated to damage morale, which should be met by immediate arrangements for the relief of this Brigade. The talk among officers and soldiers of the French Army, whom this Brigade relieved, appeared to be that constant fighting for five or six days by them excused them for falling back before the enemy. This Brigade has more than doubled the time which they considered exhausted them and has advanced against and held the enemy during all that time. I cannot too strongly urge that immediate arrangements be made for its relief to enable us to rest and reorganize.[26]

Not many marines would have disagreed. During the fighting of early June, rest was simply an impossible word. As Major Evans later wrote the Commandant:

> They've had reliefs for a few days, the battalions, for it's a battalion war now, but many people would have hardly called it rest. It was the best we could get, but the rest woods were shelled at times, there was no chance to scrub and wash clothes, and if it rained no shelter except ponchos and little dugouts that were soon flooded. But every time they went back into the lines, dead tired, but with a spirit that made any task possible. There were times when it seemed to me, with my talk over the 'phone, their official and unofficial messages and their reports of casualties, of bombardments and gas, that they must have reached their limit and could not hold.[27]

They could and would hold, they would continue to give more than they took, but none of it would prove easy. Lack of sleep, the constant pressure of fighting, of frequent artillery bombardments, the shortage of food—all was beginning to tell on the mental and physical health of the command.

This factor coupled with the tactical factors discussed above should have caused Harbord to have scrutinized Hughes's position before ordering a fresh attack. Other considerations, however, overrode them. One was the understandable desire on the part of the American and French high commands for a positive victory, in part to gain a general psychological advantage, in part to compensate for the German gains of June 10 between Montdidier and Noyon. Harbord's chief consideration, however, was the false impression of the tactical situation which he retained despite further reports from the front during the afternoon which rectified some of the earlier misconceptions.

At 2:44 P.M. Harbord telephoned division:

The attack started at 4:30 A.M. after a thorough artillery preparation. The objective was reached by 5:10 A.M. and since that hour is being consolidated. So far as known no prisoners were taken, but two large minnenwerfers [trench mortars] were captured. Our losses slight.[28]

Considering what he judged to be an impressive gain, his losses of eight killed and twenty-four wounded were very slight indeed. In his mind, part of the reason lay in the efficacy of the pre-attack artillery barrage which, according to his morning report to Bundy, "blew the wood all to hell."[29] A further barrage could only work in his favor, but if it were to include the precious guns of the French artillery regiment then it had to come soon.

Even before Harbord expressed concern to Bundy over the physical state of his command, he decided to continue the action. Field Order Number Four issued at 5:45 P.M. on June 10 called for an attack against "the northern end of the Bois de Belleau" on June 11.

This order directed Wise's 2d Battalion, 5th Marines, to strike the southwestern edge of the wood's northern portion—roughly a 500-yard front across Hill 169—with his objective the northeastern edge of the wood including Hill 133. Artillery and machine-gun barrages would support the attack as would Hughes's battalion, which was to "advance its left to conform to the progress of the attack." Once Wise gained his objective he would establish liaison with Hughes on the right while slightly refusing his left flank along the Lucy-Château Belleau ravine.

Harbord's new order set zero hour at 4:30 A.M.[30]

Notes

1. *Records*, Vol. 6.
2. *Records*, Vol. 5.
3. Ibid.
4. Ibid.
5. Ibid.
6. General Gerald C. Thomas, USMC (ret). Personal interview with the author.
7. Captain Louis F. Timmerman. Personal interview with the author.
8. *Records*, Vol. 9.
9. General Clifton B. Cates, USMC (ret). Personal interview with the author.
10. A. Golaz, "Belleau Woods June 1918." *Revue Historique de l'Armée*. Special issue 1957. Bischoff was later awarded Germany's highest decoration for his defense of the wood.
11. Ibid.
12. Kemper F. Cowing and Courtney Riley Cooper, *Dear Folks at Home—*. New York: Houghton Mifflin Co., 1919.
13. Ernst Otto, "The Battles for the Possession of Belleau Woods, June, 1918." *U. S. Naval Institute Proceedings*, November, 1928.
14. *Translations*, Vols. 1–3.
15. *Records*, Vol. 6.
16. Ibid.
17. Ibid.
18. Ibid.
19. Ibid. See also *Records*, Vol. 4: division records a telephone call from Harbord who at 7:15 A.M. stated, ". . . The artillery blew the wood all to hell."
20. E. N. McClellan, "Capture of Hill 142, Battle of Belleau Wood, and Capture of Bouresches." *Marine Corps Gazette*, September–December, 1920;

John W. Thomason, Jr., "Second Division Northwest of Château Thierry, 1 June–10 July, 1918." Washington: National War College, 1928. Unpublished manuscript; U. S. Marine Corps, *History of the Sixth Machine Gun Battalion*. Neuwied, Germany: 1919. Since June 1 Major Cole had time and again exposed himself to enemy fire while overseeing forward gun positions. On this occasion he was badly wounded and on June 10 he died. Captain Harlan Major replaced him until June 11 when Captain George Osterhout took over; on June 21 Major Littleton T. Waller, Jr., who had been commanding the 8th Machine Gun Battalion in the 3d U. S. Division, relieved Osterhout.

21. *Records*, Vol. 6.
22. Ibid.
23. Thomas, op. cit.
24. Cowing, op. cit.
25. *Records*, Vol. 5.
26. *Records*, Vol. 6.
27. Cowing, op. cit.
28. *Records*, Vol. 4.
29. Ibid.
30. *Records*, Vol. 6.

Chapter 17

*"In my judgement, the capture of the
Bois de Belleau is the most important event
that has taken place for the Allied holding in
this vicinity . . ."*
—Brigadier General Harbord to Major General Bundy,
June 11, 1918

Harbord's order to attack on June 11 (see map p.
232) started a chain of events that led to the single
most controversial action at Belleau Wood. As one
result, Wise would lose his command; as another, the
world would learn of a false victory; as a third, two
battalions of marines would miss death or capture by
a hair.

On June 10 Wise's main position, the ridge west
of the Lucy-Torcy road, was held by two companies:
considerably to the left Lieutenant Cooke's 55th Company defended the north edge of Champillon Wood;
Captain Lloyd Williams's 51st Company, which had
been attached to Turrill's line on Hill 142, was just
reporting back to battalion. The earlier fighting,
coupled with the spasmodic action of the last four days,
had prevented the men from getting much rest and
little, if any, hot food. All units were considerably

understrength; since June 1 the battalion had lost about twenty-five percent of its personnel. Officers and men both were nervous. Cooke reported:

> We had a brigade machine gun in the 18th Company sector. One night it had orders to fire at certain intervals. After it fired each time, zip-bang, zip-bang, would come some Austrian 88s. This happened several times before a runner came up to Colonel Wise and said:
>
> "Colonel Wise, Lieutenant Jackson presents his respects and says if that machine gun officer fires again he is going to kill him."
>
> It was our old friend, Gil Jackson, speaking in his natural manner. The machine gun fired no more.[1]

On the afternoon of June 10, Harbord ordered Captain Platt's 20th Company up from reserve to relieve Cooke's company, which rejoined Wise's main position. Wise, meanwhile, reported to brigade headquarters where he received Harbord's attack order. Back at his own P.C. he called in his company commanders to brief them on the forthcoming attack. His intelligence officer, Lieutenant Bill Mathews, was present:

> By early evening of June 10 the company commanders had all reported. Wise got down on his knees and spread the French hachured map on the ground. . . . The battalion was to attack at 4:30 A.M. through the big open space at the south end of the woods with the 43d Company [Dunbeck] on the left in two waves and the 51st Company [Williams] on the right in two waves. . . . The 51st was to attack due north and when it hit the road in the woods to follow it to the edge of the woods, detach one platoon to clear out the woods (a small clump) that was alongside the Belleau-Bouresches road, while the rest of the company was to turn west and bear down on Hill 133 with the hope of taking the Germans from the rear and making a bag of prisoners. The 43rd was to attack due north, but as it had more woods to

clear out . . . they were not expected to make as rapid progress as the 51st.[2]

Under cover of darkness the company commanders assembled their platoons on a ridge protected by fronting woods. Throughout the night American artillery—heavy 155s—shelled the target area. As zero hour approached, Captain Lester Wass and Lieutenant Cooke were smoking a final cigarette when, as Cooke reported:

> Suddenly, overhead sounded the rustling swish of passing shells. The sound grew louder and louder and a hurricane of steel lashed and tore at the borders of Belleau Wood.
> "What's the matter?"
> Wass had halted, facing east. A faint glow was on the misty horizon. He looked down at the luminous dial on his wrist watch. "Four thirty," he answered, in a tight, hard voice. "So long." Up from the ground rose the assaulting waves. They moved forward into a thick mist, followed by Wass and me in support. With the attack barely started, some light Maxims that had gotten inside our barrage zone opened fire. Our forward lines stumbled for a moment, then moved on through the tall wheat. Through a fence and clear of the grain—no more concealment except for the heavy clinging mist; that was a gift of Providence. The ground had been ploughed for spring planting. It was being worked again— torn and ripped into deep holes by the barrage that crept just ahead of our assault.[3]

The leading companies made it across the road and part way through the field under the cover of morning mist. But contrary to Harbord's orders, they were heading toward the lower portion of the wood's waist—the boundary between Hartlieb's battalion and the right of the 2d Battalion, 40th Fusiliers. And as they approached the angle of the woods the mist came to life. On the right Lieutenant Sam Cummings of the 51st Company watched the wave move forward at a slow pace, keeping perfect lines. Men were being mowed down like wheat. A "whizz-bang" (high-explosive shell) hit on my right, and an automatic team which was there a moment ago disappeared, while men on the right and left were armless, legless, or tearing at their faces. We continued to advance until about fifty yards from the woods, when something hit me and I spun around and hit flat.[4]

Dunbeck's 43d Company moved slightly farther before the German guns opened to punch huge gaps through its neat lines. Sergeant Thomas, sent forward by Hughes to find out what was happening on Wise's front, watched the action from the right:

About half-way from our line in the southern part of the wood to where Wise was supposed to be, I heard a hell of a lot of firing to my left. I climbed a slope, saw Wise and his command group in a wheatfield ahead. On his left and slightly forward the attacking waves were moving through the field, the men falling right and left.

I beat it up to Wise, told him who I was and what I wanted. We had to shout over the noise of the firing.

A runner came up, reported himself from the 43d Company and said, "Colonel, our men are being shot to hell in the wood—we need some help."

Wise turned to someone and said, "Tell that 18th Company to get up there to the woods."

Then he turned to the boy and said, "Who told you your company's in trouble?"

The boy said, "The wounded."

"Hell," Wise snorted, "don't you know that wounded are very poor witnesses?" He then countermanded his order and turned to me. "I tell you what you can do for me. One of your companies was supposed to attack on our right and I haven't seen them. I want you to find that company commander and tell him I want him to move out."

With no real idea of what was happening, except that Wise was getting the hell shot out of him, I followed the edge of the wood to the right until I heard heavy fire to my front. I went up there and found [Lieutenant] Megan Overton. His company was assaulting the last of the enormous machine gun nests on Wise's flank. I arrived while Megan was exchanging shots with a German officer standing on top of a huge boulder. Just as I came up to Megan his .45 automatic bucked and the German fell—dead as we later found out.

I told Megan what Wise had said. Overton answered, "Well, I've done what I was supposed to do. If Wise had brought his outfit into the woods instead of deploying them out there in the wheatfield, he wouldn't have lost all those men."[5]

Wise was meanwhile losing a great many more men, and had already lost control of his companies. Before anyone could stop them, the support companies merged with the assault. Until then, Lieutenant Cooke's 55th Company had not been hurt. And then:

Through the mist the forest loomed up as a grim shadow. We entered a deep indentation of the woods and the shadows moved to surround us. Without the slightest warning those shadows suddenly were split apart by chattering, stabbing flames. A crackling sheath of machine-gun bullets encased our battalion, doing in on us fiercely.

"Down! Down! Take cover!"

Some were already down—down to stay. Many hurled themselves into the nearest shell hole, but a few of those kids stubbornly pushed forward until their legs were shot out from under them. As the first handful of bullets whipped past my head, I hit the deck and rolled into the nearest crater. [Lieutenant] Parker followed, then Sergeant Brown; and lastly, with the pound of sprinting feet, Whitey, my runner, came hurtling in. We snuggled close in our shelter until the holocaust of steel subsided.

Peeking over the crater's edge, I saw one of my connecting files stretched close to earth in a furrow of ground. I crawled forward and shook his leg. The man was dead. To one side lay another, doubled up, both arms locked rigidly about his shattered middle. Off to the left a gun rattled and bullets searched the air a few inches above my cowering body. When the gun ceased I lifted my head and saw a third man crawling towards me, painfully dragging his right leg. It was Lieutenant Cummings of the 51st Company and his ankle was smashed.

"Where's your outfit?" I asked, as we got back to the shell hole and administered first aid.

"The machine guns got 'em. As far as I know I'm the only one left out of ten officers and two hundred and fifty men. . . ."[6]

Cummings was wrong: Captain Williams and the remnants of his company had pushed through to smash into the flank of the 2d Battalion, 40th Fusiliers. Private Steck later reported:

Hand grenades were distributed and then Captain Williams lined us up in combat formation. Soon we were going single file through the woods and charging across the open area to where the Germans were secluded in their holes.

My duties were to load a chauchat or French automatic rifle. You could run about nine steps and then another clip would have to be inserted. Bullets slit my canteen, hit my scabbard, and two or three went through my trousers without touching me. We had advanced in triangle formation about half a mile. I was in the front end of the "V" when three machine gun bullets got me. One went into the neck, another in my left shoulder, and the third in my arm.

I tried to keep on in assisting the operation of the automatic but the blood came up in my throat. I forced my way back and hid in a shell hole in the woods until a little Marine found me. This fellow dragged me 500 yards on his shoulder to a first aid dugout. There a shelter-half was used as a stretcher and I was taken back to a larger dressing station.[7]

While Williams's company was being chewed up, Overton's company of the 6th Marines was working hard to eliminate part of the flanking machine-gun fire. On Williams's left the survivors of Dunbeck's 43d Company were also pushing through against Hartlieb's left.

Not knowing the exact situation, Cooke decided that if Williams's company was wiped out, then Dunbeck's right must be exposed:

> For the first time since the battle started I actually shucked off fear like an old coat. Duty, responsibility, and something like rage took command of my thoughts. Those damn Boche couldn't go shooting up our whole outfit and get away with it like that.
>
> I stood up in plain sight and blew a blast on my whistle. From holes, furrows, and clods of dirt, faces looked up. Eyes, thankful to see someone in authority, watched expectantly. I pointed at the woods to our right front. Parker, Brown, and I walked forward.
>
> At the trees I turned, half expecting to find ourselves alone. We weren't. About twenty men were right behind us. And more came running, eager to do anything that was wanted.[8]

Pushing east, Cooke's small force ran on an enemy machine gun whose one surviving crew member quickly surrendered. He next ran into a sizable force of Germans who indicated they wanted to surrender. In the process one of them thought Cooke was going to fire and fired on him, wounding him slightly in the hip. With that his men rushed forward but the enemy threw their hands in the air, screaming *"Kamerad."* After sending them to the rear, Cooke continued east. By this time what was left of the 51st Company was slightly ahead and to his right. Dunbeck's 43d Company followed closely by Wass's 18th Company (advancing in half platoon columns—what was called "artillery formation") was on his left. Incredibly heavy undergrowth prevented contact between platoons, much less companies. It was small-unit warfare in the fullest sense; dirty, murderous fighting against entrenched machine guns flanked by other machine guns that took the most awful toll of the attacking marines. Still, yard by yard the isolated groups pushed forward across the wood to what they thought was the objective. At 6:11 A.M. Captain Dunbeck notified Wise: "All objectives reached and am mopping up with machine guns."[9]

Dunbeck was wrong: he had reached the eastern edge of the wood, not the northeastern end. His position was approximately Hughes's objective of the previous day, that is a line toward the northern end of the thin waist. On the extreme left the survivors of Wass's 18th Company stood precisely where Wise's extreme right should have been.

Less than two hours after the initial attack the marines were hopelessly disoriented.

Back in his P.C. the brigade commander was undergoing what he called the "hard waiting." A few days later he would write in his diary:

> You know your people have started forward, and the outcome is on the knees of the gods. You can do nothing more, but you wish you could, and it is sometimes hours before you know what is happening. The telephone wires are cut; runners are killed; your men are out of sight and hearing. . . .
>
> You wish more than anything else in the world to know the exact position of your troops, and exactly where the enemy is with reference to them; where you can ask the artillery to place their further fire; whether or not the casualties have been heavy among our people, and among the Germans; and the number of prisoners. This information sometimes takes a day and night to filter in, and it is difficult to be patient. The telephone gets cut at critical times. . . . Officers under fire are oblivious to the passage of time and forget the importance of reports. You can't help them unless you know where they are, how they are and when. Reports come in without the hour on them, and are worthless, for you do not know when the conditions reported existed. . . .

Meanwhile one waits, and walks the floor, or smokes (some play solitaire), or worry over whether you have left anything undone or not.[10]

In the case of Wise's attack on June 11 Harbord did not have to wait as long as usual for the first reports. At 5:00 A.M. Captain Gill, liaison officer with the 5th Marines, notified him: "Everything seems to be going along nicely." At 5:10: "Everything going well." At 5:27: "Germans retiring over hill. Regimental runner and battalion runner reported prisoners taken."[11]

Harbord's attention was now momentarily diverted by messages from Lieutenant Colonel Harry Lee, commanding 6th Marines, that the enemy was massing for an attack against Bouresches. Harbord immediately ordered an artillery barrage laid on them. At 5:55 A.M. Major Shearer reported: "Germans along railway tracks. Request barrage closer." Five minutes later he notified Harbord: "Germans attacking with machine guns and infantry."[12]

Although none of the commanders realized it, the Germans were not attacking Bouresches. The enemy formation observed and fired on was actually the reserve company of the 2d Battalion, 40th Fusiliers, hastily summoned to meet the attack in Belleau Wood. And as the right flank of that German battalion was rolled up by the marine assault with its front simultaneously hit by Hughes's battalion to the south, a good many German survivors began leaving the wood in favor of the small railroad line to the east. At 6:33 A.M. Lee notified Harbord:

2d Battalion, 5th, gained objective. Attacks on Bouresches broken up by artillery and machine guns. The Germans were caught by Shearer's machine guns while retreating from Bois de Belleau and were wiped out.[13]

In the interim, Harbord had begun receiving information from Wise, who at first was noncommittal. At 5:50 he reported: "Firing has begun again. I can hear nothing but the fire of my automatic rifles." Three minutes later: "Machine gun fire begins and stops again."[14]

Wise could have reported far more significant information at this time. About an hour earlier he had ordered his intelligence officer, Lieutenant Bill Mathews, to guide a platoon from the 6th Marines to the Lucy-Torcy road where it was to clear the fringes of any lingering enemy. At the road Mathews found Captain de Carre, commanding the Headquarters Company of Wise's battalion. Alone of the company commanders, de Carre had led his platoons toward the objective originally specified by Harbord. He had just returned from the wooded area around Hill 169 where he surprised and accepted the surrender of the better part of a German company. In passing he mentioned to Mathews that the entire left of Belleau Wood was open.

Mathews hurried back to Wise to report this vital intelligence which de Carre presently confirmed. Although Wise had not yet heard from his company commanders, he refused to believe it, an attitude reinforced minutes later by Dunbeck's message stating: "all objectives reached." At 6:50 Wise reported a message from Captain Williams who "was holding everything. Machine guns are causing damage on our right rear. Request company be sent in."[15]

At 7:00 A.M. Harbord learned from Hughes to the south that "everything is O.K. and in good shape."[16]

He then notified division:

Enemy made strong attack on Bouresches about 5 A.M. Reported en masse. Attack repulsed. Enemy masses broken by our artillery fire.

The northern end of the Bois de Belleau belongs to 5th Marines. Twenty prisoners sent back and others reported coming. Great slaughter of fleeing Germans as they left the Bois de Belleau by our machine guns from a flank.

Losses: eight killed, twenty-four wounded.[17]

The false but good news continued arriving. At 7:05 Lee reported:

About sixty prisoners have passed through and the report is that they are surrendering in numbers up in the Bois de Belleau. From Hughes: . . . Machine gun nest on my right front partly neutralized by use of mortars and rifle fire. Have had nothing direct from Wise since attack began.[18]

For over two hours Harbord learned nothing more of importance, but had no reason to believe the situation was changing. At 8:42 he notified division that 135 German prisoners were on hand "and more are coming in."[19]

But then at 9:45 he received a message written by Wise nearly an hour earlier in which the battalion commander called for a barrage from the northeast corner of the wood to run some 800 yards east. In the same message Wise reported:

> Captain Williams wounded. Casualties quite heavy as the barrage did not clean things up. We have the situation in hand but the 6th [Regiment] has not come up on right. The barrage is badly needed and artillery officer could be used as we have spotted a nest of enemy artillery.[20]

Thirty minutes later Wise submitted a situation sketch and noted, "All reports full of confidence. Artillery barrage and officer badly needed." Harbord did not receive this message until 10:15; at the same time he learned:

> Commanding officer 55th Company [Cooke] reports all companies have obtained their objectives and losses have been so heavy that we are only able to hold one line. We need barrage at once.[21]

At 10:30 Colonel Neville requested "two companies engineers to help dig in that position as losses are reported heavy. About 150 more prisoners on the way."[22]

The cautious optimism expressed in these messages now began to give way to victory tones. At 10:45 Wise reported:

> Counter battery work is needed as well as a barrage as we are being shelled regularly and it is coming from those guns on my map. In touch with 6th Regiment. If I can get the artillery I am satisfied.[23]

At the same time, Wise reported a message from Captain Wass: "Have obtained our objective. The enemy are preparing counterattack on our left flank. We need barrage immediately along Bouresches—Belleau Road, the northwest along our front." Ten minutes later Wise sent off another message by runner:

> Artillery officer arrived and will be a great help. Positions are now organized; in perfect touch with the 6th [Regiment]. I will shortly inspect and can then give an idea of losses. Think we can get more prisoners as lots of them are hiding afraid to give up, so with German speaking men we are going to comb them out. We have lost quite a few officers.[24]

As this and the other messages indicate, Wise was completely in the dark as to the true location of his companies, not to mention their shot-up state. Although he had refused to believe de Carre's earlier assertion that his left flank lay open, he had eventually sent Mathews and his small intelligence section forward to reconnoiter. Mathews later reported:

> With my men I went up through the big clearing, but when we came near the woods we ran on to scores of wounded who were lying unattended calling for help. We started giving first aid as best we could. A few minutes afterward [Marine Gunner] Mike Wordazeck came marching out of the woods with a large group of prisoners of the 40th German regiment. . . . We could find no one in the north part of the woods and when I asked Mike what was over there he said nothing. I went back into the woods with Mike and he directed me to the point where I found Dunbeck, Wass, and Lieutenant Cooke standing together. . . . I said to them:
> "Are you sure you have reached your objectives?"
> All of them spoke up and said yes, and I distinctly remember that one of them, I believe it was Dunbeck, said: "We are at the north end of the woods, because there is Torcy (pointing to Belleau) and there is Belleau (pointing to Bouresches)." When I asked them or rather told them that a

great mass of the woods to the left was totally unoccupied they insisted that it was all behind them and therefore safe.[25]

Convinced he was right, Mathews formed half of his men into an observation post on the line and with the rest returned to Wise's P.C. After telling the battalion commander where he had been, he "emphasized that the whole left flank of the woods was absolutely unprotected."

Wise's plump face flushed. "You goddamn young bonehead, you don't know what you're talking about. I have messages from my company commanders saying they are at the north end of the woods."[26]

Furious at his commander's intransigence, Mathews took his men forward to the controversial piece of wood to make still another reconnaissance. Apparently, however, his words had given Wise some doubt, for at 11:25 he sent a runner off with this message to Harbord:

I think my left flank is rather weak. The Germans are massing in our front. I can hardly spare any men. They could easily filter through tonight for counter-attack. Nothing new to report except increased artillery activity.[27]

Harbord would not receive this message until nearly two hours later and then, as will be seen, it would not greatly alter his thinking. For at 11:00 he had received the most incredible message of all from Colonel Neville, who, like Wise and himself, was remaining remote from the frontline action. Neville reported: "Do not need any more companies now. Everything O.K. Believe our casualties slight. From ravine all [the] way to Wise's flank O.K."[28]

Obviously taking those messages received at face value without checking further on their accuracy, Harbord was steadily growing more optimistic. He held ample artillery to meet Wise's barrage requests, while at division Preston Brown at once had ordered up two companies of engineers to help consolidate the new line. At

11:45, in what is probably the most premature message ever sent from one commander to another, Harbord notified Wise via Neville:

> The Division Commander [Bundy] is at Brigade Headquarters and sends hearty congratulations to you and your gallant men. He says the task could not have been performed any better. The objectives of the Brigade have been attained everywhere after days of fighting which the Division Commander has never known to be excelled. To this I add my warm personal greetings and congratulations.[29]

While Wise was reading this message, Mathews's scouts were reporting no sign of anyone in the wood to the north. Mathews, more sure than ever that he was correct, then drew a rough sketch of his position:

> I took up a position in a little group of bushes that juts out into the big clearing which was an enemy machine gun position. (The machine gun was still there.) I sent this map in to Wise with a message urging the importance of filling this gap with some troops. My messenger came back with the message that Wise could not understand my map. I had drawn it as the woods actually were at that point and of course he could not reconcile it with the French map he had. I then left my men and went back to Wise myself and pleaded the importance of filling this gap and pointed out that something must be done and done quickly. As we were talking a Marine came in with a prisoner whom he had found over in the west part of the big clearing. This marine had gone back with prisoners early in the fight and was coming back over his original ground. This prisoner was a hospital orderly and he told us that had we acted sooner all of the enemy in the woods would have surrendered, but that by now they had been reinforced. Wise now realized that I was not dreaming. When I urged the importance of getting the gap filled quickly he replied:
> "Where in the hell am I going to get them?"

I told him to take the 6th Regiment men who were lying along side the woods north of battalion headquarters,
but he said he couldn't. I went back to my men and a little
while later Lieutenant Edgar Allan Poe with a platoon of
6th Regiment men appeared followed a little later by Wise.
He then saw how serious the situation was and proceeded to
reconnoiter about six hours too late.[30]

Harbord, of course, held no idea of the new development. In
early afternoon and "owing to the inefficiency of telephone service
to Division Headquarters and repeated failures to get communication," he submitted a written report which reviewed the morning's
action and concluded:

> . . . In my judgement, the capture of the Bois de Belleau is
> the most important event that has taken place for the Allied
> holding in this vicinity. I do not believe there would be any
> advance in this region without first an attempt to dislodge
> us from the Bois de Belleau.[31]

Harbord's report could only strengthen the belief held by General
Bundy that the wood had been taken. At 12:55 P.M. he telegraphed
General Pershing:

> After a heavy artillery preparation in the northern half of
> Bois de Belleau this morning attack was delivered. Reports
> indicate that attack has reached the northern and eastern
> limits of the woods and that our troops have occupied the
> eastern edge. Approximately 250 prisoners, including three
> officers, have been taken, and a number of machine guns
> and two 7-inch minenwerfers [trench mortars]. One or two
> machine gun nests remain in the woods which will have to
> be reduced. Our casualties comparatively light considering
> the nature of this operation.[32]

Here was welcome news indeed, coming as it did with the slowing German attack on the Montdidier-Noyon front, and Pershing's

headquarters did not hesitate in releasing it to the world. On June 12 the headlines of the *New York Times* announced:

OUR MEN TAKE BELLEAU WOOD, 300 CAPTIVES.
Paris, June 11—The official statement of the War Office to-night says: South of the Ourcq River the American troops this morning brilliantly captured Belleau Wood and took 300 prisoners. . . .[33]

The War Office was wrong, Pershing was wrong, so were Bundy, Harbord and Wise. They would not learn their error for another day; they would then discover that the marines, much less than capturing the northern portion of Belleau Wood, had not even entered it.

Notes

1. Major E. D. Cooke, "We Can Take It," *Infantry Journal*, May–December, 1937.
2. William R. Mathews, "Official Report to Headquarters, U. S. Marine Corps, September 28, 1921."
3. Cooke, op. cit.
4. Kemper F. Cowing and Courtney Riley Cooper, *Dear Folks at Home—*. New York; Houghton Mifflin Co., 1919.
5. General Gerald C. Thomas, USMC (ret). Personal interview with the author.
6. Cooke, op. cit.
7. A. W. Catlin, *With the Help of God and a Few Marines*. New York: Doubleday, Page and Co., 1919.
8. Cooke, op. cit.
9. *Records*, Vol. 6.
10. James G. Harbord, *Leaves from a War Diary*. New york; Dodd, Mead and Co., 1925.
11. *Records*, Vol. 6.
12. *Records*, Vol. 5.
13. *Records*, Vol. 6.
14. Ibid.
15. Ibid.
16. Ibid.
17. *Records*, Vol. 4.

18. *Records,* Vol. 6.
19. *Records,* Vol. 4.
20. *Records,* Vol. 6.
21. Ibid.
22. Ibid.
23. Ibid.
24. Ibid. Lieutenant Mathews was with Wise when he learned of Captain Williams's death. "I would rather have lost my right arm," he said.
25. Mathews, op. cit.
26. Ibid.
27. *Records,* Vol. 6.
28. Ibid.
29. Ibid.
30. Mathews, op. cit. Wise relieved Mathews as intelligence officer, returning him to his old platoon which he subsequently commanded with distinction.
31. *Records,* Vol. 6.
32. Ibid.
33. *New York Times,* June 12, 1918.

Chapter 18

*"All objectives reached and we are
consolidating. . . ."*
—Lieutenant Colonel Wise to Brigadier General
Harbord, June 12, 1918

Had Wise's assault struck the area designated by Harbord's order, it would have met only one company of Hartlieb's battalion. Failing this opportunity, his assault companies quite by chance fell on the next weakest portion of the line: the jointure between Hartlieb's left and the right of the 2d Battalion, 40th Regiment (see map p. 268).

Since June 8 the 2d Battalion, 40th Regiment, had defended an east-west line across the wood with two companies up and two in reserve, a deployment criticized as far too weak by Major Bischoff commanding the regiment on the right. Bischoff's line, which ran from the 2d Battalion's right up the west face of the wood and then curved toward Torcy, was held by Hartlieb's 1st Battalion plus two companies of the 2d Battalion. Hartlieb placed a reserve company, the 3d, in close support and kept a final company of the regimental reserve, the 5th, back at his P.C., which was the hunting lodge in the northwest corner of the wood.

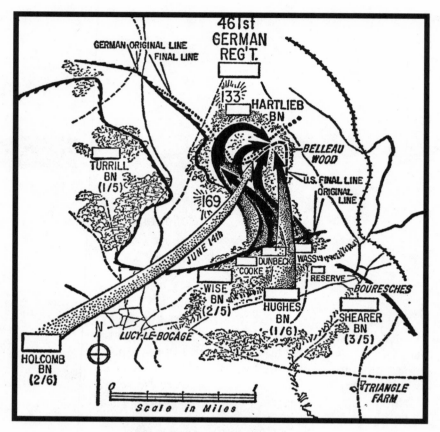

Belleau Wood

Marine Attacks
June 12–15, 1918

On June 11 the initial marine attack by Williams's 51st Company struck the extreme right of the east-west line while simultaneously Overton's company attacked it frontally. On Williams's left, Dunbeck pushed in against the front and flank of Hartlieb's 1st Company which began to yield when Wass joined the attack.

The combined assault on the right soon rolled up the east-west defensive line: while Williams and Cooke hammered its flank and Overton its front, heavy artillery fire decimated reserves hurriedly called in from east of the wood. At the same time, Dunbeck and Wass pushed back Hartlieb's 8th Company, then turned the flank of the 1st Company to expose the neighboring 4th Company. By midmorning the 1st and 4th companies were virtually eliminated, the 3d and 8th companies slowly retiring. Sometime during this day one of Hartlieb's men, Private Hebel, wrote in a letter:

> We are having very heavy days with death before us hourly. Here we have no hope ever to come out. My company has been reduced from 120 to thirty men. . . . We are now at the worst stage of the offensive, the time of counter-attacks. We have Americans (marines) opposite us who are terribly reckless fellows. In the last eight days I have not slept twenty hours. . . .[1]

At this point a less energetic commander than Hartlieb might well have retired from the wood. Instead, he collected his remnants, called up two reserve companies and led a counterattack down the west side of the wood. Finding his old positions unoccupied, he set up a series of strong points and pushed out patrols in a vain search for the 40th Regiment. When his reserves came up he reorganized his old line from about 100 yards north of Hill 181 along the western face and then slightly to the northeast where its right anchored on a rocky knoll just south of the hunting lodge.

In early afternoon a fresh battalion of the 28th Division filtered into the wood from the north and went into position on Hartlieb's left.

Once again the Germans held a defensive line.[2]

On the afternoon of June 11, Harbord received only scant information concerning enemy movement—nothing to deprive him of his earlier optimism. Wise's earlier message stating that "I think my left flank is rather weak . . ." arrived at 1:18 P.M. A little later Neville's adjutant, Captain Shuler, notified him in a delayed message:

> At 12:02 troops still reported massing on our front in the direction of Belleau and Torcy and think counter-attack is on foot. Companies 43rd, 51st and 18th have about thirty men each lost and 55th about eighty-three. I can hardly believe the latter. Increased shelling.[3]

Colonel Lee next reported:

> Overton [commanding the company on Hughes's left] just beat off Boche counter-attack. Just sent two platoons to Wise as he said enemy were on his left. Have men in good spirits.[4]

At 1:50 Wise reported that according to a prisoner a German division was in the village of Belleau.

Harbord's frame of mind was obvious from the reply he sent to Wise at 2:00 P.M.

> Artillery very watchful on your left flank. You need have no fear of it. Use your engineers to consolidate your front as rapidly as possible. Refuse your left flank slightly, along ravine or higher up along edge of woods. Let us know your losses as accurately as you can give them. What are your capture of machine guns? Your affair today was certainly well handled and is the biggest thing in prisoners that the American Expeditionary Force has yet pulled off. We are all delighted. Approximately 1000 replacements arriving for the Brigade today.[5]

Meanwhile Wise was carrying out his first frontline reconnaissance. On the extreme right of his position he found the remnants of Williams's 51st Company with "some junior in command." Wise reported:

I went on down the line. Lieutenant Cook [sic] was un-wounded, but he had lost several of his juniors and a lot of his men. . . . His outfit, too, were in fox holes and waiting for the expected German counter-attack.

Farther down the line I found Captain Dunbeck and what was left of his outfit. . . . Down on the left flank I found Captain Wass. Most of his juniors were gone, and half his men. What was left of his company had dug in, too, on the German edge of the woods. . . .

"Do we hold the extreme point of the woods at this end?" I asked Captain Wass.

"No, sir, we don't," he said. "There are a lot of Ger-mans over in that northeast corner. We didn't have enough men to extend over there."

. . . There was a problem. The Germans were evidently in that point of woods in some force. Yet I didn't have the men to attack them. I knew now that over half of my battal-ion was gone. The remnant, in fox holes, was strung out in a very thin line over nearly a two-mile front [sic]. God alone knew what minute the counter-attack was coming. We would have all we could attend to, just holding that line, when it came. And yet the presence of those Germans on our flank meant trouble unless they were cleaned out.

Also their presence put me in a devil of a fix. Based on the reports of my company commanders earlier in the day, I had reported to Colonel Neville at regimental headquarters that those woods were cleaned out. And Colonel Neville had reported that back to Brigade.[6]

According to Wise's later account, he returned to his P.C. to find Major Hughes, who agreed to lend him a company from his battalion to the south. He then informed regimental headquarters of the situation. Before the reinforcing company could come up, Wise reported that

a runner reached my P.C. with orders from General Harbord at brigade headquarters to pay no attention to the Germans on my left flank; that our artillery would take care of them. There was damned little satisfaction in that for me. I kept sending runners to regimental headquarters reiterating the fact of our losses, of the thin line with which we held the long front, and of the presence of those Germans in unknown force in those woods on our left flank.[7]

The official records contain none of these alleged messages, whose worth in any case would have been of questionable value. Harbord already knew Wise had suffered some casualties, and it was Wise's fault more than anyone else's that he did not know just how many. To repair the loss, he had sent up two companies of engineers and 150 marine replacements; in addition, Wise had one platoon from Hughes's battalion with two more on the way. At this point Harbord needed accurate information regarding the location of his front line—and in this respect Wise remained as ignorant as ever.

Wise did not receive Harbord's afternoon message until late evening. Taking Mathews with him, he went forward to withdraw his left flank in accordance with Harbord's orders. The two officers found Lieutenant Poe's platoon engaged in a hot fire fight on the left. Acting on Wise's orders, Mathews succeeded in getting them back to what Wise believed was the ravine designated by Harbord. But Harbord's ravine lay in the center of the northern portion of the wood; Wise's ravine was a small trail crossing the northern end of the wood's waist, a line over 800 yards south.

This was the incredibly muddled situation on the night of June 11 when Harbord made his twenty-four-hour report to division. After again reviewing the day's events, he noted:

> . . . Liaison is established between Bouresches, Major Hughes in the southeast corner of the Bois de Belleau, and with Lieutenant Colonel Wise's battalion to the northwest corner of the Bois near [Hill] 133, his left flank being slightly refused.[8]

If this information was slightly at odds with Harbord's earlier reports, no one at division seemed to notice. To Bundy and his staff, June 11 had proven a red-letter day as proclaimed in division's final report of operations:

. . . At 4:30 A.M. after artillery preparations, and preceded by a rolling barrage, our troops attacked the northern edge of Bois de Belleau and captured the entire woods. The attack was a complete success in every respect. Heavy losses were inflicted upon the enemy in killed and wounded. We captured more than 400 prisoners and much material including fifty-five machine guns, four trench mortars and trench mortar ammunition. . . . 200 wounded officers and men all grades have been evacuated up to 7:30 P.M. as a result of our attack this morning. No report as to number killed has been received up to the present time, but they are very light considering the operation carried out.[9]

Early on June 12, Wise carried out another inspection of his front line:

The woods had been cleared of all the wounded. The dead still lay where they fell. I was much better satisfied with the line. Those engineers and replacements had helped. It was well sprinkled with machine guns now—our own and captured German weapons. I wasn't afraid, then, of any break through.[10]

Later in the morning, Wise reported this state of affairs to Harbord, Neville and Feland. During the meeting,

[Wise] expressed the opinion that with a certain amount of artillery preparation he could capture the remainder of the Bois de Belleau. Accordingly it was arranged that artillery play on the north-western section of the Bois de Belleau until 5 P.M. when an attack is to be made. In this connection verbal orders were given to the 12th Field Artillery.[11]

The decision to attack was a curious one, completely at odds with the known facts. Although the night had proven relatively quiet in the wood, intermittent sniper, rifle and machine-gun fire still marked the presence of the enemy. Runners and stretcher-bearers working between the front line and Wise's P.C. were constantly fired on; so were the marines on Wise's left and from a distance of *only fifty feet*. Further, the commanders by now knew beyond any doubt that Wise's battalion was badly shot up, its ranks further thinned by water and ration details sent to the rear; as professional soldiers, they must have known the disadvantages inherent in attacking with green replacements, no matter how good their spirit, supported by engineer troops, no matter how good in their own specialty.

But psychological and tactical factors again asserted themselves. Having announced to the world that Belleau Wood was captured, it was incumbent upon the commanders, particularly Harbord and Wise, to capture it without further delay. So long as Wise's position was where everyone believed it to be, this did not seem too great a task: a matter of eliminating a few isolated machine-gun positions.

Even with such important factors in play, a more prudent commander might have hesitated until gaining additional information through reconnaissance or until bringing additional strength to the wood. A more prudent commander might have smelled a rat in a message sent by Wise at 10:00 A.M.:

> Men in fine shape and line is holding but getting thinner. Heavy shelling and some gas. About out of officers. Request barrage immediately. Are getting hell shelled out of us now.[12]

Unfortunately it was too late for prudence; on June 12, Harbord wanted Belleau Wood very badly.

The decision to attack was accepted more than welcomed by the tired marines. Lieutenant Cooke later recalled:

> We didn't want to make an attack. Hundreds of our men lay stiff in death already. A large part of our effectives were replacements. Reaction from the attack of the day before had left us low in morale and courage. . . .[13]

They didn't want to attack, but by midafternoon they were ready. By force of circumstances the plan was simple: three companies in line, from left to right, Cooke, Dunbeck and Wass. The pathetic remnant of Williams's 51st Company formed the reserve; when relieved by elements of Hughes's battalion from the south, it would move forward.

The American artillery began its barrage on schedule. Since the guns registered just ahead of where everyone supposed Wise's line to be, their shells struck over a thousand yards in front of the actual line. The shells thus ignored immediate German resistance, and because of the heavy trees to the north and the dispersal of the enemy's reserve companies they did precious little damage where they struck. At 4:30 P.M. Wise notified Harbord through Neville:

> The artillery officer states that barrage was entirely too light and from 3:30 to 3:40 it entirely stopped and then the Germans pushed up their guns expecting us to come across. I request that it be increased and kept up for another hour. The artillery officer could do very little spotting. I am afraid we are going to have a bit of trouble. Area to be looked out for entirely too large for the number of guns assigned to us.[14]

Harbord agreed to the request; for another hour the American guns continued to fire into the northern reaches of Belleau Wood. Then it was 5:30 P.M. and there was nothing for it but to move out. At the sound of the whistles the marines forced themselves from their scanty shelters, grabbed heavy Springfields tipped with bayonets, crouched low and moved forward under the Hotchkiss fire from their rear. On Cooke's front, he later recalled:

> The Boche heard us coming and gave us all they had. Light machine guns camouflaged in trees, heavy guns on the ground, grenades, rifles, pistols; everything was turned loose at once. In front of me Sergeant Brown was bent nearly double, pulling his men forward with beckoning arms. A burst of bullets smashed into a man's jaw beside me, carrying away the lower part of his face. A grenade fell on the other side, tearing a youngster's legs to shreds. . . .[15]

Cooke's experience belonged to the line, yet the line inched forward. On Cooke's right, a bullet soon wounded Captain Dunbeck, his place instantly taken by Lieutenant "Drink" Milner, "a mild-mannered little chap" who now fought with the strength of ten. When sergeants fell, corporals picked up their commands; when they fell, privates took over.

And as the Dunbecks and the sergeants and corporals and privates fell, the marines threw off their lethargy and began to pound. "Eyah, eyah. . . ." It was the marine yell. They had learned it at Parris Island and Quantico, it was part of the bayonet and now it rang through the wood.

Within thirty minutes the marines overran the enemy's advanced positions to strike the main line of heavy machine guns. These were protected in front and on the flanks by infantry and by light machine gunners, some of them firing from the trees. In Cooke's company, Private Gastovitch spotted one of the gunners, raised his Springfield and fired. Almost simultaneously other shots rang out. The German threw out his arms, slid from the branch, fell, bounced off a sapling and struck the ground. Oblivious to the heavy fire, Gastovitch and several of his buddies raced for the body. "He's mine, he's mine," Gastovitch yelled, and before the others could come up the boy had the German's watch and wallet.[16]

By now it was a no-quarter fight, it was a kill or get killed proposition, and here the marines were at their best. On Cooke's front, he reported:

> We crushed the Germans' forward line and reached the ravine and clearing where Poe and I had stood the previous day. . . . The hostile fire we had undergone up 'til then was only a preliminary to what we received from across the clearing. One of my lieutenants went down, writhing and clawing at his face, begging to be gotten out of there. A sergeant ducked behind the tree next to mine just as a bullet hit and exploded the canteen on his belt. We both thought we were drenched with blood.
>
> Then, in the field on our left, from where they had been working around our flank, a group of gray-clad figures got

up like a covey of frightened quail. Big, husky Huns, running over the ploughed ground with stilted awkwardness in their heavy boots.

For a stupefied moment I stared with open mouth, then, clawing out my automatic, I let go an entire clip at their retreating backs. The whole company discharged a scattered volley—and we never hit a damn one!

From over to the right came a stirring yell. Sergeant Colvin of the 18th Company was going up the side of a rocky cliff after a machine gun, like a cat chasing birds on a tin roof. Still nearer was Wass, pursuing a frightened Heinie over a pile of cordwood.

"Eyah!" one of the 43d Company men suddenly screamed . . . the kids were started by that yell. Fear, hunger, fatigue—everything seemed forgotten in a mad lust to ram two feet of steel into some Heinie's innards.

Out into the open they surged, and much against my better judgment I was carried along in the excitement. Down into the ravine—our momentum carrying us halfway up the opposite side.

The hot blast of guns beat against our faces, grenades curved over our heads, underbrush and men dying clogged our feet. We pounded across a road, crashed into some thickets bordering the clearing and stood, wild-eyed and panting.

The Boche had slipped into the underbrush and run. And streaming through the woods were the scattered remnants of our battalion, hot in pursuit. Wass and Milner had apparently joined the chase, and so had everybody else.[17]

Little semblance of organization remained in the marine ranks. As the companies moved forward from the wood's waist, their numbers depleted even more from the heavy German fire, they automatically spread out to cover the wider front. Enemy resistance, now ragged and disorganized, added to the confusion until at the end of the fierce drive the marines found themselves in small groups sometimes commanded by officers, sometimes by privates. On the left

Milner and most of his 43d Company somehow crossed Cooke's front to end at the hunting lodge in the northwestern part of the wood. Milner climbed to its top, looked over the remaining part of the wood to the village of Belleau where he saw the enemy running through the streets. Moments later he was confronted by a wounded, English-speaking German officer backed by a considerable force of men. A hasty truce resulted while Milner offered the German a cigarette and wondered if he had captured the Germans or vice-versa. Finally the officer asked him for a guide to take him and his men back to surrender. Milner had to explain that be didn't know the location of his battalion. The German thereupon oriented him, warned of an impending counterattack and ordered his men, *sans* weapons, to follow him to the American rear.[18]

Cooke's men, meanwhile, "moved through the center of the woods, following a deep, undercut ditch that was full of discarded German equipment. Already we had lost our fury of the attack. We proceeded slowly, cautiously, even fearfully."[19]

On Cooke's right, Wass had reached the northeastern edge of the wood. Seeing the chaotic situation that was rapidly developing, the senior commander wisely passed the word for the left companies to guide right, then fell back along the eastern edge until his right flank connected with Hughes's vanguard.

This was the climax of the attack which already had pushed the German left out of the wood and had smashed von Hartlieb's defense into disorganized groups similar to those of the marine companies. Hartlieb, however, had not given up the wood. And now, as the marines started crabbing sideways to the right and the pressure noticeably lessened, the German commander, hastily reinforced from Belleau, collected his surviving detachments to form a thin line across a rocky knoll south of the hunting lodge. Simultaneously artillery batteries of the 5th Guards Division and the 28th Division were alerted to fire missions that would precede a counterattack as soon as sufficient infantry could be brought up.

Wass was meanwhile receiving limited reinforcement in the form of Lieutenant Burrows, commanding what was left of Company F, 2d Engineers. On the way up this company had been struck by a German counterbarrage of high-explosive and mustard-gas shells that killed Captain Lowen and four men, and wounded some twenty others. The survivors, dispersed and wearing cumbersome gas masks, got lost in the heavy undergrowth; only fifty of 185 men reached Wass, who put them in the line to his left.

Cooke next arrived with the survivors of the 55th Company and was soon joined by Milner and his people who went into line on the left of the engineers. Lieutenant Cooke later described the final, somewhat unsatisfactory position:

> Germans were still in the woods to our rear and on our left flank as well as to our front. They got right to work and started pounding us with machine guns. We soon tired of being sniped at from in rear. With a heavy combat patrol, we drove the Heinies out of their rocky pits on the hill behind us. But when we weakened our line, those on our front and flank closed in, threatening to cut us off. When we turned to meet that threat, the ones in rear moved forward again.
>
> I finally had Milner refuse his left flank into the form of a fish hook. We dug in, prepared to hold in spite of hell and high water. We lay in our fox-holes, shook off the sand that the one pounders covered us with and listened to the machine-gun bullets snap over our heads.[20]

Only a part of this fast, confused action filtered through to the higher American commands. At 6:15 P.M., forty-five minutes after the marines jumped off, Harbord learned from Wise:

> So far no reports, but machine gun fire has now ceased. We intended to use V. B.'s [rifle grenades] if held up. Trench mortars were in woods also. I am positive that everything is going along all right. There is heavy artillery fire on our entire position.[21]

Wise next received an encouraging message from Captain Wass:

> Have reached my objective and am holding it. No connection on left yet. Am trying to connect with 51st [Company]

and machine guns on right. Need guns and send men to fill gap between me and 51st. I think other companies are too far to northeast.[22]

The battalion commander included this report in a message sent off at 6:15 and received by Harbord at 7:38:

All objectives reached and we are consolidating. From prisoners we hear that one battalion of 500 men were in there. Dunbeck and [Lieutenant] Jackson wounded. Very short of men. Quite a heavy bombardment on P.C. and the whole woods. Still think the line rather thin as our losses are heavy. Enclosed is Wass' report. Gas dropped also.[23]

At 6:45 Harbord learned: "Think all objectives have been reached but expect a counter-attack. Lost a lot of men and think the line rather lightly held. No reports except from walking wounded."[24]

During the next two hours Milner and Wass confirmed their positions and left no doubt that the line was very weakly held. At 7:35 Wise requested counter-battery fire against the heavy German shelling and at 8:15 notified Neville: "Line holding but getting thinner. Heavy shelling and some gas. Think I am entirely too weak. Do not expect any trouble before dark. Men in fine shape."[25]

At 8:40, however, Neville forwarded another message from Wise:

I know positively all positions attained and linked up. We have only two wounded Germans as they got away. Lost a great many men. We are getting a devil of a shelling, and quite accurate. Quite a few machine guns captured. They should be dug in well before dark. Everything running smooth and men in fine shape, but as I put in my report I am afraid of the [enemy] reaction.

P.S.—This is a different outfit from the one of yesterdays.[26]

Once again the overall gist of the reports seemed favorable and once again Harbord reported to division without further confirming. Preston Brown's "Report of Operations" for June 12 notes:

". . . It is now believed that the Bois de Belleau has been completely cleaned out of enemy detachments. Our losses are approximately fifty wounded, generally slight wounds. . . ."[27]

Unbeknownst to either Harbord or Brown, shortly before dark Wise learned from Lieutenant Milner of a German plan to attack. He at once informed Harbord, who did not receive the message until shortly after 11:00 P.M.: "A dying German officer states that a fresh division is in and the plan was to attack tonight. Would like artillery up on my front during night. We are in full spirits. Have now 350 old men left and seven officers. They are shelling very heavy."[28]

At Neville's headquarters his second in command, Logan Feland, had already respected this new threat by ordering 75 and 155mm fire on Belleau, its château, Torcy and surrounding roads. The only other answer was to send in fresh units, and here Harbord found himself in a nasty bite.

On June 11 Harbord had placed Holcomb's tired battalion in corps reserve *vice* Sibley's 3d Battalion, 6th Marines, which became brigade reserve. But earlier in the day he had ordered Sibley to relieve Turrill's battalion on Wise's left that night, a change even then taking place. This left him only his corps reserve, and at a little after midnight he notified Holcomb:

Information received of a possible attack from the Bois de Belleau from north and northwest tonight. Please march your battalion to the wood northwest of Lucy to arrive by 3:50 A.M. Hold it in reserve in the woods there pending further orders.[29]

Since its relief from the line, Bouresches-Triangle, Holcomb's battalion had been resting while sorting out its units and gear and working replacements into the companies. In a letter home on June 11 Lieutenant Cates wrote:

I am writing this back in the wood a few miles back of the town—we were relieved and are now in support, but it is pretty warm here, as they put a shell into us occasionally.

Each man has dug a hole big enough to stretch out in, and put some straw in it—I am sitting down in mine now, and using a board as a writing table. I wish you could look out at my bunch now—some are in their holes, some writing, some working on their little shrapnel proof dugouts, some reading of our new success, two shooting a friendly crap game, some cleaning their person and equipment, while others are just sitting looking into space—thinking, no doubt, of home and some girl. I heard, just now, that we would get mail tonight. I hope so, as nothing cheers us up more than to get mail from the ones we love. Hot chow will be in soon also, so we will feel good. It comes in only once a day, and then it is in big thermos cans.[30]

A similar routine prevailed on June 12 except that nearly continuous German shellfire kept the men confined to their shelters and prevented much real rest. Most of them were sleeping when Harbord's order reached Holcomb. He at once turned them out and ordered them on a forced march to the forward wood.

And now the German artillery stepped up its fire to turn the night into an experience that no man there would forget. For over two hours the batteries from three divisions blasted Sibley's new position on the left, Wise's and Hughes's lines in Belleau Wood, Shearer's defenses in Bouresches and the trenches fronting Malone's 23d Infantry.

Shortly after 3:00 A.M., the counterattack began: not against Wise in Belleau Wood but rather Shearer in Bouresches. Shortly after the fight was joined, a young replacement officer panicked and reported that the Germans had taken Bouresches. Learning of this at 4:10 A.M. Harbord directed Holcomb to send two companies to the valley southwest of Lucy where they would prepare to counterattack the town. Holcomb called in Robertson and Cates, the latter of whom wrote:

He told us the situation, then asked if we could take Bouresches again as on June 6.

I wasn't crazy about the idea, but we said we would try. He gave us the 78th and 96th Companies. It was daylight when we left the wood northwest of Lucy for the march toward Bouresches.[31]

Harbord now spent an anxious hour. At 4:20 he learned from Sibley: "Shelling continuous. Much H.E. [high explosive] and gas. Some Shrapnel. Casualties unknown. No rifle fire. Replacements joining company now."[32] Ten minutes later Neville reported a message from Wise:

The lines appear to be holding. Terrific barrage from my P.C. forward. And it was a real barrage. Losses must be very heavy. So far no counter-attack. If reinforcements are available they could be used. Irritating gas giving a lot of trouble. Detail requested to bring our rations as all of mine are fighting. So far have been very hard up to get runners through. Some have never returned. Morale excellent but everybody about all in.[33]

At a little after 5:00 Harbord learned Wise still had not been attacked and that Hughes was still in contact with the enemy and "was holding." Division then telephoned him:

Lieutenant Villmuth who is with 1st Battalion, 23rd Infantry, reported Germans have taken Bouresches. Have asked [for] artillery fire on town. Immediately after transmitting that message to me the 3rd Brigade repeated a pressing message from 1st Battalion, 23rd Infantry, asking that the request for artillery fire be cancelled as Bouresches was still in our hands.[34]

This welcome news was confirmed by Shearer forty-five minutes later: "Have not given up one inch of ground." As Harbord eventually learned, the German attack briefly penetrated the village only to be pushed out by accurate rifle and machine-gun fire that left fifteen

Germans dead in the streets, another forty dead in the fields just outside the town.

By early morning the German fire had slowed and in some sectors altogether stopped. Considering its intensity, the Americans came out amazingly well. Hughes's lines were hit the worst: young Captain Fuller was killed, Lieutenant Poe received bad back wounds and old Captain Burns was badly wounded in both legs.[35] At 5:50 A.M. Harbord learned from Hughes: "Everything O.K. now. Trenches badly ruined by shell fire. Casualties under twenty percent. Enemy barrage was terrific. Condition and conduct [of troops] magnificent. As far as I can find out Wise is O.K."[36] At 6:00 Sibley reported: "Shelling nearly stopped in this region. Much damage to material, trees and branches. No casualties of personnel. Very narrow escapes. Replacements have joined."[37] At 8:35 Wise notified him:

> Things quiet at present. Getting supplies up to the front line. Have one replacement officer per company left and about 300 men not including replacements. Engineers are getting well dug in. As all these woods are ranged to the yard they are absolutely torn to pieces. When this is going on it is absolutely impossible to get men or supplies up to the front. Captain Murray has been out for some time making reconnaissance of the whole line and then can give a more full report. Not having officers makes it hard to get detailed information promptly. My idea is that attack will come from the northwest. All company commanders request men.[38]

No further reference to Murray's reconnaissance is found in the records, but apparently it altered neither Wise's nor Harbord's belief that the enemy occupied only a narrow strip along the northwestern flank of the wood, a position shown on a brigade sketch of June 13.

At the moment, however, Harbord could not muster the necessary strength for a further attack. In his mind the immediate task was to consolidate: to hook up Wise's left with Sibley's right while reorganizing his brigade for its final move.

Notes

1. Kemper F. Cowing and Courtney Riley Cooper, *Dear Folks at Home—*. New York: Houghton Mifflin Co., 1919.
2. *Translations*, Vols. 2 and 3.
3. *Records*, Vol. 6.
4. Ibid.
5. Ibid.
6. Frederic M. Wise and Meigs O. Frost, *A Marine Tells It to You*. New York: J. H. Sears and Co., Inc., 1929.
7. Ibid.
8. *Records*, Vol. 6.
9. Ibid.
10. Wise, op. cit.
11. *Records*, Vol. 6.
12. *Records*, Vol. 5.
13. Major E. D. Cooke, "We Can Take It," *Infantry Journal*, May–December, 1937.
14. *Records*, Vol. 5.
15. Cooke, op. cit.
16. Ibid. See also William R. Mathews, "Official Report to Headquarters, U. S. Marine Corps, September 28, 1921."
17. Ibid.
18. Ibid. See also John W. Thomason, Jr., "Second Division Northwest of Château Thierry, 1 June–10 July, 1918." Washington: National War College, 1928. Unpublished manuscript.
19. Ibid.
20. Ibid.
21. *Records*, Vol. 4.
22. *Records*, Vol. 5.
23. Ibid.
24. Ibid.
25. Ibid.
26. *Records*, Vol. 4.
27. *Records*, Vol. 6.
28. *Records*, Vol. 5.
29. *Records*, Vol. 4.
30. General Clifton B. Cates, USMC (ret). "Personal letters, 1918." Unpublished.
31. Ibid. See also General Clifton B. Cates, USMC (ret). Personal interview with the author.
32. *Records*, Vol. 6.
33. Ibid.
34. Ibid.

35. Captain Fuller was the son of the future Commandant, Ben Fuller; Captain Burns later died from his wounds.
36. *Records*, Vol. 6.
37. Ibid.
38. Ibid.

Chapter 19

"... I am very glad to report that not-withstanding their physical exhaustion, which is almost total, and the adverse circumstances of gas, the spirit of the Brigade remains unshaken."
—Brigadier General Harbord to Major General Bundy, June 14, 1918

Since Wise and Sibley were hard up for men, the task of joining their lines was given to Turrill's battalion. Turrill turned the job over to Captain Winans who early on June 13 sent out a patrol from his 17th Company "to find the line of the Wise battalion and to examine the approaches to the new position."[1]

Led by Lieutenant Blake, the small patrol worked across the Lucy-Torcy road and around Hill 169 to the wood proper. Blake then led his men up a ravine (the one Harbord and Wise falsely believed they held) to an east-west trail where they ran into German fire. Blake now retraced his steps and reported back to Winans without having seen anything of Wise's main position.

Winans next moved his company up to the wood, halted it at the ravine and sent out scouts to the north and east with orders to find Wise's line. But now, believing himself spotted by a low-flying German plane, which would mean artillery fire, Winans called in his scouts and withdrew to just west of the Lucy-Torcy road where he dug in to watch German shells plaster his recent position. After sending two scouts south to locate Wise's line from the rear, he reported back to Turrill: obviously Wise was nowhere near the western edge of Belleau Wood; just as obviously, the Germans were in the wood and very alert.

The disquieting information did not at once reach Harbord, who was concerning himself with a reorganization of his brigade. Late in the afternoon of June 13 he issued Field Order Number Five: after dark that night, Shearer's battalion in Bouresches, upon relief by a battalion of the 23d Infantry, to move into position northwest of Lucy as brigade reserve; simultaneously, Holcomb's battalion to relieve Wise's which would go to a rear area for rest and reorganization while serving as division reserve. In order to straighten out the mix-up in battalions which was depriving his regimental commanders of proper command responsibility, Harbord assigned the left portion of his now shortened sector to Lieutenant Colonel Lee (whose new second in command was Lieutenant Colonel "Hiking Hiram" Bearrs), the right to Colonel Neville.[2]

The order primarily affected Holcomb's battalion. In late afternoon the tough little commander went forward to inspect Wise's position. Wise later wrote:

> We started out from my P.C. on the same route I took in my regular morning inspection. It was about 5 P.M. We had hardly left my P.C. when the Germans cut loose with a bombardment that, while it wasn't quite as heavy as the one we had stood the night before, still was heavy enough. Hundred-and-fifty-fives [155mm] and seventy-sevens [77mm] began to burst up and down the line. On top of them, the whizbangs [Austrian 88mm] came smashing through. Splintered trees were torn into still smaller splinters. Great masses of earth and roots, of limbs and fragments of trunks, mixed with shell-fragments themselves, began to fly through the air. The din was deafening—a solid, continuous roar.
>
> Holcomb looked at me. "Is this celebration due to my arrival?" he shouted in my ear.

"No," I shouted back. "This is only routine."

We flopped right where we stood when the shelling started and lay flat against the ground until it ended half an hour later. Then we went on with the inspection.[3]

Holcomb returned to the two companies of his battalion dug in northwest of Lucy, alerted them to the pending move, then notified his other two companies. The latter had been in a wheat field southeast of Lucy when the counterattack against Bouresches was called off. Believing that observation balloons to the north had spotted them, they at once went into bivouac, a position described by Lieutenant Cates in a letter home as

a thick woods on the side of a hill near Belleau Woods. Luckily, we had time to dig fox holes before the Germans opened up—with a heavy barrage and we had intermittent artillery fire all day. Casualties were fairly light.

During the afternoon I searched the wheat fields over which we had advanced on the 6th looking for Lieutenant Brailsford who is carried as "missing in action," but he is most probably dead. I went out alone, as I found that it's much safer than to have other men with you, as a group will draw heavy fire. I had some very close calls as I was shot at repeatedly.[4]

Back at his foxhole, Cates found his company alerted to move out at midnight. Enemy artillery was shelling to his front and right when, a few minutes before the hour, he put on his cumbersome equipment and prepared to turn out his men. He wrote:

I had not gone over twenty feet from my fox hole when I heard a salvo of shells heading our way. From the whistle I thought they were gas shells, and when they hit with a thud and no detonation my fears were confirmed. Soon I smelled the gas, and I gave the alarm to the men, and they all put on their masks. By this time there was a steady stream of incoming shells—gas, air bursts, shrapnel, and high explosives. I

reached for my gas mask, but it wasn't there. Naturally, I
was petrified. I tried to find my hole where I had left it, but
I became confused and couldn't locate it.[5]

It was an anxious moment, an easy time for panic, for the shells
were dropping fast, the fumes of the dreaded mustard gas strong as
the lethal mist began enveloping the position. But now Cates remembered that one of his men, Private Hall, had picked up a German mask for a souvenir. Forcing himself to remain calm, he crept
through the exploding wood. "Hall, Hall," he called. The fumes
were very strong now; the yellow, oily stuff trickling down on the
shrubs and trees and grass. "Hall, Hall." Cates had just about given
up when a muffled voice came out of a nearby foxhole. "Here I am,
over here. What do you . . ." Before the sentence was finished, the
lanky company commander had jumped in the small foxhole and
was donning the captured mask. It was far too small for him but it
covered his mouth, nose and eyes and that was enough to save him
from a horrible, choking death.

The German artillery had but begun its destructive work, as
Cates later reported:

> The shelling was so heavy we didn't try to move out, which
> I now realize was a mistake. It kept up for hours, and we
> suffered rather heavy casualties, both from shell fragments
> and gas, as many of our masks were defective. Heroes were
> made that night, as the wounded had to be carried to the
> dressing station, which was under a stone bridge down the
> ravine. Many of the stretcher bearers were hit while carrying
> the wounded. As soon as the Boche artillery fire stopped,
> we moved out with about half of the company remaining
> and went into this hell hole Belleau Woods.[6]

By this time the two companies had suffered considerable
wounded casualties besides evacuating 160 gas casualties. In the interim the marine lines in Belleau Wood had been badly hit by the
German guns. Although Wise's line received only limited amounts
of the deadly gas, Hughes's positions were saturated. Hughes was

evacuated, his place taken by Major Frank Garrett; his 74th Company, the one badly gassed earlier in the Verdun trenches, was virtually annihilated.[7]

Holcomb's other two companies, forced to wear masks while moving up to Wise's line, were delayed; Holcomb arrived "with one and three quarters companies" around 3:00 A.M. In the next hour or two some 150 men of the remaining companies filtered in.

Taken with the darkness and general fatigue, the gas attack produced an extremely confusing situation during which the majority of officers and men forgot their training, rudimentary at best, in gas defense. Cates did not forget; after reporting in he stripped and with water from his canteen and a piece of soap from his pack lathered his body completely and allowed the lather to dry while beating the fumes out of his uniform and letting it air. As a result of this precaution he escaped with "bad blisters between my legs, around my neck, and on my forehead where my helmet rubbed."

The rest of the gassed marines fared badly. Impressed into service as stretcher-bearers, they quickly worked up a sweat which almost immediately activated gas fumes clinging to their uniforms. In less than an hour all of the 96th Company and most of the 78th Company were being evacuated from the wood.[8]

Harbord learned part of the bad news early on June 14. He also learned that both the 9th Infantry and 23d Infantry had completed their reliefs, the 23d suffering about 150 gas casualties with one of its companies "badly shot up" in the process. At 6:05 A.M. he received a discouraging report from Wise:

Holcomb arrived with 1-3/4 companies at 3 A.M. and other two companies badly broken up, from shells and gas. About 150 of these have showed up. My men physically unable to make another attack. Have just made another reconnaissance of the line and consider my present line unsafe unless whole woods are in our possession and not enough troops on hand and if these woods are taken there must be enough troops to hold them, or it will be the same story again; that is they [the enemy] will filter in. The woods are larger than shown [on the map]. Request permission to withdraw slightly to make the line safer and that Holcomb be given more men as many of them here have had gas. Some gas here.[9]

Harbord was in no better shape regarding replacements than he had ever been. If he held any designs on Shearer's battalion, just relieved from the Bouresches-Triangle sector, they were shattered by a message from Major Ralph Keyser, Shearer's second in command, received at 9:00 A.M.: ". . . officers and men are exhausted. They are doing good work but on their nerve only; physically they are all in. Major Shearer is in care of the 6th Regimental Surgeon suffering from temporary exhaustion."[10]

The only remedy for this unit was time—time to eat and sleep and get replacements. Until time repaired exhaustion, the line units, including Wise's shattered battalion, would have to hold on. This was a difficult demand for Harbord to make, and he made it with apology as indicated in a message of that afternoon to Holcomb: "Regret necessity of having to put your fine battalion in again with so little rest, and when so many have been gassed, but do it with perfect confidence that you and they can be depended upon under adverse circumstances."[11]

The circumstances were certainly adverse enough to discourage even so ebullient a commander as Harbord. Perhaps sensing this, Colonel Neville during one of Harbord's morning visits handed him a pair of Marine Corps collar devices and said, "Here, we think it is about time you put these on." Harbord later said:

. . . I was as much thrilled by his brusque remark and his subsequent pinning them on my collar the next few minutes as I have ever been by any decoration of the several that have come to me. I wore those Marine Corps devices until after I became a Major General, and I still cherish them as among my most valued possessions. I think no officer can fail to understand what that little recognition meant to me, an Army officer commanding troops of a sister service in battle. It seemed to me to set the seal of approval by my comrades of the Marine Corps, and knowing the circumstances, it meant everything to me.[12]

After this pleasant interlude Harbord set about reorganizing his brigade. So long as Wise, Holcomb and Garrett defended Belleau Wood with Sibley's battalion on the left, he could not effectively divide his command into regimental sectors. When he learned further that on the following day the French 167th Division was going to relieve the left of his sector, he directed Logan Feland, second in command to Colonel Neville, to command the overall defense of Belleau Wood.

Feland went up to the forward line that afternoon. Wise later described their meeting:

> "General Harbord is sore as hell because you didn't clean out the wood," he told me.
>
> "We've done the best we could, Logan," I told him, "but on the original attack the men got a great deal of punishment from the right. They naturally drifted toward it to take the machine guns in that sector. We simply didn't have enough men to cover the whole front. More than half the battalion are casualties now. I've got one captain left. Now you know how we stand. You've got a map. You can read it as well as I can."
>
> He agreed with me that things didn't look very well, with the Germans in those woods at the left of our line. When the shelling eased up a little bit, we made an inspection.[13]

Feland took Captain Winans along. Winans and Turrill had already reported the results of the earlier patrols to Feland, Winans suggesting that if supported by one-pounders, trench mortars and machine guns he could push through from his present position to Wise's left. Agreeing with this logic, Feland now telephoned Neville to report the situation as he saw it. What he had seen completely contradicted what Neville believed, and the senior commander did not hesitate to state this. Only when Feland asked to be relieved of his command did Neville quiet down and listen. And when Feland recommended that Winans attack early the following morning, Neville agreed.[14]

While Feland was on reconnaissance, Harbord had ordered still another change in the wood's defense. Alarmed by a new gas attack in the southern portion of the wood—at 4:30 P.M. Garrett was still evacuating what would reach a total of 185 men—the brigade commander directed Garrett to shift the bulk of his battalion west, leaving only one company to hold the eastern position: "The enemy is not liable to attack within several days a wood which he has filled with Yperite gas."[15] To discourage him further, Harbord ordered the artillery to gas the German line to the east and to lay heavy barrages on Torcy and the Château Belleau.

For the moment Harbord could do little more. After summing up the day as "unfavorable" in his evening report to Bundy, he tersely described the planned relief, the gas attack that disrupted it, the extreme casualties, the countermeasures. As if to cheer himself more than the division commander, he concluded: "I am very glad to report that notwithstanding their physical exhaustion, which is almost total, and the adverse circumstances of gas, the spirit of the Brigade remains unshaken."[16]

Unbeknownst to the marines, this spirit was about to get a tremendous lift. For some time, General Bundy and his chief of staff, Preston Brown, had been unsuccessfully urging the corps commander, General Degoutte, to furnish a relief for the marine brigade. On June 14 Degoutte moved up to command of the French Sixth Army. His successor, General Naulin, proved no more amenable: after pointing out that the French 167th Division had already been ordered to take over one of Harbord's battalion sectors, the French general suggested that the 3d Brigade should go into line while Harbord's people came out for rest and reorganization.

Bundy and Brown refused to consider this. The situation on either side of the American position was far from stable, the 3d Brigade was already defending a large sector; to weaken the line at this stage could very well cause an American setback with fantastic repercussions in France, England and America. Pressed by Brown, the division commander argued that the French XXXVIII Corps on his right was not fully utilizing the 3d U. S. Division, specifically Colonel Anderson's 7th Infantry Regiment sitting idle on the Marne—why couldn't Bundy temporarily borrow this unit? When Naulin demurred, Bundy threatened as the senior American commander in the area to take command of all American troops. Seeing the point, Naulin changed his mind and ordered the immediate transfer of the 7th Infantry to the 2d Division.

Harbord did not learn of this development until early on June 15. In the interim the marines had spent a sleepless night, the result of an artillery duel that petered off toward dawn. Winans's position on the left remained untouched, however, and in early light he struck into the western face of the wood. His well-coordinated attack, supported by heavy machine-gun fire, quickly ran over German outposts defending the right flank of von Hartlieb's remaining line and continued on to the east. In overcoming new resistance and in attempting to establish a line behind him, Winans soon grew short of men. Turrill responded to his predicament by sending up two platoons. Winans then caught a bullet in the foot but fortunately Captain Quigley came up to take over. By 8:00 A.M. the marines, at a cost of twenty-two casualities, had succeeded for the first time in sealing off the bulk of the wood.

Feland, who from his first reconnaissance had "exposed himself time after time to heavy fire" and who "was on the go day and night,"[17] spent the rest of the morning in consolidating the welcome gain and in assessing his future course of action. It did not look too bright. An attempt by Quigley to advance his left up the western side of the wood failed almost immediately. Wise's battalion had all it could do to hold its present line still under fire from both front and rear; Holcomb's companies were still reorganizing with officers and men frequently falling from the effects of the earlier gas.

At this crucial moment Feland learned that help was on the way. Early in the afternoon Lieutenant Colonel Adams and his company commanders from the 1st Battalion, 7th Infantry, arrived at Feland's P.C. to arrange for the relief of Wise's and Holcomb's battalions that night. A later written order from Harbord directed these two battalions to proceed to the rear; simultaneously the French would relieve Sibley's battalion which would form division reserve. Other reliefs would take place on the following nights upon the arrival of the rest of the 7th Infantry.

Late that afternoon Feland informed Harbord that the remaining opposition in Belleau Wood consisted of an estimated "forty or sixty Germans with several machine guns" defending "a small knoll in the western part of the north end of the wood." The enemy, he believed, was contained: artillery and machine-gun fire would prevent either escape or reinforcement. Although his attempt to maneuver around the position during the day failed, and although he believed he could force the line by direct assault "in a few minutes," he wished to take a "little more time" and thus save lives.[18]

The new battalion commander agreed and so did Harbord. That night Adams led his battalion of fresh infantry into the wood while the French came up on his left. By dawn the first of the marines had reached the rear.

The marines went back with a pride justified by official reports of the enemy. On June 16 Corps Conta noted:

> The 2d American Division can be rated as a very good division, if not possibly as an assault division. The various attacks by both the Marine Regiments were carried out with vigor and without consideration of losses. The moral effect of our firearms did not materially check the advance of the infantry. The nerve of the Americans is still unshaken.

As for replacements:

> The personnel may be considered excellent. They are healthy, strong, physically well set-up men from eighteen to twenty-eight years old, who, at present, only lack the necessary training to make them a dangerous foe.
>
> The spirit of the troops is high and they possess an innocent self-confidence. A characteristic expression of the prisoners is "we kill or get killed."[19]

According to the War Diary of the 28th Division:

> The prisoners are mostly members of the better class, many of them artisans and they consider their membership in the Marine Corps as something of an honor. They proudly resent any attempts to place their Regiments on a par with

other Infantry Regiments; call themselves "Soldiers of the Land and the Sea" and are well informed as far as the glorious history of their Regiments during the period of the Revolutionary War is concerned. . . . Their training in rifle marksmanship is remarkable. Once as they broke through our left flank they settled down behind rocks and by their rifle fire broke up every counter-attack.[20]

It was a good reputation, but it came at a price. Having paid the price, the marines were now glad to go back. For what seemed like years, life had consisted of death in a thousand forms, of rifle and machine-gun fire, of artillery barrages, of attack and defense, of woods and shattered trees, broken bodies, cries of the wounded, tiny gouges of earth as home, a candle in a tin can for a stove, a thirst never assuaged, a body never clean, the same clothes, filthy and lice-infested, bowels tortured by foul rations and relieved in stinking slit trenches, cold nights without blankets, hot days in wool uniforms, everywhere the stench of dead—the complete, awful, humiliating sordidness of combat that once they supposed would be grand.

Lieutenant Cooke remembered the relief:

My nerves were completely shot. I cowered in a foxhole at the sound of every shell and cringed at any unexpected noise. If a man had suddenly yelled in my ear I'd have probably shot him dead. [Lieutenant] Jackson came through on his way to the hospital and I thought him lucky.

Then, on the night of June 15th, our whole outfit was relieved. Another battalion was to finish what we were too few to accomplish. My company, with some of the 43d [Company] attached, filed silently back through the spectral forest and the ruins that had once been Lucy. Stealthily we slipped past buildings that were tumbled to the ground, under beams reared on end, around shell holes gaping in the streets. Smoke eddied about our feet while gas clung to the broken walls and dripped from crevices.

We kept no formation. Each man simply followed the one in front. No one was going to let himself be left behind.

We wanted to hurry but our legs acted as though gripped by an undertow. Weak, starved, and apprehensive we bent forward, painfully propelling ourselves up the hill from Lucy, pathetically eager for escape.

But shells suddenly dropped along the road. The battle reached out, diabolically determined not to let us go. . . . We plodded on, praying for no more shells. Just a little longer and we would be beyond their reach. With each step we gained confidence and strength. Someone laughed! We hadn't heard a laugh for days. Someone whistled!! Well, why not? We were safe. Safe! They hadn't gotten us that time. No, by God, we'd fooled 'em.[21]

For the moment that was enough: "We were safe. . . . We'd fooled 'em." It was a matter of survival, the most basic of human drives; it was a logical feeling and it pervaded those pathetic columns stumbling in the darkness toward the temporary light of sanctuary: Sibley's men to Platerie Wood about a mile northwest of Harbord's headquarters; Holcomb's men farther to the rear to the Gros-Jean Wood; Wise's men farther still, on foot to Montreuil, then by trucks to Néry, a sleepy little village on the Marne, the same route for Turrill's and Garrett's battalions during the next two days.

Survival having been established, the men turned to the fruits of survival: to baths, no matter how crude; to clean underclothing, fresh uniforms; to treatment of skin infections and sour stomachs; to sleep uninterrupted by staccato bursts of machine-gun fire, brilliant flares, exploding shells; to hot food, not particularly good but *hot* food and *hot* coffee to wash it down followed by cigarettes and chocolate and jam distributed by the Red Cross; to mail from home and to the writing of long-overdue letters.

These were simple pleasures, but to seemingly condemned men suddenly reprieved they loomed as riches. Lieutenant Cooke later recalled: "But best of all was a bath. I lay full length in a tub of hot water and critically regarded my naked body. Incredible, but it was all there—bony ribs, skinny shanks, and hairy legs. Maybe not beautiful but it looked plenty good to me."[22] On June 18 Lieutenant Cates wrote in a letter home:

We are now a few miles back of the lines in support, and we have been resting very well as we have not been shelled here. It sure is good to get back where we can get hot food and a little sleep. Can you imagine men nibbling old hard bread and enjoying it—for many days we didn't get that in the front lines—really, we lived on excitement. I didn't average one hour's sleep a day. The strain has been terrible, but the few that have come through will soon recuperate back here. Honest, when I look out at the few men left I really cry—I am the only officer out of two companies and I am in charge of the remains of both companies—one good platoon. I didn't realize how I loved the old bunch until it had been broken up.[23]

The old bunch had certainly been broken up. In two weeks of combat the once splendid 4th Marine Brigade had taken over fifty percent casualties in officers and men. Despite replacements no one unit stood at full strength. Some had lost all of their original officers and most of their NCOs; a few had ceased to exist. Casualties by battalions were appalling. Major J. C. Montgomery, sent down by division to inspect the relieved units, reported that between May 31 and June 18 Holcomb had lost twenty-one officers and 836 men; Sibley fourteen officers and 400 men; Turrill sixteen officers and 544 men.[24] In a separate report to Colonel Neville, Wise listed his losses at nineteen officers and 615 men.[25]

The brigade was scarcely finished. The survivors were young; they were resilient. And if their minds would remain forever scarred, their bodies responded amazingly to sleep and food. In addition they had their pride—pride of what they had accomplished, pride that they could accomplish more—and they had passed this on to replacements who already considered themselves part of the brigade, as indeed they were.

And now more replacements came up to flesh out reorganized units already being supplied with new weapons, equipment and clothing. On June 18 Major Montgomery reported to division that Sibley's battalion "is now being reequipped and reorganized. Replacements are being incorporated in the squads and platoons and appear to be in excellent condition."[26] On June 19 he reported the morale of Holcomb's "officers and men is excellent"; on the same day Major Montgomery reported that Turrill's battalion "is now well located in comfortable billets. The companies are being reorganized, re-equipped and cleaned up. Arrangements are being made for suitable drill grounds and the instruction is to be resumed tomorrow."[27]

The newcomers could use the instruction. Unfortunately they would not receive much of it before the word came to form into columns and move out. As they would shortly find out, the marines were not yet finished at Belleau Wood.

Logan Feland's appreciation of the enemy situation, which Harbord approved, was over-optimistic. The remaining German defenses in Belleau Wood were not as weak as he believed. Neither were they isolated; holding a larger portion of the wood than Feland yet realized, the enemy remained comparatively free to come and go through the northern re-entrant.

Although the enemy's numbers were considerably greater than Feland's estimate, he was growing steadily weaker. Attrition is a two-edged sword, and in mid-June at Belleau Wood, by asserting its inexorable effect on both the Americans and the Germans, it was foreshadowing what would happen in the months ahead.

On June 11 the 237th German Division was defending nearly a two-mile front with a total 3,200 infantry troops. Without exception officers and men were exhausted, generally hungry and increasingly ill from Spanish flu, a mysterious disease already prevalent on the Flanders front.[28] According to a diary entry by Lieutenant Breil, commanding the 12th Company, 461st Regiment:

> He who escaped being wounded during the days around here may surely boast of exceptionally good fortune. But there was no time to worry about that; we were too exhausted. *What our men did here can only be judged by one who was on the scene himself.* How feeble and sick we were, with fever (the influenza), and diarrhea, all of us without exception, and yet we held out! Here we had a good example of the influence of a leader. Major Bischoff, the veteran African

fighter, said to his men: "I know you are all sick. Any physician would have you put on the side list. But will you allow the successes won with our blood to be jeopardized or even lost? A man can endure anything so long as he has the will to do so. Clench your teeth, then! Pull yourselves together! When we get out of this place we will have time to recuperate." Not a man reported himself sick.[29]

Other troops of the division did report themselves sick, however, and these coupled with heavy combat losses rapidly eliminated the fighting value of the 237th Division. On June 12 the 461st Infantry reported only nine officers and 149 men fit for duty in Belleau Wood. On June 13 the division's entire rifle strength numbered 47 officers and 1,482 men. The division commander now ordered all rear units stripped to provide frontline reinforcement, an effort resulting in a gain of some 340 generally motley, ill-equipped, untrained troops. With this he scraped the bottom of his barrel. He could gain help neither from his right where the French were slowly chewing up the 5th Guards Division nor from the 28th Division on his left. Since May 27 the 28th Division counted seventy officers and over 2,000 enlisted casualties—on June 13 its 40th Regiment reported: "Due to exhaustion, malnutrition, and above all to lack of junior officers, the fighting value of these troops is practically nil."[30]

Some relief appeared on June 13 when the 87th German Division, in reserve behind First Army, was transferred to Seventh Army and given to von Conta. On June 14 he ordered it to relieve the 237th besides taking over the 28th Division's right.

Never a top unit, the 87th Division was rated by the spring of 1918 as fourth class, good only for holding purposes in quiet sectors. Perhaps because of this, its commander, Major General Feldkerr, wanted to evacuate Belleau Wood in favor of building a main line of resistance along the slopes behind the villages of Belleau and Torcy. Since this would cause von Conta to pull back the 5th Guards Division on the right, thus yielding the line of the Clignon, the corps commander refused and ordered Feldkerr to proceed with the relief.

Feldkerr's three regiments began moving up on the night of June 15, the same night the American relief began. On the right and left the regimental commanders put one battalion forward, one in close support and one in reserve. In the center the 347th Regiment moved one battalion into Belleau Wood, placed another to the west and held a third in reserve. The Belleau Wood commander, in turn, placed two companies in line in the wood, two in reserve.[31]

Instead of the short, weakly defended line imagined by Feland and Harbord, by June 18 the enemy was again defending the northernmost portion of the wood in considerable strength and in defensive terrain that more than compensated for the dubious quality of the troops.

Notes

1. John W. Thomason, Jr., *Fix Bayonets!* New York: Charles Scribner's Sons, 1925.
2. *Records*, Vols. 5 and 6.
3. Frederic M. Wise and Meigs O. Frost, *A Marine Tells It to You*. New York: J. H. Sears and Co., Inc., 1929.
4. General Clifton B. Cates, USMC (ret). "Personal letters, 1918." Unpublished.
5. Ibid.
6. Ibid.
7. E. N. McClellan, "Capture of Hill 142, Battle of Belleau Wood, and Capture of Bouresches," *Marine Corps Gazette*, September–December, 1920.
8. Cates, op. cit. See also *Records*, Vol. 6.
9. *Records*, Vol. 6.
10. Ibid.
11. Ibid.
12. McClellan, op. cit.
13. Wise, op. cit.
14. William R. Mathews, Official correspondence, Headquarters, U. S. Marine Corps, 1928.
15. *Records*, Vol. 6.
16. Ibid.
17. William R. Mathews, personal correspondence with the author.
18. *Records*, Vol. 6.
19. *Translations*, Vol. 1.
20. *Translations*,Vol. 4.

21. Major E. D. Cooke, "We Can Take It," *Infantry Journal*, May–December, 1937.
22. Ibid.
23. Cates, op. cit.
24. *Records*, Vol. 7.
25. Ibid.
26. Ibid.
27. Ibid.
28. Barrie Pitt, *1918 The Last Act*. New York: W. W. Norton and Co., 1963. For an excellent history of this disease which would eventually cause more American deaths than combat, see A. A. Hoehling, *The Great Epidemic*. Boston: Little Brown and Company, 1961.
29. Ernst Otto, "The Battles for the Possession of Belleau Woods, June, 1918." *U. S. Naval Institute Proceedings*, November, 1928.
30. Ibid.
31. Thomason, op. cit.

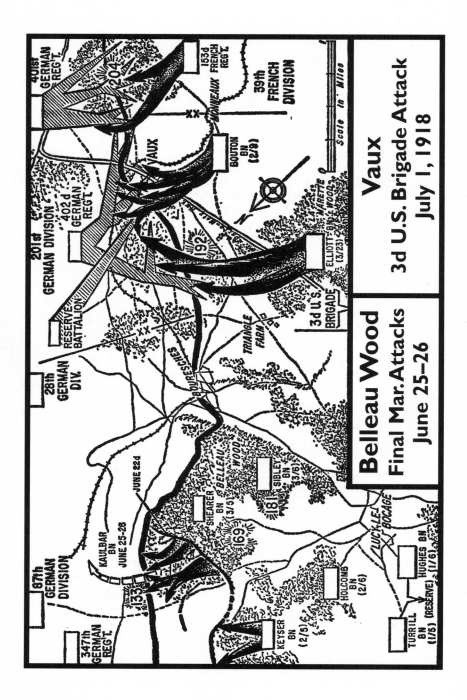

Belleau Wood
Final Mar. Attacks
June 25–26

Vaux
3d U.S. Brigade Attack
July 1, 1918

Belleau Wood map labels:

87th GERMAN DIVISION

347th GERMAN REGT.

28th GERMAN DIV.

KAULBAR BN JUNE 25–26

JUNE 22d

153

KEYSER BN (2/5)

69 BN (3/5)

SHEARER BN (3/5)

BELLEAU WOOD

181 BN (3/6)

SIBLEY BN (3/6)

HOLCOMB BN (2/6)

TURRILL BN (1/5) (RESERVE)

HUGHES BN (1/6)

LUCY-LE-BOCAGE

BOURESCHES

TRIANGLE FARM

Vaux map labels:

40ist GERMAN REGT.

204

163d FRENCH REGT.

201st GERMAN DIVISION

402d GERMAN REGT.

RESERVE BATTALION

VAUX

MONNEAUX

39th FRENCH DIVISION

BOUTON BN (2/9)

192

LA MARETTE

ELLIOTT BN (N. WOOD)

ELLIOTT BN (3/23)

3d U.S. BRIGADE

N

Scale in Miles

Chapter 20

"Belleau Woods now U. S. Marine Corps entirely."
—Major Maurice Shearer to
Brigadier General Harbord,
June 26, 1918

General Bundy's decision to put the untried and relatively untrained 7th Infantry Regiment into line at Belleau Wood is curious. A more logical course would have been to use it to relieve one of the 3d Brigade's blooded regiments. Either the 23d Infantry or the 9th Infantry could easily have moved into the wood and would have picked up the fight with an enthusiasm kindled by desire to get some of their own back from the headline-featured marines.

Bundy was probably influenced in his thinking by Harbord's reports which painted an altogether too optimistic picture of remaining German strength in the wood, and also by a desire to keep the 3d Brigade intact for the pending Vaux operation. Whatever the case, it was a sad mistake.

Sometime around noon on June 15, Colonel Anderson, commanding 7th Infantry, and Lieutenant Colonel Adams, commanding its 1st Battalion, conferred with Harbord and Neville. To Anderson's surprise he learned he would not command his three battalions; Colonel Neville would retain command of the sector with Logan Feland in direct command of Belleau Wood. According to Harbord, although Adams's primary mission was to hold the present defensive line, he would also carry out Feland's plan to envelop the remaining German defense.[1]

When that afternoon Adams and his company commanders visited Wise's and Holcomb's positions, they were not greatly impressed. Wise later wrote:

> I took them over the front line. It was very quiet. They couldn't understand why they had heard the place was such a hot box. It was their first experience in the front lines. They didn't seem to understand what they were up against. They were courteously unimpressed when I tried to tell them. I impressed it upon them that they must get into position before daybreak. I pointed out the German sausages [observation balloons], and told them they had to come over a lot of open ground, explained that the German artillery had that whole sector plotted and had damned near perfect observation, and told them they would get the hell shelled out of them the first time a column was seen in open ground in daylight.[2]

The infantry officers returned to the rear after dark, met their units marching up from Montreuil and, toward morning on June 16, proceeded with the relief. As predicted by Wise, enemy artillery caught them coming in, a sudden, sharp barrage costing six casualties before they closed the frontline area. Then, upon beginning the actual relief, they encountered a series of German patrol actions, a sharp fight described by Lieutenant Cates in a letter written two days later:

> We were relieved from the front line last night by an Army unit. It is the first time they have been in action, and it's a tough spot to put them in for their first baptism of fire. I felt sorry for them last night when they came in. They had just

arrived and were starting the relief when all hell broke loose. The Boche in our rear started firing, then our men returned it, the Germans to our front started firing, we answered, then both their artillery and ours opened up. We thought they were attacking, and they probably thought we were. It kept up for over thirty minutes, and it was a madhouse. Imagine the poor Army boys that have not been under fire before.[3]

The remaining army battalions fared slightly better. On the night of June 16, Captain Hurley's 2d Battalion relieved Garrett's marines in the southern portion of the wood, and on the following night Major Gaston's 3d Battalion relieved Sibley's companies on the wood's left. By June 18 the 7th Infantry occupied the old marine lines which, with the help of the 2d Engineers, they were improving with deeper individual shelters and barbed-wire defenses.

The first note of discord appeared in a message sent by Harbord to Lieutenant Colonel Adams on June 18:

> . . . It is understood that you are wiring an east and west line through the woods between you and the party of Germans on whom you are supposed to exert pressure. It is not believed that you have anything to fear from any aggression on the part of these people and it is not desired that you wire yourself in to prevent the pressure which it is desired you exert steadily until these people are killed or driven out.
>
> There has been nothing heard from you in the way of reports since early morning. You are supposed to report at least once each day whether anything is happening or not to keep your C.O. [commanding officer] informed of exactly what is going on.[4]

Very little in fact was going on, either here or elsewhere in the sector where Anderson's battalions were still consolidating their new positions, an effort accompanied by spasmodic enemy shelling which held movement to a minimum during daylight.

Darkness brought the first serious actions. On Adams's front, Company B, in an unsuccessful attempt to straighten its line on the left, lost five men killed and sixteen wounded. West of the wood, Gaston's left company pushed forward to a ravine a kilometer south of Torcy, a bloodless gain acknowledged by Harbord in a message to the battalion commander the following morning:

> Congratulate you on your good work in occupying the ravine to the crossroads without loss. Be on the lookout in this foggy weather for a surprise counter-attack. Find out if the French on your left have occupied the fringe of woods to your left. . . . If they have, send out some small patrols and ascertain if the enemy occupy the line along the road half a kilometer south of Hill 126, and in what force if any. If not occupied by the enemy, I desire you to send a company through the woods to the left and take it as you did the ravine, and bring another company to the ravine at the cross roads as support. Of course these movements must be under cover of woods and not across the open. If your patrols find the line occupied, give Colonel Neville a report on it before attempting to send a company in there.[5]

While Gaston prepared to carry out these orders, Adams was planning his first serious attack in Belleau Wood, a relatively small action to take place early on June 20 and involving two platoons from Company D supplemented by one platoon each from two other companies. In the event, the force from Company D failed to get into proper position, which left the attack up to the other platoons, an abortive effort gaining nothing but sixty-three casualties plus the fury of the brigade commander who informed Bundy:

> . . . Attack ordered on machine gun nest of northwestern edge of Bois de Belleau failed because companies of 7th Infantry fell back when a few casualties [sic] occurred. One company commander, Captain Russell, 7th Infantry, relieved by Battalion Commander for inefficiency and sent to report to Regimental Commander.[6]

Harbord might well have come up with some second thoughts at this particular point. The action already suggested an enemy in better position with greater strength than that estimated by Feland; just as important, it showed that the newly arrived, sadly inexperienced battalion lacked the drive and determination necessary for a final assault.

Seemingly oblivious to any such considerations, Harbord ordered Adams to attack on the following morning. In one of the more extraordinary documents of military history the brigade commander wrote:

> Your battalion will be relieved tomorrow night. Tomorrow morning is its only chance to redeem the failure made this morning. If you clear the northern half of the Bois de Belleau the credit will belong to the 1st Battalion, 7th Infantry, and will be freely given. The battalion cannot afford to fail again.[7]

Adams could do very little but accept the orders and plan the new attack as outlined in his return message:

> Company A, Lieutenant Helms commanding, will make attack at 3:15 [A.M.] tomorrow. . . . It is absolutely necessary to have 1000 hand [grenades] and 500 V.B. [rifle grenades] delivered this morning early to give to this company. Stokes [mortars] will open fire at 1 A.M. and fire until 3 A.M. Request artillery barrage on north and east of woods from 3 A.M. to signal to cease by rocket. If possible would like to get some food here before 11 P.M. that the company may have supper before beginning fight.[8]

On the surface these seemed the words of a competent, confident battalion commander. But any comfort which they bestowed on Harbord was immediately shattered by a confidential enclosure:

> . . . Orders have been issued for an attack tomorrow morning. Information has reached me that the Germans have filtered through and have in place at least fifteen machine guns

in and around Belleau Woods. They are now firing into rear of Companies D and C and have moved two guns up toward right flank of Company B. Under the conditions noted I do not believe any attack without a heavy artillery fire preceding can move the guns from the woods. They are all emplaced and strongly held. The woods is almost a thicket and the throwing of troops into the woods is filtering away men with nothing gained. Recommend that Companies D and C be drawn back to line occupied by Company B. That a heavy artillery fire be placed on the woods and an advance made afterwards. I can assure you that the orders to attack will stand as given, but it cannot succeed. This is only my individual expression and has not reached the ears of any one else. Further: the line held by Company B can be crushed at any time and it leaves the woods open. Please consider this. It is serious and requires immediate action, for I can assure you that it is only made after careful consideration, and earnest thought. Let me hear by return messenger.

Underneath his signature Adams added: "The two Stokes [mortars] won't even worry the German machine guns."[9]

Yielding to Adams's fears, Harbord ordered the necessary barrage, a decision given to the army commander at 6:00 P.M. with the concluding words: "Your troops will attack at 3:15 [A.M.] and capture or destroy the enemy."[10]

Late in the evening Adams issued revised orders to his company commanders, who shortly before midnight began the necessary retirement to the rear. At 2:00 A.M. the American artillery opened fire on the northern part of the wood, a barrage which Adams and the other battalion commanders judged "light in volume and ineffective." At 3:15 the two attack companies, A and B, began to move out in two waves each. Company B, whose left was supposed to advance along the western face of the wood, almost immediately lost direction, with the result that its right found itself on the edge of the wood—in other words this company was advancing outside the wood altogether.

The error utterly confused Lieutenant Helms, commanding Company A, who lost considerable time in attempting to make contact with Company B. By 4:00 A.M. he had advanced only about 200 yards. At this point the Germans opened a counter-barrage that stopped, then dispersed the attacking waves while simultaneously hidden machine guns belched out a devastating, flanking fire from behind trees and rocks. In short order Helms lost some 150 men while Company C, coming up in support from the rear, suffered another thirty casualties. Small groups of enemy dressed in American uniforms added to the confusion by infiltrating the American line to give conflicting orders in English. According to a report made immediately after the action:

> . . . a German in American uniform approached Lieutenant Paysley of Company A saying to him: "My God, you are not going to fire on your own men out there in front of you, are you? You are not going to kill your own men?" It being so apparent to Lieutenant Paysley that this officer was an enemy in our own uniform that he immediately shot and killed him.[11]

The frantic action ended shortly after it began. Seemingly content with having stopped the attack, the Germans remained in position, their snipers harassing the tired, confused Americans trying to gain a semblance of cohesion while getting out their wounded. By 7:30 A.M., Companies A and C were back in their original positions; Company B, which saw virtually no action, was coming up on the right rear of Gaston's 3d Battalion.

The confusion now spilled over to the higher commands. At 7:00 Harbord received Adams's awkward understatement: "Everything is not going well."[12] At 8:20 Harbord heard from Gaston: the commanding officer of Company A, Lieutenant Helms, had gotten lost and had turned up at Gaston's P.C. to report his company "all shot to pieces." Minutes later Gaston reported Company B coming up on his rear with the information that "the Germans have broken through" and "there is fighting going on to the right rear of M Company."

Harbord now ordered a reserve company of marines to march on Hill 169, clean out any enemy and continue on into the wood. Simultaneously he told Gaston to order Company B to march "towards the sound of the firing it reported, keeping an eye out for Marines that had been sent there, and to proceed to its entrenched position in the Bois de Belleau."

At Neville's P.C., Harbord next listened to Lieutenant Helms's account of the action (which he plainly doubted), then directed Colonel Anderson to go to the wood "to investigate [the] condition of his troops, and to get them back into the positions held yesterday."[13]

By noon Harbord again controlled the situation. Company B's report of a German breakthrough had proven false, Adams's other companies were back in their old positions and his right had been repaired by two platoons from Hurley's 2d Battalion. Shearer, again in command of the 3d Battalion, 5th Marines, and his company commanders were reconnoitering the position for the relief scheduled that night.[14] At 1:00 P.M. Harbord reported the details of the catastrophe to Bundy in a long message which concluded:

> . . . This whole situation arises in my opinion from the inefficiency of officers of the 7th Infantry and the lack of instruction of the men. . . . The 7th Infantry needs a period of instruction under a strong commanding officer, with disciplinary drills and the weeding out of inefficient officers. It is unreliable at present.[15]

By June 21 the war was moving slowly beyond Belleau Wood. In anticipation of the coming German offensive, *Friedensturm*, Schoeler's VIII German Corps began relieving von Conta's exhausted and decimated divisions. On the Allied side General Lebrun's III French Corps relieved Naulin's XXI Corps. Neither relief affected the 2d U. S. Division or the thorny problem of capturing Belleau Wood.

Adams's final failure unfortunately did not cause Harbord to revise his estimate of enemy strength in the wood. Convinced it consisted of a "little machine gun nest," he refused to believe any evidence to the contrary, including the final paragraph of Colonel Anderson's report made on June 21:

> It is estimated by Lieutenant Colonel Adams and Captain Carter that the Germans in this position are between 150 and 200 strong. The ground is exceedingly rough, ravined, covered with dense underbrush and all trails and paths in the direction of this stronghold seem to be covered by machine gun fire and in one or two cases of 37mm [cannon].[16]

Rather than investigating the situation as demanded by prudence, Harbord's obduracy continued to rule his thinking. That afternoon he instructed Major Shearer, commanding 3d Battalion, 5th Marines, which would relieve Adams's battalion that night:

> It is believed that by the judicious use of sharpshooting snipers you can reduce the German positions without much expenditure of men. These men should operate in pairs, should be provided with canteens of water, with some rations, and crawl out toward the German position exerting every effort, exercising the patience of Indians and waiting for shots without exposing themselves. Pairs to be sent in from all sides. Additional pairs to be sent at night along the west edge of the Bois from both north and south. These will stop any further infiltration if any has taken place. . . .
>
> The wiring-up on the east and north of the Bois must proceed. Just as soon as it is completed the line can be held with comparatively few men and remainder dug-in support and out of shell fire.
>
> *It is not practicable to withdraw again and give further artillery preparation.* [Author's italics.] With the sniping which should worry the enemy you should be endeavoring to get the machine gun nests surrounded so you can rush them when ready and put an end to them.[17]

Before Shearer could embark on the new tactics, a German deserter supplied some disturbing information: the Germans held the entire northern end of the wood. On June 22 Logan Feland confirmed this by personal reconnaissance as reported by Harbord to Bundy:

> . . . Colonel Feland is certain no trenches run through the north end of the woods, but undoubtedly the Germans have access to that part of the woods, and have been free to come and go. The undersigned has been misled as to affairs in that end of the woods, either consciously or unconsciously, ever since its first occupation by the battalion under command of Lieutenant Colonel Wise and later by the battalion of the 7th Infantry.[18]

Incredibly enough the information, which clearly made envelopment an impossibility, did not cause Harbord to significantly alter his tactics. His report to Bundy continued:

> The Commanding Officer 3d Battalion 5th Marines [Shearer], now in there, has been told that this [situation] is intolerable and that he will clean the woods by ten o'clock tomorrow night; further that the space does not permit the use of more troops than he now has and that it is not practicable to make artillery preparation by withdrawing his troops. He is to use V.B.'s [rifle grenades] and trench mortars and at the same time of the assault provide his men plentifully with hand grenades. Snipers in pairs have been out all day today and Colonel Feland reports they believe that they have accomplished something by their fire. Major Shearer, the battalion commander, has been directed to submit his plan for approval before making the attack.[19]

Force of circumstance called for a relatively simple attack plan. Shearer's defensive position consisted of four companies in line—from left to right, the 45th, 16th, 20th and 47th. At 7:00 P.M., on June 23, Captain Yowell's 16th Company and Captain Platt's 20th Company, preceded by special assault groups armed with rifles and hand grenades, would advance from this line which would then close behind them.

The attack kicked off on schedule. Covered by heavy machine-gun fire, the assault groups moved out, quickly contacted enemy outposts which at first gave way to the grenadiers backed by bayonet-wielding riflemen. At 8:00 Shearer reported to Harbord, ". . . making progress slowly. Little shelling on front line companies." But now the marines were discovering that as soon as one machine-gun position yielded, "immediately a new and unexpected fire opened" from the flanks. On the right Platt's company overran three machine-gun nests to advance about twenty yards to the top of a fire-swept rocky knoll where they were pinned down both by frontal and flanking fires preventing either further advance or consolidation. On the left Yowell's company, already out of contact with Platt, pushed in about 200 yards before it was stopped. In less than three hours the Americans suffered over 130 casualties, the attack was bogged down, and the advance companies began retiring to their old lines now under German artillery fire. Lieutenant Laurence Stallings, leading a platoon in the supporting 47th Company, later described the scene:

Men in supporting platoons, inching forward to plug the gaps in a decimated company where there was no artillery roar to drown the cries of human beings, sometimes thought this duty the worst of war's alarms. The cries of men as blood drained from them and they lost self-control were almost not to be endured. Officers restraining men who wished to administer first aid to such sufferers felt themselves unconscionable brutes as they hazed the kindhearted into gaps littered with corpses, crawling forward hugging the ground, the blood of other men on their sleeves, their hands, their faces. Wounded lads on their backs, a kneecap still on its ligaments caught in brambles where it had been shot out of a leg, begging for someone to release it so they might inch back farther to some slight depression, might find succor; but the ones who needed tourniquets and compresses—and precious time—could not be accommodated. The gaps had to be plugged. This last failure in Belleau Wood would be remembered by some as the worst afternoon of their lives no matter what fortune later befell them.[20]

At 11:20 P.M. Colonel Neville reported to Harbord "that attack is held up for the night and will continue in the morning."[21]

Shearer held no intention of continuing the attack. After reviewing the night's action he informed Harbord:

> . . . [Captain Yowell] could not now reoccupy his advanced position of last night without repeating the attack of last night and there is no reason to believe that circumstances would not be the same. . . .
>
> The enemy seems to have unlimited alternate gun positions and many guns. Each gun position covered by others. I know of no other way of attacking these positions with chance of success than one attempted and am of opinion that infantry alone cannot dislodge enemy guns. Water is difficult to obtain and rations scarce. Men and officers very tired but retain their spirit.[22]

Shearer's failure caused the American commanders to once again reassess the situation. By now the 4th Brigade had completed the relief of the 7th Infantry: on the left the 2d Battalion, 5th Marines, under Major Ralph Keyser (who that day relieved Wise),[23] held the line from Hill 142 to the Lucy-Torcy road; Shearer's battalion, stretched across the north edge of the wood, tied in on the right with Sibley's battalion which carried the marine line back to Bouresches; Holcomb was in brigade reserve northwest of Lucy, Turrill and Hughes in reserve in Gros-Jean Wood.

At a meeting on June 24 between Bundy, Harbord, Chamberlaine (the division artillery commander), Colonel Neville, Lieutenant Colonel Lee and the battalion commanders of the 4th Brigade, a new plan emerged: that night Shearer to withdraw his line slightly while Keyser extended his line over to the double-tree road skirting the western edge of the wood; with the enemy thus screened, Chamberlaine's artillery supplemented by French batteries to open a barrage at 3:00 A.M., a massive effort lasting until 5:00 P.M. when Shearer would begin a methodical advance not to "exceed 100 meters each three minutes. The objective of the advance is the north edge of the Bois de Belleau."[24]

Shortly before daylight on June 25 Chamberlaine's hastily reorganized artillery opened fire both on the northern end of the wood and on adjacent areas. The pattern fire from both 75s and 155s continued throughout the sunny morning into an afternoon of increasing clouds and haze. While the big guns tore up the terrain, aircraft of both sides filled the skies—the result of French attempts to bomb deep behind the German line. On the previous day a pilot of Richtofen's squadron, Lieutenant Udet, had made his 33d kill; now on June 25 it was his turn to be shot down.[25]

At 4:00 P.M. the ground war again took over. Chamberlaine's guns increased fire, a murderous concentration exploding in the trees to rain shrapnel on the German positions. An hour later the barrage rolled back, the marines moved up.

Shearer attacked with three companies in line, one in close support. Although counter-artillery fire hurt the advancing waves, the dreaded enemy machine guns for the most part remained silent. At 5:55 Shearer reported:

> Attack started O.K. at 5 P.M. Heavy firing on us just before we jumped off. Several casualties. Very little machine gun fire. Telephone line out. Runner reports seven prisoners and one captain also prisoner, carrying back wounded. The two left platoons 16th Company reported grenades and snipers working on them. No report from companies yet. Will go through if humanly possible.[26]

Shearer's companies were doing just fine. Fighting "like a bunch of wild cats," the marines quickly worked forward of their old lines. Although they made little progress on the right, they continued to push through in the center and on the left where increasing numbers of enemy were surrendering.

The German commander of the 1st Battalion, 347th Regiment, Captain von Kaulbars, now realized the seriousness of the situation. Pre-attack artillery fire had caused him considerable casualties, including one company commander killed, one mortally wounded. Even worse, the bursting shrapnel had either knocked out or temporarily disorganized the bulk of his machine-gun nests, the *sine qua non* of his entire defensive line. A little after 6:00 P.M. he committed the 1st Company, his only reserve. An hour later he sent an urgent wireless message asking for reinforcement.

Fortunately for the Americans, the enemy was not functioning at peak performance. Upon receipt of Kaulbars's request, his regimental commander alerted his reserve, the 3d Battalion. But higher headquarters, disturbed by the heavy artillery fire and subsequent attack, refused to release this from division reserve. Instead a message went to the commander of the 3d Reserve Ersatz Regiment on the left to send Kaulbars two companies.

The delay proved fatal. At 7:00 P.M. in a message received by Harbord's headquarters at 8:40 Shearer reported:

> 47th Company gained objective—20th and 47th digging in. 45th still in reserve but will occupy positions just as soon as things settle. 16th [Company—Yowell] still working into position. Estimated 150 prisoners by 20th and 47th Companies. No report of 16th as to prisoners. More prisoners just coming in too numerous to count. I am making prisoners dig and carry wounded. Every one doing fine work. Yowell, 16th [Company] meeting resistance. Will send him help. Will need all my company to hold new line. Can't Keyser send me two platoons. Just reported counter-attack on 47th [Company]. Am sending two platoons 45th [Company] to help. Report capture of some of the 47th Company. Our casualties will make help necessary. Please keep artillery and machine guns going to stop reinforcements of enemy.[27]

By this time Harbord knew from prisoner interrogation that the enemy was defending with three companies in line, one in reserve. He now told Neville to send Shearer two platoons from Sibley's battalion and authorized him to send up a company if necessary. He also informed Neville:

> Contingent upon Major Shearer obtaining his objective, orders were this afternoon sent Major Keyser to advance his line tonight and bring the right of the line on the double-

tree road just west of Bois de Belleau. This will begin shortly after dark. Please notify Major Shearer that the movement is going to take place so that in the dark he will not confuse it with a possible counter-attack.[28]

This was a sound precaution. Although Shearer's center and right companies had gained their objectives, Yowell's 16th Company on the left was "still meeting resistance." In the center the 47th Company was reduced to about seventy survivors and was still fighting hard; in an attempt to bolster the left platoon of this company, Lieutenant Stallings and nine men walked into a fire fight that stopped them cold and badly wounded Stallings.

Shearer's incomplete knowledge of the situation coupled with reports of heavy casualties was making him increasingly nervous. After reporting what he knew of the action to Harbord, he wrote: ". . . Need reinforcements badly. Have got to have reinforcements to hold on. Counter attack will be bad."[29]

Far from thinking in terms of counterattack, Captain von Kaulbars was trying desperately to survive. By 9:00 P.M. he had received no reinforcement, his left and center were shattered, his right in serious jeopardy. Fifteen minutes later he ordered the remnants of his companies to begin withdrawing from the wood to a new line along the Torcy-Belleau road.

Since Kaulbars's order did not reach many of his units, it scarcely affected the immediate tactical situation. At 9:30 Shearer reported to Harbord:

20th and 47th [companies] are in position. 47th apparently too far east but am trying to rectify the same. 16th has not made position yet and reports machine guns still in their front. They are forward of last advance position held during last attack. They are still trying to work forward to objective. Reported about 100 enemy on 47th Company's left who want to surrender but Boche machine gun shoots them as they try to come out. Companies may have passed some enemy. Our casualties so heavy can't spare men to patrol to rear. Any counter-attack by enemy would be fatal to us in present condition. Can't some force come in east and west line advancing north and clean up woods and thicken our lines? We must not lose what we have now. Enemy shelling woods continually. Please get heavy counter-battery work on them. Estimate 150 prisoners. Impossible estimate enemy casualties. Heavy though. Sending prisoners back to Sibley to send in. Had to use reserve company in line so Sibley is filling up gap on right of 20th Company east side woods and Sibley's left. *We have taken practically all of woods but do need help to clean it up and hold it. Do we get it?* [30]

Harbord received this message just after 11:00 P.M. Although refusing to share Shearer's anxiety, he did undertake to strengthen the battalion commander's left by notifying Keyser:

In moving your line forward it is important that you send a platoon to clean up in the edge of the Bois, parallel to the double-tree road. The 16th Company in trying to come out to position on that side of the road is meeting some resistance. Send your platoon by your right rear to come up now on the left [of the wood] and clean it out. I do not believe the remainder of your line will meet with much resistance. [31]

A few minutes later he informed Colonel Neville:

Your Shearer Battalion has done splendid work. I have no fear of a counter-attack by the Germans tonight. You are in charge of the Bois de Belleau and can divert such part of Major Sibley's Battalion as you think best. His front is practically wired in. In connection with the movement of Keyser's Battalion to connect up with the west side of Bois de Belleau, I have ordered him to send a platoon by his right rear to come up on the left of the 16th Company and help clean that edge of the woods. It is very important that Shearer be told of this in order that the 16th Company may not, in the dark, confuse that platoon with the enemy. . . . Artillery are trying to neutralize some of the enemy artillery. [32]

Harbord's appraisal was correct.

By midnight Captain Kaulbars had cleared the wood of those units with whom he held contact. When the reinforcing companies of the 3d Reserve Ersatz Regiment reported to him, he used them to bolster his new line along the Torcy-Belleau road. Throughout the night small groups of Germans continued to evacuate the wood; others remained to fight; still others happily gave themselves up as prisoners.

Although both sides held action to a minimum, confusion filled the night. Shortly before daylight Private Leonard, one of Captain Yowell's runners, got lost and wandered into a German position. To Leonard's surprise he was immediately confronted with a very tired German captain who told him in excellent English, "I am on a salient, and the companies of the 3d Battalion, 5th Marines, around it in front of me are the 16th and 20th. Are there any troops in back of them?"

"Yes," Leonard said quickly, "the 6th Regiment is in back of them and they are going to pass through and attack you at the coming of daybreak, in the morning."

After a hurried conference with his officers, the captain asked Leonard to take him and his men prisoner. As if this were an everyday occurrence, the young marine ordered his prisoners to discard their arms, then calmly took the lead of four officers and seventy-eight men. On the way the captain stopped him; according to his compass they were going in the wrong direction. Leonard thanked him, changed course and without being challenged led the procession back to brigade headquarters. Not quite sure to whom to report, his doubt was answered by the appearance of one of Harbord's staff officers. Leonard walked up to him. "What will I do with these prisoners I have just captured?"[33]

While Private Leonard was making his way back to the front, daylight had brought the Belleau Wood fighting into its final phase. By dawn Keyser had moved his right to the double-tree road from where his men were observing and occasionally firing on the enemy. On the right, one of his platoons was beating up to Captain Yowell's company now pushing forward against only slight resistance.

Yowell's marines found a hideous wood. Groups of enemy wounded surrounded by their dead spoke for the dreadful accuracy of the American artillery. In places the big shells had torn swaths through the dense wood to leave once proud timber standing forlornly, skeletal sentries over the wrath of humans. Farther north the marines found the hunting lodge still standing, its octagonal facade scarred by a 155mm shell which left its entrance covered with seven mangled German bodies; the torso of one rested in the crotch of a nearby tree. Arms and equipment of both the falling and fleeing littered the wood's soft floor otherwise spotted with the refuse of destroyed ammunition and supply dumps.

Although no one recorded the exact time, Yowell reached the north edge of the wood about 7:00 A.M. on June 26. This was Shearer's last objective, the last objective of the 4th Marine Brigade. It was still early when the tired battalion commander received the welcome word from Captain Yowell. The wood was quieter now, the sun already up, the day hot when Shearer sent Harbord the long-awaited message of victory: "Belleau Woods now U. S. Marine Corps entirely."[34]

Reports received throughout the morning confirmed the victory. It cost Shearer's people some 250 casualties; the Germans lost about 450 men, of whom nearly 300 were prisoners, as well as thirty light and heavy machine guns.

Neither Harbord nor Bundy desired to pursue the marine action any further. With Belleau Wood in American hands, the Germans could no longer defend the line of the Clignon. Once Vaux was taken on the right, the 2d Division would hold a more than satisfactory defensive position.

Harbord's task now was to consolidate his gains. After ordering Holcomb's battalion to relieve Shearer that night, he instructed Neville and Lee to prepare a defense in depth: "Please see that Battalion Commanders reduce the number of men in their front lines to the lowest number consistent with safety in holding the line when attacked until their supports can be brought up."[35]

The battle was not yet over, artillery shells would continue to kill and wound, patrols to fire on one another, rifles and machine guns to occasionally break the new-found quiet. But on June 26, for the marines, for the survivors and the replacements, the offensive at last was over.

Notes

1. John W. Thomason, Jr., "Second Division Northwest of Château Thierry, 1 June–10 July, 1918." Washington: National War College, 1928. Unpublished manuscript.
2. Frederic M. Wise and Meigs O. Frost, *A Marine Tells It to You.* New York: J. H. Sears and Co., Inc., 1929.
3. General Clifton B. Cates, USMC (ret). "Personal letters, 1918." Unpublished.
4. *Records*, Vol. 6.
5. *Records*, Vol. 5.
6. *Records*, Vol. 6.
7. Ibid.
8. *Records*, Vol. 5.
9. Ibid.
10. *Records*, Vol. 6.
11. Ibid. Lieutenant Paysley was killed the following day.
12. *Records*, Vol. 5.
13. *Records*, Vol. 6.
14. Ibid. The 7th Infantry suffered a total 350 casualties.
15. Ibid.
16. Ibid.
17. Ibid.
18. Ibid.
19. Ibid.
20. Laurence Stallings, *The Doughboys.* New York: Harper and Row, 1963.
21. *Records*, Vol. 6.
22. *Records*, Vol. 5.
23. *Records*, Vol. 6. See also Wise, op. cit. During the temporary relief of the marines from Belleau Wood, Harbord severely criticized Wise for reporting the woods free of Germans. After acrimonious discussion, Wise lost his temper. According to his later account he asked Harbord: "If you had so much doubt about those woods being clear, why the hell didn't somebody from Brigade come out and take a look?" The very germane question infuriated Harbord while the entire episode undoubtedly explained Wise's relief a few days later. After considerable rear area adventures, Wise resumed command of his battalion after the Soissons campaign.
24. Ibid.
25. U. S. Army, *The German Offensive of July 15, 1918.* Fort Leavenworth: The General Service Schools Press, 1923. See also *Translations*, Vol. 1. Lieutenant Udet safely parachuted and continued to fly as one of Germany's greatest aces.
26. *Records*, Vol. 5.
27. Ibid.

28. *Records,* Vol. 6.
29. *Records,* Vol. 5.
30. Ibid.
31. Ibid.
32. Ibid.
33. *Records,* Vol. 6. See also George V. Gordon, *Leathernecks and Doughboys.* Chicago: privately printed, 1927; John J. Pershing, *My Experiences in the World War.* Vol. 2. New York: F. A. Stokes Co., 1931. When Harbord told this story to Pershing the latter replied ". . . that if he told such stories as that it was little wonder he was popular with the Marines." Pershing later discovered it was true.
34. Ibid.
35. Ibid.

Chapter 21

"The whole attack went off like a dress rehearsal and I regret we did not take moving pictures of it."
—Colonel Upton to Major General Bundy, July 2, 1918

The battle for Belleau Wood had not yet finished when the first congratulatory telegrams began arriving at Harbord's headquarters. Late on June 25 the commander of the III French Corps, General Lebrun, sent "his compliments for the very fine success" of the marine attack. On June 28 Pershing's inspector general paid a personal visit to Harbord; the following day brought Major General Hunter Liggett, commanding I U. S. Corps, who delivered a letter to Bundy containing General Pershing's personal congratulations to the marines.

The brigade and its regiments had already been cited in Sixth French Army orders which automatically brought Harbord, Neville and Lee the Croix de Guerre with Palm and added the citation to regimental colors.[1] More honors were to come but the officers and men of the brigade would gladly have traded them for immediate relief from the combat area. Not that the war was particularly active. Up in the north end of the wood the marines of Holcomb's battalion spent the nights attempting to capture a German—a feat for which division headquarters promised ten days of leave in Paris. One of the aspirants, Lieutenant Cates, reported: "I went out one night to get my prisoner. I ran into three distinct groups and each time thought they were Germans only to learn they were my own people. I finally gave up in disgust."[2] On the eastern side of the wood Lieutenant Timmerman of Sibley's battalion held, as he described it,

> a curious sort of position. In the daylight we looked across a field several hundred yards to the German lines behind the railroad embankment. I soon found that if my men fired even one round the enemy answered with a battery of Austrian 88s. I took the hint and ordered the men not to fire unless we were under an obvious attack.[3]

To guard against attack the marines worked hard wiring in the wood. After an inspection of June 29 Harbord noted in his official diary:

> The bringing out of salvage is progressing. . . . The woods are still very full of salvage of all sorts. There are a great many unburied dead near the edge of the wood but they are being buried as fast as possible. The wiring on the front of the south half of the wood from Bouresches north is practically completed. The wire for the north half will be gotten in tonight and the wiring will be done tomorrow night.[4]

Such labors were both boring and hazardous, marked as they were by frequent enemy artillery and sniper fire. Although supply details considerably improved the delivery of rations to the front line, the food was neither good nor in sufficient quantity to assuage the hunger of weeks. The men had had enough of warm, slightly sour meat and cabbage; of canned beef eaten cold; of bread fried in bacon fat and covered with sugar—the famous "trench doughnut." They had had enough of filthy clothes and primitive sanitation, of constipation and diarrhea, of shot nerves, enough of the shattered, filthy wood with everywhere the cloying stench of death that failed to vanish even with the burial of the bloated, flyblown corpses.

Even under more pleasant conditions the troops would have wanted to leave. They were no longer tired. They were exhausted, their bodies thin and sickly, their minds haunted by experiences so ghastly as to produce living nightmares. It was not yet time, however. In Harbord's later words:

> Everybody recognized that the 4th Brigade needed rest. The 3d Brigade had not been so actively engaged and did not need rest so badly. Neither had the 3d Brigade had the opportunity to distinguish itself as had the 4th. As early as the twentieth of June we knew informally that if the Division Commander would ask it a division would relieve us. For some reason he would not ask it. You could not possibly convince a member of the Marine Brigade that it was not because he had made up his mind to stay until the 3d Brigade also had a chance to "pull off a stunt." Eventually a "stunt" was staged for them with most elaborate artillery preparation, and they took the town of Vaux, or rather its flat ruins, for the artillery pounded it to pieces.[5]

Harbord had a valid point, but he was oversimplifying. The attack of Vaux had been brewing since General Degoutte's initial orders on June 12 and a conference a few days later between Degoutte, his successor, General Naulin, and Bundy. On June 25, with the fall of Belleau Wood imminent, the commander of the III French Corps, General Lebrun, issued detailed orders for an American attack against Vaux and La Roche Wood to the west including Hill 192 (the scene of Malone's abortive attack on June 6–7). Simultaneously the 153d French Regiment, 39th French Division, on the right would strike Hill 204 dominating Château-Thierry (see map p. 304).

Lebrun's orders fell on enthusiastic ears. Since early June, with the exception of Malone's catastrophic attack of June 6, the 3d Brigade had been fighting position warfare which held most of the disadvantages of offensive war without such compensations as ground gained, prisoners and guns captured and glory given. Since it was a regular army brigade in a regular army division, it rather resembled vis-à-vis the marines the legitimate son forced to look on while the bastard son received the titles.

The sidelines of this war were no fun. Major Whiting, commanding 2d Battalion, 23d Infantry, later wrote:

> . . . To keep contact with the enemy, we pushed our lines as close to them and as rapidly as conditions permitted. My battalion held the flanks of the salient the Germans had driven into the French line in the Château-Thierry road, nearest to Paris.
>
> Each night we dug trenches and put out wire, while in the daytime we constructed little splinter-proof dugouts in the woods and ravines where we lived. We could not work in the open during the day as so doing immediately attracted shell or machine gun fire. Each night our trenches grew and improved. Under these conditions our dugouts were crude and offered little shelter from the rain of shell and so they often proved some poor fellow's grave. . . .[6]

On June 11 Lieutenant Lambert Wood of the 9th Infantry wrote home: ". . . My best sergeant was killed yesterday, fifteen feet from me. A true and fine soldier. I wish every German in the world were dead. . . . We are blocking the road to Paris. So we don't die in vain. . . ." On June 16: ". . . Some blank-blank Boche appears to be sniping at me with a six-inch howitzer. Two hit within forty feet of my pitiful little hole in the ground, and covered me with dirt this morning. But I am hardened. . . ."[7] On June 20:

> . . . It is mostly artillery pounding—we are standing now, which is wearing on the nerves. . . . We are living like moles in the ground to escape shell fire, but all of us have feather beds, comfortable, and blankets gotten from the abandoned village and I, in my little hole shaped like a grave, have sheets; but I haven't had my clothes off in twenty days. So it isn't as pleasant as it sounds. I've had men killed and wounded all about me, but have not been scratched. . . . This is a great fight. The men are splendid, splendid; some of the men under me are as brave as any men on earth, I know. Standing

by and working the guns under a hell of fire of shell and bullets that seemed impossible for men to live through. . . .[8]

It was not easy for men to keep up their spirits under such conditions and it is greatly to the credit of these American soldiers that they did so. An exchange of messages between Major Whiting and Colonel Malone showed something of the prevalent attitude. On June 13 Malone directed Whiting:

Do everything you can to encourage and inspire your officers and men and keep them in fine morale.

American troops are performing great feats and contributing largely to the feat of stopping the [German] drive. Other American divisions are coming up behind us. Let the men know it and feel that the situation is secure.

Whiting replied:

I think the morale of my men is at present splendid. They are working under a great nervous strain due mostly to constant and heavy shell fire. I believe they are all sorry the Boche did not come over this A.M. for a little hand to hand work. . . .

Seemingly determined to have the last word, Malone replied: "I do not doubt the morale of your men. I merely appreciate the effect of keeping the men in fine temper by encouraging news from their associates."[9]

The encouraging news from Belleau Wood, if it could be called that, scarcely kept the soldiers in fine temper. Quite to the contrary. As the marines kept claiming the headlines of the western world and the soldiers remained the victims of static warfare, tempers frayed and occasionally flared. On June 20 Major Elliott exploded in a message to Malone:

As some of the requests, orders, and reports of some of the [regimental] staff are so absurd, ludicrous and in many cases impossible I request that the following officers visit my C.R. [center of resistance] as soon as possible to see situations for themselves. Regt. Gas Officer, Regt. I.O. [Intelligence Officer], Regt. Sig. [Signal] Officer, Regt. Surgeon. For instance to receive instructions that no one will sleep within 1200 yards of the front line unless in a gas proof dugout and with gas sentries over each dugout would keep us all awake all of the time as such things are not possible in a minute. Another is that a man who is exposed to mustard gas should have a warm bath with soap and change of clothing, when as a matter of fact we don't get enough water to wash regularly and some are about to fall through their clothes even though requisitions were submitted some time ago. We are supposed to have two O.P.s [observation points]—doubtful if they can be found. Liaison with left company by lamp, telephonic communication with light wire in shelled areas and a few other things which sound fine theoretically. When we are doing all in our power and are as capable of handling all of the foregoing more efficiently from the practical side it becomes exasperating to receive so many orders and requests which someone has "doped" out of a book and from the maps. Another thing they should remember is that the *actual defense* of this position must be considered and that it takes some time each day.[10]

In view of the abject pettiness of such life, it is little wonder that company officers and battalion commanders greeted the new orders with open arms and turned eagerly to preparations for attack.

They were greatly aided by Colonel Conger, Bundy's intelligence officer, who belatedly compensated for his costly ignorance of Belleau Wood. Over some weeks and through exhaustive interrogation of former Vaux residents, including the village stonemason, Conger produced a special map of the town which showed "every one of the eighty-two houses with floor and cellar plans, thickness of house walls and dimensions of all garden walls."[11] From other sources such as aerial reconnaissance, patrols and prisoner interrogation, Conger had learned an enormous amount concerning enemy order of battle and defenses in the target area, all of which he published in a special *Information Bulletin* dated June 29.[12]

The target area had been occupied since June 15 by the 201st German Division, a third-class unit primarily composed of men from eastern provinces. Veterans of the Russian front, the troops were reasonably well trained, but illness was prevalent and martial spirit lacking. They had, however, worked quite hard fortifying the new line.

Defense consisted of three carefully delimited regimental sectors. The 402d Infantry Regiment, a total sixty-nine officers and 2,062 men, held *Sector Wald*—the American objective. Two of its three battalions were in line, the third in reserve five miles to the rear. Of the two line units, the 2d Battalion held *Sector Wald West* with two companies in La Roche Wood, a third in support and a fourth in reserve. The 1st Battalion defended *Sector Wald East* with one company in the village of Vaux, one extending to the slope of Hill 204 and two in reserve to the rear. Lieutenant Adamson, commanding the 2d Company of two officers and 217 men defending Vaux, was reinforced with a detachment of four trench mortars supported by machine guns.[13]

Colonel Conger's detailed intelligence allowed the most thorough preparations and plans for the attack which Bundy on June 30 scheduled for 6:00 P.M., July 1. Division Field Order Number Nine directed General Lewis's 3d Brigade, supported by machine gun and engineer units, to attack the line Hill 192-La Roche Wood-Vaux. To support his attack Lewis was given all of division artillery (only six guns of 12th Battery could fire on the area) plus twelve French batteries including three of heavy 155s. In addition he gained the division trench mortar battery which had just reached the battlefield; for counter-battery and long-range fire he could count on corps artillery. Further, since June 30 American airplanes of Billy Mitchell's newly organized 1st Brigade were flying overhead, the single-seater Spads hotly contesting the superiority hitherto enjoyed by Richtofen's Fokkers.[14]

Under these auspicious conditions, Lewis chose a simple attack plan: after a twelve-hour artillery preparation, Elliott's 3d Battalion, 23d Infantry, to pass through Whitley's battalion in line and attack along a thousand-yard front from Hill 192 to the right of La Roche Wood; simultaneously Major Bouton's 2d Battalion, 9th Infantry, already in line, to attack along an 800-yard front from the right of Vaux to the eastern edge of La Roche Wood. Each rifleman would "carry two extra bandoleers" of ammunition, "two grenades in pack. Hand bombers will carry twelve grenades. Grenadier riflemen will carry twelve V.B.s [rifle grenades]." Bundy's orders also attached machine gun and engineer units to each battalion.[15]

Thanks to Conger's extraordinary intelligence, the ranks knew exactly where they were supposed to go and what they were supposed to do; in Bouton's case support units such as signalmen received assignments to specific buildings in Vaux.[16] The regimental surgeon of the 9th Infantry, Captain Marvin Cappel, established reserves of medical officers and corpsmen which in the event "allowed an elasticity which kept wounded from congregating at any station, and kept a steady, constant stream of evacuations to the rear."[17]

Early on July 1 the heavy guns of the American and French batteries opened a steady, preparatory fire concentrating on enemy infantry positions on Hill 204 and along the Vaux-La Roche line. The fire continued throughout the morning, the lighter 75s variously joining to register on assigned targets.

Shortly before noon the commander of the 201st German Division ordered a general alert along the line. In early afternoon, when the American and French guns began a heavier fire including a mustard-gas barrage behind La Roche Wood, the German commander asked for artillery support from the 10th Division on the left and the 28th Division on the right. By midafternoon a general artillery duel was causing casualties on both sides although support companies ordered up to the German lines were still too distant to suffer. Nor did the exploding shells prevent one of Major Lewis's machine gun companies from enjoying a midafternoon dinner of "bread, ham, cabbage and coffee."[18]

By 5:00 P.M. all American and French guns were firing, a murderous barrage finally consuming 21,000 75mm and 1,600 155mm shells of which 6,000 held mustard gas.[19] Under this cover the Americans on the left and in the center and the French on the right moved up to attack positions. At 5:57 the nine French batteries of 75s opened a rolling barrage toward the objectives, the remaining guns including heavy trench mortars shifting fire to rear areas. Three minutes later the 75s began moving north a hundred yards every three minutes; at Vaux they paused with lethal lovingness, then continued slightly beyond while machine guns hurled curtain fire on the target.

At 6:00 P.M. the infantry moved out.

In the center, Major Bouton's battalion attacked with two companies in line—Company H on the left, Company E on the right—one company in support and one in reserve. On hand observing them was a small party composed of Upton's adjutant, Lieutenant Hanford MacNider, Lieutenant Gray and four battalion scouts. MacNider reported to Upton three hours later:

[We] came up the small ravine of brook towards Vaux, reached the small bridge (Mont Monneaux-Vaux road) just after H-hour and stopped to watch the assaulting companies come over the top. The formations were perfect and the groups advanced smoothly and without interruption until they came opposite us at 6:05. They hesitated in wire at 6:06 for a moment but took up the advance at once. We proceeded along ravine about fifty meters when Lieutenant Gray suddenly discovered five Boche in brush. We took them prisoners, sent them back under guard.

The assaulting troops passed directly through what was left of the south side of Vaux—demolition was complete—marched directly to position defined in orders as objective, threw out outposts and were organizing shellholes on eastern side of railroad on reverse slope. They were in place at 6:20 P.M. and when the adjoining elements were visited immediately afterward they were hard at work on the line indicated. Saw no American wounded, or dead.[20]

There would be American wounded and dead, but not many in Vaux. Accurate artillery fire had early severed the garrison's communication with the rear; houses once hiding fortified positions were flattened, observation points destroyed, the infantry and trench mortar men driven into cellars from where most emerged in a state of shock to surrender. Bouton later reported:

> The Germans were only too willing to surrender in most cases and tried in many cases to induce men in front of our lines to come in and give themselves up.
>
> Almost their first act on being captured was to discard their equipment and throw away their helmets.[21]

Not all surrendered. When two signalmen entered a preassigned cellar to set up a telephone they found nine armed Germans still in the war. They shot two with pistols, the others surrendered.[22]

Within half an hour after the initial advance, Bouton's support company was mopping up Vaux while Company E consolidated its objective, the railroad line east of the village.

Meanwhile Company H moving northwest of the village toward La Roche Wood, had run into an entrenched German position of seven machine guns. After eliminating the guns by a costly grenade assault, the Americans pushed through the wood across the Vaux-Bouresches road. Around 7:00 P.M. the soldiers were digging in, their right east of the railroad tied in with Company E's left, their own left refusing the edge of the wood. A short time later a platoon from Company I of Elliott's battalion on the left came up but reported itself isolated, the rest of the company in trouble.

Elliott had attacked with three companies in line and one in support. On his left, Captain Green's Company M moved across the fields toward the wood of Hill 192, a route marked by bloated American corpses from the June 6 attack. Encountering only slight resistance, Green quickly stood on his objective. In the center, Captain Eaton's Company L pushed through to the left of La Roche Wood, overcame heavy resistance and gained their objective. On Eaton's right, Captain Moore's Company I ran into trouble at the start of the attack when enemy artillery caused five casualties. Twelve minutes later, heavy machine-gun fire cut into his lead squads, a short but nasty fire fight causing heavy losses on his left. After knocking out immediate resistance, the company again moved forward toward La Roche Wood. At 6:20 the Germans opened another heavy fire that wounded both Moore and his assistant commander, Lieutenant Furbush. Lieutenant Cole took command, ordered the survivors into shell holes which he organized into a temporary defensive position. Just over an hour later, detachments from the flanking companies worked in toward the wood and knocked out the enemy machine guns. With that Cole moved to his objective, which he quickly consolidated with the help of following engineers and machine gunners.

By 8:30 P.M. the two battalions were consolidating a line running from Hill 192 east across the northern face of La Roche Wood to the railroad line north of Vaux and on to the viaduct on the right where Bouton's flank company tied in with a French detachment from the 153d Regiment charged with the attack against Hill 204. Communications were rapidly being established with the rear, engineers were wiring in the front, detachments were emplacing captured German machine guns to bolster the new line.

Part of the reason for the American success stemmed from the simultaneous French attack against Hill 204 on the right. Correctly regarding this position as vital, the Germans defended it with an entire regiment, the 401st, which held one battalion in line and two in reserve.

At 6:00 P.M. the French had moved up to their old lines, continued up the wooded slopes of Hill 204 and met the German outposts guarding their objective, the east-west trail halfway across the hill. In the ensuing fight the French pushed in the German right, but now the Germans brought up the bulk of the two reserve battalions to restore the position. At 7:40 P.M. the French commander reported himself unable to proceed farther.[23] As it turned out, the enemy would successfully hold his line, but only by committing division reserves to the hill rather than to the west where the 402d Regiment was desperately trying to organize a counterattack against the Americans.

For the counterattack the regimental commander of the 402d held only his reserve 3d Battalion supplemented on the flanks by two companies released from the 28th Division and one company from the 401st Regiment. The 3d Battalion had been on the march since late afternoon, its movement greatly hindered by artillery fire. Sometime around midnight it deployed between La Roche Wood and Vaux with orders to attack at 2:15 A.M. After a thirty-minute delay caused by heavy fire from both sides, the Germans struck in small storm groups supported by machine guns.

The Americans were ready. Prisoners had already alerted them to the German reinforcement and now with the first attacks they called down artillery barrages which, with heavy and accurate machine-gun and rifle fire, quickly took the steam out of what was a halfhearted venture at best. One company, ordered to continue the attack despite severe losses, simply disintegrated—one sergeant took a group of some fifty men to a cellar from where they later surrendered.[24]

By early morning of July 2 the Americans indisputably held the new line and with it the last objective of the 2d U. S. Division. On the right the French would continue attacking Hill 204 until it fell some days later. In the interim the war would continue for the American soldiers, but like the marines on their left they would now be fighting a battle of artillery fire, of patrols, of a few brief individual encounters while consolidating their gains.

These had not come cheaply. In the short action the 3d Brigade suffered nearly 300 casualties of whom fifty-four were killed; French losses, known to be heavy, were never precisely stated.[25] The enemy lost over 1,200 men of whom at least 500 were taken prisoner. The bulk of the German losses occurred in the 402d Regiment opposite the Americans.[26]

Perhaps more important than the tactical gains and the damage done to the enemy was the morale value accruing to the 3d Brigade. For the first time since early June a superior commander congratulated an army unit without mention of the marines. Late on July 1 General Lebrun notified Bundy: "The 3d Corps sends its congratulations to the 2d Division U. S. on its complete success. It begs the staff of the 2d Division [to] convey them to the 3d Brigade and its splendid troops."[27]

For the first time in brigade history its officers could report favorably on the offensive performance of their units. Also late on July 1 Hanford MacNider informed Colonel Upton: "Attack on right by 9th Infantry went off in splendid shape. Saw no lost men, nor badly wounded Americans. Immediate consolidation and efficient handling of men worthy of mention. Everything organized and functioning well."[28] Major Bouton reported:

> I consider the manner in which the company officers and all men performed their duty to have been perfect. Practically all officers and men whose duty required their presence in rear of the assaulting companies had to be restrained to prevent them from joining the assaulting troops; in fact some of them begged so strongly to accompany the assault, that where their presence could be spared they were allowed to join the attack and did most excellent work. Some men even went forward without authority and also did excellent work, but I know not of a single case of anyone attempting to go to the rear.[29]

In a dispatch recommending immediate promotion for Lieutenant MacNider, Major Bouton and Lieutenant Gray, Colonel Upton noted:

> . . . Disinterested French observers remarked on the dash and spirit of our soldiers and made special mention of the fact that they had seen no lost or badly wounded [men] thus proving good control and efficient evacuation. . . . The whole attack went off like a dress rehearsal and I regret we did not take moving picture of it.[30]

Upton unconsciously verified Harbord's earlier criticism of the operation: its theatrical quality. The observation in no way denigrates the sacrifice and bravery of the individual soldiers involved; but one cannot examine the detailed preparations and orders and action reports without concluding that the attack was a little too perfect to prove very much; that it was a show piece made possible only by disproportionate advantages in men and armament, a set of circumstances not often occurring in war and not again to occur to the Americans in World War I.

Notes

1. James G. Harbord, *Leaves from a War Diary*. New York: Dodd, Mead and Co., 1925. A further citation gained at Soissons allowed all members of the regiments to wear the fourragère, an honor still respected today.
2. General Clifton B. Cates, USMC (ret). Personal interview with the author.
3. Captain Louis F. Timmerman. Personal interview with the author.
4. *Records*, Vol. 6.
5. Harbord, op. cit.
6. Oliver L. Spaulding and John W. Wright, *The Second Division American Expeditionary Force in France 1917–1919*. New York: The Hillman Press, Inc., 1937.
7. Lambert Wood, *His Job—Letters written by a 22-year-old lieutenant in the World War to his parents and others in Oregon*. Portland, Oregon: Metropolitan Press, 1956.
8. Lambert Wood, *Certain Brief Conclusions*. Portland, Oregon: Binfords and Mort, 1939.
9. *Records*, Vol. 5.
10. Ibid.
11. Spaulding and Wright, op. cit.
12. Major General Omar Bundy, "The Second Division at Château Thierry," *Everybody's Magazine*, March, 1919.
13. Spaulding and Wright, op. cit.
14. Alfred Goldberg, editor, *A History of the United States Air Force, 1907–1957*. Princeton: D. Van Nostrand, Inc., 1957.
15. *Records*, Vol. 3.
16. *Records*, Vols. 1 and 3. See also Bundy, op. cit.
17. *Records*, Vol. 7.
18. *Records*, Vol. 8.
19. Ibid. See also Spaulding and Wright, op. cit.
20. *Records*, Vol. 7.
21. Ibid.
22. Ibid.
23. *Records*, Vol. 4.
24. John W. Thomason, Jr., "Second Division Northwest of Château Thierry, 1 June–10 July, 1918." Washington: National War College, 1928. Unpublished manuscript.
25. *Records*, Vol. 6.
26. *Translations*, Vol. 1. The 402d Regiment lost 928 officers and men; 254 killed, 164 wounded, 510 missing. The 401st Regiment lost 184 officers and men. Remaining casualties occurred in the 403d Regiment and in attached units.
27. *Records*, Vol. 4.
28. *Records*, Vol. 7.
29. Ibid.
30. Ibid.

Chapter 22

"...The General commanding the Sixth [French] Army orders that henceforth in all official papers the Bois de Belleau shall be named 'Bois de la Brigade de Marine.'"
—General Degoutte, commanding Sixth Army,
June 30, 1918

The German movements essential to Ludendorff's new offensive, code-named *Friedensturm,* did not escape the notice of Foch or Pétain who, although differing in detail, agreed to a general counter plan: from Reims west along the line of the Marne the French armies to build an elastic defense in depth; if the Germans then struck in the vicinity of Reims or along the Marne, as seemed likely, Mangin's Tenth French Army, in bivouac southwest of Soissons, to strike east, thus severing enemy communications and trapping the German divisions between the Aisne and the Marne.

The plan held a major drawback in that Foch's chronic shortage of troops—soon to be repaired by new American divisions—caused him to strip Sir Douglas Haig's front to a dangerous degree. Although his decision caused another round of inter-allied arguments, in the event it was more than justified by Foch's accurate divination of enemy intentions.[1]

As part of Degoutte's Sixth French Army and Lebrun's III French Corps, the 2d U. S. Division played a part in Foch's overall plan. Lewis's soldiers were still taking prisoners in the La Roche-Vaux area when Bundy's headquarters issued detailed orders for both brigades to build a defense in depth. From July 2 on, the division sector would be called *Sector Pas Fini,* a name apparently stemming from the early June action when American soldiers and marines, told by retreating French that the war was *"fini,"* replied *"Pas fini."*

Bundy's new orders called for no great reorganization. *Sector Pas Fini* was to consist of *Sub-Sector Marine* on the left and *Sub-Sector Regular* on the right. It would maintain the present frontline positions in a Zone of the Advanced Posts backed by a Zone of Principal Resistance and finally by a Zone of the Reserves. Each subsector would be broken down into regimental sectors, which would mean four battalions holding the division's front.[2]

The major effect of Bundy's memorandum was to dampen the hopes of officers and men for immediate relief from the combat area. If the soldiers and marines were the heroes of France, as the newspapers had informed them, then it seemed only reasonable that they should receive their due homage during long leaves in Paris. As they were soon to find out, there would be no long leaves anywhere (except for the wounded); a few, however, did get to Paris.

For now Bundy learned the French Parliament "by unanimous vote" had decided to celebrate "July 4th the anniversary of the Declaration of Independence of the United States" as a French national holiday. The event would include a gigantic parade in Paris in which a provisional battalion (one company from each regiment) would represent the 2d U. S. Division.

Word went out for battalion commanders to select one officer and twenty men from each company. In the reserve units this presented only the difficult problem of choice. It was not that simple in the line battalions. In a letter dated July 13, 1918, Lieutenant Cates described the event:

> [On the night of July 2 in Belleau Wood] I took thirty-two men and put up 450 yards of double apron wire out in no man's land. As luck would have it, it was real dark and the

Boche did not spot us, so we did not get shelled. The major said we would be relieved as soon as we finished the wire, so I worked the men very hard so as to complete it that night—and I did—(a record though).

We had just finished eating our daily meal and had gotten into our small holes (just about daybreak) when the Boche put a heavy barrage on our trenches. I thought they were going to try to come over, but I knew that they would get slaughtered as they knew nothing of our new wire and would run into it, and would be shot down by my men and machine guns, but none came within sight. As soon as it started, I jumped out of the captain's dugout and ran up to mine where I could be with my men. . . . Some of the machine guns had opened up, so I sent up a few sky rocket flares so as to take a good look. Just as I fired one, a shell hit a tree, just six feet above my head, tearing it to pieces. It also tore a box about two feet from me into splinters—of course it knocked me down and gave me a little shell shock, but I got up and continued to send a flare occasionally. I left there and went back to report to the captain—just as I entered his dugout, another shell hit directly over me. Then I was sore sure enough. Both shells knocked me down and God only knows how they missed me, but I did not get a scratch. The left side of my face and head are very sore—it even gave me a toothache. All is well now though. The rest of the day was reasonably quiet—just an occasional shell. We were all waiting for the night so as to get out. I had just crawled out of my hole (about 5 P.M.) when word came that I was to pick twenty men and proceed to Paris at once, as I was to have charge of our battalion in the parade the next day (4th). I was some happy mortal. I took as many old men as possible, as they deserved it. It was a risky business getting out in open daylight, but we were more than willing to take the chance. The men soon had their packs rolled and we started out. We took as much cover as possible in woods and ravines and the Boche did not spot us until we were almost out of range (ten kilometers). They then shot three shells at us—

two missed us by 150 yards, but the other hit within twenty
feet of my sergeant and myself, but we had heard it coming
and had hit the dirt (as they call it in baseball) into a ditch,
so all was well. We literally ran out of that woods and we all
heaved a sigh of relief when we got beyond range of their
guns—the first time since May 31st. We met the other details from the other companies at a designated place and
proceeded to gay Paree. . . . [We] marched out to a good
camp where the men had their first good washing for weeks
and really slept in a bunk. . . . I didn't feel natural as I had
been sleeping on the bare ground so long.[3]

A new crisis now arose. On July 4 Lieutenant Cates learned that
neither his twenty men nor the additional sixty men who had joined
his command held a thin dime between them. He himself had drawn
4,600 francs—nearly a thousand dollars. Keeping 600 francs for himself, he turned the rest over to Gunnery Sergeant Ben Taylor who
gave each man fifty francs, "which was enough for a good meal,
drinks and entertainment for the one afternoon and night" of their
leave.[4] The lieutenant continued:

The morning of the 4th, we got up early and cleaned up and
tried to look half way decent, but we still looked like a bunch
of bums. At eight we left our camp and marched to where
the parade formed. Mother, you cannot imagine the cheer
that would go up as the French people would recognize the
Marine flag—it was one continual shout—Vive la Marines—
la Marines, etc. They literally covered us with roses—I would
carry each bouquet a piece and then drop it—then another
girl would load me down with more flowers. It was truly
wonderful and it made us Marines feel very good as they
give us all of the credit. Even every little kid going to and
from Paris would yell, "Vive la Marines." We have certainly
made a name in France. . . . Most of all Paris witnessed the
parade, and it was one grand sight and adventure for us—
one that I will never forget. The parade ended at noon—
then three hundred men and four officers and myself went

out to the largest ammunition factory in the world for lunch. We rode out and first went through the factory. It was a wonderful big factory and employed 10,000 girls—a very good class of girls. . . . They gave us Marines another grand welcome as we filed through. We then marched into an enormous dining room. At each table there was an American ribbon on one chair so a soldier would sit at each table. We were above in the club rooms where we could look down on that angry mob—over 10,000 and mostly girls. . . . At each table there was red wine and champagne. It was wonderful to look at that mob in one dining room. They had a fine band and the dinner was swell. We had the same and we ate with a lot of generals, colonels, etc. Also a lot of pretty girls. At a given signal they twisted the wire on the champagne bottles and hit them on the table—imagine two thousand corks popping about forty feet into the air at once. It sounded like a German barrage. Of course, champagne flew in every direction. After filling the glasses, toasts were made and responded to. After lunch they set the chairs up on the table and danced for two hours—the girls literally fought over the men. After that we went back to our barracks and discarded our arms and went up town on liberty. Until 6 A.M. the next morning. . . . We left about 2 P.M. on the 5th and came back towards the front. My company had come out of the line and we have been out since, so we have had a nice rest.[5]

By the time Cates and his men returned to the front, the 2d Division had been assigned to Hunter Liggett's I U. S. Corps which had ordered its immediate relief. On the night of July 4 the first units of the 26th U. S. Division reached *Sector Pas Fini*. These were National Guard troops from New England, good, tough men under the competent command of Major General Clarence Edwards. For several nights running they came up, marched to their appointed places, quietly took over their new tasks. One of them, Platoon Sergeant Holden, temporarily commanding a platoon in Company L of the 103d Regiment, remembered relieving Garrett's battalion in Belleau Wood:

As we were practically full strength, 250 men per company, we found that there were not by any means enough foxholes to accommodate all of our men. Accordingly we set to work digging enough holes to fill the need. Sergeant Burke and I picked out a nice round knoll and dug a fairly elaborate hole some six and a half feet by five. We gathered poles and covered the top and put the excavated earth on top of these poles. We hung a blanket at the door so that we could use candles and were quite cozy.

In front of our new home was a grave with a rude cross thereon and, hanging on the cross, a Marine helmet with the whole front torn off. We soon discovered that there was quite an odor emanating from this grave and found, upon inspecting it, that the whole area was alive with maggots. I told two of the men to find enough clean earth to cover this grave with six inches of soil. In a few minutes they came back to report they couldn't find any clean earth. I thought they were merely alibying and went out to show them that, if they went far enough from the grave, they could find clean earth. I kept making larger and larger circles and still found, upon taking up a shovel full of earth, that it was still alive. I went at least fifty yards and found it all the same, and by that time I came to another grave. I gave up and just lived with the condition until we moved. The next morning the Germans shelled the woods heavily.[6]

The last unit of the 2d Division left the front on the night of July 8. The division was still not far from the war, but it was far enough for men to sleep and wash and see their units filled with replacements and enjoy clean underclothing and fresh uniforms and equipment.

It was also a time for honors. On June 5 General David Meyer, Adjutant General of the Royal Marines, cabled from London: "On behalf of the Royal Marines I send you and all ranks of the United States Marine Corps our heartiest congratulations on the auspicious day and may the future years bring us still closer together."[7] On

June 30 Harbord published a special order signed by the Sixth French Army commander, General Degoutte:

> In view of the brilliant conduct of the 4th Brigade of the 2d U. S. Division, which in a spirited fight took Bouresches and the important strong point of Bois de Belleau, stubbornly defended by a large enemy force, the General commanding the VIth Army orders that henceforth, in all official papers, the Bois de Belleau shall be named "Bois de la Brigade de Marine."[8]

On July 10 the mayors of the Meaux District sent the 2d Division a "heartfelt expression of their admiration and gratefulness" for "the generous and efficacious deeds of the American Army in the stopping of the enemy advance."[9]

The price of glory was high. From June 1 to July 10 the 2d U. S. Division counted 217 officer and 9,560 enlisted casualties. Of these the 3d Brigade lost sixty-eight officers and 3,184 men; the 4th Marine Brigade 126 officers and 5,057 men.[10] It was a high price but in paying it without reserve the 2d Division could hold its collective head very high indeed.

More then was the shame of a schism which began developing between soldiers and marines when the first headlines announced marine victories. The immediate envy of the soldiers was understandable and it would largely dissipate as the 2d Division went on to earn a fantastic combat record by November, 1918. More serious was the mean feeling of deep, smoldering resentments held principally by ranking army officers who should have known better.

This had exerted itself mildly during the fighting: on one occasion Pershing personally intervened to gain the army better publicity; on another, when Clemenceau visited 2d Division headquarters, neither Harbord nor senior marine commanders were invited to meet him.[11] It flared after the battle when higher American headquarters unsuccessfully attempted to nullify Degoutte's order changing the name of Belleau Wood to the Wood of the Marine Brigade.[12] It asserted itself officially after the war when the army designated the battle of Belleau Wood as a mere local engagement—a part of the

Aisne-Marne defensive not even worthy of a bronze battle star; unofficial postwar writings kept the flame burning: Generals Dickman, Hunter Liggett, Bullard—each went to considerable effort to denigrate marine achievements at Belleau Wood.[13]

It is a great pity that these and other envious senior army officers failed to recognize the true symbol of the wood in preference to petty trees, that they failed to appreciate and respect the manner in which accidental participants lived up to the highest traditions of American arms.

The detractors should first of all have appreciated the momentous events leading to the emergency commitment of the 2d Division: the horrendous, partially successful series of German offensives during March and April which chewed the British and French armies to pieces before being met and contained. Then the interim period, a nerve racking time for the Allies who wondered where next Ludendorff would strike and if he could again be held. Then the terrible, unprecedented, utterly crushing blow of May 27 when Crown Prince Wilhelm's assault divisions tore across the Chemin-des-Dames, decimated Duchêne's army, raced across the heartland of France, knocked on the bastion walls of Reims, poised on the banks of the Marne, threw the French from Château-Thierry and the line of the Clignon, swept down to Villers-Cotterêts and through Soissons—a massive human arrow which the French thought was aimed at Paris.

It makes no difference that Ludendorff never quite made up his mind, that one cannot positively say whether or not he planned to take Paris, whether or not he thought the seizure of Paris would decide the war in his favor. That is not important because Pétain and Foch and their staff officers *thought* that is what Ludendorff wanted, and most of them thought that the loss of Paris would prove tantamount to the loss of the war.

Nor was this feeling confined to the military professionals. As the German legions plunged ahead, unchecked and virtually unchallenged, something akin to panic broke out in Paris. At first thousands, then hundreds of thousands of citizens left their city; the French government, as in 1914, once again prepared to evacuate—the American ambassador was warned, papers were burned, archives crated, emergency plans made.[14] The feeling spilled over to the western world: no amount of censorship could hide the single, awful fact that the Germans again stood on the Marne, that the French continued to fall back, that Paris was in mortal danger.

Enter the Americans.

"I am very glad that America has entered the war," Pétain had told Pershing nearly a year earlier. "I hope it is not too late."[15]

At the end of May, 1918, it seemed much too late. Admittedly the Americans had fought well at Seicheprey and Cantigny, but these were brief, very limited actions undertaken in reasonably auspicious circumstances. They could not really be compared to the fight now at hand—a fight of seemingly hopeless odds when one coldly considered the force of the German drive. What conceivably could two new and virtually untried American divisions accomplish?

As it turned out—a great deal.

They went to the Marne—first a single, motorized machine gun battalion that within hours covered itself with enormous glory while its infantry plodded in behind to fight long and well. Second, the vanguard units of another division, hastily routed from billets northwest of Paris, rushed to the crumbling front, committed to chaos and confusion, almost at once to face an oncoming line of several battle-wise if weary German divisions, to face them almost alone, for if the Germans were weary the French were exhausted.

The world now waited, its single question: Can the Americans hold? On the battleline the question was asked by General Degoutte, and it was answered first by Preston Brown, then by 27,000 soldiers and marines—young Americans who did not know that they alone believed in themselves. It didn't really matter so far as they were concerned which battalion or which regiment or which brigade would stop the Germans, if one or if all would stop them. As it turned out, the hot part of the line went to the marine brigade, an accident due solely to the change in orders in initial deployment which placed the marine brigade on the left, the infantry brigade on the right of the Paris-Metz highway—an order solely of circumstance and one given by Major General Omar Bundy. The hot part of the line scarcely meant the only part of the line, however, and while it is true that marine riflemen and machine gunners scored heavily against the

German vanguards, it is also true that the soldiers on their right contributed—and of course exploding German shells knew no favorites during that midnight of Allied fortune.

The matter might have ended there. The world might have learned that its question was answered—that the Americans could hold—but for another accident due solely to the lifting of censorship to permit news-starved correspondents the use of the generic term "marines"—also an order of circumstance, an army order issued by Pershing's own headquarters.

There, too, the matter might have ended. The world might have credited the American stand to the marines and gone on with the rest of the war. But while news-starved correspondents were telling the world about the marine stand, the generals decided to attack Belleau Wood. And with this decision the former question—Can the Americans hold?—gave way to a new question: Can the Americans win? And because the Americans had been accidentally divided onto either side of a French road and because Belleau Wood lay on the left side of this road, it fell to the marines to provide the answer.

The world waited while the marines gave it the foot-by-foot, yard-by-yard, killing, wounding answer. The world of course knew none of the details—knew nothing of faulty command decisions, nothing of command ignorance and confusion, very little of the incredible sacrifices and courage of junior officers, non-coms and men, very little of the filth, the pain, the utter depravity of omnipresent death. It was not in the nature of this battle for non-participants to know such details.

The world did know, however, that when the 2d Division went to battle the future of western civilization was being held in considerable jeopardy. Citizens and soldiers everywhere expressed immense relief when the Americans stopped the Germans. They everywhere exploded with pride when the Americans attacked and kept on attacking the Germans. When the 2d Division finally emerged from the battle, the future of the western world seemed far more secure. The people of this world and particularly of France and England and Italy now knew that the Americans had met and defeated the enemy—that America was finally in the war, that her sons would and could fight and win.

It was an immense revelation with world-shaking consequences, for while the slugging match was being fought to the finish, time was on the side of the Allies. Time for Haig and Pétain to rest and reorganize their whipped divisions; time for Great Britain to round up troops from other theaters of war and ship them to the western front; time for men and more men from America to cross the Atlantic, to train and form divisions for Pershing's new army; time especially for Allied leaders and soldiers to regain confidence to wage war to victory.

In that July no one yet realized that victory was near. No more than the rest of the world had the marines sorted out the gigantic issues at stake, no more did they realize that they had created a combat milestone that would later mark the turning point of a war. When they left Belleau Wood and its environs they knew only they had won, they knew they had paid an enormous price for winning—a tired and sad pride covering their ranks as they slogged back to the Marne, slept, cleaned up, ate decent food, reorganized. Many familiar faces were gone: many killed, more wounded, a few like Wise transferred; new faces daily, a few old ones turning up. Wise would return to fight again, so would many of the wounded; company rosters would change and change again in those next few months of Soissons, Saint-Mihiel, Mont Blanc, Meuse-Argonne. Not many of the veterans of Belleau Wood would survive to the end.

Neither marines nor soldiers knew it at the time. They had no way of learning that while they enjoyed halcyon days of lazy baths in the sluggish, warm Marne their immediate future was being planned. On July 10, the same day Pershing visited the division to award decorations to officers and men, he also conferred with Foch. After discussing the formation of an American army, Foch "then referred to a proposed attack that might occur between July 20th and 31st, and indicated that he expected the 1st and 2d Divisions to take part."[16]

For the soldiers and marines resting on the Marne, this decision numbered the days of peace. On July 14 Pershing put Harbord in command of the 2d Division with Colonel Neville moving up to command the 4th Brigade.[17] On July 15 the Germans launched *Friedensturm*: forty-nine divisions struck on either side of Reims.

Foch visited Mangin on the same day. Learning that Pétain had canceled the French attack finally scheduled for July 18, Foch angrily countered Pétain's decision by ordering Mangin "to press forward with his arrangements with all possible speed."[18]

The arrangements included the 1st and 2d U. S. Divisions which, with the French Moroccan Division, were to form Mangin's spearhead for what would become the bloody Soissons campaign.

The 2d Division of U. S. Regulars received its marching orders on July 16. In Lieutenant Cates's words:

> We were still very tired. When we received the alert we thought we were being transferred to another rest area. Then we saw the *camions*, and then we knew the truth: we never rode to rest.

Notes

1. Ferdinand Foch, *The Memoirs of Marshal Foch*. New York: Doubleday, 1931. See also John Terraine, *Douglas Haig*. London: Hutchinson, 1963; Barrie Pitt, *1918 The Last Act*. New York: W. W. Norton and Co., 1963.
2. *Records*, Vols. 4 and 5.
3. General Clifton B. Cates. "Personal letters, 1918." Unpublished.
4. General Clifton B. Cates. Personal interview with the author. Lieutenant Cates did not ask to be repaid, but about sixty percent of the troops nonetheless repaid him. One man came up to him just before the 1919 victory parade in New York and handed him a ten-dollar bill with appropriate thanks.
5. General Clifton B. Cates, "Personal letters, 1918." Unpublished.
6. A. E. Holden, personal correspondence with the author.
7. *Records*, Vol. 6.
8. Ibid.
9. Oliver L. Spaulding and John W. Wright, *The Second Division American Expeditionary Force in France 1917–1919*. New York: The Hillman Press Inc., 1937.
10. John W. Thomason, Jr., "Second Division Northwest of Château Thierry, 1 June–10 July, 1918." Washington: National War College, 1928. Unpublished manuscript.
11. James G. Harbord, *The American Army in France, 1917–1918*. Boston: Little Brown and Co., 1936.

12. Robert D. Heinl, Jr., *Soldiers of the Sea*. Annapolis: U. S. Naval Institute, 1962. General Degoutte told Franklin D. Roosevelt, then Assistant Secretary of the Navy, of this attempt.
13. General A. A. Vandegrift, USMC (ret), personal interview. See also A. A. Vandegrift and Robert B. Asprey, *Once A Marine*. New York: W. W. Norton and Co., 1964. Heinl, op. cit., and works of cited generals. Incredibly enough the army attitude persisted. Shortly before General MacArthur left Corregidor for Australia he recommended all units except the marines and navy for a Presidential Unit Citation. When the omission was pointed out to General Sutherland, MacArthur's chief of staff, he said that the marines had received far too much credit in World War I—that they weren't going to get it all in World War II. This attitude partially explained the Saipan debacle and of course lay behind Department of Army attempts to absorb the Marine Corps, a campaign actually begun during World War II. After the war, in April, 1947, General Eisenhower, then Army chief of staff, pointedly referred to marine publicity at Belleau Wood in a talk with General Vandegrift, Commandant of the Marine Corps at the time. Three years later President Truman, who had served as an army artillery captain in France, expressed his sentiments of the Marine Corps in terms so virulent that public opinion forced him to an apology.
14. Lee Meriwether, *The War Diary of a Diplomat*. New York: Dodd, Mead and Co., 1919.
15. James G. Harbord, *Leaves from a War Diary*. New York: Dodd, Mead and Co., 1925.
16. John J. Pershing, *My Experiences in the World War*. Vol. 2. New York: F. A. Stokes, Co., 1931.
17. After a distinguished military career General Harbord became president of the Radio Corporation of America. After World War II he was promoted to lieutenant general by a special act of Congress.
18. Foch, op. cit. See also Pitt, op. cit.

American Battle Monuments Commission. *American Armies and Battlefields in Europe.* Washington: U. S. Government Printing Office, 1938.

_____. *2d Division Summary of Operations in the World War.* Washington: U. S. Government Printing Office, 1944.

_____. *3d Division Summary of Operations in the World War.* Washington: U. S. Government Printing Office, 1944.

Andriot, Captain R. *Belleau Wood and the American Army.* Translated by W. B. Fitts. Washington: Belleau Wood Memorial Association, no date.

Army Times (the editors of). *A History of the United States Signal Corps.* Washington: The Army Times Publishing Co., 1961.

Asprey, Robert B. See Vandegrift.

Balck, William. *Development of Tactics—World War.* Translated by Harry Bell. Fort Leavenworth: The General Service Schools Press, 1922.

Baldwin, Hanson W. *World War I.* New York: Harper and Row, 1962.

Binding, Rudolf. *A Fatalist at War.* London: Allen and Unwin, 1929.

Blakeney, Jane. *Heroes, U. S. Marine Corps, 1861–1955.* Washington, 1957.

Brooks, Alden. *As I Saw It.* New York: Knopf, 1929.

Bugnet, Charles. *Foch Speaks.* New York: The Dial Press, 1930.

Bullard, Robert L. *Personalities and Reminiscences of the War.* New York: Doubleday, Page and Co., 1925.

_____, with E. Reeves. *American Soldiers Also Fought.* New York: Longmans Green and Co., 1936.

Bundy, Major General Omar. "The Second Division at Château Thierry." *Everybody's Magazine,* March, 1919.

Butts, E. L. *The Keypoint of the Marne*. New York: The George Banta Publishing Co., 1930.

Callwell, Major General Sir C. E. *Field Marshal Sir Henry Wilson—His Life and Diaries*. 2 vols. London: Cassell, 1927.

Carter, W. A. *The Tale of a Devil Dog*. Washington: The Canteen Press, 1920.

Cates, General Clifton B., USMC (ret). "Personal letters, 1918." Unpublished.

_____. *History of the 96th Company, 2nd Battalion, 6th Regiment, United States Marine Corps*. Washington: Headquarters U. S. Marine Corps, 1935.

_____. Personal interview with the author.

Catlin, A. W. *With the Help of God and a Few Marines*. New York: Doubleday, Page and Co., 1919.

Chicago Daily Tribune, June 1–30, 1918.

Churchill, Winston S. *The World Crisis 1916–1918*. London: Butterworth, 1927.

Clark, Paul H. "Letters and Messages to John J. Pershing, 1918–1919." Washington: Manuscripts Division, Library of Congress. Unpublished.

Clemenceau, Georges. *Grandeur and Misery of Victory*. Translated by F. M. Atkinson. New York: Harcourt Brace and Co., 1930.

Cooke, Major E. D. "We Can Take It." *Infantry Journal*, May–December, 1937.

Cooper, Courtney Riley. See Cowing.

Cooper, Duff. *Haig*. London: Faber and Faber Ltd., 1935.

Corbin, Louise. See Hamilton.

Cowing, Kemper F., and Courtney Riley Cooper. *Dear Folks at Home—*. New York: Houghton Mifflin Co., 1919.

Crozier, Emmet. *American Reporters on the Western Front 1914–1918*. New York: Oxford University Press, 1959.

De Weerd, Harvey A. *Great Soldiers of the Two World Wars*. New York: W. W. Norton and Co., 1941.

Dickman, Joseph T. *The Great Crusade*. New York: Appleton and Co., 1927.

Du Puy, W. A., and J. W. Jenkins. *The World War*. Chicago: National Historic Publishing Association, 1919. Vols. 5 and 6 of 6 vols.

Erskine, General Graves B., USMC (ret). Personal correspondence with the author.

Esposito, Colonel V. J. See Stamps.

Eyck, Erich. *The Generals and the Downfall of the German Monarchy 1917–1918*. Fifth Series, Vol. 2. London: Offices of the Royal Historical Society, 1952.

Falls, Cyril. *The Great War*. New York: G. P. Putnam's Sons, 1959.

Feland, Logan. "Retreat Hell!" *Marine Corps Gazette*, June, 1921.

Field, H. B., and H. G. James. *Over the Top with the 18th Company, 5th Regiment, U. S. Marines, a History*. Rodenbach, Germany: no date.

Foch, Ferdinand. *The Memoirs of Marshal Foch*. Translated by Colonel T. Bentley Mott. New York: Doubleday, 1931.

_____. See also Joffre.

Frost, Meigs O. See Wise.

Gatzke, Hans W. *Germany's Drive to the West*. Baltimore: The Johns Hopkins Press, 1950.

George, David Lloyd. *War Memoirs of David Lloyd George*. London: Ivor Nicholson and Watson, 1934. Vols. 4 and 5 of 5 vols.

Gibbons, Floyd. *And They Thought We Wouldn't Fight*. New York: George H. Doran and Co., 1918.

Golaz, A. "Belleau Woods June 1918." *Revue Historique de l'Armée*. Special Issue, 1957.

Goldberg. Alfred, editor. *A History of the United States Air Force, 1907–1957*. Princeton: D. Van Nostrand Co. Inc., 1957.

Gordon, George V. *Leathernecks and Doughboys*. Chicago: privately printed, 1927.

Gulberg, Martin Gus. *A War Diary*. Chicago: The Drake Press, 1927.

Hagan, Lieutenant Colonel J. A., USMC (ret). Personal correspondence with the author.

Hamilton, Craig, and Louise Corbin. *Echoes From Over There*. New York: The Soldier's Publishing Co., 1919.

Hankey, Lord. *The Supreme Command 1914–1918*. London: Allen and Unwin, 1962. Vol. 2 of 2 vols.

Hanssen, Hans Peter. *Diary of a Dying Empire*. Translated by O. O. Winther. Bloomington: Indiana University Press, 1955.

Harbord, James G. "Personal War Letters." Washington: Manuscripts Division, Library of Congress. Unpublished.

_____. *Leaves from a War Diary*. New York: Dodd, Mead and Co., 1925.

_____. *The American Army in France 1917–1919*. Boston: Little Brown and Co., 1936.

Harding, E. F. See Lanham.

Heinl, Robert D., Jr. *Soldiers of the Sea*. Annapolis: U. S. Naval Institute, 1962.

Hertzler, R. H. *C'Est la Guerre*. Newton, Kansas: 1928.

Hindenburg, Marshal Paul von. *Out of My Life*. 2 vols. New York: Harper & Brothers, 1921. Translated by Frederic Appleby Holt.

Hoehling, A. A. *The Great Epidemic*. Boston: Little Brown and Co., 1961.

Holden, A. E. Personal correspondence with the author.

Hopper, James. *Medals of Honor*. New York: The John Day Co., 1929.

Howland, C. R. *A Military History of the World War*. Fort Leavenworth: The General Service Schools Press, 1923.

Hubbard, S. T. *Memoirs of a Staff Officer 1917–1919*. Tuckahoe, N. Y.: Cardinal Associates, Inc., 1959.

James, H. G. See Field.

Jenkins, J. W. See Du Puy.

Joffre, Marshal, General Ludendorff, Marshal Foch, Crown Prince Wilhelm. *The Two Battles of the Marne*. New York: Cosmopolitan Book Corporation, 1927.

Johnston, C. H. L. *Famous Generals of the Great War.* Boston: The Page Co., 1919.

King, Jere Clemens. *Generals and Politicians.* Berkeley: University of California Press, 1951.

Kruger, Rayne. *Good-Bye Dolly Gray.* Philadelphia: J. B. Lippincott Co., 1960.

Lanham, C. T. and E. F. Harding. "Infantry in Battle." Washington: *The Infantry Journal,* 1939.

Lejeune, John A. *Reminiscences of a Marine.* Philadelphia: Dorrance and Co., 1930.

Liddell Hart, Basil Henry. *Reputations, Ten Years After.* Boston: Little, Brown and Co., 1928.

_____. *A History of the World War 1914–1918.* Boston: Little, Brown and Co., 1930.

Liggett, Hunter. *AEF Ten Years Ago in France.* New York: Dodd, Mead and Co., 1928.

Lucas, P. M. *The Evolution of Tactical Ideas in France and Germany During the War of 1914–1918.* Paris: Berger-Leorault, 1923. Translated by P. V. Kieffer.

Ludendorff, Erich. *Ludendorff's Own Story.* New York: Harper & Brothers, 1919.

_____. See also Joffre.

March, General Peyton C. *The Nation at War.* New York: Doubleday, Doran and Co., 1932.

Mathews, William R. "Official report to Headquarters, U. S. Marine Corps, September 28, 1921." Copy furnished author by Mr. Mathews.

_____. Official correspondence, Headquarters, U. S. Marine Corps, 1928. Copy furnished author by Mr. Mathews.

_____. Personal correspondence with the author.

Maurois, André. *Semper Fidelis.* New York: Marine Corps League of New York booklet. no date.

McClellan, E. N. *The United States Marine Corps in the World War.* Washington: U. S. Government Printing Office, 1920.

_____. "Operations of the Fourth Brigade of Marines in the Aisne Defensive." *Marine Corps Gazette,* June, 1920.

_____. "Capture of Hill 142, Battle of Belleau Wood, and Capture of Bouresches." *Marine Corps Gazette,* September–December, 1920.

_____. "The Battle of Belleau Wood." *Marine Corps Gazette,* September–December, 1920.

_____. "The Nearest Point to Paris in 1918." *Sea Power,* June, 1921.

McEntee, G. L. *Military History of the World War.* New York: Charles Scribner's Sons, 1943.

Meriwether, Lee. *The War Diary of a Diplomat.* New York: Dodd, Mead and Co., 1919.

Metcalf, Clyde H. *A History of the United States Marine Corps.* New York: G. P. Putnam's Sons, 1939.

Metcalf, Stanley W. *Personal Memoirs.* Auburn, N.Y.: privately printed, 1927.

Miller, Henry W. *The Paris Gun.* London: Jonathan Cape Ltd., 1930.

Moore, William E. "The 'Bloody Angle' of the A.E.F." *The American Legion Weekly,* February 24, 1922.

_____. See Russell.

Müller, Georg Alexander von. *The Kaiser and His Court.* London: McDonald, 1961. Edited by Walter Görlitz.

Neame, Philip. *German Strategy in the Great War.* London: Edward Arnold and Co., 1923.

New York Herald, Paris Edition, June 1–30, 1918.

New York Times, June 1–30, 1918.

Otto, Ernst. "The Battles for the Possession of Belleau Woods, June, 1918." *U. S. Naval Institute Proceedings,* November, 1928.

Palmer, Frederick. *America in France.* New York: Dodd, Mead and Co., 1918.

_____. *Newton D. Baker—America at War.* New York: Dodd, Mead and Co., 1931. 2 vols.

_____. *With My Own Eyes.* Indianapolis: Bobbs-Merrill Co., 1933.

Pattullo, George. *Hellwood.* Philadelphia: Curtis Publishing Co., 1918.

Pershing, John J. Personal letter to Major General Barnett, November 10, 1918. Washington: U. S. Marine Corps Archives.

_____. *Final Report of General John J. Pershing.* Washington: U. S. Government Printing Office, 1920.

_____. *My Experiences in the World War.* New York: F. A. Stokes Co., 1931. 2 vols.

Pierrefeu, Jean de. *French Headquarters 1915–1918.* Translated by Major C. J. C. Street. London: Geoffrey Bles Ltd., 1929.

Pitt, Barrie. *1918 The Last Act.* New York: W. W. Norton and Co., 1963.

Pogue, F. C. *George C. Marshall: Education of a General.* New York: The Viking Press, 1963.

Recouly, Raymond. *Foch—My Conversations with the Marshal.* New York: Appleton and Co., 1929. Translated by Joyce Davis.

Reeves, E. See Bullard.

Repington, Charles à Court. *The First World War.* 2 vols. New York: Houghton Mifflin Co., 1920.

Robinson, Fielding S. Personal correspondence with the author.

Rockey, Lt. General Keller E., USMC (ret). Personal correspondence with the author.

Rogerson, Sydney. *The Last of the Ebb.* London: Arthur Barker, Ltd., 1937.

Rouvier, Jacques. *Present-Day Warfare.* New York: Charles Scribner's Sons, 1918.

Russell, J. C., and W. E. Moore. *The United States Navy in the World War.* Washington: Pictorial Bureau, 1941.

Shepherd, General Lemuel C., USMC (ret). Personal interview with the author.

Simonds, F. H. *They Won the War.* New York: Harper & Brothers, 1931.

Sioux City [Iowa] *Journal,* June 1–30, 1918.

Smith, L. N. *Lingo of No Man's Land.* Chicago: Jamieson Co., 1918.

Spaulding, Oliver L. and John W. Wright. *The Second Division American Expeditionary Force in France, 1917–1919.* New York: The Hillman Press Inc., 1937.

St. Joseph [Missouri] *Gazette,* June 8, 1919.

Stallings, Laurence. *The Doughboys.* New York: Harper and Row, 1963.

Stamps, T. D., and V. J. Esposito, editors. *A Short History of World War I.* West Point: Military Academy, 1950.

Terraine, John. *Douglas Haig.* London: Hutchinson, 1963.

Thomas, General Gerald C., USMC (ret). Personal interview with the author.

Thomas, S. *The History of the A.E.F.* New York: G. H. Doran Co., 1920.

Thomason, John W., Jr. *Fix Bayonets!* New York: Charles Scribner's Sons, 1925.

_____. "Second Division Northwest of Château Thierry, 1 June–10 July, 1918." Washington: National War College, 1928. Unpublished manuscript.

_____. "The Marine Brigade." *U. S. Naval Institute Proceedings,* November, 1928.

Timmerman, Captain Louis F. *War Diary, 1917–1919.* Unpublished manuscript.

_____. Personal interview with the author.

U. S. Army. *Histories of 251 Divisions of the German Army Which Participated in the War (1914–1918).* Washington: U. S. Government Printing Office, 1920.

_____. *The Aisne and Montdidier-Noyon Operations.* Washington: U. S. Government Printing Office, 1922.

_____. *The German Offensive of July 15, 1918.* Fort Leavenworth: The General Service Schools Press, 1923.

_____. *Records of the Second Division (Regular).* Washington: The Army War College, 1927. Vols. 1–9.

_____. *Translations of War Diaries of German Units Opposed to the Second Division (Regular), 1918. Château Thierry.* Washington: Army War College, 1930–32. Vols. 1–4.

_____. *The Ninth U. S. Infantry in the World War.* No place, no date.

_____. *The Official History of the Second Regiment of Engineers and Second Engineers Train United States Army in the World War.* No place, no date.

_____. *United States Army in the World War, 1917–1919.* Washington: U. S. Government Printing Office, 1943. Vols. 3, 4, 15 of 17 vols.

U. S. Marine Corps. *History of Second Battalion, 5th Regiment, U. S. Marines.* No place, no date.

_____. *History of the First Battalion, 5th Regiment, U. S. Marines.* No place, no date.

_____. *A Brief History of the Sixth Regiment, United States Marine Corps.* No place, no date.

_____. *History of the Third Battalion, Sixth Regiment, U. S. Marines.* Hillsdale, Michigan: Akers, MacRitchie and Hurlbut, 1919.

_____. *History of the Sixth Machine Gun Battalion.* Neuwied, Germany: 1919.

_____. *History of Second Battalion, Fifth Marines.* Quantico, Virginia: Marine Barracks, 1938.

U. S. Navy. *Medal of Honor, The Navy.* No place, no date.

_____. *The Medical Department of the United States Navy with the Army and Marine Corps in France in World War I.* Washington: U. S. Navy Department, 1947.

Van Every, Dale. *The AEF in Battle.* New York: D. Appleton and Co., 1928.

Vandegrift, General A. A., USMC (ret), and Robert B. Asprey. *Once A Marine.* New York: W. W. Norton Co., 1964.

_____. Personal interview with the author.

Viereck, G. S. *As They Saw Us.* New York: Doubleday, Doran and Co., 1929.

Westover, Wendell. *Suicide Battalions.* New York: G. P. Putnam's Sons, 1929.

Wilhelm, Crown Prince. *My War Experiences.* London: Hurst and Blackett, 1922.

_____. *The Memoirs of the Crown Prince of Germany.* London: Thornton Butterworth Ltd., 1922.

_____. See Joffre.

Wise, Frederic M., and Meigs O. Frost. *A Marine Tells It to You.* New York: J. H. Sears and Co., Inc., 1929.

Wood, Lambert. *Certain Brief Conclusions.* Portland, Oregon: Binfords and Mort, 1939.

_____. *His Job—Letters written by a 22-year-old lieutenant in the World War to his parents and others in Oregon.* Portland, Oregon: Metropolitan Press, 1956.

Wright, John W. See Spaulding.

Wright, Peter E. *At the Supreme War Council.* London: Nash Co., 1921.

Wyly, Mr. and Mrs. William. Personal correspondence: Copy of Sergeant Al Sheridan's letter.

A.7.V, tank, 42
Abbéville conference, 47–48, 224
Adams, Lt. Colonel, 295, 296, 305–13
Adamson, Lt., 331
Adrian barracks, 18, 24
Ailette River, 45
aircraft. *See* under respective armies
Aisne River, 3, 51, 52, 132, 339
Aisne-Marne defensive, 339, 345–46
Albert, King of Belgium, 35
Albert-Bapaume line, 37, 40
Alland Creek, 71, 72
Allied blockade, 31
Allied Supreme War Council, 95, 222
Allies, 3, 4, 13, 17, 28, 34–35, 36–39, 43, 51, 95, 129, 218, 222–25, 227, 294, 339, 346
America. *See* United States of America
American army. *See* U.S. Army
American Battle Monuments Commission, 1
American Expeditionary Force. *See* U. S. Army

American marines. *See* U. S. Marine Corps
Amette, Cardinal, 62
Amiens, 37–40, 42, 46
Anderson, Colonel, 294, 305, 307, 312, 313
Anizy, 45
Anthoine, General, 50, 51, 96
Arbuckle, Private, 181
Argaut, Pfc. Tom, 184
Arizona, 12
Armentières, 41
Arnim, General von, 41, 42
Aronde valley, 230
Arras, 32
Artillery. *See* under respective armies
Ashmead-Bartlett, Ellis, 216
Ashurst, Lt., 197
Associated Press, 217
Aulnois, 89
Ausborn, Sgt. Major Matthew, 114
Ayencourt, 228
Azy, 100, 108

Bailey, Leo J., 13, 14
Bailey, Major, 126–27
Bailleul, 41
Baker, Newton, 47
Bar-le-Duc, 60
Barescut, General de, 54–55, 130

Barnett, Maj. General George, 8, 236
Bastien, Lt., 12
Battle of the Frontiers, 3
bayonet drill, 14, 19
Bearrs, Hiram, 9, 288
Beauvais, 47, 56, 60, 80
Beauvais agreement, 222, 223
Beauvais conference, 39
Belfry, Sgt., 184–85
Belgian army, 35, 41, 48
Belgium, 3
Belleau, 3, 102, 112, 139, 142, 161,
        163, 192, 193, 239, 261,
        270, 281, 301
Belleau Wood, 76, 102, 116, 139,
        142, 159, 160, 161, 162,
        163, 165, 178, 194, 195,
        196, 198, 200, 203, 204,
        209, 213, 225, 233, 235,
        238, 239, 241–47, 250, 259,
        264, 274, 288, 290, 293,
        300, 301, 305, 306, 308,
        312, 315, 316, 319, 325,
        328, 330, 340, 343–44, 345,
        347, 349
    description, 1–2, 4, 5, 161, 211,
        244, 251, 261–62, 271, 279,
        281–82, 284, 288–89, 290–
        91, 306–307, 310, 315
    German defensive positions, 141,
        154, 163–64, 238, 239–42,
        258, 267, 269, 271, 288,
        295–96, 300, 302, 309–310,
        311, 316
    German seizure of, 111–12, 163
    U.S. seizure of: June 6–8, 143–
        213; June 9–10, 237–247;
        June 11, 252–74, 281–82;
        June 12, 274–84; June 13–
        15, 287–302; June 15–21,
        305–312; June 21–26, 313–
        20; final assault of, 317–22
Belleau-Bouresches road, 251, 278
Belloy, 230
Below, General von, 37

Berry, Major Ben, 9, 61, 110, 139,
        144, 147, 149, 150, 152,
        153, 159–60, 164, 165,
        166–67, 169, 173, 174–77,
        181, 192, 193, 194, 195,
        196, 197, 198, 202, 203,
        204, 235, 237
Berry-au-Bac, 45
Bessell, Colonel, 69
Bessières, Vivien, 19
Betz, 219
Bézu, 76
Bischoff, Major, 163–64, 240, 241–
        42, 267, 300–301
Bissell, Lt. John T., 59, 60
Blake, Lt., 287
Blanchfield, Captain John, 9, 105,
        106, 121, 129, 200
Blévaincourt, 18
Bliss, Maj. General Tasker H., 34
Blue Devils. See French army
body lice. See cooties
Boehn, General von, 45, 131, 132,
        230, 241
Boer War map, 140
Bois de Belleau. See Belleau Wood
Bombon, 39
Bonneil, 125
Bonner, Pvt. Paul, 200
Bordeaux, 12
Bourbetin Wood, 186
Bouresches, 3, 76, 84, 87, 112, 131,
        139, 159, 160, 161, 162,
        164, 167, 168, 169, 179,
        180, 182, 183, 184–85, 186,
        188, 192, 193, 194, 195,
        196, 203, 209, 210, 211,
        212, 213, 219, 236, 237,
        239, 241, 242, 258, 259,
        272, 282, 283, 288, 289,
        316, 326
Bouresches-Belleau road, 210, 261
Bouresches-Torcy road, 160, 163, 193
Bouresches-Triangle line, 195, 239,
        281
Bourmont, 12–13

Bouton, Major, 332, 333, 334, 335, 337
Bowley, Colonel, 116–17
Bowling, Lt., 183
Brailsford, Lt., 289
Breil, Lt., 300–301
Bremoiselle, 77
Briane, 51
British Army, 14, 32, 35, 36–39, 40–42, 46, 47, 49, 53, 54, 95, 220, 221, 223, 227, 230, 346
British Expeditionary Force, 3
Britton, Sgt., 128
Brooks, Alden, 97
Brown, Colonel Preston, 27, 48–49, 69, 70, 72, 73, 76, 77, 79, 87–89, 90, 140, 141–42, 160, 163, 191, 244, 262, 280–81, 294
Brown, Sgt., 254, 256, 275
Bruchmüller, Colonel, 33, 36, 228
Brumetz, 101
Buford, Gunnery Sgt., 127–28
Bullard, Maj. General R. L., 48, 346
Bundy, Maj. General Omar, 13, 25, 27, 56, 60, 62, 87, 90, 91, 92, 93, 94, 100, 101, 107, 108, 110, 117, 124, 125, 137, 139, 141, 150, 154, 159, 163, 188, 203, 207, 209, 213, 244, 247, 263, 264, 265, 272–73, 294, 295, 305, 308, 312, 314, 316, 322, 325, 327, 329, 331, 332, 336, 340
Burke, Sgt., 344
Burns, Captain, 284
Burr, Lt. Carlton, 24
Burrows, Lt., 278
Bussiares, 3, 87, 100, 107, 112, 115, 116, 142, 160, 161, 204, 207
Butler, Smedley, 9
Byng, General, 35, 37, 40

Cable, Pvt., 129
California, University of, 12
Canadian Army Corps, 35
Canadian Mounted Police, 218
Cantigny, 48, 52, 56, 60, 97, 216, 226
Cappel, Captain Marvin, 332
Carre, Captain de, 258, 261
Carrières, 107
Carter, Captain, 313
Carter, Pvt., 78
Case, Captain, 181
Castelnau, General de, 35, 95
Cates, Lt. Clifton B., 11, 22, 167–68, 182–83, 184–85, 194, 195, 281–83, 289–90, 291, 298–99, 306–307, 326, 340–43, 350
Catlin, Colonel Albertus W., 9, 10, 18–19, 77–78, 90, 91, 101, 103, 104, 109, 110, 117, 122, 123–24, 125–26, 159, 162, 165–66, 167, 168, 169–70, 177–78, 192, 193, 205–206
Central Powers, 30
Châlons, 80
Chamberlaine, Brig. General W., 27, 92, 93, 116, 142, 242, 316, 317
Champagne, province of, 35
Champigneulles, 18
Champillon, 91, 105, 106, 117, 137, 139, 142–43, 149, 151, 152, 197, 198
Champillon-Bussiares road, 107, 118, 143
Champillon Wood, 208, 250
Chantilly, 49
Château Belleau, 1–2, 281, 294
Château de Vaudencourt, 61, 63
Château-Thierry, 4, 56, 58, 59, 60, 63, 71, 76, 81, 83, 84, 87, 88, 94, 95, 96, 102, 130, 216, 221, 224, 226, 327, 328, 346

Châteauvillain, 58
Chauchat rifle, 15, 19–20, 103, 107,
    152, 193, 255
Chaumont, 12, 56, 62, 92
Chaumont-en-Vexin, 56, 60, 62, 116
Chaumont-la-Ville, 18
Chemin-des-Dames, 45, 49, 50, 53,
    62, 64, 81, 97, 220, 221,
    346
Chézy-en-Allier, 73
Chézy-en-Orxois, 87
Chicago, Illinois, 165
Chicago Daily Tribune, 164–65, 217
China, 9
Churchill, Winston, 227–28
Cierges, 53
Clark, Major Paul H., 48–49, 52, 54–
    55, 79, 80, 96, 130, 224,
    225–26
Clemenceau, Georges, 22, 38, 39, 51,
    95, 221, 223, 345
Clerembauts Woods, 92, 112
Clignon Brook, 71, 76, 83, 84, 102,
    103, 104, 116, 139, 159,
    301, 322, 346
Clignon villages, 2
Cobbey, Lt., 60
Cocherel, 76, 92, 93
Coffenberg, Captain, 235
Cole, Lt., 335
Cole, Major Edward, 9, 91, 101, 108,
    191, 194, 212, 243
Collins, Pvt., 165
Colvin, Sgt., 277
Committee for the Defense of Paris,
    219
Communists, 4
Compans-la-Ville, 92
Compiègne, 45, 228
Conachy, Captain, 150, 154, 159,
    160, 166, 167, 202, 208–
    209
Condé-en-Brie, 59
Conger, Colonel, 330–31, 332
Congress of the United States. *See*
    U.S. Congress

Connolly, Chaplain J. N., 62
Conroy, Lt., 167
Conta, General von, 46, 54, 82, 83,
    112, 124, 131, 133–34, 239,
    240, 242, 296, 301, 312
Conte, Colonel de, 49
Cooke, Lt. E. D., 65, 76–77, 105–
    106, 197, 199, 201, 208–
    209, 250, 251, 252, 254–55,
    256, 260, 261, 269, 271,
    274, 275–77, 278, 279,
    297–98
cooties, 26
Corbin, Captain, 120
Coulombs, 94, 101, 102
Coulommiers, 97
Coupru, 86
Courcelles, 61
Courchamps, 83
Courlandon, 51
Courtmont, 83
Craig, Malin, 69
Croiselles, 36
Croix de Guerre, 325
Crouy-sur-Ourcq, 73, 77
Crowther, Captain, 143–44, 146
Crozier, Emmet, 215–16
Cuba, 9
Cummings. Lt. Sam, 252, 255

Daly, Gunnery Sgt. Dan, 9, 173,
    218
Damblain, 13
Darche, Chaplain, 61
Davis, Lt. Colonel, 116, 188
Debeney, General, 48, 227
Dederer, Captain, 210
Degoutte, General, 86, 87–89, 94,
    101, 110, 112, 124, 137,
    138, 140–41, 142, 154, 159,
    160, 161, 213, 235, 294,
    327, 340, 345
Delaware, 109
Departed Days, 61
Dépôt de la Guerre, 140
D'Esperey, General Franchet, 35

Destler, Pvt., 210
Devil Dogs, 218
Dickman, Maj. General J. T., 56, 58,
    59–60, 131, 346
Diepenbroick-Grüter, General von,
    102
Distinguished Service Cross, 188, 200
Dockx, Corporal, 127–28
Domptin, 89, 90, 116
Dormans, 60, 81
Dorrell, Corporal, 184
Doullens conference, 38–39
Doyen, Colonel Charles, 9, 12–13, 27
Duchêne, General, 50, 52, 58, 71, 72,
    73, 79, 97, 130, 346
Duffieux, Colonel, 54, 55, 225
Duffour, Colonel, 130
Dunbeck, Captain Charles, 105, 106,
    107, 251, 253, 256, 257,
    259, 261, 269, 271, 274,
    276, 280
Duncan, Captain Donald, 160, 167,
    182, 183
Dunkirk, 222

Eaton, Captain, 334
Ecoute Plet, 101
Eddy, Lt. William, 162, 163, 244–45
Edwardian Age, 2
Edwards, Maj. General Clarence, 343
Elliott, Major, 101, 168, 186–87, 188,
    189, 204, 329–30, 331, 334
Eloup, 154
Ely, Colonel Hanson, 52
England, 2, 31, 42, 95, 348
Epernay, 131
Epieds, 76
Erskine, Lt. Graves B., 12, 182, 185
Escadrille Sol 252, 162
Etheridge, Lt., 237–38
Etrépilly, 76, 81, 83, 90
Evans, Major Francis, 10, 122, 123,
    192, 194–95, 212, 246

Fadden, Sgt., 181
Falkenhayn, General von, 30

Farnum, Colonel, 49
Fayolle, General, 54, 227, 229
Feland, Lt. Colonel Logan, 9, 110,
    118, 120, 143, 149, 160,
    167, 193, 194, 197, 198,
    202, 273, 281, 293, 294,
    295–96, 300, 302, 306, 309,
    314
Feldkerr, Maj. General, 301, 302
Fère-en-Tardenois, 53, 71
Ferme Paris. See Paris Farm
Filley, Lt., 187
Finn, Corporal, 184
Fismes, 54, 79
Flanders, 17, 46, 227, 230, 300
Flanigan, Pvt., 165
Flesquières salient, 37
Foch, Ferdinand, 34, 35, 38, 42, 43,
    47, 48, 50, 51, 53–54, 55,
    56, 79, 80, 87, 95, 120, 129,
    140, 220, 221, 222, 223–24,
    229, 230, 233, 339–40, 346,
    349, 350
Fokker airplane, 331
Fox, Major, 196
France, 12, 13, 31, 38, 79, 88, 95, 97,
    215, 220, 221–22, 294, 340
Frazier, Lt., 65, 197
French, Pvt., 65
French army, 3, 24, 27, 35, 46, 49,
    72, 79, 89, 97–98, 102, 103,
    107, 116, 117, 130, 131,
    134, 149, 154, 161, 188,
    192, 193, 207, 219, 220,
    221, 223, 226, 227–28, 243,
    245, 296, 301, 308, 312,
    316, 332–33, 337, 346, 350
  aircraft, 162, 163, 220, 245, 317
  artillery, 87, 101, 102, 105, 108,
    115, 119, 142, 162, 182,
    228–30, 316, 331, 333
  casualties, 3, 51, 81, 87, 140, 187,
    225, 226, 336
  Chasseurs, 106, 107, 119
  communications, 51, 81, 109, 160
  Dépôt de la Guerre, 140

GQG, 43, 49, 50, 52, 54–55, 63,
80, 81, 96, 224, 225
intelligence, 23, 50, 51, 54, 79,
161, 220
morale, 32, 38, 47, 55, 88, 96, 97–
98, 111, 120, 130, 224
operations:
attack against Hill 204, 335–36
Château-Thierry defense, 87,
94, 95, 98
Chemin-des-Dames defense,
49–50, 221
June 6 attack, 139–41, 143,
144, 147, 149, 150–51, 152,
157, 159, 161–62
Marne defense, 54–56, 60, 62,
86–134, 294, 327
Marne retreat, 54, 73, 77–78,
86–87, 120
Montdidier-Noyon defense, 247
strategy, 3, 31, 38–39, 49–56,
79–81, 87–89, 129, 220–21,
224, 339–40
strength, 39, 47, 48, 52–56,
124–25, 220, 339–40
tactics, 50–56, 71–77, 87–89,
110, 115–16, 124–26, 139–
43, 154, 159–61, 171, 193,
207, 221, 222, 293, 332–33
French army units:
Army Detachment of the North, 54
Army Group of the North, 35
Army Group of the East, 35, 95
Reserve Group of Armies, 54
1st Army, 48, 224
3d Army, 220, 224
5th Army, 47, 48, 54
6th Army, 50–56, 58, 69–73, 97,
130, 294, 325, 340, 345
III Corps, 312, 325, 327, 340;
39th Division, 327; 153d
Regiment, 327, 335
VII Corps, 71, 87, 94, 101, 108
XI Corps, 52
XXI Corps, 76, 86, 94, 137,
312; 43d Division, 87, 90,

91–92, 101, 103, 109, 112,
115, 119, 125; 133d
Regiment, 103, 119; 164th
Division, 87; 33d Infantry,
89; 167th Division, 125,
137, 139, 159, 207, 293,
294; 116th Regiment, 143;
2d US. Division. See U.S.
Army; 3d U.S. Division. See
U.S. Army
XXXVIII Corps, 59, 87, 125,
294; 10th Colonial Division,
59, 64, 129, 168;
10th Army, 54, 56, 339
miscellaneous: 115th Chasseurs
Alpins (Blue Devils), 14,
150; Escadrille Sol 252, 162;
French Moroccan Division,
350
French Chamber of Deputies, 221
French refugees. See Refugees
Fuller, Captain, 242–43, 244, 284
Furbush, Lt., 335

GQG. See French army
Galicia, 31
Gallipoli, 216
Gandelu, 71, 72, 84, 94, 102, 115
Gare de l'Est, Paris, 37
Garlow, Peter, 218
Garrett, Major Frank, 291, 293, 294,
298, 343
gas masks, 15, 18–19, 65, 279, 289–
90, 291
gas warfare, 18, 24, 51, 182, 192,
278–79, 280, 283, 290,
291–92, 294, 332
Gaston, Major, 307, 308, 311, 312
Gastovitch, Pvt., 276
Gaucher, General, 87
Germainvillers, 18
German army, 13, 17, 24, 30–34, 43,
49–55, 59–61, 71–72, 79,
81–84, 86, 87, 88, 90, 102,
116, 119, 162–63, 179, 193,
199, 210, 211–13, 217–18,

220, 229, 237, 258, 262,
267, 275, 277, 279, 283,
287, 295–96, 317–21, 335–
36, 346–47
aircraft, 32, 76–77, 78, 90, 115,
140, 166, 220, 221, 222,
229, 230, 288, 289, 306,
317
appreciation of U.S. forces, 296–97
artillery, 17, 32, 33, 36, 78, 82,
102, 105–106, 107, 111,
115, 117, 119, 120–21,
122–24, 125, 132, 140, 142,
154, 162, 166, 170, 173,
178, 186, 188, 197, 199,
201, 219, 228, 238–39, 251,
282, 317, 326, 334, 335
campaigns, 3, 17, 339
casualties, 25, 42, 51, 116, 124,
129, 133, 144, 146, 154,
205, 209, 226, 254, 269,
273, 283–84, 301, 311,
321–22, 332, 336
intelligence, 23, 140, 166, 186,
226, 237–38, 306
morale, 40, 42, 82, 116, 131, 133,
226, 245, 269, 301–302,
331, 347
operations:
    advance to the Marne, 45–46,
        51–56, 81–134, 220
    attack on Montdidier-Noyon
        line, 220, 224, 227–30, 264
    defense of Belleau Wood, 142,
        144–45, 162–68, 172–89,
        191–94, 197, 258, 267–69,
        270–72, 275–81, 288–96,
        300–302, 304–22
    defense of "Hill 142," 144–58
    defense of Vaux, 331, 332–34
strategy, 36, 37, 40–43, 45–46, 81–
    84, 131–34
strength, 33, 110, 131, 163, 220,
    222, 225, 228, 240, 300–
    301, 313
supply, 40, 53, 81, 131, 133, 239,
    240

Sturmtruppen, 32, 228
Supreme Command (OHL), 31,
    33, 81, 84, 131–34, 220,
    226–27, 230, 241–42, 312,
    317–21
tactics, 32, 33–34, 36–37, 46, 51–
    54, 82, 83–84, 102–105,
    111–12, 122–24, 131, 132,
    141, 152, 163–64, 226–27,
    229, 230, 239–42, 267–79,
    309–10, 317–21
German army units:
    Army Group Rupprecht, 46, 53,
        54, 81, 222, 230
    Army Group Wilhelm, 45, 131,
        132, 346
    lst Army, 37, 45, 83, 131, 301
    2d Army, 37, 42, 46
    3d Army, 3
    4th Army, 41, 42
    6th Army, 41, 50, 51
    7th Army, 45, 53, 81, 82, 83, 84,
        131, 132, 230, 301
    Corps Conta (IV Reserve
        Corps), 46, 53, 54, 81, 82,
        83, 84, 102, 104–105, 111–
        12, 116, 124, 133, 239, 301,
        312; 5th Guards Division,
        53, 81–82, 83, 105, 112,
        124, 134, 154, 239, 278,
        301; 10th Division, 81, 102,
        112, 131, 164, 239, 332;
        47th Regiment, 102, 131;
        6th Grenadier Regiment,
        131; 398th Regiment, 131,
        164; 19th Division, 83; 28th
        Division, 54, 81, 83, 239,
        240, 242, 269, 278, 296–97,
        301, 332, 335; 40th Fusilier
        Regiment, 240, 241, 252,
        255, 258, 261, 267, 269,
        301; 2d Battalion, 240, 241,
        245, 252, 258, 267; 36th
        Division, 83, 112; 87th
        Division, 301; 3d Reserve
        Ersatz Regiment, 267, 318,

321; 347th Regiment, 302,
317–18; 1st Battalion, 317;
3rd Battalion, 318; 197th
Division, 83, 102, 104–105,
112, 116, 134, 144, 154,
239; 273d Regiment, 144,
154, 163; 231st Division, 81,
83, 112; 237th Division, 83,
102, 104–105, 112, 116,
134, 144, 192, 240, 300,
301; 460th Regiment, 144,
150, 163; 461st Regiment,
163, 192, 240, 267, 300,
301; 1st Battalion, 267
Corps Schmettow, 53, 82, 83
Corps Schoeler (VIII Corps),
312; 201st Division, 331,
332; 401st Regiment, 335;
402d Regiment, 331, 335,
336; 1st Battalion, 331; 2d
Battalion, 331; 3d Battalion,
335–36
Corps Winkler, 83, 84, 131
18th Army, 32, 35, 37, 45–46, 53,
83, 132, 133, 228–30
German Foreign Office, 33
Germigny, 94, 101
Gibbons, Floyd, 164, 174–77
Gilfillan, Lt., 148
Gill, Captain, 191, 258
Gleeson, Sgt. Joseph, 114–15
Gondrecourt, 165
Gordon, Lt., 61, 64, 167, 172–73,
204
Gotha aircraft, 219
Gough, General, 35, 36, 37
Grand Courmont, 101
Gray, Lt., 333, 337
Green, Captain, 186, 187, 334
Groff, Sgt., 180
Gros-Jean Wood, 298, 316
Gulberg, Martin, 61

Hagan, Lt. J. W., 120
Haig, General Sir Douglas, 34–35,
37–39, 41, 47, 56, 79, 220,
221, 222, 223–24, 339, 349

Haiti, 9
Hall, Pvt., 290
Hamilton, Captain George W., 143,
144, 145, 146–47, 148, 150,
152–53
Hamilton, General Sir Ian, 216
hand grenade, 14, 19, 148, 161, 194,
255, 309, 314, 317, 332
Hankey, Lord, 222–23
Harbord, Brig. General James G., 27,
61, 63, 71–72, 73, 76, 77,
86, 87, 90, 91–92, 93, 101,
103–104, 105, 108, 109–
110, 111, 112, 118, 119,
137, 139, 140, 141, 142,
143, 149, 150–52, 159, 160,
161, 162, 163, 164, 166,
167, 168, 177, 191, 192,
193–94, 194–95, 196, 197,
203–204, 207–208, 209–
210, 212, 213, 218, 233–36,
237, 239, 242–43, 245–46,
250–52, 257–60, 262–63,
264–66, 269, 271–72, 273–
75, 279, 280, 281–82, 283,
284, 288, 291, 292–93, 294,
295, 296, 298, 300, 302,
305, 307, 308–309, 310,
311, 312–21, 322, 325, 326,
337, 345, 349
Hardin, Lt. John, 165
Hartlieb, Major von, 163, 240, 245,
252, 256, 267, 269, 278,
295
Hartzell, Lt. Oscar, 164, 174–77
Harvard University, 12, 49
Hausen, General von, 3
Hautevesnes, 83, 103, 111
Hazebrouck, 41
Hearington, Captain, 186
Hebel, Pvt., 269
Helms, Lt., 309, 311, 312
Henry, Pvt., 179–80
Herald Tribune. See New York Herald
Tribune
Hess, Lt. Elmer, 126–27

Hill 126, 105, 112, 197
Hill 133, 160, 193, 196, 197, 248,
    251, 272
Hill 142, 91, 92, 100, 101, 103, 105,
    107, 110, 112, 117, 118,
    139, 142, 143, 144, 150,
    153, 154, 159, 160, 197,
    250, 316
Hill 165, 122, 150, 193
Hill 169, 248, 259, 287, 312
Hill 181, 203, 242, 269
Hill 183, 106
Hill 190, 90
Hill 192, 168, 188, 237, 331, 332,
    334, 335
Hill 204, 76, 83, 87, 124, 168, 327,
    331, 335, 336
Hill 219, 83
Hindenburg, Marshal Paul von, 5, 30–
    31
Hoffman, Gunnery Sgt. Charles, 148
Holcomb, Major Thomas, 9–10, 13,
    18, 22, 91, 109, 110, 111,
    125, 137, 140, 159, 160,
    167, 168, 182, 193–94, 195,
    196, 203, 209, 236, 237,
    239, 253–54, 281, 282,
    288–89, 291–92, 293, 295,
    298, 299, 300, 306, 316,
    322, 325–26
Holden, Platoon Sgt. A. E., 343
Holladay, Lt., 196
Hope, Lt., 150
Horne, General, 37
Hotchkiss machine gun, 19, 104, 152,
    239, 275
Hôtel de Ville, Montreuil, 90
Houghton, Captain C. F., 59
House, Colonel, 34
Hubbard, Captain S. T., 49–50
Hughes, Major John, 9, 160, 235,
    237, 238, 239, 242, 243,
    244, 245, 247, 248, 253,
    257, 259, 270–71, 272, 275,
    278, 282–84, 290–91, 316
Hughes, Pvt. John, 115

Humbert, General, 220, 227
Hunt, Lt. Leroy, 12, 149
Hunter, First Sgt. "Beau," 146
Huntington, Colonel, 9
Hurley, Captain, 179, 180, 181, 307,
    312
Hurley, Lt., 178
Hutier, General von, 32, 35, 37, 39–
    40, 83, 131, 133, 228, 229,
    230

Inter-Allied Supreme War Council,
    34, 95
Italian army, 4
Italy, 31, 34, 248

Jackson, Lt. Gil, 197, 199, 251, 280,
    297
Jacobi, General von, 102
Janson, Ernest. See Hoffman
Jaulgonne, 54, 60, 83, 84, 131
Johnson, Jamey, 27

Kaemmerling, Lt., 186
Kansas, 183
Kauffman, Reginald, 216
Kaulbars, Captain von, 317–18, 319,
    321
Keyser, Major Ralph, 316, 318–19,
    320, 321
Kingman, Captain, 118
Knapp, Corporal, 128
Kreuznanch, 34

La Basée, 40, 41
La Cense ravine, 182
La Fère, 32, 36
La Gonetrie, 90
La Loge Farm, 94, 116, 139, 142,
    191
La Maison Blanche Farm, 160, 165
La Nouette, 125, 137
La Roche Wood, 327, 331, 332, 334,
    335, 336
La Voie du Châtel, 92, 122, 124, 164
Lagore, Lt., 12

Larsen, Captain Henry, 64, 167, 172, 173
Larsen, Corporal, 179
Laspierre, Captain, 170, 177–78, 192
Laure, Commandant, 80–81
Lawe River, 41
Lawrence, General, 223
Le Bout de Bois, 61
Le Pletriere, 101
Le Thiolet, 89, 91, 92, 102, 124
Le Valdahon, 17
Lebrun, General, 312, 325, 327, 336
Lee, Lt. Colonel Harry, 9, 178, 192, 193–94, 195, 210, 235–36, 242, 243, 244, 258, 259–60, 270, 288, 316, 322, 325
Legendre, Lt., 198, 205
Lejeune, General John A., 9
Leonard, Pvt., 321
Les Glandons, 101
Les Mares Farm, 105, 107, 117, 127, 148, 149
Lewis, Brig. General E. M., 27, 71, 72, 73, 77, 90, 100–101, 104, 110, 137, 160, 168, 186, 187–88, 189, 331, 332, 340
Lewis, Major, 332
Lewis gun, 19
Licy Farm, 83
Liggett, Maj. General Hunter, 325, 343, 346
Lizy-sur-Ourcq, 116
Lloyd George, David, 222, 223, 227
Lockhart, Lt., 183
Loire River, 48
London, 218, 222, 223, 344
Lorraine, 39
Louisiana, 12
Lowen, Captain, 279
Lucy-Bouresches road, 195
Lucy-Château Belleau ravine, 248
Lucy-Clignon, 118, 142, 161
Lucy-le-Bocage, 91, 92, 102, 112, 142, 151, 160, 163, 165, 166, 169, 170, 178, 181, 192, 195, 196, 198, 203, 206, 207, 235, 238, 239, 281, 283, 287, 289, 316
Lucy-Torcy road, 198, 236, 250, 258, 288, 297–98, 316
Ludendorff, General Erich, 5, 30–34, 40–42, 45–46, 52, 81–83, 131, 132, 220, 226, 227, 230, 233, 339, 346
Lys River, 41, 43, 80, 81, 87

McCabe, Colonel, 215, 216, 217
McCloskey, Colonel, 116, 142, 144, 167, 170
Macedonia, 31
McEvoy, Captain Tom, 169
McIndoe, Colonel, 78, 92
MacNider, Lt. Hanford, 333, 336–37
Madagascar beef, 93
Maggione, Pvt. Charles, 104
Malone, Colonel Paul, 76, 90, 92, 93, 94, 101–103, 104, 105, 107, 108, 110, 117, 125, 137, 140, 160, 168, 185–86, 187, 188, 191, 210, 211, 282, 327, 328
Mangin, General, 229, 230, 339, 350
March, General Peyton, 34, 130
Mares Wood, 150
Mareuil, 72, 73
Marigny, 84, 102, 105, 107, 112, 124
Marines. See U. S. Marine Corps
Marines, town of, 64
Marne River, 3, 5, 7, 8, 46, 53, 59, 80, 81, 82, 83, 87, 96, 97, 98, 100, 108, 112, 126, 132, 141, 217, 220, 221, 223, 226, 227, 298, 339, 346, 349
Marshall, Lt., 181
Martin, Don, 216–17
Martin, Pvt., 200
Marwitz, General von der, 37, 39–40, 42
Mathews, Lt. William, 12, 128–29, 166, 198, 245, 251–52, 258, 261–62, 263–64, 272

Mathews, Pvt. Sam, 104
Matz River, 228
Max, Prince of Baden, 34
Maxim machine gun, 145, 146, 150, 154, 172, 183, 252
May-en-Multien, 71, 72, 73, 77
Meaux, 63, 64, 65, 69, 71, 77, 78, 94, 97, 345
Meaux-Soissons highway, 71, 73, 78
Meriwether, Lee, 62, 219
Méry, 229
Messersmith, Captain, 185, 186
Messines, 41
Metcalf, Lt. Stanley, 61, 64, 78
Meuse-Argonne, 349
Mexico, 9
Meyer, General David, 344
Meyers, Corporal Sam, 104
Michel, General, 87, 90, 91–92, 94, 101, 103, 104, 112, 115, 119, 125
Micheler, General, 47, 48, 54
Millet, Commandant, 130
Milner, Lt., 276, 277, 278, 280, 281
Milner, Lord, 38, 39, 222–23
Minnesota, University of, 10, 11
Mitchell, Billy, 331
Moltke, Helmuth von, 3
monkey meat, 20, 93, 107
Monneaux, 168
Mont Blanc, 349
Mont Debonneil, 89
Mont des Chats, 41
Mont Kemmel, 41, 42
Mont Monneaux-Vaux road, 333
Montdidier, 48, 220, 221, 227, 247
Montdidier-Noyon line, 53, 79, 220, 227, 264
Montgivrault, 151
Montgivrault-le Grande Farm, 108
Montgomery, Major J. C., 299–300
Monthiers, 83
Montigny, 72, 94
Montigny-Gandelu road, 73
Montmirail, 59

Montreuil-aux-Lions, 76, 77, 78, 86, 87, 90, 91, 92, 93, 94, 298, 306
Moore, Captain, 191, 335
Moore, Lt. William, 12, 192, 195–96
Moorey, Gunnery Sgt., 185
Moulin-du-Rhône, 101
Mudra, General von, 45
Murphy, Lt. Richard, 11, 196
Murray, Captain, 284

Napoleon, 111
Naulin, General, 294–95, 312, 327
Néry, 298
Nesles, 59
Neuilly, 61, 71
Neville, Colonel Wendell, 9, 93, 101, 103, 104, 105, 109, 110, 111, 117, 118, 119, 120, 124, 125, 143, 148, 149, 150, 151–52, 153–54, 164, 192, 193, 194, 229, 236, 260, 262, 263, 270, 271, 273, 275, 280, 283, 288, 292, 293, 299, 305, 306, 308, 312, 316, 318, 320, 322, 325, 349
New England, 9, 215, 343
New York, 12, 218
New York Herald Tribune, 22, 216–17
New York National Guard, 49
New York Times, 164, 217, 218, 219
Nicaragua, 9
Nivelle, General, 229
Noble, Lt. A. H., 165, 169, 178, 179, 182, 195, 196, 210, 211, 212
Nouvron plateau, 54, 79
Noyon, 80, 220, 227, 247
Noyon-Montdidier line, 83, 132

O'Brien, First Sgt. John, 9
Oeuilly, 51
Oise River, 36, 45, 48, 50, 79, 220, 228
Ormoy-le-Daviens, 78

Osborne, Dental Surgeon Weedon,
183
Otto, Ernst, 95
Ourcq River, 54, 71, 72, 73, 76, 79,
94, 265
Overton, Lt. John Megan, 12, 254,
256, 269, 270

Paillé, Colonel, 130, 224
Paris, 3, 22, 38, 53, 55, 62, 65, 79,
81, 87, 96, 129, 133, 215,
218, 219, 221, 222, 223,
224, 227, 326, 328, 340–43,
346
Paris, bombardment of, 32, 37, 219
Paris Farm, 89, 91, 92, 237
Paris-Metz highway, 64, 71, 76, 89,
90, 100, 102, 110, 116, 349
Parker, Lt., 254, 256
Parris Island, 10, 11, 276
Passy, 81
Patterson, Sgt., 204–205
Paysley, Lt., 311
Peabody, Lt., 127
Pegler, Westbrook, 216
Pennsylvania, 7
Péronne, 37
Perrin, Lt., 242
Pershing, General John J., 8, 12, 22,
27, 34, 35, 39, 43, 46–47,
48, 49, 54, 55, 60, 63, 79–
80, 87, 88, 130, 164, 215,
216, 217, 224–25, 233, 264,
265, 325, 345, 347
Pétain, General Henri, 34–35, 36–37,
38, 43, 47, 48, 49, 50, 51,
52, 54, 55, 60, 63, 79, 80,
95, 96, 97, 129, 130, 220,
222, 224, 225, 339, 346,
349, 350
Philadelphia, 12
Piave River, 4
Pierrefeu, Jean de, 43, 96, 97, 225
Pinon, 45
Plan Blücher, 45–46
Plan Friedensturm, 312, 339, 349

Plan Mars, 40
Plan St. George I, 40–41
Plan St. George II, 40–41
Plan St. Michael, 32, 40, 41, 42
Platerie Wood, 238, 298
Platt, Captain, 167, 251, 314, 315
Ploegsteert, 41
Plumer, General, 42
Poe, Lt. Edgar Allan, 264, 272, 276,
284
Poincaré, Monsieur, 38
Pontoise, 64
Port Royal, South Carolina, 11
Portuguese divisions, 35, 41
Prémont, 101, 103, 104
Prémont-Les Glandons road, 119
Prince Max of Baden. See Max
Princeton University, 12
Prommelfeur, 17
Provence, 96
Provins, 50, 62, 96
Pulkowsky, Captain, 33
Punch magazine, 140
Pyramid Farm, 93, 105, 110

Quantico, Virginia, 9, 11–12, 276
Quast, General von, 41, 42
Quay de Seine, Paris, 37
Quick, Sgt. Major John, 9, 195–96,
236
Quigley, Captain, 295

Rainbow Division. See U. S. Army
Rawlinson, General Sir Henry, 34
Red Cross, 22, 72, 298
Redford, Lt. David, 63
Refugees, 59, 65–66, 69, 71, 72, 92
Reims, 35, 45, 50, 53, 54, 55, 79, 80,
81, 82, 131, 132, 227, 230,
339, 346, 349
Renouard, General, 59
Rhode Island, 63
Ribécourt, 229
Richtofen, Baron von, 317, 331
Ris, Forêt de, 54
Robecourt, 18

Robertson, General, 222
Robertson, Lt., 184, 185, 194, 282
Robinson, Lt. Fielding, 61, 63, 177–
    78, 196
Rochets Wood, 102
Rockey, Captain Keller, 143, 145, 148
Rogers, Sgt., 105
Rollot, 228
Roode, Captain de, 102
Rotenbücher, Lt. Colonel, 102
Royal Marines, 344
Rozet, Colonel, 48, 55, 96, 130
Rumania, 31
Rupprecht, Crown Prince, 46, 53, 222
Russell, Captain, 308
Russia, 31

Saint-Denis, 64
Saint-Mihiel, 23, 47, 349
Saint-Nazaire, 12, 18
Saint-Quentin, 36, 73
Sainte Aulde, 94
Sainte-Claude plateau, 228
Sarcus, 55, 80
Savatier, General, 24
Scarpe River, 37
Schmidt, General, 125, 137
Schoeler, General, 312
Schulenburg, General, 131
Seicheprey, 226, 347
Shearer, Major Maurice, 9, 91, 103,
    109–110, 111, 117–18, 119,
    126, 139, 237, 239, 258,
    282, 283, 288, 292, 312,
    313, 314, 315, 316, 317,
    318–20, 322
Shepherd, Lt. Lemuel C., 11, 20–21,
    61, 63, 106–107, 121, 122,
    123, 129, 198, 200
Sheridan, Sgt. Al, 183–84
Shuler, Captain, 270
Sibley, Major Berton, 9, 143, 159–60,
    165, 168–69, 177, 178, 179,
    181, 182, 183, 193, 194,
    195, 196, 203, 209, 209–
    211, 212, 213, 233, 235,

    238, 239, 244, 281, 283,
    284, 287, 293, 295, 298,
    299, 300, 307, 316, 318,
    320, 326
Sioux City, Iowa, 217
Sioux City Journal, 217
Sissler, First Sgt., 183
Smith, Captain Dwight, 169, 178,
    179, 182, 212
Smith, Captain Mark, 179, 180, 212
Smith, Major Holland M., 9, 149
Smith, Pvt., 205–206
Snow, Pvt., 165
Soissons, 3, 52, 53, 54, 71, 79, 83,
    84, 132, 230, 339, 346, 349,
    350
Soissons-Fismes railroad, 81
Soissons-Hartennes road, 54
Soissons-Reims line, 45
Somme River, 36, 48, 80, 81, 87, 220,
    221
Soulacourt, 13, 14
Spad airplane, 331
Spanish-American War, 8
Spanish flu, 300–301
Springfield rifle, 13, 19, 198, 275
Stallings, Lt. Laurence, 13, 315, 319
Stanley, Pvt. Robert R., 206
Stars and Stripes, 22
Steck, Pvt., 205, 255
Stohl, Captain George, 237–38
Stokes mortar, 210, 309, 310
Storey, Corporal Adel, 26, 27
Sturmtruppen, 32, 228
Submarine warfare, 31
Sumner, Captain, 118
Supreme War Council. *See* Allied
    Supreme War Council
Sweet Caporal cigarettes, 12, 22
Swenson, Pvt., 179, 180
Swiss border, 55
Sydow, General, 131
Syracuse, 14

Tardieu, Monsieur, 80
Taylor, Gunnery Sgt. Ben, 342

Taylor, Major James G., 59, 60
Tennessee, University of, 11
Teufelhünden. See Devil Dogs
Texas, 7, 215
Tharau, Gunnery Sgt. "Babe," 129
Thiescourt, 228
Thomas, Gerald C., 24, 27, 61, 63,
    237–38, 244–45
Thomason, John, 144–45
Thompson, Gunnery Sgt., 165
Tillmann, Lt., 240–41, 245
Timmerman, Lt. Louis S., 12, 165,
    178–82, 195, 196, 211, 212,
    238, 326
Torcy, 3, 87, 102, 111, 112, 115, 116,
    139, 142, 147, 161, 162,
    163, 192, 193, 197, 219,
    240, 261, 267, 281, 294,
    301, 308
Torcy-Belleau road, 319, 321
Touchon, Major, 14
Treloup, 54
trench mortar, 19, 161, 211, 242,
    243, 247, 314, 331, 333
trench rats, 26–27
trench warfare, 15, 21, 80, 216, 289
Tromblon, 19
Triangle Farm, 91, 102, 109, 112,
    137, 160, 168, 195, 203,
    204, 239
Triangle Wood, 182, 188
Trilport, 69, 79
Turrill, Major Julius, 9, 94, 101, 103,
    104, 107, 109, 110, 118,
    139, 142, 143, 144, 148,
    149, 150, 151–52, 153, 154,
    159, 160, 161, 166, 167,
    193, 202, 250, 281, 287,
    288, 293, 295, 298, 299,
    300, 316

Udet, Lieutenant, 317
United States Army:
    aircraft, 245, 331
    American Expeditionary Force, 8,
        22, 101, 270

artillery, 78, 92, 95, 125, 126, 142,
    144, 153, 159, 161, 167,
    188, 193, 194, 196, 207,
    209, 212, 213, 235–36, 238,
    243, 252, 269, 275, 281,
    309–310, 331, 332, 336
campaigns, 24–27, 52, 101
casualties, 25, 104, 105, 108, 123,
    127–28, 129, 153, 154, 160,
    165, 173, 180, 182, 186,
    187, 189, 193, 196, 204,
    208, 209, 212, 238, 242,
    247, 259, 260, 264, 270,
    275, 276, 280, 284, 289,
    290, 291, 295, 299, 308,
    311, 315, 318, 319–20, 322,
    332, 336, 345
communications, 60, 64, 94, 103,
    107, 108–109, 117, 125,
    140, 162, 166, 167–68,
    186–99, 213, 234, 237–38,
    242–43, 246–47, 251, 253,
    258–63, 264, 270–75, 283,
    292–95, 307–20, 335
field orders, 76, 89, 90, 93–94,
    142, 159, 166, 234–35, 243,
    247, 251, 288, 309–11,
    313–14, 347
General Staff, 96
G-2-D, 49, 215
GHQ France, 48–49, 215, 264,
    347
intelligence, 49, 103, 110, 140,
    149, 161–63, 237, 244–45,
    251, 259, 261, 272, 284,
    309–10, 313–14, 318, 330–
    31, 332
maps, 95, 105, 106, 108, 109, 117,
    119, 140, 143, 146, 167,
    169, 173, 244, 245, 251,
    263, 293, 330–31
medical support, 93, 94, 108, 111,
    148, 153, 165, 174, 183–84,
    186, 187, 192, 206–207,
    255, 290, 292, 332
military police, 94
mobilization, 7–15

morale, 26–27, 97, 130, 212, 238, 246–47, 251, 270, 274, 276–77, 280, 283–84, 300, 315, 326, 329, 336, 340
National Guard, 49, 216, 343
operations:
    attack against Hill 142, 139, 142–54, 159
    attack against Vaux, 305, 322, 327–34
    Belleau Wood: June 6–8, 157–213; June 9–10, 237–47; June 11, 252–265, 267–272, 281–82; June 12, 273–84; June 13–15, 287–95; June 15–21, 295–311; June 21–26, 311–22; final capture of, 321–22
    Marne defense, 59–60, 100–134, 225, 226, 347
    Marne deployment, 64–80, 86-97
    ordered to Marne front, 58–66
    Verdun trenches, 23–25, 48
press policy, 215–17, 336–37
rations, 18, 20, 63, 64, 69, 91, 93, 100, 107, 114, 117, 140, 211, 238, 250, 283, 298, 309, 326, 332
Regular Army, 89, 216
relations with Allies, 22, 24, 34–35, 43, 46–49, 95, 130, 224, 225, 348–49
relations with U. S. Marine Corps, 8–9, 292, 327–28, 329, 336, 345–46
reliefs, 125, 137, 139–40, 197, 236, 239, 246, 251, 281, 288, 291, 294, 295, 306, 332, 343
replacements, 226, 236–37, 281, 295, 282, 296, 298–99, 343
Selective Service, 216
strategy, 39, 47–48, 87–88, 213, 305
strength, 13, 35, 47, 87, 107, 125, 137, 139, 250–51

supply, 53, 66, 69, 87, 92, 93, 94, 103, 104, 107, 110, 116, 117, 152, 153, 193, 284
tactics, 71, 87–88, 89–91, 103–104, 141, 169, 213, 227, 235, 245, 247, 251–52, 274, 313, 316–17, 319–20, 331–32, 336
training, 11–12, 14–15, 17–23, 27, 47, 56, 297, 299
War Department, 8, 12, 47, 265
United States Army units:
I Corps, 325, 343
1st U. S. Division, 7, 47, 48, 56, 60, 216, 349, 350; 28th Infantry Regiment, 52
2d Division of U. S. Regulars, 5, 7, 12, 15, 17, 23, 27–28, 30, 47, 48, 49, 56, 60, 63, 71, 72, 73, 76, 84, 94, 100, 105, 129, 130, 137, 139, 141, 151, 159, 162, 168, 187, 216, 217, 224, 238, 295, 296, 312, 322, 336, 340, 343, 345, 346, 347, 349, 350
3d U. S. Brigade, 13, 24, 27, 72, 73, 76, 97, 100–101, 116, 130, 131, 137, 168, 188, 283, 294, 305, 327–28, 331, 336, 344, 345
9th Infantry Regiment, 13, 24, 25, 72, 77, 87, 88, 89, 91, 100–101, 104, 108, 114, 168, 187, 291, 305, 328, 332, 336–37; 1st Battalion, 88, 331; 2d Battalion, 18, 88, 109, 332; Company E, 333, 334; Company H, 333, 334; 3d Battalion, 89, 101; Company I, 25; Company M, 13
23d Infantry Regiment, 13, 73, 86, 90, 92, 93, 94, 107, 117, 119, 125, 140, 160, 167, 168, 187, 203, 282, 283,

288, 291, 328, 331; 1st
Battalion, 101, 103, 104,
168, 283; Company A, 2d
Battalion, 101, 118, 168,
328; 3d Battalion, 144, 150,
166, 168, 197, 331–32;
Company I, 103, 108, 334;
Company K, 186; Company
L, 343; Company M, 186,
334; Detachment, AEF, 101
5th Machine Gun Battalion, 92,
94
4th Marine Brigade, 27, 110,
116, 137, 151, 159, 160,
161, 162, 189, 204, 247,
251, 263, 271, 281, 282–83,
292, 294, 299, 316, 322,
327, 345, 349
5th Marine Regiment, 8–9, 18,
20, 65, 72, 76, 86, 92, 93,
101, 103, 110, 118, 139,
142, 143, 149, 191, 194,
196, 203, 204, 237, 248,
258, 259, 312, 313, 314,
321; 8th Machine Gun
Company, 118, 139, 142,
143, 148; Headquarters
Company, 103; 1st Battalion,
94, 139, 142, 152, 272; 17th
Company, 148, 287; 49th
Company, 143, 147, 153;
66th Company, 148, 153;
67th Company, 143, 146,
147, 152–53; 2d Battalion,
103, 117, 139, 147, 159,
160, 166, 196, 198–200,
204, 206, 236, 237, 239,
245–46, 248, 251–65, 258,
316; 18th Company, 251,
253, 256, 257, 270, 277;
43d Company, 245, 251,
252, 253, 256, 270, 277,
278, 297; 51st Company,
107, 149, 151, 154, 160,
196, 250, 251–52, 255, 256,
269, 270, 275, 279–80; 55th

Company, 106, 107, 200,
208, 250, 254, 260, 270,
279; 3d Battalion, 61, 110,
139, 142, 152, 159–60,
165–66, 169, 174–75, 192,
194, 195–98, 201, 203, 204,
235, 237, 239, 258, 282,
288, 292, 312, 313, 314,
321; 16th Company, 167,
314, 317, 318, 319, 320,
321; 20th Company, 167,
251, 314, 318, 319, 320,
321; 45th Company, 150,
166, 167, 172, 314, 318;
47th Company, 167, 181,
194, 314, 315, 318, 319
6th Marine Regiment, 9, 10, 18,
26, 61, 77, 78, 90, 93, 101,
103, 107, 117, 121, 137,
162, 163, 191, 192, 203,
235, 258, 259, 260, 261,
264, 281, 321; 1st Battalion,
24, 91, 92, 109, 117, 126,
139–40, 160, 235, 243, 247,
282, 288, 290–91, 307; 74th
Company, 242, 291; 75th
Company, 242–43; 2d
Battalion, 18, 91, 92, 109,
111, 125–26, 137, 140, 159,
168, 182, 196, 203, 209,
236, 270, 288, 289, 291,
295, 298, 316, 322; 78th
Company, 185, 186, 283,
291; 79th Company, 160,
182, 185; 80th Company,
210, 235, 254, 288–89; 96th
Company, 160, 167, 182,
283, 291; 3d Battalion, 92,
143, 159, 165, 167, 169,
177, 181–83, 193–94, 203,
209–13, 233, 238, 281–84,
287, 293, 298, 299, 307,
316, 318, 320, 326; 82d
Company, 169, 178, 179,
182, 210, 213; 83d Com-
pany, 165, 169, 182, 210,

211, 212; 3d Platoon 165, 185; 84th Company, 169, 179, 212; 97th Company, 169

6th Machine Gun Battalion, 76, 91, 92, 101, 191, 243; 15th Machine Gun Company, 144; 23d Machine Gun Company, 142, 143; 77th Machine Gun Company, 159

2d Field Artillery Brigade, 17, 116, 159

12th Field Artillery, 114, 116, 273, 331; Battery D, 114

15th Field Artillery, 116, 126, 188; 1st Battalion, 126; Battery C, 115

17th Field Artillery, 61, 64, 78, 117

2d Trench Mortar Battery, 331

2d Engineer Regiment, 18, 60, 86, 92, 116, 143, 195, 208, 260, 262, 273, 278, 279, 284, 307; Company A, 196; Company B, 196; Company D, 143; Company F, 278

4th Machine Gun Battalion, 13, 92

16th Ambulance Company, 206

1st (Air) Brigade, 331

3d U. S. Division, 56, 58, 60, 63, 84, 97, 131, 224–25, 294

7th Machine Gun Battalion, 59, 137; Company A, 59; Company B, 59

7th Infantry Regiment, 294, 295, 305–309, 314, 316; 1st Battalion, 295, 305, 309; Company A, 309, 310–11; Company B, 308, 310–11, 312; Company C, 310, 311; Company D, 308, 310; 2d Battalion, 307, 312; 3d Battalion, 307, 311; Company M, 311

26th "Yankee" Division, 47, 58, 216, 225, 343

103d Infantry Regiment, 343

42d "Rainbow" Division, 47, 216, 226

United States of America, 5, 7, 8, 12, 209, 248, 249

United States Congress, 8, 12, 218

United States Marine Corps: casualties. *See* U. S. Army Commandant of, 8, 236, 246 field orders. *See* U. S. Army morale. *See* U. S. Army operations. *See* U. S. Army publicity at Belleau Wood, 217–18, 265, 325, 329 replacements. *See* U. S. Army strategy. *See* U. S. Army strength, 7–15 tactics. *See* U. S. Army training. *See* U. S. Army units. *See* U. S. Army

United States Navy, 8, 148, 174

Unruh, Colonel von, 46, 51, 82, 133

Upton, Colonel Leroy, 24, 25–26, 72, 73, 76, 77, 89–90, 93, 100–101, 108, 110, 117, 124, 125, 168, 188, 189, 210, 211, 333, 336–37

Vailly, 51

Valentine, Captain, 186

Vandélicourt, 229

Vaurichart Wood, 101, 103, 109

Vaux, 76, 84, 87, 102, 112, 164, 168, 240, 327, 330–34, 335, 336

Vaux-Bouresches road, 102, 334

Vaux-La Roche line, 332, 340

VB grenade, 19, 279, 309, 314, 332

Ventelet Farm, 110

Verdun, 23–24, 35, 291

Verry, Lt., 150

Vesailles, 34

Vesle River, 46, 51, 52

Veuilly-Champillon line, 139

Veuilly Wood, 101, 105, 106, 112, 117, 118, 119, 124, 217

Ville-en-Tardenois, 53
Villers-Cotterêts, 54, 79, 84, 132, 346
Villmuth, Lt., 283
Virginia Military Institute, 11
Vosges, 18, 35, 58

Waddill, Major, 101, 103, 104,
    108, 168, 185, 186, 187,
    188, 189
Waller, L. W. T., 9
Waller, Major L. W. T., Jr., 9
war correspondents, 164–65, 174–75,
    215–19
War Department. *See* United States
    Army
Washington, D. C., 217, 236
Wass, Captain Lester, 9, 76, 105, 106,
    107, 197, 199, 201, 252,
    256, 257, 261, 269, 271,
    274, 277, 278, 279, 280
Welte, Frank, 174
Westover, Captain Wendell, 13–14
West Point (USMA), 59
Weygand, General Maxime, 34, 223
White Farm, 78
Whiting, Major, 101, 118–19, 168,
    328
Whitley, Major, 331
Wiggins, Mess Sgt., 25
Wilhelm, Crown Prince, 131, 132–33,
    346
Wilhelm, Emperor of Germany, 41, 46
Wilhelmi, General von, 45, 102
Williams, Captain Lloyd, 105, 107,
    117, 120, 121, 149, 151,
    152, 154, 160, 165–66, 193,
    196, 250, 251, 255, 256,
    259, 260, 269, 270, 275
Williams, Lt. Norris, 72, 168–69
Wilson, General Henry, 34, 38, 39,
    222–23

Wilson, President Woodrow, 8, 12, 34,
    95
Winans, Captain, 148, 153, 154, 287–
    88, 293, 295
Winkler, General von, 83
Wischura, General von, 131
Wise, Major Frederic, 9, 10, 14–15,
    20–21, 61, 63–64, 65, 76,
    103, 105, 107, 108, 109,
    110, 115, 117–18, 119, 120,
    121, 125, 137, 139, 149,
    151, 160, 161, 166, 196,
    197, 197–98, 199–200, 201,
    203, 205, 207, 208, 236,
    239, 243, 245, 248, 250,
    251, 253, 254, 257–64, 265,
    267, 270–73, 274, 275,
    279–80, 281, 282, 283, 284,
    287–89, 290, 291–92, 293,
    295, 298, 299, 306, 314,
    316, 349
Wood, Lt. Lambert, 188, 328–29
Wood, Sgt., 210
Wordazeck, Marine Gunner Mike, 261
Worton, Lt. Arthur, 12, 182

YMCA, 22, 61
Yale University, 12, 27
"Yankee" Division. *See* United States
    Army
"Yankee Doodle Dandy," 218
Yowell, Captain, 167, 314, 315, 316,
    318, 319, 321–22
Ypres, 41, 42, 222
Yssonge Farm, 93

Zachio, Pvt. Provet, 104
Zane, Captain Randolph, 160, 182,
    185, 195, 212
Zischke, Lt., 197